North Eurasian Trade in World History, 1660–1860

This book offers the first long-term analysis of the protracted struggle between Britain, France, Prussia, Russia, and Sweden for economic power and political influence in the northern part of the Eurasian continent between 1660 and 1860. This book shows how their commercial, diplomatic, and military entanglements determined the course of Baltic trade from the late seventeenth to the mid-nineteenth century, provoking, among other things, the decline of the Dutch Republic and the partitions of Poland-Lithuania.

The author conceptualizes the Baltic Sea as one of North Eurasia's western border basins, alongside the White, Black, and Caspian Seas, and employs novel statistical series of Baltic trade as a proxy for the long-term development of North Eurasian trade in world history. Based on extensive quantitative evidence and sources for the history of international relations, this book outlines how North Eurasian trade became an object of growing tensions between various larger and smaller powers with a stake in North Eurasia's riches. The book addresses the long-term impact of mercantilist policies, territorial greed, and military conflicts in North Eurasia's border basins, and accentuates the significance of developments in the preindustrial transport and commercial infrastructure of the North Eurasian landmass. Employing the concept of North Eurasia and its different borderlands and border basins, this book overcomes previous limitations in the historiography of globalization and sheds light on a large, continental landmass, which researchers tend to leave aside for the benefit of a predominant maritime perspective in historical studies of globalization.

North Eurasian Trade in World History, 1660–1860 will be invaluable reading for students and scholars interested in world history, East European history, and the history of international relations and trade.

Werner Scheltjens is Professor of Digital History at the University of Bamberg, Germany.

Perspectives in Economic and Social History
Series Editors: Andrew August and Jari Eloranta

Fiscal Policy in Early Modern Europe
Portugal in Comparative Context
Rodrigo da Costa Dominguez

Workers, Unions and Truck Wages in British Society
The Fight for Real Wages, 1820–1986
Christopher Frank

Early Modern Overseas Trade and Entrepreneurship
Nordic Trading Companies in the Seventeenth Century
Kaarle Wirta

Credit and Debt in Eighteenth-Century England
An Economic History of Debtors' Prisons
Alexander Wakelam

Luxury, Fashion and the Early Modern Idea of Credit
Edited by Klas Nyberg and Håkan Jakobsson

The Nordic Economic, Social and Political Model
Challenges in the 21st Century
Edited by Anu Koivunen, Jari Ojala and Janne Holmén

North Eurasian Trade in World History, 1660–1860
The Economic and Political Importance of the Baltic Sea
Werner Scheltjens

For more information about this series, please visit www.routledge.com/series/PESH

North Eurasian Trade in World History, 1660–1860

The Economic and Political Importance of the Baltic Sea

Werner Scheltjens

Routledge
Taylor & Francis Group
LONDON AND NEW YORK

First published 2022
by Routledge
2 Park Square, Milton Park, Abingdon, Oxon OX14 4RN

and by Routledge
605 Third Avenue, New York, NY 10158

Routledge is an imprint of the Taylor & Francis Group, an informa business

British Library Cataloguing-in-Publication Data
A catalogue record for this book is available from the British Library

Library of Congress Cataloging-in-Publication Data
A catalog record has been requested for this book

ISBN: 978-0-367-68346-7 (hbk)
ISBN: 978-0-367-68348-1 (pbk)
ISBN: 978-1-003-13704-7 (ebk)

Typeset in Bembo
by codeMantra

Contents

Figures

Tables

Maps

About the author

Prior to his recent appointment as professor of digital history at the University of Bamberg (2021), Werner Scheltjens (1978) obtained a master's degree in East European languages and cultures (University of Leuven, 2001), a PhD degree in history (University of Groningen, 2009), and a senior doctorate, or Habilitation, in economic and East European history at the University of Leipzig (2020). Scheltjens specializes in preindustrial trade and transport history, maritime history, East European history, digital research methods, and historical metrology.

Preface

Some straightforward questions crossed my mind in 2013, when the first version of *Sound Toll Registers Online*, an electronic database of ship movements and cargoes passing through the narrow strait between the North Sea and the Baltic, was published: What do these data tell us? How could I use these data? Would it be possible somehow to analyse the entire database and observe it as a whole? Before I realized, I was wading through the fascinating, but muddy pool of premodern weights and measures. Without some sort of standard (metric) unit, how would I be able to tackle this 'whole,' to produce general statements about the development of shipping and trade between the North Sea and the Baltic, and eventually come up with a novel analysis based upon it? The traditional rule of thumb saying that 'one *last* = two tonnes' may be helpful in a number of cases, but it is neither accurate, nor can it be applied to the many different weights and measures in the electronic database.

My encounters with premodern weights and measures were enriching, to be sure, but they also left me in doubt on numerous occasions. Many issues of conversion could not be solved, and several decisions made during the conversion from a *raw* to a metric database may be criticized by specialists with in-depth knowledge of local weights and measures. Therefore, in addition to this monograph, I provide information about all my decisions regarding the conversion of premodern weights and measures in Sound Toll Registers Online to metric units. Online access to the methodology of the conversion as well as to selected annual statistics of tonnage estimates of trade through the Danish Sound from 1670 until 1856, further referred to as: Tetradas, is provided by the Journal Data Archive of the Leibniz Information Centre for Economics (*Leibniz Informationszentrum Wirtschaft*, ZBW).

Tetradas served as the starting point for (re)assessing the role of the Baltic Sea in international trade and politics, taking into account both the commodities that were exchanged, and the actors that were involved in this exchange. Again, this turned into a preoccupation with 'the whole': Can 'the Baltic' be observed as such, or should it be seen as part of an (even) bigger unit of space? What might be the consequences of embedding 'the Baltic' in a larger unit of space? How would this affect my empirical observations about the development of trade through the Danish Sound from the mid-seventeenth to the mid-nineteenth century?

In the following analysis, the mass of information about commodities flowing in and out of the Baltic Sea provides a novel starting point for examining the meaning of North Eurasian trade in world history. Without *Tetradas*, it would have been much harder, if not impossible, to embark on such endeavour. I have relied on *Tetradas* to identify, scrutinize, and contextualize the different stages of a quest for North Eurasian trade, which experienced its breakthrough in the latter part of the seventeenth century, reached its peak by the end of the eighteenth century, and was over by the mid-nineteenth century. In the following chapters, I argue that the quest for North Eurasian trade represents a significant episode in world history. Protracted political and military disputes determined the quest, which coincided with the heyday of mercantilism, the rise of state politics, and the breakthrough of industrial modes of production and fossil-energy fuelled means of transportation. The quest for North Eurasian trade lasted from ca. 1660 until the abolition of the Sound dues in 1857. Although the available literature on Baltic trade during this period is vast, only few studies adopt a world historical perspective. I hope that my way of putting the pieces of the quest for North Eurasian trade together – using the tonnage estimates of trade through the Danish Sound as glue – convinces the reader.

Abbreviations

AUX	Auxiliary Tables (in *Tetradas*)
Bex	Exports from the Baltic, through the Danish Sound (in *Tetradas*)
BIE	Balance of Imports and Exports (in *Tetradas*)
BTR	Bilateral Trade Relations (in *Tetradas*)
C	Commodity statistics (in *Tetradas*)
CIES	Commodity Import and Export Series (in *Tetradas*)
EI	Export and import statistics (in *Tetradas*)
FS	Foodstuffs (in *Tetradas*)
MF	Manufactures (in *Tetradas*)
m.u.	metric unit (1 kg or 1 liter)
PIES	Port Import and Export Series (in *Tetradas*)
PSZ	Polnoe Sobranie Zakonov Rossijskoj Imperii
RGADA	Rossijskij Gosudarstvennyj Archiv Drevnich Aktov
RM	Raw materials (in *Tetradas*)
STRO	Sound Toll Registers Online
T	Transport services statistics (in *Tetradas*)
Tetradas	Tonnage Estimates of Trade through the Danish Sound
Wim	Imports to the Baltic, through the Danish Sound (in *Tetradas*)

Maps

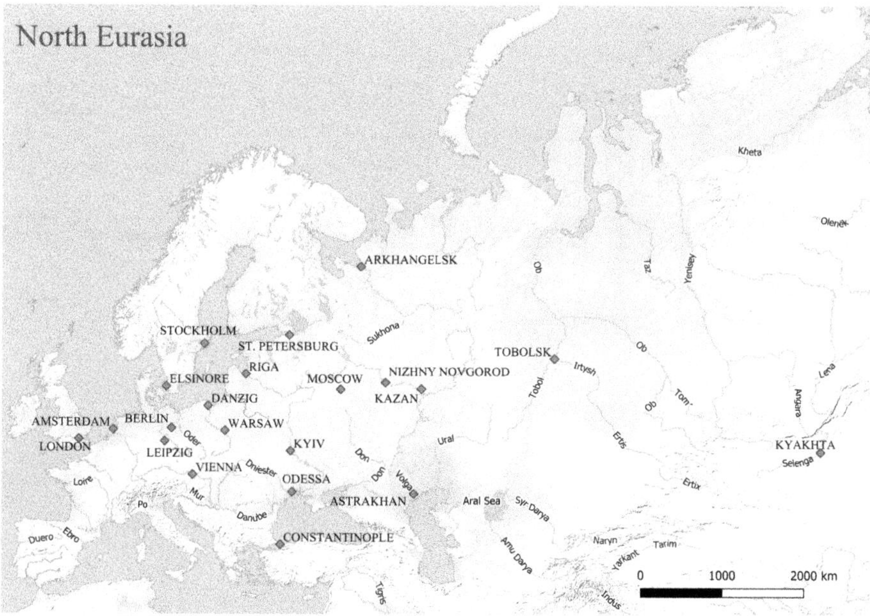

Map 0.1 North Eurasia

Map 0.2 Baltic Sea Region

Map 0.3 Black Sea Region

1 An exploratory analysis of trade through the Danish Sound, 1670–1856

Introduction

Based on a conversion into tonnes of one thousand metric units of the commodities carried through the Danish Sound and meticulously inscribed in the toll registers of the Øresund between 1670 and 1856, it was found that in 1670 the estimated total tonnage of Baltic commercial exchange (i.e. imports and exports) amounted to 426,978 tonnes, whereas in 1856 it had risen to 2,802,175 tonnes (see Figure 1.1).[1] In other words, between 29 May 1669, when the much-reduced and largely irrelevant *Hansetag* gathered for the very last time in Lübeck,[2] and 14 March 1857, when the leading advocates of *free trade* – the United Kingdom and the United States – finally achieved the abolition of the Danish Sound dues in the Copenhagen Convention,[3] the estimated tonnage of commercial exchange with the Baltic underwent a fivefold increase. During this period of almost two centuries, different commodities started to dominate imports and exports, while new centres of gravity emerged and replaced formerly dominant *gateways*. Like the *Hansetag* in 1669, the abolition of the Danish Sound dues in 1857 had a significant symbolic meaning. It confirmed, once again, the commercial dominance of the British Empire, and showed that the 'young' United States had established themselves on the international arena, even in supposedly peripheral 'Baltic affairs'. At the same time, the eradication of the Sound dues in 1857 also made clear that 'Baltic affairs' were anything but peripheral: whereas in 1669 a small, regional gathering of cities concluded that their method of doing business had become outdated, the abolition of the Sound dues in 1857 had been preceded by years of negotiations between the leading maritime and political powers of the world. Alongside the United Kingdom and the United States, Russia, Hamburg, and Lübeck contributed to the one-time fee, which was paid to Denmark in compensation of the Sound dues.[4]

This chapter presents a concise overview of the long-term development of trade through the Danish Sound, and it formulates a set of research questions based on the exploratory analysis of flows and commodities passing through the Danish Sound and registered at Elsinore (*Dk.* Helsingør) between 1670 and 1856. The flows are described based on annual series of total tonnage

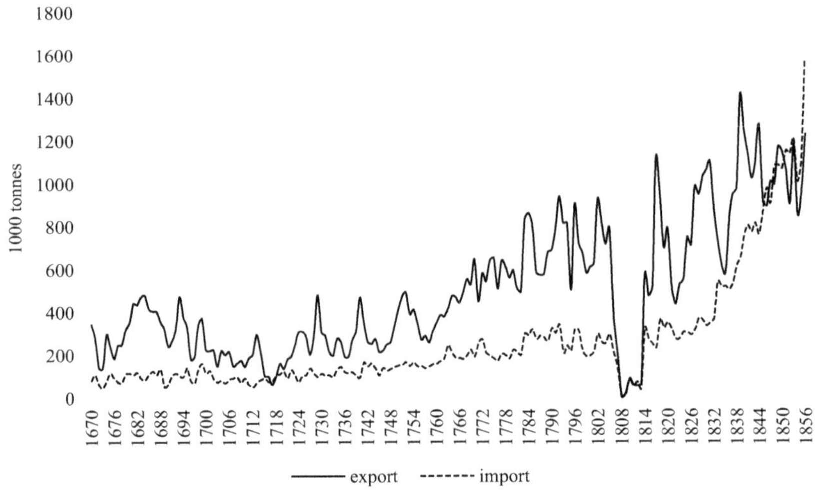

Figure 1.1 Estimated total tonnage of imports and exports through the Danish Sound, 1670–1856. Includes estimates of Swedish tax-free shipping between 1670 and 1720.

Source: *Tetradas* [VSWG-JDA], 1_Turnover: *Estimated total turnover.*

estimates of imports and exports through the Danish Sound. The survey of commodities shipped through the Sound relies on a broad categorization into foodstuffs, raw materials, and manufactured goods. Since the latter typically had a higher value-to-weight ratio than foodstuffs or raw materials, the use of tonnage estimates might seem to be misleading. At the same time, value-based analyses of the development of international trade tend to underestimate (or even ignore) the economic *significance* of low-value bulk commodities, such as salt, coal, grain, naval stores, and perhaps even wine. Though their exchange value was low, especially compared to manufactured goods, their intrinsic value (i.e. economic significance) was potentially high and as D.A. Iredale had noticed, "(…) salt, like coal, had an economic importance which value of exports belied."[5] Similar concerns are expressed with regard to the contribution of grain and naval stores to the British Industrial Revolution.[6] The value of these commodities in export trade statistics was usually low, especially when expressed in terms of a value-to-bulk ratio, but the high volumes shipped had an economic significance that is difficult to express in monetary terms. Since trade through the Danish Sound was defined primarily by bulk goods, volumes rather than values were taken as the starting point for analysing long-term changes in the economic significance of commercial exchange with the Baltic.[7] However, tonnage estimates typically cannot provide any information about the value of the registered commodity flows. Hence, whereas the volume of commodity flows (mostly) remains unchanged during its movement in space and time, this cannot be the case for the value of these flows.

The tonnage estimates used throughout this study have an important advantage over estimates of monetary value. Tonnage estimates provide an indication of the volume of commodity flows; while monetary address the value of such flows. Both are subject to the same reasonable doubt, inaccuracies and restrictions towards their interpretation. However, whereas monetary estimates and the trade statistics based upon them provide information about the value of trade at a certain node in a network (in which the node may be a single port, region or nation), typically, they contain much less information (or none at all) about the connections between different nodes. The tonnage estimates based on STRO, however, provide precisely this kind of information. Moreover, thanks to the structure of the original data and the bottom-up methodology of conversion, information about the connections between different nodes is preserved at all times. Using tonnage estimates, commodity flows and their geography can be analysed both at the level of single cargo items, ships, ports, or transport routes and at higher levels of aggregation, such as port clusters, regions, nation-states, or even the Baltic Sea as a whole.

The most significant foodstuffs exported through the Danish Sound comprised different types of grain: rye, wheat, barley, and oats.[8] During the entire period covered in this book, they account on average for more than 92% of the estimated total tonnage of foodstuffs exported through the Danish Sound. Different types of timber, tar, pitch, iron, tallow, hemp, flax, and linseed largely determined the volume of raw materials exports.[9] These commodities (except tallow and linseed) are commonly referred to as *naval stores*, indicating their significance for (naval) shipbuilding in the Age of Sail. The exportation of potash was significant as well, but because of its resemblance to other raw materials, it is not treated separately in this study. During the entire period, the estimated tonnage of these raw materials accounted for 86% on average of all raw materials exports through the Sound. The tonnage of manufactures exported through the Danish Sound was small compared to that of foodstuffs and raw materials. The most significant manufactured goods exported from the Baltic were sailcloth and raven duck.[10]

Whereas the vast historiography of Baltic trade tends to rely on selective observations and case-studies (or the ‘sum’ thereof) to describe long-term changes in trade through the Danish Sound, the goal of this chapter is to describe the whole, i.e. all commodities and all directions, as observed and registered in the Danish Sound between 1670 and 1856. The bulk of the historiography of Baltic trade deals with bilateral trade relations, the study of ports, the role of the Baltic in the commercial history of a certain region or political entity (often during limited periods of time), or trade in specific commodities. One will look in vain for a general, long-term history of Baltic commercial exchange, which places the water basin in a *Braudellian* framework encompassing geographical expansion, international politics, infrastructural development, and conflicting commercial interests. Previous general histories of the Baltic have dealt with trade through the Danish

Sound mostly in the broader context of cultural exchange. Typically, they have based their insights on the historiography of Baltic trade rather than a critical appraisal of available primary sources.[11]

At least partly, the lack of a general, long-term history of Baltic commercial exchange is due to the predominance of the famous *Tabeller over skibsfart og Væretransporte gennem Øresund*, a seven-volume quantification of the original Danish Sound toll registers, which was compiled by a team of researchers supervised by Nina Ellinger Bang (1866–1928) and Knud Korst (1894–1962) in the first half of the twentieth century.[12] The Sound Toll Tables (STT), as they are often called, cover the period from 1497 until 1783, and thus remain silent about the following period of fundamental changes in the European economy. Until quite recently, the *Tabeller* were the foremost important source for research into the history of trade through the Sound. Despite severe, but often justified criticism with regard to their content,[13] a large number of studies on a wide range of topics dealing (directly or indirectly) with the Baltic has relied on them. Alongside known issues, such as the loss of information due to the abridged quantification and categorization of textual data items (like names of ports, commodities and shipmasters),[14] the critical lack of information about the final 74 years of the original Sound toll registers in Bang and Korst's *Tabeller* was recognized soon. In the early 1950s, a group of French historians led by Pierre Chaunu (1923–2009) attempted to compute the Sound toll data from 1784 to 1793. Two journal articles notwithstanding, the project has not resulted in the publication of a database.[15] In the 1970s, the Danish historian Hans Christian Johansen undertook a similar effort, which eventually led to the release of an electronic database of the Danish Sound toll registers from 1784 to 1795, published on microfiches as appendix to the author's dissertation.[16] In the early twenty-first century, the Dutch historian George Maria Welling converted Johansen's work to a relational database format.[17] But even so, Baltic commercial exchange in the first half of the nineteenth century has attracted scholarly attention only quite recently, when Kalevi Ahonen and later Klas Rönnbäck "discovered" the Sound Toll Chamber commodity records, a statistical compilation of the original registers for the years 1773–1856, which was maintained by the Danish customs office for internal use.[18] However, these data are neither available to the public in electronic form nor do they allow adopting a truly long-term perspective.

Since 2013, the situation has changed drastically with the release of *Sound Toll Registers Online*, or STRO, the electronic database of the Danish Sound toll registers. STRO is "a relational database set up to make the Sound toll registers' data instantaneously available to all".[19] STRO documents about 1.5 million passages of ships through the Danish Sound between 1497 and 1857 as well as almost 5 million registrations of cargoes carried by these ships. Even if the release of STRO seems to have made both the Sound Toll Tables (1497–1783) and the Sound Toll Chamber commodity records (1773–1856) obsolete, novel results can only be expected if traditional quantification practices, which often involve the counting of ships, are replaced with a bottom-up methodology, which preserves the richness and variety of the original data while also providing a broad range of options for data aggregation. *Tetradas*, the tonnage estimates of trade through the Danish Sound from 1670 to 1856, documents and applies such methodology.[20] The observations made in the following sections are based on *Tetradas*. The exploratory analysis provides the backbone for claims about the role of the Baltic in the history of international trade at the end of this chapter.

Flows

Imports and exports

Long-term changes in the structure of supply and demand as well as short-term fluctuations caused by climatic variation and warfare determined the fivefold increase in the tonnages shipped through the Danish Sound between 1670 and 1856 (see Figure 1.1). Climatic variation had an extensive impact on harvests and the duration of the sailing season, which could result in sudden up- or downswings in the turnover of trade through the Danish Sound. Warfare had a clear, but diverse impact on the estimated total tonnage of Baltic commercial exchange.[21] Warfare put downward pressure on trade through the Danish Sound in the late seventeenth century and during the Great Northern War (1700–1721) (see Chapter 3), but the quick recovery in the late 1710s and during the first half of the 1720s did not result in sustained growth. Short upswings in 1729 and 1740–1741 were related to subsistence crises caused by bad harvests in parts of Western Europe. In general, however, the estimated total tonnage of Baltic commercial exchange stagnated until the mid-1740s. Only after 1745, when another low point was reached, a rapid increase in the volume of Baltic commercial exchange led to a relative boom lasting from 1750 until 1754. In 1751 and 1752, for the first time since the eradication of the *Hanse* almost a century earlier, the estimated total tonnage of Baltic commercial exchange exceeded 600,000 tonnes. A decade later, in 1763, this happened again. From then on, the character of Baltic commercial exchange started to change. In contrast to the long depression caused by the Great Northern War, the Seven Years' War (1756–1763) led to an acceleration in the estimated total tonnage of Baltic commercial exchange (see Chapter 4). Between 1764 and 1805, the annual tonnage shipped into and out of the Baltic increased from 684,155 to 1,081,921 tonnes.[22]

A comparison of the balance of Baltic commercial exchange, i.e. the estimated tonnages of imports and exports through the Danish Sound, helps to clarify the differences and similarities between both periods of warfare (see Table 1.1). Compared to the latter decades of the seventeenth century (1670–1699), the average estimated tonnage of exports from the Baltic during the relatively peaceful period 1721–1755 was somewhat lower and a little less volatile. The average estimated tonnage of imports to the Baltic, on the

Table 1.1 Key figures of exports and imports through the Danish Sound in designated periods

	1670–1699	*1700–1720*	*1721–1755*	*1756–1763*	*1764–1805*	*1806–1813*	*1814–1839*	*1840–1856*
Exports from the Baltic								
Maximum	478,724	294,214	490,725	417,039	936,903	386,162	1,411,626	1,267,999
Minimum	139,397	61,042	179,910	257,286	444,051	1,471	435,399	849,673
Average	320,493	173,243	297,683	331,684	647,401	108,197	795,118	1,062,162
Imports to the Baltic								
Maximum	159,748	126,824	165,376	243,477	339,519	209,076	652,210	1,577,630
Minimum	46,873	49,878	72,697	137,607	169,904	8,894	231,097	754,262
Average	98,563	87,351	125,328	167,372	239,105	76,947	378,430	1,003,117
Ratio of exports to imports								
	76:24	65:35	70:30	66:34	73:27	50:50	67:33	52:48

Source: *Tetradas* [VSWG-JDA], 1_Turnover: *Estimated total turnover.*

contrary, was about 25% higher and less volatile in 1721–1755 than in 1670–1699. The changes in the estimated tonnage of exports during the Great Northern War and the Seven Years' War were more remarkable. During the former, exports declined strongly, whereas imports remained almost stable. Contrastingly, during the latter, both average exports and imports increased significantly. The growing absolute tonnages of exports *and* imports during the Seven Years' War marked a departure from the previous periods. Although during the Seven Years' War the Baltic became one of the scenes of a truly global conflict, which, in one way or another, involved all the European powers, warfare did not cause a general disturbance of trade through the Danish Sound. Similarly, warfare does not seem to have had a negative impact on trade through the Danish Sound during the American War of Independence (1776–1783), the Fourth Anglo-Dutch War (1780–1783), and the French Wars (1793–1813), at least until 1806, despite Britain's and France's increasing adversity towards neutral shipping (see Chapter 5).[23] During the first half of the nineteenth century, fluctuations remained large and seem to have been the consequence of short-term downswings in otherwise growing tonnages of Baltic commercial exchange.

A closer look at the share of imports and exports highlights a further characteristic of Baltic commercial exchange. During most of the period under survey, the classical axiom of trade through the Danish Sound as driven and dominated by the exportation of large tonnages of bulk goods applies.[24] This axiom plays a prominent role in the traditional historiography of Baltic trade. It relies strongly on Bang and Korst's *Tabeller over Skibsfart* and perhaps even more so on Willem Sybrand Unger's (1889–1963) succinct tabular overview of the main structural changes in Baltic trade, which he summarized based on

Bang and Korst's tables.[25] In the long term, the predominance of exports over imports changed from a 70:30-relation during most of the 1670s to 80:20 in the relatively stable years from 1679 until 1688. This period was followed by a decline from 70:30 during the Nine Years' War to 65:35 during the first decade of the Great Northern War. The modest upswing in the estimated total tonnage of Baltic commercial exchange in 1712–1713, which was probably due to a sense of relief in the wake of the Treaty of Utrecht (1713) and the end of the War of the Spanish Succession (1701–1713), resulted in a temporary drop in the share of imports to pre-war levels (80:20).[26] Two years later, the opposite was true. Between 1715 and 1720, the estimated tonnages of imports and exports were almost equal. Imports even slightly exceeded exports in 1717 and 1718. The end of the Great Northern War resulted in a return to pre-war export-to-import-ratios (between 70:30 and 80:20), which lasted until 1805. During the Continental Blockade (1806–1813), the relationship between exports and imports reversed again, this time even more outspoken than in the closing years of the Great Northern War. However, as *registered* traffic through the Danish Sound was interrupted almost completely during the Continental Blockade, it is obvious that commodity flows were not captured adequately (see Chapter 5).

After the abolition of the Continental System, the tonnage of trade through the Danish Sound almost immediately returned to pre-1805 levels (see Figure 1.1). In 1814, an estimated 898,646 tonnes passed through the Danish Sound. Probably affected by Napoleon's brief return to the scene, famous in historiography as the Hundred Days,[27] the estimated tonnage declined to 747,748 tonnes in 1815. Although a swift recovery could be expected in 1816, the eruption of the Tambora volcano on the Island of Sumbawa in Dutch East India shook the climate and caused a 'year without summer' with bad crops, inundations, and epidemics across large parts of Europe and in the United States.[28] Baltic commercial exchange felt the effects of the Tambora eruption only in 1817 and – to a lesser extent – 1818, when extraordinary grain exports resulted in a massive increase in the total tonnage of trade through the Danish Sound.[29] The 1817 and 1818 statistics reveal record highs of 1,345,897 and 1,309,856 tonnes. In 1817, exports from the Baltic accounted for an exceptional 82.8% of the total turnover in the Danish Sound. In 1819 and 1820, the volume of Baltic commercial exchange declined to pre-1805 levels, and the share of imports increased. Between 1821 and 1824, however, the Greek War of Independence and the French Invasion of Spain seem to have contributed to a slump in the estimated tonnage of trade through the Danish Sound, even though the direct impact of these wars on Baltic commercial exchange was limited. Rather, the French and Greek wars seem to have increased insecurity at sea, which resulted in a (brief) upsurge in marine insurance premiums.[30]

In 1825, Baltic commercial exchange resumed its previous course. From then on, it would never drop below one million tonnes. A new peak was reached during the revolutionary years 1830–1831, when the July Revolution in France and the Belgian Revolution intertwined with the November

Uprising in Congress Poland and resulted in the brief, but violent, Russo-Polish War (1830–1831).[31] The position of the European powers towards this *in se* local conflict prevented a decline of exports from the Baltic during these years. Quite differently, the bad harvest in the Russian Empire in 1833 – "one of the worst of the century"[32] – caused a sudden decline of exports from the Baltic, which was matched partly by a strong upsurge of imports. Whereas the volume of exports continued to decline in 1834 and 1835, imports maintained their 1833 level and now accounted for more than 40% of the total trade through the Danish Sound. Exports recovered rapidly from the 1833–1835 crisis and reached a record high in 1839, when 1,411,626 tonnes of goods left the Baltic Sea via the Danish Sound.

From the early 1840s onwards, the total tonnage of exports stagnated at about one million tonnes per year. Contrastingly, the total tonnage of imports increased threefold between 1833 and 1856. In 1846, the total tonnage of imports exceeded that of exports for the first time since the closing years of the Great Northern War. While the turn of the balance in favour of imports to the Baltic had been a temporary and short-lived phenomenon before, the 1840s marked the start of a new era in Baltic commercial exchange. After having crossed the two million tonnes-mark in 1846, total turnover remained more or less stable, but it was no longer determined by exports through the Danish Sound alone. The tide was changing for trade through the Danish Sound. Between 1836 and 1844, the ratio of exports and imports was 65:35 to 60:40. From 1845 onwards, their shares were almost equal; from 1851, the volume of imports exceeded that of exports. After the Continental Blockade, imports became the driving force of further growth in the total tonnage of Baltic commercial exchange. Whereas early industrialization on the European continent led to ever-larger volumes of coal imported to the Baltic,[33] the estimated tonnage of exports stagnated and even declined in the turbulent years immediately preceding the abolition of the Sound dues.

Departure and destination

The main exporters of commodities through the Danish Sound to destinations in Western Europe and across the Atlantic coast, originated mainly from Poland-Lithuania, Sweden, Prussia, and Russia. Denmark played a secondary role in trade through the Danish Sound, even though it controlled the narrow entrance to the Baltic Sea. During the earlier period, the contribution of Prussia and Russia was small, and in the case of the latter, direct exports were non-existent until the second decade of the eighteenth century. However, the trade of both Russia and Prussia grew significantly in the course of the eighteenth century, not at the least thanks to territorial expansion at the cost of Sweden and Poland-Lithuania (see Chapters 3 and 5). As a result, for the entire period from 1670 until 1806, Prussia and Russia accounted for 52% of the total estimated tonnage of exports from the Baltic (see Table 1.2). In the first

Table 1.2 Distribution of exports, imports, and transport through the Danish Sound per designated period, annual averages in '000 tonnes

Exports from the Baltic						*Shares*	
Departure	*PR*	*RU*	*SW*	*PLC*	*other B*	*% PR*	*% RU*
1670–1806	90	115	73	96	16	23	29
1814–1856	348	339	109	1	72	40	39
Destination	*nsea*	*UK*	*atl/med*	*scan W*	*other W*	*% nsea*	*% UK*
1670–1806	200	106	49	29	9	51	27
1814–1856	219	494	85	68	35	24	55
Imports to the Baltic						*Shares*	
Departure	*nsea*	*UK*	*atl/med*	*scan W*	*other W*	*% nsea*	*% UK*
1670–1806	22	43	67	19	1	14	28
1814–1856	24	386	112	85	18	4	62
Destination	*PR*	*RU*	*SW*	*PLC*	*other B*	*% PR*	*% RU*
1670–1806	24	22	36	20	50	16	15
1814–1856	188	204	61	1	171	30	33
Carriers of trade						*Shares*	
West	*nsea*	*UK*	*atl/med*	*DK*	*other W*	*% nsea*	*% UK*
1670–1806	219	126	3	39	6	56	32
1814–1856	154	492	16	67	43	20	64
Baltic	*PR*	*RU*	*SW*	*PLC*	*other B*	*% PR*	*% RU*
1670–1806	39	3	66	20	7	10	1
1814–1856	306	91	264	1	92	20	6

Source: Tetradas [VSWG-JDA], 3_EI: Exports and imports; 4_T: transport services.
Note: PR = Prussia; RU = Russia (including Finland from 1809); SW = Sweden; PLC = Poland-Lithuania; other B = other places in the Baltic Sea region; nsea = North-West Europe; UK = United Kingdom; atl/med = Atlantic and Mediterranean; scan W = Scandinavia west of the Danish Sound; other W = other places west of the Danish Sound; DK = Denmark.

half of the nineteenth century, their dominance increased further. Whereas the average annual tonnage exported from Prussia and Russia experienced a three- to fourfold increase compared to the period before the Continental Blockade, Sweden's average annual exports grew much slower. Between 1814 and 1856, the average share of Prussia and Russia in exports through the Danish Sound was as high as 79%. The same development, though with slightly less extreme figures occurred for imports to the Baltic. Between 1670 and 1806, Prussia and Russia accounted for 31% on average of all imports to the Baltic; between 1814 and 1856, their share rose to 63% (see Table 1.2).

For the most part, exports from the Baltic were destined to ports in North-West Europe (*nsea* in Table 1.2) and on the British Isles (*UK* in Table 1.2). Together, their share varied between 60% and more than 90%, and dropped to 60% or less only on three occasions: on the eve of the Third Anglo-Dutch War in 1671 and 1672; in 1782, during the Fourth Anglo-Dutch War (1780–1783); and during the Continental Blockade.[34] Between 1674 and 1740, their average share was as high as 86%. Then, from the outbreak of the Austrian War of Succession (1740–1748) and until 1782, it declined to 77%, and during the next period, from 1783 until 1807, it stagnated at an average of 74%. After the Continental Blockade, the North Sea basin resumed its previous course. Between 1814 and 1856, 79% of all exports went to ports in North-West Europe or on the British Isles (see Table 1.2). Remarkably, however, the role of ports in North-West Europe declined, whereas British ports became increasingly important.

The share of Scandinavian ports west of the Sound (*scan W* in Table 1.2) in exports from the Baltic rarely exceeded 10%. Sudden upswings occurred only when external circumstances required a shift of export routes towards western Scandinavian ports. Thus, the relatively high shares in 1671–1673, 1690–1692, 1696, 1705–1708, 1742–1743, and – of course – 1806–1814 resulted from (the threat of) warfare in Western Europe and increased risks of exporting commodities to the North Sea (or beyond).[35] The hardships of carrying out trade during these years perhaps explain why the volumes exported to Scandinavian ports west of the Sound remained relatively low. Like the ports in West Scandinavia, the share of overseas destinations in the estimated total tonnage of exports from the Baltic was never high, except for two years during the Continental Blockade, 1809 and 1811, when the United States benefited the most from the neutrality of their ships.[36] However, interpreting the share of overseas destinations as such may be deceptive. Destinations across the Atlantic Ocean were new to commercial exchange with the Baltic and literally started from zero. Some unsuccessful and rather exotic attempts in the seventeenth century notwithstanding,[37] the first direct exports to overseas destinations occurred in the late 1740s, albeit with very small volumes. From the start of the American War of Independence (1776–1783), overseas destinations obtained a more regular character. The volumes traded increased rapidly; exports from the Baltic to overseas destinations experienced a tenfold increase between 1784 and 1796.[38]

Two exceptions notwithstanding, 1797 and 1800, the average annual tonnage exported to overseas destinations stabilized at 1796 level during the next ten years: 12,340 tonnes on average were sent from the Baltic overseas during the 1797–1806 period. Insofar as American shipping managed to maintain its neutral status during the Continental Blockade, exports to overseas destinations continued. Although the estimated total tonnage of overseas exports grew at increasing rates after the Continental Blockade and almost tripled between 1806 and 1837, a breakthrough was never achieved. On the contrary, the estimated total tonnage of overseas exports declined rapidly between 1838 and 1843 and stagnated at 21,340 tonnes between 1844 and 1856.[39]

The areas of origin of imports to the Baltic, which had a much lower volume than the exports until the late 1830s (see Figure 1.1), did not have the same relative shares as the destinations of exports from the Baltic. In fact, only the long-term development of imports from overseas areas was similar to that of its exports, even if overseas imports grew faster and achieved higher volumes than the corresponding exports to overseas destinations.[40] The differences in the other regions, however, indicate that – even at the highest level of observation – complex transport patterns rather than 'simple' bilateral exchange relations were at play. Insofar as these patterns were related to the Dutch commercial system of the seventeenth and eighteenth centuries, the high shares of direct imports from the Atlantic and Mediterranean are hardly surprising. The so-called *voorbijlandvaart*, a common Dutch term to describe direct sailing routes between the Baltic and Southern Europe bypassing the Dutch Republic, has received considerable attention in the historiography of the preindustrial Dutch commercial system.[41] Remarkable is the relative decline of the Atlantic and the Mediterranean as regions of origin for imports to the Baltic from the late 1780s onwards, and particularly after the Continental Blockade. Compared to West Scandinavia and the North Sea basin, the volume of imports from the South grew only marginally and remained below its peak level of 1785 (161,140 tonnes).[42] Southern Europe's share in total imports to the Baltic declined rapidly and dropped below 10% in 1853.[43] The long-term development of imports from West Scandinavia (i.e. ports in Norway, Denmark, and Sweden west of the Danish Sound) followed a different path. Imports from West Scandinavia rose clearly above the long-term trend on three occasions in the late seventeenth and early eighteenth centuries: during the Third Anglo-Dutch War (1672–1673), at the start of the Nine Years' War (1689–1690) and during the initial phase of the Great Northern War (1705–1708).[44] However, the volumes imported during these periods were modest and hardly exceeded 20,000 tonnes per year. During the rest of the Great Northern War and until 1743, the volume of West Scandinavian imports to the Baltic remained very low. From 1744, imports started to rise and reached a first peak in 1796. Due to the sevenfold increase in the volume of imports, the share of West Scandinavia in total imports to the Baltic rose from 5% in the early 1740s to about 20% at the end of the eighteenth century. This was clearly an effect of the famous Bohuslän herring period (1747–1809).[45] The share of West Scandinavia was exceptionally high during the Continental Blockade, when ports such as Gothenburg seem to have served, inasmuch as possible, as alternatives to the blockaded ports on the continent.[46]

Carriers of trade

Until the second half of the eighteenth century, merchants and carriers from the Dutch Republic dominated trade through the Danish Sound and secured commercial ties between the Baltic and most of continental Europe, including the Mediterranean. Dutch shipmasters carried an overwhelming share of all imports and exports, but their relative position was weakened during the Third Anglo-Dutch War (1672–1674), the Dutch War with France (1672–1678), the Nine Years' War (1688–1697), the Spanish War of Succession (1702–1713), and – most importantly – the Northern Crisis (1715–1720) (see Chapter 3). A major share of total turnover in the Danish Sound went through the hands of Dutch merchants. Amsterdam functioned as a gateway for both merchants and shipmasters, not at the least because of the highly developed financial and insurance markets upon which they could rely for carrying out their business.[47] However, other European powers openly contested their predominant role. The British, who had established the Muscovy (Russia) Company and the Eastland Company in the middle of the sixteenth century, gradually increased their share in commercial exchange with the Baltic, although their turnover remained limited until the late seventeenth century.[48] The French also pursued a leading role in northern commerce (*Fr.* Commerce du Nord), which comprised, but was not limited to the Baltic alone. Their attempts were ineffective, at least insofar as the volume of French shipping was concerned.[49] Sweden, on the other hand, used its military and political strength in the Baltic to expand its commerce and mercantile fleet (see Chapter 3).

Throughout the seventeenth century, Sweden was the dominant supplier of maritime transport services located in the Baltic, followed at a considerable distance by Denmark. In the course of the eighteenth century, Prussia joined Sweden and Denmark as major supplier of maritime transport services located in the Baltic, whereas Great Britain joined the Dutch Republic as the second supplier of such services located in the North Sea basin. The Dutch Republic lost its predominant position in the wake of the Fourth Anglo-Dutch War.[50] On the one hand, the decline of the Dutch Republic and its annexation by Napoleon in 1795 strengthened British shipping in the Baltic. On the other hand, it also gave way to the emergence of other areas of origin in the North Sea basin, such as East Frisia (then Prussian), Oldenburg, Papenburg, and the Hanseatic Towns (Hamburg and Bremen), which attracted carriers from the (former) Dutch Republic by offering neutral passes.[51] The effects of the Fourth Anglo-Dutch War (1780–1783) and the start of the Napoleonic Era coincided with a growth spurt in Baltic carrier services, which continued after the Continental Blockade. Whereas the share of Dutch shipping declined and rapidly lost its significance after 1783,[52] Danish, Swedish, and, from the late eighteenth century onwards, American merchant fleets successfully pursued their neutral role until the early nineteenth century.[53] In the late eighteenth century and until 1806, the suppliers of carrier services in the Baltic were Prussia, Sweden, and Denmark; after 1814, they were joined by Mecklenburg and the Grand Duchy of Finland (then part of the Russian Empire).[54] In the North Sea basin, there was only one major player left: the United Kingdom. The Netherlands played a secondary role. The rise of the *states* in the Baltic Sea region as suppliers of maritime transport services in the eighteenth century, and the fact that they obtained a dominant share by the end of that century, indicates that the long-term development of Baltic commercial exchange also entailed a process of economic integration between the North Sea and the Baltic.

Commodities

Exports from the Baltic

Two major product groups dominated westward commodity flows through the Danish Sound: foodstuffs and raw materials.[55] Westward traffic through the Danish Sound of manufactured goods, the third major product category comprising manufactures such as sailcloth and raven duck, was low until the early 1720s. Then, their estimated total tonnage started to rise quickly to reach a first peak in 1750. Afterwards, the pattern reversed, and the estimated total tonnage of exported manufactures declined until 1767, when it resumed its former course and rose to unprecedented levels towards the end of the eighteenth century.[56] In 1798, an estimated 83,609 tonnes of manufactures were exported from the Baltic; in 1802, as much as 86,903 tonnes.[57] A sudden rise in the exportation of manufactures occurred immediately after the Continental Blockade, but the decline that followed was just as abrupt. Exports started to grow rapidly again between 1819 and 1836, fell by about 30% between 1837 and 1843, and maintained roughly the same level for the remaining period of this study.[58] The long-term development of manufactures exports differed significantly from both the irregular pattern of foodstuffs exports and the more or less steady growth of raw materials exports. The latter seem to have been determined by more or less predictable conditions, whereas climatic variation, warfare, and *ad hoc* regulations in reaction to rapidly changing market conditions promoted or restricted the exportation of foodstuffs.

Until the end of the seventeenth century, foodstuffs clearly dominated exports. After 1700, however, the share of raw materials (in a declining estimated total tonnage exported) rose gradually. It surpassed the share of foodstuffs for the first time during the final years of the Great Northern War. The tonnage of foodstuffs exports remained low and returned to the level of the 1680s only around the mid-eighteenth century. From 1727 onwards, the share of raw materials in total exports from the Baltic almost permanently exceeded that of foodstuffs (see Figure 1.2), rising above 50% of the estimated total tonnage of exports through the Danish Sound between 1731 and 1792. Only exceptional foodstuffs exports occasionally caused a temporary drop below 50%. Between 1792 and until the Continental Blockade, the shares of raw materials and foodstuffs exports were almost equal.

The estimated total tonnage of raw materials exports peaked in 1792. The following decline of raw materials exports continued throughout the closing decade of the eighteenth and during the first years of the nineteenth century. After the Continental Blockade, raw materials exports recovered quickly and resumed their previous growth path. Contrastingly, the volume of foodstuffs exports fluctuated strongly throughout most of the period under survey. Peak levels were reached in one, two, or, exceptionally, three consecutive years. Such upswings in the volume of grain exports from the

Figure 1.2 Estimated tonnage of foodstuffs and raw materials exports from the Baltic, 1670–1856. Five-year moving averages, in tonnes.

Source: *Tetradas* [VSWG-JDA], 2_C_Bex: *Commodity categories.*

Baltic occurred in 1681–1684, 1693, 1698–1699, 1713, 1729, 1740, 1751–1752, 1770, 1783–1785, 1793–1794, 1796, 1802, 1817–1818, 1829–1831, 1839–1840, 1843–1844, and 1849–1850.[59] They relate directly to harvest and, in some cases, hunger crises across Europe. Several such episodes have been the subject of historical analysis and various causes have been discussed, ranging from the climatic impact of volcanic eruptions to crop failures due to bad weather conditions, and bad harvesting during periods of war.[60] During each of the upswings, the volume of exports lay within a range of 300,000–500,000 tonnes before the Continental Blockade. In the post-1814 period, peak volumes exploded and reached more than 800,000 tonnes in 1817–1818, when the eruption of the Tambora volcano (1816) caused a bad harvest in large parts of Europe,[61] and in 1839, when bad wheat harvests had struck the United Kingdom.[62] During three more modest upswings (1829–1831, 1843–1844, and 1849–1850) annual volumes between 550,000 and 650,000 tonnes of foodstuffs were exported through the Danish Sound. From 1840 onwards, the very large fluctuations that characterized the preceding three decades became less outspoken and the shares of foodstuffs and raw materials in total exports from the Baltic seem to have become more or less stable (see Figure 1.2).

Compared to the *hausses* described above, periods of diminishing foodstuffs exports were typically longer and lasted between 7 and 12 years. Depressions, when foodstuffs exports were extremely low during one or more consecutive years, did not last long: 1672–1673, 1697–1698, 1703, 1707–1708,

1710, 1715–1720, 1727, 1732–1733, 1736–1737, 1745–1746, 1756, 1758, 1787–1788, 1806–1813, 1822–1824, and 1833–1835. In a number of cases, these depressions coincided with warfare. Depending on the area where the war was waged, its impact was different. Warfare in Western Europe hindered the trade and distribution of foodstuffs across Western European destinations, as was the case during the Anglo-Dutch War (1672–1673), the Seven Years' War (1756, 1758), and the Franco-Spanish War (1822, 1824). Warfare in the Baltic disturbed the supply to Western Europe, which happened during the Great Northern War and the Continental Blockade. Finally, warfare in the areas of production, e.g. the Polish War of Succession (1736–1737), could also have a negative impact on the harvested and traded volumes.

Imports to the Baltic

The tonnage of eastward commodity flows (imports) through the Danish Sound and their long-term development differed completely from that of exports. The tonnage of eastward traffic was much lower than that of westward traffic until the late 1830s, its commodity structure was different for most of the period, and neither its general growth pattern nor that of single product groups resembles that of westward traffic through the Danish Sound. The tonnage of imported manufactures was low during most of the eighteenth century, except for two years: 1769 and 1771.[63] The import of manufactures started to increase dramatically after the Continental Blockade and peaked in 1844–1846, when almost 25,000 tonnes of manufactured goods were imported. Afterwards, the tonnage of imports declined to jump up again only in 1855 and 1856, when a record 32,779 tonnes of manufactures were imported to the Baltic.[64]

The tonnage of foodstuffs imports (including wine and salt) rose steadily during most of the period.[65] The lowest tonnages were registered, not surprisingly, in 1673, during the Anglo-Dutch War, between 1690 and 1697, during the Nine Years' War, in 1705, during the Great Northern War, and during the Continental Blockade. Overall, however, a fourfold increase in the estimated total tonnage of foodstuffs imports to the Baltic can be observed from 55,517 tonnes in 1670 to 256,547 tonnes in 1805. Growth continued in the first half of the nineteenth century and stagnated at an annual average of 355,339 tonnes only in the final years of observation.[66]

The pattern of raw materials imports was different. Until 1721, raw materials imports were very low. From 1722 onwards, they started to rise in a more or less regular fashion until 1797. During this long period, the highest tonnages of raw materials imports were registered in 1769, 1771, 1788, 1790, and 1796.[67] Although the estimated total tonnages were relatively low, particularly in comparison with the corresponding raw materials exports from the Baltic, the growth of raw materials imports from 18,382 tonnes in 1722 to 79,711 tonnes in 1797 also resulted in more than a fourfold increase. Between 1798 and 1832, the registered tonnage of raw materials imports to the Baltic diminished to an average of about 26,000 tonnes annually. This decline was probably related to the under-registration of coal imports during this period. Then, quite suddenly, an entirely different pattern emerged. Rapidly increasing volumes of raw materials – mostly coal – were imported to the Baltic from 1833 onwards; their estimated tonnage rose to more than one million tonnes in 1856.

Framework of analysis

Questions

Between the establishment of the Sound dues by the Danish king Erik VII in 1429 and their abolition in 1857, the Baltic had evolved from a basin of regional trade, where members of individual cities could successfully defend their commercial interests, to an arena of world trade, where the leading powers of the time tried to secure and leverage their national interests. Between these extremes lies a period of protracted political and military disputes, which coincided with the heyday of mercantilism and the rise of state politics, the breakthrough of industrial modes of production and fossil-energy fuelled technologies. This period, which lasted from about 1670 until the abolition of the Sound dues in 1857, is central to this study.

The succinct exploratory analysis of the preceding sections and additional statistics of the long-term development of bilateral trade relations between countries east and west of the Danish Sound[68] underline the fundamental character of the changes that occurred during this period. Great Britain (from 1801: the United Kingdom) replaced the Dutch Republic; Prussia and Russia (quite literally) replaced Poland-Lithuania. After the Continental Blockade, tonnage shipped between the United Kingdom and Prussia grew faster than tonnage shipped between the United Kingdom and Russia. By the mid-nineteenth century at the latest, the centre of gravity in trade through the Sound had shifted towards Prussia and the southern Baltic coast, close to the entrances to the Baltic. Trade through the Danish Sound with Russia stagnated and experienced a relative decline. Finally, in the course of the eighteenth century, the Dutch commercial system, which had dominated trade through the Danish Sound since the late sixteenth century,[69] was overthrown by a novel structure in which the pursuit of commercial gains for the benefit of the state occupied a central position. Although the British system propagated the freedom of trade, it bore in mind the freedom of its own commerce in the first place (if not exclusively).[70]

Remarkably, even though the available literature on many aspects of Baltic trade is vast,[71] no analysis is available that addresses some inevitable questions with regard to the empirical observations outlined in the previous sections. The questions themselves are deceptively simple: What has provoked these fundamental changes in trade through the Danish Sound between 1669 and 1857? How can the changes observed at the macro level be explained? What is the larger political and economic context of these changes? How were they embedded in *longue durée* processes of transition (in particular, from pre-industrial to industrial modes of production)? If at all, how can answers to these questions inform us about the relative significance of trade through the Danish Sound?

The latter question is tricky, however. Even though it may seem that the empirical observations made above are conclusive in their own right, they cannot provide an answer to the issue of the relative significance of trade through the Danish Sound. Most importantly, in light of previous research on the Black Sea (grain) trade in the nineteenth century,[72] a recent effort to compile statistics about the Greek contribution to this trade,[73] and published annual statistics of France and the United Kingdom, which distinguish between the 'northern' (Baltic and White Sea) and 'southern' (Black Sea) ports of the Russian Empire from the early 1840s onwards,[74] it must be taken into account that the *opening* of the Black Sea for foreign trade might have had significant impact on the development of trade through the Danish Sound.[75] This, in turn, leads to another set of questions: How large was this impact? Besides grain, were other commodities affected as well by the opening of the Black Sea for foreign trade? How large was the impact of other supply areas on the development of trade through the Danish Sound? Finally, if we expand our view on trade through the Danish Sound in this way, what was its role in world history? To tackle these questions, we introduce four hypotheses, which constitute the pillars of this study.

Hypotheses

First, this study postulates that the fundamental changes in trade through the Danish Sound between 1669 and 1857 are embedded in a perception of the world, which, for some time at least, saw the northern part of the continental landmass depicted as Eurasia as an area of special interest in international politics and trade. The study introduces the concept of *North Eurasia* as a unit of world history and places its emergence in the context of a changing worldview promoted, among others, by Gottfried Wilhelm Leibniz (1646–1716) at the turn of the eighteenth century (see Chapter 2). This changing worldview had its roots in long processes of nation building in the western part of the landmass, which had led to the emergence of the Polish-Lithuanian Commonwealth in 1569, almost two hundred years after the establishment of a personal union between the Kingdom of Poland and the Grand Duchy of Lithuania. Further eastward, the Grand Duchy of Muscovy absorbed the Republic of Novgorod in 1478, which marked the beginning of expansion across the Ural Mountains into Siberia and – less successful at first – in southern direction towards the Black Sea, which had become an 'Ottoman lake' after the fall of Constantinople (1453). Decisive achievements were the conquest of Kazan and Astrakhan, both strategically located on the Volga, around the mid-sixteenth century. In 1558, Muscovy gained access to the Baltic Sea via the port of Narva; roughly at the same time, it established trading posts on the White Sea coast, and founded the city and port of Arkhangelsk. With Narva lost to the Swedes in 1581, Archangel remained Muscovy's only direct maritime connection to Western Europe throughout the seventeenth century. Muscovite travellers and explorers reached the Pacific coast in 1654, granted Armenian merchants privileges in the transit trade of Persian goods through Muscovy via the Caspian Sea and signed an anti-Ottoman treaty with Poland-Lithuania (both in 1667). Having acknowledged its vital economic importance long before, the Muscovite rulers never abandoned their wish to obtain direct access to the Baltic Sea. However, this wish would only be fulfilled during the Great Northern War (1700–1721) (see Chapter 3). Muscovy's territorial expansion, which had started back in 1478, culminated in the establishment of the Russian Empire and the (reluctant) international acceptance of the title *Tsar'* in the Treaty of Nystadt (1721).

Second, in view of these territorial developments, the study argues that competition between the (western) *borderlands and border basins* of North Eurasia, i.e. the White Sea, Black Sea, Caspian Sea, and the Baltic, and conflicts in and about the border basins and borderlands of North Eurasia, had a significant impact on trade through the Danish Sound between 1669 and 1857. The study relies on statistical data about commodity flows and traded values in the borderlands and border basins to assess the impact of competition and complementarity between the different borderlands on processes of development and change as well as on the outcome of international conflicts. Although exchange along the North-South axis (e.g. with Persia and China) constituted a vital element in the development of North Eurasia as a unified landmass, North Eurasian trade was driven for the most part by the westward orientation of its constituent political units. In particular, Russia's expansionism led to drastic border regime changes in the wake of the partitions of Poland-Lithuania (1772, 1793 and 1795) and the Peace Treaty of Küçük Kajnarca (1774). Access to the Black Sea was recovered and a third western borderland of North Eurasia was opened for international trade in the last quarter of the eighteenth century.

The study ends around 1860, shortly after the defeat of the Russian Empire in the Crimean War (1854–1855), the abolition of the Danish Sound dues (1857), the Second Treaty of Beijing (1858), and the foundation of Vladivostok on the Pacific coast (1860). Among other things, the Crimean War makes clear that Russia's state organization and economic structure were no longer competitive in the international constellation, but it also shows how strongly intertwined the different western borderlands of North Eurasia had become. The abolition of the Danish Sound dues underlines the profound changes in the institutional framework of international trade through the Danish Sound. The Second Treaty of Beijing and the foundation of Vladivostok provide evidence for the growing importance of the "new" borderlands in the Far East, where competition between the United Kingdom and Russia (and later Japan as well) provoked the next fundamental change in the intellectual, economic, and political focus of the parties involved. The political and economic issues between Russia and the United Kingdom, in particular, now shifted towards the borderlands between North and South Eurasia, eventually leading to what is known in historiography as the 'Great Game'.[76] The analysis of international commercial and diplomatic relations between the main political entities with interests vested in North Eurasia helps to assess the role of North Eurasian trade in world history from the second half of the seventeenth century until the mid-nineteenth century.

Third, the study underlines the contribution of *infrastructure and logistics* to long-term changes in the structure of trade through the Danish Sound. It argues that infrastructural development in North Eurasia, on the one hand, and the logistics of commercial interaction in the borderlands of North Eurasia, on the other, need to be taken into account to forward our understanding of North Eurasia as a unit of world history. The infrastructure addressed in this study precedes the emergence of a 'modern' transport infrastructure and 'modern' logistics. It comprises the various surfaces of the earth that may be used for transportation (solid ground, rivers, lakes, seas, and oceans), the different means of covering distances across these surfaces (ships, waggons, animals, etc.), and the manmade physical infrastructure (roads, canals, and portages) that was developed, controlled, and exploited with the goal of obtaining political power, supporting the domestic economy, or promoting trade.[77] Due to their impact on the intensity and directions of cross-border exchange as well as their vulnerability and susceptibility to conflict and even disruption, the political and economic functions of infrastructure are key to understanding the long-term development of cross-border commercial exchange relations and thus to understanding North Eurasia as a unit of world history. Moreover, the focus on infrastructure and logistics contributes to understanding processes of integration and unification and allows tracing the origins of a North Eurasian system of commercial exchange. Although the central role of infrastructure at the crossroads between society, economy, and politics, recently has become the object of innovative studies in modern and contemporary history, it is not fully acknowledged that infrastructure may have played a similar role in the preindustrial period. Few noteworthy exceptions notwithstanding, the predominant empirical research into the history of infrastructure is preoccupied mostly with the (late) nineteenth and twentieth centuries.[78] In modern history, infrastructure is understood as an element that 'pre-structures' the market,[79] and its central role in such matters as state intervention in the economy, the location of economic activity, and the implementation of regional economic policies[80] is widely acknowledged. Preindustrial infrastructure, on the other hand, often is regarded merely as a loose collection of 'isolated initiatives.'[81] Such viewpoint seems to rely on a limited understanding of the scope of preindustrial infrastructural developments and thus carries the risk of underestimating the efforts of engineers, economists, government officials, and publicists to realize large-scale infrastructural improvements.[82]

Dealing essentially with 'infrastructure before infrastructure' (to paraphrase Kriedte et al.'s famous formulation about the process character of the industrial revolution),[83] the term 'preindustrial infrastructure' is introduced to denote a particular phase in the transition from local infrastructural development initiatives to 'national' systems in the sense of Friedrich List. In contrast to most current research on the history of infrastructure, which usually takes the railway as starting point, it is argued that 'modern' ideas about infrastructural development experienced a breakthrough in the wake of the Peace of Westphalia,[84] and that preindustrial infrastructure signifies more than just isolated, premodern examples of later developments.[85] Rather, preindustrial infrastructure emerged because of increasingly modern ideas about the economy and the state, but was realized and exploited with non-mechanical means. The study maintains that the planning and construction of canals, but also of ports, markets, warehouses, and transport facilities was an important (but often neglected) element of mercantilist discourse and policy-making in post-Westphalian Europe,[86] but acknowledges that the available means to realize these plans and ideas remained *pre*modern. In this sense, preindustrial infrastructure is typical of a transitory phase of societal development on the road to modernity.

Fourth, the study argues for a distinction between the actual and perceived economic significance of infrastructural developments. Rather than the construction of transport infrastructure *per se*, which is part of the history of technology, this study deals with domestic and international transport and trade policies (as found in tariffs, customs regulations, diplomatic correspondence, bilateral and multilateral commercial and shipping treaties). Transport and trade statistics reflect the long-term outcome of such policies. However, alongside the actual economic significance of transport infrastructure, which can be traced in statistical data, the development and exploitation of transport infrastructure, and even just plans to develop new infrastructure, could provoke reactions of fear or envy but also of hope and even admiration. Such 'emotions' are documented in diplomatic and private correspondence, memoirs, pamphlets, and other (printed) media rather than statistics. Therefore, this type of documentation should also be taken into account when assessing the impact of infrastructural developments on North Eurasian trade.

Method

Two elements account for the novelty of the following analysis. The first element is the creation and use of a large, uniform data set of commodities flows through the Danish Sound between 1670 and 1856. The present study could not have been executed without the groundbreaking digitization of the Danish Sound toll registers, a unique source for European economic history of the pre- and early industrial period (for details, see Appendix A). The second element is the elaboration of the geographical concept of North Eurasia, which includes the Baltic as one of its western border basins, alongside the White, Black, and Caspian Seas, and the western overland border. The analysis focuses on political entities with a stake in North Eurasian trade; they were the main drivers of internal and external processes of continuity and change on the North Eurasian landmass. Gaining insight into the internal processes requires the study of infrastructure and logistics on the North Eurasian mainland, whereas the analysis of commercial exchange in North Eurasia's borderlands and border basins furthers knowledge and understanding of external processes of continuity and change. This, in turn, allows taking into account the contribution of North Eurasia to Europe's overseas expansion, on the one hand, and the impact of Europe's overseas expansion on the northern, continental part of Eurasia and its transit trade, on the other hand.

Throughout the study, the Baltic as a whole serves as the starting point of empirical observations, rather than preselected bilateral relations or other variables. The Baltic is not seen as an (almost entirely) closed basin with a relatively small coastal strip and a few main ports along that coast, as is often the case in traditional accounts of 'the Baltic' as a space of cultural and commercial interaction. Rather, we see 'the Baltic' as one of several border basins of a large continental landmass depicted as North Eurasia. In line with these statements, the concept of North Eurasia as unit of analysis provides an alternative to more common geographical demarcations that are often found in historical studies of international politics and trade, such as divisions into historical regions or countries (e.g. Pomerania, Prussia, East Prussia, etc.), the (anachronistic) use of modern countries and their borders, or politically inspired historiographical concepts. The present study differs significantly from the bulk of the historiography of 'Baltic trade', with its predominant focus on bilateral trade relations, the study of ports, the role of the Baltic in the commercial history of a certain region or political entity (often during limited periods of time), or trade in specific commodities. The present study also distinguishes itself from previous 'general histories' of the Baltic, which deal with trade through the Danish Sound mostly in the broader context of cultural exchange, and typically base their insights on the traditional historiography of 'Baltic trade' rather than asking novel questions. Finally, rather than observing the borderlands of North Eurasia separately, this study pursues a holistic approach in which the different western borderlands and border basins of North Eurasia are seen as constituent parts of this landmass.

In so doing, I hope to shed light on a large, continental landmass, which is often left aside for the benefit of a predominant maritime perspective in historical studies of globalization. Moreover, I hope to provide indications towards a novel appraisal of the historical roles of the Baltic, the Black Sea, the Russian Empire, and Eastern Europe in world history. Rather than being pictured plainly as arenas of 'peripheral' or at best 'semi-peripheral' developments, the concept of North Eurasia and its borderlands and border basins may help to overcome the limitations of previous, often politically inspired historical concepts of space. Finally, the concept of North Eurasia may also help to address "(…) the constantly changing relationships between bodies of water and masses of land, (…)"[87] in a novel way.

This chapter started with an exploratory analysis of the tonnage estimates of trade through the Danish Sound between 1670 and 1856, which revealed structural changes in its main actors, the commodities exchanged between east and west, the main areas of departure and destination of goods carried through the Danish Sound, and the origin of the carriers of this trade. Based on the results of this exploratory data survey, questions and hypotheses were formulated about the long-term impact on the structure of trade through the Danish Sound of geographical expansion, international politics, infrastructural development, and conflicting commercial interests, and the method for dealing with these questions was outlined briefly. The next chapter digs deeper into the concept of North Eurasia as a unit of world history, provides further specifications about the role of the Baltic as one of North Eurasia's border basins, and underlines the need for a holistic approach towards North Eurasia, including its borderlands and border basins.

Notes

1 For more information about the Danish Sound toll registers, the creation of an electronic database of these registers, and recent research examples using them, see Veluwenkamp and Scheltjens, *Early modern shipping and trade.* The history of the toll has been treated in detail in: Gøbel, "The Sound Toll Registers Online project"; Degn (ed.), *The Sound Toll at Elsinore*, or its Danish version Degn (ed.), *Tolden i Sundet*, and the elder, but still valuable: Scherer, *Der Sundzoll*; Hill, *The Danish Sound Dues.* The methodology for the conversion of data from the Danish Sound toll registers online into tonnage estimates is described in: Scheltjens, "Tetradas." Selected trade statistics based on the converted data can be accessed at: *Tetradas* [VSWG-JDA]. Throughout the text, the term *tonnes* refers to a metric unit, equivalent to 1,000 kilograms or litres. The similar term *ton* is a unit of measurement corresponding to a variety of different values. Throughout the book, I refer to the statistics available online in the following abridged manner: *Tetradas* [VSWG-JDA], <series number>_<series abbreviation>_<subseries>: <short title(s) of the series>. For example, the time series underlying figure 1 is: Tetradas [VSWG-JDA], 1_turnover: *Estimated total turnover.*

2 Dollinger, *Die Hanse*, 469–477; Graichen and Hammel-Kiesow, *Die deutsche Hanse*, 341–360; Selzer, *Die mittelalterliche Hanse*, 125; Ressel, "Von der Hanse."

3 The documentation about the process of abolishing the Sound dues between 1854 and 1857 is vast and remains largely unexplored. For introductory surveys of the issue, see Ahonen, "Den dansk-amerikanske strid"; Tønnessen, "Nord Amerikas Forente Stater"; Krauel, "Die Ablösung des Sundzolls"; Rubin, "Sundtoldens afløsning"; Wehrmann, "Die Betheiligung Lübecks."

4 Alexandersson, *The Baltic straits*, 73.

5 Iredale, "John and Thomas Marshall," 80.

6 Evans, "The gift of the sea"; Evans, "Transport, economics and economists."

7 At the same time, in a slightly different form, one could use these volumes to address the demand for maritime transport services, since it is the volume rather than the value of trade, which determines employment of shipping. However, maritime transport services are not determined by the volume of the transported

goods alone; distances between ports are another important element in estimating the productivity of maritime transport services. See Davis, *The rise*, 169–193. A method for generating tonkm-estimates using tonnages as well as distances between ports has been described in: Scheltjens, *Dutch deltas*, Introduction.

8 *Tetradas* [VSWG-JDA], 8_CIES_Bex_FS: *Barley, Oats, Rye, Wheat.*

9 *Tetradas* [VSWG-JDA], 8_CIES_Bex_RM: *Flax, Hemp, Iron, Linseed, Pitch, Tallow, Tar, Timber.*

10 *Tetradas* [VSWG-JDA], 8_CIES_Bex_MF: *Raven-duck, Sailcloth.*

11 Most recently: North, *Geschichte der Ostsee* [Eng. translation: North, *The Baltic*]. Earlier examples include: Klinge, *Östersjövärlden*; Kirby, *Northern Europe*; and Kirby and Hinkkanen, *The Baltic and the North Seas.* An early, unsuccessful attempt to institutionalize the history of the Baltic (*Ger.* Ostseeraumgeschichte) as a discipline of the historical sciences in the 1930s is documented in: Hanssen-Decker, "Geschichtswissenschaft für den Ostseeraum?"

12 Bang and Korst (eds.), *Tabeller over skibsfart.*

13 Criticism of the Sound toll tables has been formulated since the publication of the first volume of the *Tabeller.* See Christensen, "Der handelsgeschichtliche Wert"; Friis, "Sundtoldregenskaberne"; Jeannin, "Les Comptes du Sund"; Kownatzki, "Die Bedeutung der Sundzoll-Listen"; Heckscher, "Øresundsrakenskaperna." Smaller reviews of the publication of the *Tabeller* are listed in the bibliography to: Degn (ed.), *The Sound Toll at Elsinore.* The history of the scientific perception of the Danish Sound toll registers, and the particular role of Bang and Korst's *Tabeller* therein, is yet to be written. Relevant starting points for such undertaking include: Schäfer, "Zur Orientierung"; Schäfer, "Die Sundzollrechnungen"; Schäfer, "Die Sundzoll-Listen"; [s.n.], "Zur Frage der Herausgabe"; [s.n.], "Bericht über die Arbeit"; Schäfer, "Die Sundzoll-Tabellen"; Unger, "De Sonttabellen"; Unger, "Een nieuw deel der sonttabellen"; Unger, "De publikatie der Sonttabellen voltooid"; Jeannin, "Les Comptes du Sund"; Gøbel, "De Sonttolregisters"; Pourchasse, "Danish Sound Dues"; Gøbel, "Øresundstoldens arkivalier 1497–1858"; Gøbel, "The Sound Toll Registers Online project"; Frandsen, "Neue entwicklungen."

14 For a summary of recurrent points of criticism with regard to the *Tabeller,* and a discussion of the advantages of the electronic database, see Scheltjens and Veluwenkamp, "Sound Toll Registers Online"; Veluwenkamp, "Die 'Sound Toll Registers Online'"; Scheltjens, "Maße und Gewichte"; Scheltjens, Veluwenkamp, and Van der Woude, "A closer look." Recently, a modest attempt was made to 'rehabilitate' Bang and Korst's tables: Kumar, "A note in defense."

15 Desfeuilles, "La Navigation" [1959]; Desfeuilles, "La Navigation" [1961].

16 Johansen, *Shipping and trade.*

17 Unfortunately, this database is no longer available.

18 Ahonen, *From sugar triangle to cotton triangle*; Rönnbäck, "New and old peripheries"; Rönnbäck, "The sound toll chamber commodity records"; Rönnbäck, "Balancing the Baltic trade."

19 www.soundtoll.nl

20 Scheltjens, "Tetradas."

21 For general surveys of warfare and trade in the Baltic, see Anderson, *Naval wars in the Baltic*; Kirby, *Northern Europe*; Oakley, *War and peace in the Baltic*; Heckscher, *The continental system.*

22 *Tetradas* [VSWG-JDA], 1_Turnover: *Estimated total turnover.*

23 Heckscher, *The continental system*, 13–29; Melvin, *Napoleon's navigation system*, 2–5.

24 *Tetradas* [VSWG-JDA], 1_Turnover: *Estimated total turnover.*

25 Scheltjens, Veluwenkamp, and Van der Woude, "A closer look," 2–3.

26 *Tetradas* [VSWG-JDA], 1_Turnover: *Estimated total turnover.*
27 Price, *Napoleon*, 251–262.
28 Stothers, "The Great Tambora eruption"; Behringer, *Tambora*; D'Arcy Wood, *Tambora.*
29 *Tetradas* [VSWG-JDA], 1_Turnover: *Estimated total turnover,* and 8_CIES_Bex_FS: *Barley, Oats, Rye, Wheat.*
30 Denzel, *Die Hamburger Seeversicherung* (mimeo).
31 Morley, "European Significance."
32 Blackwell, *Beginnings of Russian Industrialisation*, 178.
33 *Tetradas* [VSWG-JDA], 8_CIES_Wim_RM: *Coal (Kuller), Coal (Stenkul).*
34 *Tetradas* [VSWG-JDA], 3_EI_Bex: *Countries (areas) of destination.*
35 *Tetradas* [VSWG-JDA], 3_EI_Bex: *Countries (areas) of destination.*
36 Heckscher, *The continental system*, 127–148; Golden and Lewis, "The role of exports"; Adams, "American neutrality"; Keene, "American shipping and trade"; Hunter, "Wheat, war, and the American economy." See also: *Tetradas* [VSWG-JDA], 4_T: *Transport services by countries (areas).*
37 Hundt, " *Woraus nichts geworden*"; Kalisch, "Pläne zur Belebung des Orienthandels"; Hassinger, "Die erste Wiener orientalische Handelskompagnie"; Mattiesen, "Die Versuche zur Erschließung"; Eckert, *Kurland unter dem Einfluss*, 164–190.
38 *Tetradas* [VSWG-JDA], 3_EI_Bex: *Countries (areas) of destination.*
39 *Tetradas* [VSWG-JDA], 3_EI_Bex: *Countries (areas) of destination.*
40 *Tetradas* [VSWG-JDA], 3_EI_Bex: *Countries (areas) of destination*; 3_EI_Wim: *Countries (areas) of departure.*
41 Van Tielhof, *The 'Mother of all Trades'*, 71–75; Scheltjens, 'The changing geography,' 21–30.
42 *Tetradas* [VSWG-JDA], 3_EI_Wim: *Countries (areas) of departure.*
43 *Tetradas* [VSWG-JDA], 3_EI_Wim: *Countries (areas) of departure.*
44 *Tetradas* [VSWG-JDA], 3_EI_Wim: *Countries (areas) of departure.*
45 Lindquist, "Herring periods of Bohuslan," and the literature cited there.
46 Heckscher, *The continental system*, 236–237.
47 About the 'gateway' function of Amsterdam, see Lesger, *The rise of the Amsterdam market.* The Amsterdam insurance market has been analysed in detail in: Go, *Marine insurance in the Netherlands.* The Amsterdam financial market and the role of the *Wisselbank* is treated extensively in: Dehing, *Geld in Amsterdam.*
48 The Muscovy Company, later called 'Russia Company,' was active in the White Sea and the port of Narva. The Eastland Company's area of commercial activity comprised "Norway, Sweden and Finland, Copenhagen and Elsinore in Denmark, and the whole Baltic coast from Estonia to the Oder, (...)". Finally, in the rest of Denmark, Pomerania and Mecklenburg the spheres of commercial interest of the Eastland Company and the Merchant Adventurers overlapped. See Aström, *From Stockholm to St. Petersburg*, 11–12. On the activities of the different companies, mostly during the sixteenth and seventeenth centuries, see the following introductions: Van Brakel, "Die Entwicklung"; Hinton, *The Eastland Company*; Groth, "Angielska Kompania Wschodnia"; Willan, "The Russia Company."
49 Boissonade and Charliat, "Colbert et la Compagnie."
50 *Tetradas* [VSWG-JDA], 4_T: *Transport services by countries (areas).*
51 Scheltjens, *Dutch Deltas*, Chapter 4.
52 De Vries, *De economische achteruitgang.* For a critical assessment of the decline of the Dutch Republic, see Riley, "The Dutch Economy"; Van Zanden, "De economie van Holland."
53 *Tetradas* [VSWG-JDA], 4_T: *Transport services by countries (areas).*
54 *Tetradas* [VSWG-JDA], 4_T: *Transport services by countries (areas).*

55 For details about the categorization of commodities, see Scheltjens, "Tetradas," and *Tetradas* [VSWG-JDA], 9_AUX: *Replication data for commodities.*
56 *Tetradas* [VSWG-JDA], 2_C_Bex: *Commodity categories.*
57 *Tetradas* [VSWG-JDA], 2_C_Bex: *Commodity categories.*
58 *Tetradas* [VSWG-JDA], 2_C_Bex: *Commodity categories.*
59 Remarkably, there was only one longer period of steadily rising foodstuffs export, between 1759 and 1770. *Tetradas* [VSWG-JDA], 2_C_Bex: *Commodity categories*; 2_C_Bex: *Itemized commodities.*
60 See, for example: Rössner, "The 1738–1741 harvest crisis in Scotland"; Collet, "Hunger ist der beste Unterhändler des Friedens"; Veale and Endfield, "Situating 1816"; Behringer, *Tambora*; Schanbacher, *Kartoffelkrankheit*; Ó Gráda (ed.), *When the Potato failed*; Bass, *Hungerkrisen in Preußen*; Abel, *Massenarmut und Hungerkrisen*; and the article series "Great Historical Events that were significantly affected by the weather", published in the Bulletin of the American Meteorological Society.
61 Behringer, *Tambora.*
62 Wallis, "What caused the crisis of 1839?"
63 *Tetradas* [VSWG-JDA], 2_C_Wim: *Commodity categories.*
64 *Tetradas* [VSWG-JDA], 2_C_Wim: *Commodity categories.*
65 *Tetradas* [VSWG-JDA], 2_C_Wim: *Commodity categories.*
66 *Tetradas* [VSWG-JDA], 2_C_Wim: *Commodity categories.*
67 *Tetradas* [VSWG-JDA], 2_C_Wim: *Commodity categories.*
68 *Tetradas* [VSWG-JDA], 6_BTR: *Exports from Poland-Lithuania, Prussia, Russia, and Sweden*; 6_BTR: *Imports from France, Netherlands, United Kingdom, and United States.*
69 North, *Geschichte der Ostsee*, 149.
70 As goes the classical argument of Friedrich List, which was rephrased in a more popular fashion by Ha-Joon Chang. See Chang, *Kicking away the ladder.*
71 The bibliographical appendix in Degn's *Tolden i Sundet* (English version: *The Sound Toll at Elsinore*) provides a good starting point for getting acquainted with the literature. See Degn (ed.), *The Sound Toll at Elsinore*, 549–590.
72 E.g. Puryear, "Odessa"; Fairlie, *The Anglo-Russian grain trade*; Herlihy, *Russian grain*; Družinina, *Južnaja Ukraina*; Zolotov, *Vnešnjaja torgovlja*; Kardasis, *Diaspora merchants.*
73 www.blacksea.gr
74 See *Tableaux générales* for France, and *Tables of the revenue* for the United Kingdom.
75 Recent historiography treats the *opening* of the Black Sea since 1774 as the opposite process of the *closure* of the Black Sea since the fall of Kaffa (1475) and Kilia (1484) and its becoming an 'Ottoman lake' in the sixteenth century. See Kołodziejczyk, "Inner lake or frontier?"; Popescu, "La mer noire ottomane."
76 Ewans, *The great game.*
77 The term infrastructure appeared for the first time in 1875, but has obtained its broad contemporary meaning only after World War II. The history of the term is reviewed in: Van Laak, "Der Begriff."
78 Van Laak, "Technological infrastructure." One noteworthy exception is: Förster and Bauch (eds.), *Wasserinfrastrukturen und Macht.*
79 Van Laak, "Der Begriff," 293.
80 Van Laak, "Der Begriff," 293–294.
81 Van Laak, "Infra-strukturgeschichte."
82 See Mukerji, *Impossible engineering.*
83 See Kriedte et al. (eds.), *Industrialisierung vor der Industrialisierung*; Schremmer, "Industrialisierung vor der Industrialisierung."
84 Mukerji, *Impossible engineering.*
85 Van Laak, "Infra-strukturgeschichte."
86 Helander, "Merkantilistische Verkehrspolitik."
87 Bentley, "Sea and ocean basins," 217.

References

www.blacksea.gr: *The Black Sea Research Project Web*

www.soundtoll.nl: *Soundtoll Registers Online*

[s.n.]. "Bericht über die Arbeit an den Sundzollregistern." *Hansische Geschichtsblätter* 21 (1915): 394–395.

[s.n.]. "Zur Frage der Herausgabe und Bearbeitung der Sundzoll-Tabellen." *Hansische Geschichtsblätter* 19 (1913): 603–606.

Abel, Wilhelm. *Massenarmut und Hungerkrisen im vorindustriellen Europa. Versuch einer Synopsis.* Hamburg / Berlin 1974.

Adams Jr., Donald R. "American neutrality and prosperity, 1793–1808. A reconsideration." *The Journal of Economic History* 40, 4 (1980): 713–737.

Ahonen, Kalevi. "Den dansk-amerikanske strid om Øresundstolden." In *Tolden i Sundet. Toldopkrævning, politik og skibsfart i Øresund 1429–1857*, edited by Ole Degn, 527–566. København 2010.

Ahonen, Kalevi. *From sugar triangle to cotton triangle. Trade and shipping between America and Baltic Russia 1783–1860.* Jyväskylä 2005.

Alexandersson, Gunnar. *The Baltic straits.* Leiden 1982.

Anderson, R.C. *Naval wars in the Baltic during the sailing-ship epoch, 1522–1850.* London 1910.

Åström, Sven-Erik. *From Stockholm to St. Petersburg. Commercial factors in the political relations between England and Sweden, 1675–1700.* Helsinki 1962.

Bang, Nina Ellinger; Korst, Knud (eds.). *Tabeller over skibsfart og Varetransport gennem Øresund / Tables de la navigation et du transport des marchandises passant par le Sund 1497–1660. I: Tabeller over skibsfarten / Tables de la navigation.* København / Leipzig 1906; *II.A. Tabeller over Varetransporten / Tables du transport des marchandises.* København / Leipzig 1922; *II.B. Tabeller over Varetransporten / Tables du transport des marchandises.* København / Leipzig 1933.

Bang, Nina Ellinger; Korst, Knud (eds.). *Tabeller over skibsfart og Varetransport gennem Øresund 1661–1783 og gennem Storebælt 1701–1748 / Tables de la navigation et du transport des marchandises passant par le Sund 1661–1783 et par le Grand-belt 1701–1748. I: Tabeller over Skibsfarten.* København / Leipzig 1930; *II.1. Tabeller over varetransporten. Halvbd. 1: 1661–1720.* København / Leipzig 1939; *II.2. Tabeller over varetransporten. Halvbd. 2: 1721–1760.* København / Leipzig 1945; *II.2. Transport gennem Øresund 1661–1783 og gennem Storebælt 1701–1748.* København 1953.

Bass, Hans H. *Hungerkrisen in Preußen während der ersten Hälfte des 19. Jarhunderts.* St. Katharinen 1991.

Behringer, Wolfgang. *Tambora und das Jahr ohne Sommer. Wie ein Vulkan die Welt in die Krise stürzte.* München 2015.

Blackwell, William L. *The beginnings of Russian industrialization, 1800–1860.* Princeton 1968.

Boissonade, P.; Charliat, P. "Colbert et la Compagnie de Commerce du Nord." *Revue d'histoire économique et sociale* 17, 2 (1929): 156–204.

Chang, Ha-Joon. *Kicking away the ladder. Development strategy in historical perspective.* London 2003.

Christensen, Aksel E. "Der handelsgeschichtliche Wert der Sundzollregister." *Hansische Geschichtsblatter* 59 (1934): 29–142.

Collet, Dominik. "'Hunger ist der beste Unterhändler des Friedens'. Die Hungerkrise 1770–1772 und die Erste Teilung Polen-Litauens." In *Die Teilungen Polen-Litauens.*

Inklusions- und Exklusionsmechanismen – Traditionsbildung – Vergleichsebenen, edited by Hans-Jürgen Bömelburg, Andreas Gestrich, and Helga Schnabel-Schüle, 155–170. Osnabrück 2013.

D'Arcy Wood, Gillen. *Tambora. The eruption that changed the world.* Princeton 2015.

Davis, Ralph. *The rise of the English shipping industry in the seventeenth and eighteenth centuries.* St. John's Newfoundland 2012 (reprint 1962).

De Vries, Johannes. *De economische achteruitgang der Republiek in de achttiende eeuw.* Leiden 1968.

Degn, Ole (ed.). *The Sound Toll at Elsinore. Politics, shipping and the collection of duties.* Copenhagen 2018.

Degn, Ole (ed.). *Tolden i Sundet. Toldopkrævning, politik og skibsfart i Øresund 1429–1857.* København 2010.

Dehing, Pit. *Geld in Amsterdam. Wisselbank en wisselkoersen.* Hilversum 2012.

Denzel, Markus A. *Die Hamburger Seeversicherung 1736–1859.* Leiden / Boston (forthcoming).

Desfeuilles, Paul. "La Navigation à travers le Sund en 1784: d'après les registres de la Douane danoise." *Annales: Histoire, Sciences Sociales* 14, 3 (1959): 492–520.

Desfeuilles, Paul. "La Navigation à travers le Sund et la guerre russo-suédoise de Finlande (1788–1790)." *Vierteljahrschrift für Sozial- und Wirtschaftsgeschichte* 48, 1 (1961): 56–74.

Dollinger, Philippe. *Die Hanse. 6. vollständig überarbeitete und aktualisierte Auflage (Neu bearbeitet von Volker Henn und Nils Jörn).* Stuttgart 2012.

Družinina, Elena Ioasafovna. *Južnaja Ukraina v 1800–1825 gg.* Moskva 1970.

Eckert, Walter. *Kurland unter dem Einfluss des Merkantilismus (1561–1682). Ein Beitrag zur Verfassungs-, Verwaltungs-, Finanz- und Wirtschaftsgeschichte Kurlands im 16. und 17. Jahrhundert.* Marburg 1926.

Evans, Laurence. "The gift of the sea. Civil logistics and the Industrial Revolution." *Historical Reflections / Réflections historiques* 15, 2 (1988): 361–415.

Evans, Laurence. "Transport, economics and economists. Adam Smith, George Stigler et al." *International Journal of Maritime History* 5, 1 (1993): 203–219.

Ewans, Martin (ed.). *The great game. Britain and Russia in Central Asia.* London 2004.

Fairlie, Susan Elisabeth. *The Anglo-Russian grain trade 1815–1861 [Thesis submitted for the degree Doctor of Philosophy (Faculty of Arts) in the University of London].* London 1959.

Förster, Birte; Bauch, Martin (eds.). *Wasserinfrastrukturen und Macht von der Antike bis zur Gegenwart.* Berlin / Boston 2014.

Frandsen, Karl-Erik. "Neue Entwicklungen mit altem Material. Die Öresund-Zollisten und die Möglichkeiten moderner Technik: Das STR-Online-Projekt." *Hansische Geschichtsblätter* 129 (2011): 247–254.

Friis, Astrid. "Sundtoldregenskaberne." *Scandia. Tidskrift för historisk forskning* 8, 1 (1935): 129–146.

Go, Sabine. *Marine insurance in the Netherlands 1600–1870: a comparative institutional approach.* Amsterdam 2009.

Gøbel, Erik. "De Sonttolregisters." In *Goud uit graan. Nederland en het Oostzeegebied 1600–1850*, edited by Remmelt Daalder et al., 25–47. Zwolle 1998.

Gøbel, Erik. "Øresundstoldens arkivalier 1497–1858." In *Tolden i Sundet. Toldopkrævning, politik og skibsfart i Øresund 1429–1857*, edited by Ole Degn, 569–588. København 2010.

Gøbel, Erik. "The Sound Toll Registers Online project, 1497–1857." *International Journal of Maritime History* XXII, 2 (2010): 305–324.

Goldin, Claudia D.; Lewis, Frank D. "The role of exports in American economic growth during the Napoleonic Wars, 1793 to 1807." *Explorations in Economic History* 17 (1980): 6–25.

Graichen, Gisela; Hammel-Kiesow, Rolf. *Die deutsche Hanse. Eine heimliche Supermacht*. Reinbek bei Hamburg 2013.

Groth, Andrzej. "Angielska Kompania Wschodnia w handle bałtyckiem." *Studia Maritima* 28 (2015): 5–18.

Hanssen-Decker, Ulrike. "Geschichtswissenschaft für den Ostseeraum? Der Conventus primus historicorum Balticorum 1937 in Riga." *NORDEUROPAforum* 19, 1 (2009): 65–82.

Hassinger, Herbert. "Die erste Wiener orientalische Handelskompagnie, 1667–1683." *Vierteljahrschrift für Sozial- und Wirtschaftsgeschichte* 35, 1 (1942): 1–53.

Heckscher, Eli F. *The continental system. An economic interpretation*. Oxford / New York 1922.

Heckscher, Eli F. "Øresundsrakenskaperna och deras behandlings." *Historisk Tidskrift* 62 (1942): 170–186.

Helander, Sven. "Merkantilistische Verkehrspolitik." *Weltwirtschaftliches Archiv* 48 (1938): 420–453.

Herlihy, Patricia Anne McGahey. *Russian grain and Mediterranean markets, 1774–1861*. University of Pennsylvania Dissertation 1963.

Hill, Charles E. *The Danish Sound Dues and the command of the Baltic. A study of international relations*. Durham 1926.

Hinton, Raymond William King. *The Eastland Company and the Common Weal in the seventeenth century*. Cambridge 1959.

Hundt, Michael. *"Woraus nichts geworden" – Brandenburg-Preußens Handel mit Persien (1668–1720)*. Hamburg 1997.

Hunter, Brooke. "Wheat, War, and the American economy during the Age of Revolution." *The William and Mary Quarterly, Third Series* 62, 3 (2005): 505–526.

Iredale, D.A. "John and Thomas Marshall and the Society for improving the British salt trade. An example of trade regulation." *The Economic History Review, New Series* 20 (1967): 79–93.

Jeannin, Pierre. "Les comptes du Sund comme source pour la construction de l'activité économique en Europe (XVIe–XVIIIe siècle)." *Revue historique* 121 (1964): 55–102 and 307–340.

Johansen, Hans Chr. *Shipping and Trade between the Baltic and Western Europe 1784–95*. Odense 1983.

Kalisch, Johannes. "Pläne zur Belebung des Orienthandels über Kurland und Polen am Ausgang des 17. Jahrhunderts." In *Hansische Studien. Heinrich Sproemberg zum 70. Geburtstag*, edited by Gerhard Heitz, Manfred Unger, 190–200. Berlin 1961.

Kardasis, Vassilis. *Diaspora Merchants in the Black Sea: The Greeks in Southern Russia, 1775–1861*. Lanham / Boulder / New York / Oxford 2001.

Keene, Charles E. "American shipping and trade, 1798–1820. The evidence from Leghorn." *The Journal of Economic History* 38, 3 (1978): 681–700.

Kirby, David. *Northern Europe in the early modern period. The Baltic world, 1492–1772*. London / New York 1990.

Kirby, David Gordon; Hinkkanen, Merja-Liisa. *The Baltic and the North Seas*. London 2000.

Klinge, Matti. *Östersjövärlden*. Stockholm 1985.

Kołodziejczyk, Dariusz. "Inner lake or frontier? The Ottoman Black Sea in the sixteenth and seventeenth centuries." In *Enjeux politiques, économiques et militaires en mer noire (XIVe–XXIe siècles). Études à la mémoire de Mihail Guboglu*, edited by Faruk Bilibi, Ionel Cândea, Anca Popescu, 125–140. Braïla 2007.

Kownatzki, Hermann. "Die Bedeutung der Sundzoll-Listen nach den Elbinger Pfundzoll-Listen." *Historisches Jahrbuch* 57 (1937): 358–365.

Krauel, Richard. "Die Ablösung des Sundzolls und die preussische Politik." *Hansische Geschichtsblätter* 13 (1907): 319–341.

Kriedte, Peter; Medick, Hans; Schlumbohm, Jürgen; Kisch, Herbert; Mendels, Franklin F. *Industrialisierung vor der Industrialisierung. Gewerbliche Warenproduktion auf dem Land in der Formationsperiode des Kapitalismus*. Göttingen 1977.

Kumar, Manish. "A note in defense of Bang and Korst's Sound Toll Tables." *International Journal of Maritime History* 30, 2 (2018): 343–348.

Lesger, Clé. *The rise of the Amsterdam market and information exchange: merchants, commercial expansion and change in the spatial economy of the Low Countries, c. 1550–1630*. London 2016 (reprint 2006).

Lindquist, Armin. "Herring periods of Bohuslan: a cross-sectorial approach." *ICES Marine Science Symposia* 215 (2002): 343–351.

Mattiesen, Heinz. "Die Versuche zur Erschließung eines Handelsweges Danzig-Kurland-Moskau-Asien, besonders für Seide, 1640–1655." *Jahrbücher für Geschichte Osteuropas* 3, 4 (1938): 533–567.

Melvin, Frank Edgar. *Napoleon's navigation system. A study of trade control during the Continental Blockade*. New York 1919 (University of Pennsylvania Dissertation).

Morley, Charles. "The European Significance of the November Uprising." *Journal of Central European Affairs* 11, 4 (1952): 408–416.

Mukerji, Chandra. *Impossible engineering: Technology and territoriality on the Canal du Midi*. Princeton 2009.

North, Michael. *The Baltic. A history*. Cambridge, MA / London 2015.

North, Michael. *Geschichte der Ostsee. Handel und Kulturen*. München 2011.

Ó Gráda, Cormac (ed.). *When the Potato failed. Causes and effects of the last European subsistence crisis*. Turnhout 2007.

Oakley, Stewart P. *War and peace in the Baltic, 1560–1790*. London / New York 1993.

Popescu, Anca. "La mer noire ottomane: Mare clausum? Mare apertum?" In *Enjeux politiques, économiques et militaires en mer noire (XIVe–XXIe siècles). Études à la mémoire de Mihail Guboglu*, edited by Faruk Bilibi, Ionel Cândea, and Anca Popescu, 141–170. Braïla 2007.

Pourchasse, Pierrick. "Danish Sound Dues." In *Oxford Encyclopedia of Maritime History*, edited by John Hattendorf. New York 2007. DOI: 10.1093/acref/9780195130751.001.0001

Price, Munro. *Napoleon. The end of glory*. Oxford 2014.

Puryear, Vernon J. "Odessa. Its rise and international importance, 1815–1850." *Pacific Historical Review* 3, 2 (1834): 192–215.

Ressel, Magnus. "Von der Hanse zur hanseatischen Gemeinschaft. Die Entstehung der Konsulatsgemeinschaft von Bremen, Hamburg und Lübeck." *Hansische Geschichtsblätter* 130 (2012): 127–174.

Riley, James C. "The Dutch economy after 1650: Decline or growth?" *The Journal of European Economic History* 13 (1984): 521–569.

Rönnbäck, Klas. "Balancing the Baltic trade. Colonial commodities in the trade on the Baltic, 1773–1856." *Scandinavian Economic History Review* 58, 3 (2010): 188–202.

Rönnbäck, Klas. "New and old peripheries. Britain, the Baltic and the Americas in the Great Divergence." *Journal of Global History* 5, 3 (2010): 373–394.

Rönnbäck, Klas. "The sound toll chamber commodity records. Estimating the reliability of a potential source to international trade history." *International Journal of Maritime History* 22, 1 (2010): 229–238.

Rössner, Philipp Robinson. "The 1738–1741 harvest crisis in Scotland." *The Scottish Historical Review* 90, 1 (2011): 27–63.

Rubin, Marcus. "Sundtoldens afløsning." *Historisk Tidsskrift* 6 (1905–1906): 172–311.

Schäfer, Dietrich. "Die Sundzoll-Listen." *Hansische Geschichtsblätter* 14 (1908): 1–33.

Schäfer, Dietrich. "Die Sundzollrechnungen als internationale Geschichtsquelle." *Internationale Wochenschrift für Wissenschaft, Kunst und Technik* 1 (1907): 365–373 and 401–409.

Schäfer, Dietrich. "Die Sundzoll-Tabellen." *Hansische Geschichtsblätter* 28 (1923): 162–164.

Schäfer, Dietrich. "Zur Orientierung über die Sundzollregister." *Hansische Geschichtsblätter* 9 (1899): 95–114.

Schanbacher, Ansgar. *Kartoffelkrankheit und Nahrungskrise in Nordwestdeutschland 1845–1848.* Göttingen 2016.

Scheltjens, Werner. "The changing geography of demand for Dutch maritime transport in the eighteenth century." *Histoire & Mesure* 27, 2 (2012): 3–48.

Scheltjens, Werner. *Dutch deltas. Emergence, functions and structure of the Low Countries' maritime transport system, ca. 1300–1850.* Leiden / Boston 2015.

Scheltjens, Werner. "Maße und Gewichte. Konvertierungsmöglichkeiten am Beispiel der Sundzollregister." In *Wiegen – Zählen – Registrieren. Handelsgeschichtliche Massenquellen und die Erforschung mitteleuropäischer Märkte (13.–18. Jahrhundert)*, edited by Peter Rauscher and Andrea Serles, 455–479. Innsbruck / Wien / Bozen 2015.

Scheltjens, Werner. "Tetradas: Tonnage Estimates of Trade through the Danish Sound, 1670–1856." *Vierteljahrschrift für Sozial- und Wirtschaftsgeschichte* (forthcoming 2021).

Scheltjens, Werner; Veluwenkamp, Jan Willem. "Sound Toll Registers Online. Introduction and first research examples." *International Journal of Maritime History* XXIV, 1 (2012): 301–330.

Scheltjens, Werner; Veluwenkamp, Jan Willem; Van der Woude, Siem. "A closer look. STRO as instrument for the study of early modern maritime history." In *Early modern shipping and trade. Novel approaches using Sound Toll Registers Online*, edited by Jan Willem Veluwenkamp and Werner Scheltjens, 1–18. Leiden / Boston 2018.

Scherer, Hermann. *Der Sundzoll. Seine geschichte, sein jetziger Bestand und seine staatsrechtlich-politische Lösung. Nebst einem Anhang über die Sundzollfreiheit der Pommerschen und Preusischen Städte.* Berlin 1845.

Schremmer, Eckart. "Industrialisierung vor der Industrialisierung. Anmerkungen zu einem Konzept der Proto-Industrialisierung." *Geschichte und Gesellschaft* 6, 3 (1980): 420–448.

Selzer, Stephan. *Die mittelalterliche Hanse*. Darmstadt 2010.

Stothers, Richard B. "The great Tambora eruption and its aftermath." *Science* 224, 4654 (1984): 1191–1198.

Tableau général du commerce de la France avec ses colonies et les puissances étrangères pendant l'année... [1829–1860]. Paris 1829–1861.

Tables shewing the trade of the United Kingdom with different Foreign countries and British possessions, in each of the years 1831 to 1840. Compiled from official returns. London 1842.

Tetradas [VSWG-JDA]: *Tetradas: Tonnage estimates of trade through the Danish Sound, 1670–1856 (Replication data and selected statistics). Version: 1.* VSWG – Journal of Social and Economic History. Dataset, edited by Werner Scheltjens. https://journaldata.zbw.eu/dataset/tetradas

Tjaden, Anja. "The Dutch in the Baltic, 1544–1721." In *In quest of trade and security. The Baltic in power politics 1500–1990, volume I: 1500–1890*, edited by Göran Rystad, Klaus-R. Böhme and Wilhelm L. Carlgren, 61–136. Stockholm 1994.

Tønnessen, John N. "Nord Amerikas Forente Stater og opphevelsen av Øresundstollen 1857." *Historisk Tidskrift* 47 (1968): 293–310.

Unger, W.S. "De publikatie der Sonttabellen voltooid." *Tijdschrift voor Geschiedenis* 71 (1958): 147–205.

Unger, W.S. "De Sonttabellen." *Tijdschrift voor Geschiedenis* 41 (1926): 137–155.

Unger, W.S. "Een nieuw deel der Sonttabellen." *Tijdschrift voor Geschiedenis* 55 (1940): 272–277.

Van Brakel, S. "Die Entwicklung und Organisation der Merchant-Adventurers." *Vierteljahrschrift für Sozial- und Wirtschaftsgeschichte* 5, 3 (1907): 401–432.

Van Laak, Dirk. "Der Begriff "Infrastruktur" und was er vor seiner Erfindung besagte." *Archiv für Begriffsgeschichte* 41 (1999): 280–299.

Van Laak, Dirk. "Infra-strukturgeschichte." *Geschichte und Gesellschaft* 27, 3 (2001): 367–393.

Van Laak, Dirk. "Technological infrastructure, concepts and consequences." *Icon* (2004): 53–64.

Van Tielhof, Milja. *The 'mother of all trades'. The Baltic grain trade in Amsterdam from the late 16th to the early 19th century*. Leiden / Boston 2002.

Van Zanden, Jan Luiten. "De economie van Holland in de periode 1650–1805. Groei of achteruitgang? Een overzicht van bronnen, problemen en resultaten." *Bijdragen en mededelingen betreffende de Geschiedenis der Nederlanden* 102, 4 (1987): 562–609.

Veale, Lucy; Endfield, Georgina H. "Situating 1816, the 'year without summer', in the United Kingdom." *The Geographical Journal* 182, 4 (2016): 318–330.

Veluwenkamp, Jan Willem. "Die "Sound Toll Registers Online" als Instrument für die Erforschung des frühneuzeitlichen Ostseehandels." In *Wiegen – Zählen – Registrieren. Handelsgeschichtliche Massenquellen und die Erforschung mitteleuropäischer Märkte (13.–18. Jahrhundert)*, edited by Peter Rauscher and Andrea Serles, 365–385. Innsbruck / Wien / Bozen 2015.

Veluwenkamp, Jan Willem; Scheltjens, Werner (eds.). *Early modern shipping and trade. Novel approaches using Sound Toll Registers Online*. Leiden / Boston 2018.

Wallis, John Joseph. "What caused the crisis of 1839?" *NBER Working paper series on historical factors in long run growth* 133 (2001): 1–57.

Wehrmann, Carl. "Die Betheiligung Lübecks bei der Ablösung des Sundzolls." *Zeitschrift des Vereins für Lübeckische Geschichte und Alterthumskunde* 6 (1892): 405–430.

Willan, T.S. "The Russia Company and Narva." *The Slavonic and East European Review* 31, 77 (1953): 405–419.

Zolotov, Vladimir Aleksandrovič. *Vnešnjaja torgovlja Južnoj Rossii v pervoj polovine XIX veka*. Rostov 1963.

2 The Baltic as arena of a quest for North Eurasian trade

North Eurasia as unit of world history

Leibniz and Kilburger

In 1697, two very different events coincided. Tsar Peter I (1672–1725) travelled incognito as a member of the so-called Great Embassy to Western Europe (*Ru.* Velikoe Posol'stvo) with the aim of 'making Russia a part of Europe,'[1] and Gottfried Wilhelm Leibniz (1646–1716)[2] published his *Novissima Sinica*,[3] in which he proclaimed a *commerce de lumières*, an exchange of ideas between East and West.[4] Peter's Embassy provided a strong impetus for Leibniz' desire to (re)unite Christianity against the enduring Islamic threat,[5] which had reached a peak only a decade earlier with the Ottoman siege of Vienna (1683), and to realize his lasting 'dream' of establishing an overland connection and exchange of ideas between Western Europe and China,[6] the universal centres of civilization in his worldview. In the wake of growing European interests in Persia, India, and China, and ongoing Jesuit efforts to secure the land route to China,[7] the vast landmass between both ends of the Eurasian continent attracted travellers, political leaders, and scholars alike. Supported by an impressive network of correspondents,[8] Leibniz' ideas about Muscovy as bridge between Western Europe and China culminated in several appeals to the Tsar.[9] At first, Leibniz' appeals took the form of memoranda; they were followed by meetings with the Tsar in Torgau and Karlsbad, and direct correspondence with the Tsar. As scattered as these documents may be,[10] they provide ample evidence of the emergence of the concept of Eurasia as a means to describe the landmass between Western Europe and China, underlining Muscovy's crucial role in it.

Among the contemporary reports, travel accounts, and memoirs on the 'exotic' areas of Muscovy and *Tartary*, one document seems to have been particularly important for the development of Leibniz's understanding of North Eurasia: A handwritten copy of Johann Philipp Kilburger's (1642–1721) *Kort underrättelse om den ryska handeln såsom denna bedrevs år 1674 med ut- och införda varor in hela Ryssland.*[11] The value of this document has hardly been recognized in the historiography of Leibniz' ideas about Russia, which is probably because it appeared in Leibniz's collected works for the first time only in 2011.[12] Although an abridged version of Kilburger's concise review of Russian trade around the mid-seventeenth century had been printed only in 1769,[13] different handwritten versions of the manuscript had circulated long before.[14] Possibly, Leibniz learned about Kilburger's manuscript through Nicolaas Witsen (1641–1717), author of the influential *Noord-en Oost-Tartarye*,[15] and a member of Leibniz' network of correspondents.[16] In 1697, Leibniz received the manuscript from Lorenz Hertel (1659–1737), who assisted him in his duties as director of the Herzog August Library in Wolfenbüttel.[17] Kilburger's manuscript probably inspired Leibniz in his correspondence with Tsar Peter. Leibniz' excerpts from the manuscript underline his keen interest in Muscovy's potential as the 'power of the middle' between Western Europe and China.

Kilburger wrote his account of Russian trade in 1674, during a Swedish diplomatic mission to Muscovy.[18] The goal of this mission was to convince Muscovy to sign a treaty with Sweden and move its trade from the White Sea port of Arkhangelsk, Muscovy's only direct point of access to Western Europe at that time, to Swedish ports in the eastern Baltic.[19] Kilburger wrote his manuscript shortly after his return to Sweden, relying strongly on the earlier travel accounts of Adam Olearius (1599–1671), Johan de Rodes (?–1655), Johan Palmqvist (?–1716), and Grigoriy Karpovich Kotoshikhin (c. 1630–1667) during the process.[20] Besides a detailed description of the commodities of Russian trade, an overview of imports to Russia via Arkhangelsk and the Baltic in 1671 and 1672, and a price-current of 1674, the manuscript also contains statements addressing Muscovy's potential to increase its international trade with Persia, China, and the Black Sea region through infrastructural developments and (economic) policy measures. Some of these statements were original, more often they were borrowed from earlier accounts. Kilburger was conscious about Muscovy's central role in emerging global commodity flows and the consequences of its eastward expansion. He was well aware of the fact that, following exploratory missions in the Amur area between 1643 and 1653, and the foundation of Anadyr and Okhotsk on the Pacific coast in the late 1640s, Muscovy was about to institutionalize its commercial relations with Persia and China and consolidate its expansion across the northern part of the Eurasian continent.[21]

Kilburger criticized the Muscovite government for adopting the wrong policies with regard to the Persian silk trade. He claimed that Muscovite policy obstructed the reorientation of the Persian silk trade towards Muscovy and away from the camel trade to Alexandria and Hormuz or the Turkish road to Smyrna and Aleppo. Kilburger maintained that the transportation of Persian goods via Astrakhan to Moscow and then to Reval or Narva was faster and shorter than the routes to the Red Sea and the Mediterranean, which the Dutch and English East India and Levant Companies commonly used.[22] However, following De Rodes' calculations, Kilburger also noted that the exportation of Persian goods via Arkhangelsk was less expensive than via the Baltic and therefore posed a threat to Sweden's trade with commodities originating from or moving in transit through Muscovy.[23] Adhering to De Rodes' opinion about the fundamental role of Persian trade in Russian commercial exchange, Kilburger proposed several measures for promoting the reorientation of Persian trade to the Baltic, which the Swedes controlled at that time. Among other things, the Muscovite government would have to restructure the transit of Persian goods through Muscovy, (re)build Swedish *guesthouses* (Ru. *gostinyj dvor*) in Novgorod, Pskov, Moscow, and Yaroslavl and develop Astrakhan as the centre of Muscovy's Persian trade.[24] Improvements to the transport infrastructure between Moscow and the Baltic ports, in particular, in Vyshny Volochyok, were essential for the reorientation of Muscovy's Persian trade to the Baltic. Kilburger observed that a connection between the Tsna and Tvertsa would eventually connect Lake Ladoga, and thus the Baltic Sea, with the Caspian Sea.[25] With regard to Muscovy's trade with China, Kilburger proposed to pursue the further development of Tobolsk as the centre of this trade and hinted at the possibility of river and overseas transportation on the Ob to China and India.[26] Finally, 'Greek trade' could be promoted by establishing centres of trade on the shores of the Black Sea or in Constantinople.[27]

Although Leibniz' plans to leverage the unique role of Russia as the 'true' Empire of the Middle, or "*das wahre Reich der Mitte*", between the Asia and Western Europe were far-reaching, they were highly practical as well.[28] In fact, many of his ideas, which were based on his correspondence with Witsen and others as well as his reading of Kilburger's manuscript, would be realized during the eighteenth century, e.g. the canal of Vyshny Volochyok. The expanding geographical scope of Leibniz' writings and his increasing awareness of a vast North Eurasian space that tied Western Europe and China may be seen as a sublime account of the significant changes that occupied European minds. In the wake of Muscovy's eastern expansion, the 'world' was 'encompassed' not only by sea, but also by land, and Leibniz may have been the first to acknowledge Muscovy's pivotal role in North Eurasia.[29] Leibniz' desire to reunite Christianity and establish an overland connection between Western Europe and China, his acquaintance with Witsen's cartographic works, his knowledge and use of Kilburger's illustrious manuscript, and – last but not least – his correspondence with Tsar Peter, all made an important contribution to the promulgation of the (geopolitical) concept of North Eurasia. At the same time, it must be clear that North Eurasia never was equal to Muscovy or the Russian Empire.[30]

The contours of North Eurasia

The concept of North Eurasia became a hallmark of Muscovy's expansionist policies at the turn of the eighteenth century. The term North Eurasia itself, however, was coined for the first time by the Finnish historian and later Prime Minister Aimo Kaarlo Cajander (1879–1943).[31] In the present study, the use of the term has its roots in the recent reassessment of Eurasia as a paradigm that "(...) rejects (...) monolithic and static cultural determinism (...) and tries to account for the importance of longer-term ecological, demographic, economic, and cultural structures for understanding the processes and outcomes of tremendous change (...)",[32] but its application has a more limited geographical scope. The concept of North Eurasia does not coincide with the Russian Empire (or its predecessors or successors), even though the Russian Empire does comprise the majority of the territory of North Eurasia. Besides Russia, the main actors on the North Eurasian landmass include Prussia, Poland-Lithuania, and the political entities of Southern Russia (Cossacks, Tatars, and others); states with no direct territorial interest in North Eurasia, such as Great Britain (later: United Kingdom), France, the United States and the Dutch Republic (later: Netherlands); and – last but not least – the adjacent political entities of Denmark, Sweden, and the Ottoman Empire. The meaning of the term North Eurasia has nothing in common with the politico-ideological concept of Eurasia and the Eurasianist movements of the 1920s and the present day.[33]

The geographical concept of North Eurasia embraces the poly-ethnic composition of the landmass and distinguishes it from the southern part of the Eurasian continent, South Eurasia. Although one might be tempted to speak of the 'Slavic world' rather than North Eurasia, this would create more problems than it solves. Hence, a significant part of the landmass under survey is not inhabited by Slavic peoples, but by Armenians, Kalmyks, Tatars, and others, who all had their role to play in North Eurasian trade. Moreover, the 'Slavic world' would necessarily have to encompass significant parts of South-East Europe. Inspired by David Christian's broad distinction between Inner and Outer Eurasia,[34] North Eurasia is determined by its borderlands and border basins (see Map 1).

The Caucasus, Tien Shan, and Altai mountain ranges constitute the borderlands between North and South Eurasia. The White, Baltic, Black, and Caspian Sea basins serve as its border basins. Finally, the rivers Danube, Elbe, and Oder, including their adjacent rivers, constitute a borderland between North Eurasia and the westernmost part of the Eurasian landmass – 'Europe.' Thus, 'Europe' is not an integral part of North Eurasia but rather a connected geographical unit, where North and South Eurasia collide and intersect. The border basins of North Eurasia, with the exception of the White Sea, are virtually cut in half in the proposed demarcation. Scandinavia and the part of Finland bordering the Gulf of Bothnia are not part of North Eurasia or continental 'Europe' in the same way as the Turkish mainland is not part of North Eurasia or 'Europe.' Like 'Europe,' they are geographical units adjacent to North Eurasia.

The peoples inhabiting the earth's different *landmasses* (continents) interact – either among themselves, across the landmass or between landmasses divided by *water basins* (seas and oceans). Insofar as the latter is concerned, the water basin itself becomes an area of interaction. The interaction between peoples takes place across real, territorial *borders*, i.e. "the legal lines separating different jurisdictions,"[35] and imagined social and cultural *boundaries* and *frontiers*,[36] as "broad zone[s] of transition between different societies and centres of power (…)."[37] Imagined boundaries are "part of the production of territory/territoriality that occurs concomitantly at all spatial scales and (…) brings various social and cultural processes together 'topographically,' in a non-hierarchical way."[38] Territorial borders are inherent to the cross-border exchange of ideas, peoples, and goods. Through exchange and interaction, be it cross-border exchange across territorial borders or human interaction across social and cultural boundaries, real borders, frontier areas, and imagined boundaries obtain a dynamic character.[39]

Borders are never "a simple borderline,"[40] they are always subject to change,[41] and always remain an integral part of larger spaces of interaction and exchange.[42] The terms *borderland* and its maritime counterpart *border basin* underpin the embeddedness of territorial borders and imagined, social and cultural boundaries in larger spaces of interaction and exchange. Borderlands and border basins are the spaces where "(…) border motions are manifested, considered and contested (…)."[43] Borderlands are dynamic (because of their inherent conflict potential); they can move in space and expand. Border basins, however, are fixed. They cannot move in space and cannot expand (at least insofar as expansion is beyond human capabilities). Borderlands are essentially manmade; border basins are natural. Moreover, border basins typically extend beyond territorial claims and control; they are 'shared waters,' in which the concepts of border and boundary intertwine.

Any human activity in a border zone (i.e. a borderland or border basin) produces cross-border exchange, but for as long as this exchange remains a singular, one-directional event, which other human beings do not adopt, it will not produce *border effects*. The latter are the cumulative result of enduring cross-border exchange. Border effects appear at different levels of observation, thus acquiring distinct meanings. In the economic sciences, the term has become part of the econometric study of trade flows and barriers using gravity theory or the law of one price.[44] Quite differently, adhering to its geographical meaning, historians tend to employ the terms borderlands and related notions such as border, boundary, and frontier rather loosely to address the spatial dynamics of (long-term) societal change.[45] For example, prominent historians of the Russian Empire and Eurasia, such as John LeDonne and Alfred Rieber, have employed the terms frontier and borderland as synonyms in their recent works. But whereas LeDonne subscribes to a geopolitical approach, in which military conflict and conquest are seen as part of a 'grand strategy' of the Russian Empire in different 'theatres' on its borders,[46] Rieber adopts a more encompassing geo-cultural definition.[47]

Conflict is inherent to borderlands and border basins. *Border regimes*, changes therein, and conflicts resulting from their establishment affect cross-border exchange, making borderlands and border basins relevant topics of international political economy. Finally, borderlands and border basins share two distinct features: (1) they may compete with or complement each other, providing access to the same landmass or water basin; (2) they may serve as areas where interest groups meet, cooperate and compete with other interest groups. Comprehensive observation of North Eurasia's borderlands and border basins is a precondition for understanding the structure of its trade. Similarly, any study analysing a borderland or border basin must take into account – as explicitly and as comprehensively as possible – the territories for which this border zone has a function in commercial exchange relations, including its *other* border zones.

The proposed concept of North Eurasia as a unit of world history calls into question the appropriateness of the term Eurasia in the historiography of globalization. Mainstream accounts of the history of globalization tend to focus on Europe's overseas expansion, the establishment of colonial empires, and related issues such as the rise of the Atlantic economy, the emergence of global networks of trade (including illicit and diaspora networks), and the (early modern) consumer revolution.[48] In light of the frequent use of the term Eurasia in such accounts, it is remarkable that the northern part of the continent is often treated superficially and is sometimes even overlooked entirely in favour of a predominant interest in its extremities: (Western) Europe and China. Immanuel Wallerstein (1930–2019), for example, depicted most of the landmass between (Western) Europe and China as an 'outer arena,' which was not yet incorporated in the world-system, and admitted "(...) not [being] very interested in what actually happens in this outer arena."[49] Quite differently, the term Eurasia figures prominently in Eric L. Jones' famous *The European miracle*. Jones employs the term as title of both the opening and concluding part of the book, implying that the development of (Western) Europe took place in a larger Eurasian context. However, Jones fails to define Eurasia and does not explain which part of it is Europe and which part is Asia. This poses particular problems for the northern part of the Eurasian continent, which – according to the geographical conventions that Jones seems to accept – belonged to both Europe and Asia. A few scattered references to Russia, which continues to occupy most of the North Eurasian landmass, seem to place it in Europe.[50] However, the demarcation of Europe as the part of the continent west of the line Trieste-Leningrad,[51] which originated from Hajnal's research on European marriage patterns,[52] sharply contradicts with this demarcation. It turns out that Jones' focus is on North-West Europe exclusively,[53] and that Eurasia seems to be relevant only insofar as it hosts India and China as counter-examples for the miraculous Western European developments in the wake of North-West Europe's overseas expansion.[54] Maritime connections prevail in Jones' understanding of the term Eurasia. Similarly, Geoffrey Gunn's *First Globalization: The Eurasian exchange, 1500–1800* deals with "(...) complex crossovers of ideas, languages and philosophies that engaged and transformed Europe and Asia in the sixteenth to eighteenth centuries (...),"[55] but only takes into account what he describes as "the Eurasian maritime world system."[56] Similarly, a tacit focus on the maritime dimension of Europe's expansion seems undeniable in Osterhammel and Petterson's concise history of globalization.[57] They employ the term Eurasia as a geographical "container term" indicating that Europe and Asia are both part of the same landmass and make a claim for recognizing "(...) the occurrence of expansionist movements throughout all of Eurasia (...)."[58]

Finally, if globalization is understood as a process that would eventually lead to an 'encompassed world,'[59] it is notorious that mainstream accounts of its history hardly pay attention to the emergence of intercontinental competition between productive areas in the emerging world economy and remain silent on the necessary conditions for such process to unfold. Favouring a predominant focus on (barter) exchange and consumption, production seems to be taken into account only insofar as efficiency gains in manufacturing are involved. Productive areas, where the raw materials for manufacturing and the commodities for exchange and consumption are grown, only figure in standard economic theories as one element of the 'factor-price' of goods. Other aspects of the (international) competition between productive areas, such as the quality and unique features of its produce or the international political framework of its exchange usually are not taken into account. Rather, productive areas are reduced to abstract notions such as 'external arena' or 'ghost acreage,'[60] depriving them of their qualitative features.

The Baltic as border zone of North Eurasia

This book frames the Baltic as a border basin of North Eurasia, and conceptualizes the latter as a unit of world history. Such framing overlaps partly with Michael North's cultural concept of the Baltic as a contact zone, determined by encounters and interactions between different European and Asian cultures.[61] The book argues that processes of economic development and change can be observed most clearly in borderlands, and that the study of border effects and border regimes illuminates the impact of these processes on the lives of peoples controlling and exploiting borderlands and continental landmasses. In this way, the broad concept of the Baltic as a border basin of North Eurasia, which is inspired by insights from borderlands studies, complements North's cultural borderlands concept.

The proposed geographical framework marks a firm departure from previous historiographical concepts of the lands surrounding the Baltic Sea basin, such as Oskar Halecki's (1891–1973) 'Ostmitteleuropa,'[62] Klaus Zernack's (1931–2017) 'Nordosteuropa,'[63] or David Kirby's 'Northern periphery.'[64] These classical concepts of the Baltic Sea area apply politically inspired *boundaries* based on distinct worldviews and carry the risk of providing biased accounts of complex historical processes. The classical historiographical concepts are undermined by their (tacit) ideological origins and weakened by the significance attributed to time as a factor for including or excluding territories. Moreover, consciously or unconsciously, they reflect personal research interests and thus give room to *imagined boundaries* based on personal (research) experience rather than sticking to more objective (but not necessarily more precise) demarcations. The evolution of the historiographical concept of 'Northeastern Europe' (*Ger.* Nordosteuropa) is exemplary.[65] In contrast to the notion's narrower original meaning,[66] it comprised the entire Baltic Sea region in Zernack's work on East European history.[67] Based on an earlier definition of the 'space of Northeastern Europe and the Baltic' (*Ger.* Nordosteuropa-Ostseeraum) as "(...) an area of contact of Scandinavian with hanseatic and of native Baltic and Slavic with German colonial factors"[68] in the Middle Ages, Zernack argues for the *temporal* expansion of this concept into 'premodern' times.[69] Whereas the spatial demarcation of this area is inspired by a combination of political borders and historical evidence,[70] its temporal component is extremely precise. According to Zernack, Nordosteuropa is a typical 'large space'-concept (*Ger.* Großraum-Konzept) of 'premodern history' from the times of Vikings until 1809, when Finland became part of the Russian Empire and the latter's imperial history became dominant.[71] In geographic terms, Zernack defines 'Northeastern Europe' as one of four regions of East European history, alongside *Ostmitteleuropa*, *Südosteuropa*, and *Rußland*,[72] and dismisses of the use of 'The Baltic' (*Ger.* Ostseeraum) as a synonym.[73] Thus, the concept 'Northeastern Europe' obtains its meaning "through its precise regional and temporal boundaries (...)."[74] A remarkable extension of the historiographical concept of 'Northeastern Europe' has been proposed by Stefan Troebst, who pleads for the inclusion of Northern Russia "(...) at least until the beginning of the eighteenth century."[75] Roughly at the same time, Ralph Tuchtenhagen "(...) pleaded for a differentiation of the notions of Northeastern Europe and Baltic Sea area in order to propose a more restricted definition of Northeastern Europe in terms of historical space semantics."[76]

Finally, the book studies border regimes and border effects from the perspective of transport and trade, and it includes the latter's political economy as well as its real, anticipated, and perceived economic significance. In this way, the book hopes to overcome the limitations of previous concepts of economic space, most importantly the foreland-hinterland and core-periphery dichotomies. The 'catchiness' of such concepts inevitably reduces large, interconnected landmasses to abstract categories and carries the risk of producing a one-sided narrative of the history of globalization. Klas Rönnbäck's thought-provoking effort to give 'the Baltic' a place in the so-called 'divergence debate'[77] has not been able to overcome the traditional view of 'the Baltic' as a peripheral area in the history of globalization. Rönnbäck argues that "[i]t was to a very large extent [the] growth in demand for specific raw materials, rather than a generally stagnant economy in the Baltic region itself, that can explain why the Baltic became of less importance than the Americas during the Great Divergence."[78] This statement is problematic in a number of ways. First, it has a weak empirical basis and lacks the necessary source criticism, even though the findings rely on a novel source for the study of Baltic trade. One is left wondering about the obvious gaps in Rönnbäck's data (especially between 1815 and 1830), the calculation underlying the tonnage and hectolitre estimates in the text, and the choice of commodities for the analysis.[79] Second, the sweeping metaphor of "[t]he Baltic region, which for such a long time had been a winner in the commodity lottery, [and now] simply drew a blank around the time of the British Industrial Revolution (...),"[80] should not conceal the fact that the concept of space is hardly elaborated in the text. One looks in vain for a definition of 'the Baltic region' beyond ambiguous descriptions in which 'the Baltic region' means either the ports around the Baltic Sea (east/south of the Sound) and their effective hinterlands,[81] or the countries in eastern Europe which had access to the Baltic, such as Poland, the Baltic States and Baltic Russia.[82] It can only be concluded that 'the Baltic region' is used as an alternative to Kenneth Pomeranz' equally vague understanding of 'eastern Europe.'[83] However, whereas Pomeranz "hardly ever mentions the Baltic as a region in his book,"[84] Rönnbäck's conclusions provide a very strong statement in this regard: "(...) Pomeranz' claim of an economic stagnation in the Baltic region is not supported by empirical data."[85] Might this be the consequence of not having properly defined 'the Baltic' in the first place?

The issue of space does not end there. Although space is at the centre of Rönnbäck's argument in the abstract form of 'ghost acreages,' its physiography, economic and political geography are almost entirely disregarded in favour of a bold opposition of the 'old' periphery of the Baltic with the 'new' periphery of 'the Americas.' Whereas 'the Americas' in fact refer to the United States with its proper institutions and policies, 'the Baltic' refers to a profoundly different unit of space: a water basin, where several political entities pursued conflicting policies and developed different institutions. By reducing 'the Baltic region' to an abstract space, the path is paved for sweeping general statements about its economy and counterfactual analysis of its 'unrealized' potential.[86] Can 'the Baltic region' really be reduced to a passive 'agent' in the production of raw materials, which just happened to produce the 'wrong' commodities at the 'wrong' time?

This study argues that the novel perspective of *borderlands studies* is well-suited for dealing with the impact of the process of globalization on contested areas of human interaction, and that it contributes to overcoming some of the previous limitations in the historiography of 'Baltic trade' and of East and East-Central Europe. Consequently, it is argued that trade through the Danish Sound was essentially North Eurasian trade, and that its careful study in this vein may forward our understanding of the changing role of 'the Baltic' during the first wave of globalization. Moreover, the focus on North Eurasia and its productive areas, on the one hand, and on North Eurasia's borderlands and border basins, on the other, helps to overcome some of the limitations of mainstream accounts of the history of globalization.

That said, this book postulates that the Baltic obtained the status of a privileged outlet for North Eurasian trade in the closing decades of the seventeenth century and that it maintained its special role for some time during the eighteenth and part of the nineteenth century. It is argued that a general awareness of the crucial role of 'the Baltic' in transnational commercial networks emerged in the closing decades of the seventeenth century, culminated in the foundation of St. Petersburg (1703) and provoked the reorganization of Baltic commerce during and immediately after the Great Northern War. Around the turn of the eighteenth century, the Baltic became an area of vested interest under the impact of changing international commercial and diplomatic relations. This special role was part of an international quest for North Eurasian trade, in which Great Britain, France, Russia, Prussia, Sweden, and later the United States played a major role. Incessant needs for raw materials and foodstuffs, which were themselves the result of global processes of development and change in the political, military, naval, and economic sphere, fuelled the quest for North Eurasian trade. Until the end of the eighteenth century, the Baltic maintained its special role in North Eurasian trade. However, when Russia's advances towards the Black Sea culminated in the defeat of the Ottoman Empire, the necessary conditions for the much-awaited consolidation of the Russian Empire along the Black Sea coastline were created. At the same time, the reconfiguration of Baltic commerce, which had started during the Great Northern War was terminated in the Third (and final) Partition of Poland. By the late eighteenth century, the Baltic's near monopoly position as preferred maritime outlet for North Eurasian trade was threatened from different sides, but the French Wars and the Continental Blockade delayed the impact of these threats for another two decades. In the first half of the nineteenth century, however, it became clear that the advantageous geographical position of the Black Sea, now open for international commerce, caused significant changes to the role of North Eurasia's southern border basins in international commerce and politics. Moreover, the ongoing British search for alternative supplies of raw materials as well as their preference for ready-to-use commodities, such as wheat flour rather than mere wheat, became more and more effective. Although the estimated annual tonnages exchanged at the Sound in Elsinore continued to rise in the first half of the nineteenth century, the relative decline of the Baltic as preferred maritime outlet for North Eurasian commercial exchange becomes undeniable. It can be readily observed in the rapid growth of Odessa during the first half of the nineteenth century, but it also finds expression in Russia's political and economic isolation, and in the successes of the British reorientation towards India, East Asia, North America, Egypt, and Latin America as the main suppliers of raw materials and foodstuffs. By the end of the Crimean War, the quest for North Eurasian trade was over.

The composition of the remainder of the book reflects this 'grand thesis' about the long-term development of the Baltic and the quest for North Eurasian trade between ca. 1660 and 1860. Tailor-made statistical series derived from the Danish Sound toll registers online are used to identify changes in the volume, geographical and commodity structure of transport and trade between the North Eurasian landmass and 'Europe.' These statistics shed light on the relations between commercial exchange partners and their development over time, i.e. on the political economy of North Eurasian trade. Moreover, in combination with other relevant sources, they also inform about the geographical structure of North Eurasian trade and the Baltic's changing role as one of its outlets. Chapter 3 discusses the emergence of the Baltic as a privileged outlet for North Eurasian trade. Chapter 4 describes how the special role of the Baltic found consolidation by means of infrastructural and commercial developments in the North Eurasian landmass, and it highlights the increasing importance of novel patterns of international trade, which started to complement and replace the 'traditional' Dutch Baltic trade. Chapter 5 is devoted to the latter part of the eighteenth century, when conflicting commercial and political interests in North Eurasian trade culminated in the Baltic, before its trade collapsed during the Continental Blockade. Finally, Chapter 6 outlines how North Eurasian trade was reconfigured in the first half of the nineteenth century in the wake of the opening of Black Sea trade, the onset of industrialization in parts of Europe and the Russian Empire, and the emergence of competing productive areas in Western Europe, the Mediterranean, the United States, and Latin America.

Notes

1 Massie, *Peter the Great*, 156–285. Research on the Russian Great Embassy of 1697/98 has produced a significant number of publications in several languages, including both general works and detailed, day-to-day accounts of the Tsar's travels across Europe. In addition to Massie's descriptive account, the most valuable work with a good critical survey of earlier historiography is: Guzevič and Guzevič, *Velikoe posol'stvo*. For smaller contributions, in particular, with regard to Peter the Great's time in the Netherlands (and Flanders), see Tavernier, *Russia and the low countries*, 154–169. All relevant literature on the Great Embassy (published until 2006) was gathered in the magnificent bibliography: Guzevič and Guzevič, *Pervoe evropejskoe putešestvie carja Petra*.

2 The literature about Leibniz and his works is vast. Relevant bibliographies are: Ravier, *Bibliographie*; Müller (ed.), *Leibniz-Bibliographie*; Heinekamp (ed.), *Leibniz-Bibliographie*; and Heinekamp (ed.), *Leibniz-Bibliographie. Band 2*. Good starting points for acquaintance with the man's life and works are: Guhrauer, *Gottfried Wilhelm Freiherr von Leibniz*; Müller and Kronert, *Leben und Werk von Gottfried Wilhelm Leibniz*; Ariew, *G.W. Leibniz*; Fischer, *Gottfried Wilhelm Leibniz*; Antognazza, *Leibniz*. Leibniz' works and correspondence are published under the auspices of, among others, the Prussian Academy of Sciences since 1923. See Leibniz, *Sämtliche Schriften und Briefe*.

3 Leibniz, *Novissima Sinica*. Modern edition: Nesselrath and Reinbothe, *Das neueste von China*.

4 Reinhard, *Die Unterwerfung der Welt*, 650.

5 This aspect of Leibniz' thought is treated extensively in: Fischer, *Gottfried Wilhelm Leibniz*.

6 Leibniz' fascination with China is analyzed in, e.g.: Widmaier, *Leibniz korrespondiert mit China*; Li and Poser (eds.), *Das Neueste über China*.

7 Osterhammel, *Die Entzauberung Asiens*, 99–100.

8 Roll, "Barbaren? *Tabula rasa*?" 328–353.

9 Earlier historiography has focused on Leibniz' image of Russia as 'unchartered territory'. See, e.g. Guerrier, *Leibniz in seinen Beziehungen zu Russland*; Benz,

Leibniz und Peter der Grosse; Richter, *Leibniz und sein Russlandbild*; Groh, *Russland und das Selbstverständnis Europas*, 32–43. Roll's recent discourse analysis argues that this image was part of Leibniz' 'strategy of argument' rather than being his 'metaphor for Russia'. See Roll, "Barbaren? *Tabula rasa*?" 307.

10 As Roll points out, Leibniz never published directly on Muscovy; his ideas are found throughout his correspondence and writings. See Roll, "Barbaren? *Tabula rasa*?" 315–316.

11 Title taken from: Arne, "En svensk handelsspion," 143.

12 Leibniz, *Sämtliche Schriften und Briefe*, Reihe IV, Band 7, 683–716. Christine Roll briefly mentions the excerpts from Kilburger's manuscript in Leibniz' works, but maintains a focus on his correspondence rather than written sources for his ideas. See Roll, "Barbaren? *Tabula rasa*?" 328–353.

13 Kilburger, "Kurzer Unterricht von dem rußischen Handel." The final part of the manuscript, curiously omitted in the first printed edition of 1769, contains a copy of Bajkov's 1654 voyage of exploration to China, which is generally regarded as the take-off of Muscovite-Chinese relations. This part was published in 1781 (Schmidt). A further addition to the text, describing the route from Stockholm to Tobolsk, was published in 1823 (Jazykov). The first complete publication of the manuscript, with an extensive commentary, was published in Russian by Kurc in 1915. See Schmidt, "Kilburger's Unterricht"; Jazykov, "Opisanie puti"; Kurc, *Sočinenie Kil'burgera*. The most recent review of the entire manuscript dates from 1937. See Nyström, "Mercatura Ruthenica."

14 Leibniz, *Sämtliche Schriften und Briefe*, Reihe IV, Band 7, 683–684.

15 Witsen, *Noord en Oost Tartarye*.

16 Roll, "Barbaren? *Tabula rasa*?" 339–345.

17 Leibniz, *Sämtliche Schriften und Briefe*, Reihe IV, Band 7, 683–684.

18 Arne, "En svensk handelsspion," 138; Kurc, *Sočinenie Kil'burgera*, 2. Kilburger's manuscript is one of three descriptive accounts of Muscovy, which were written during that mission. See Zernack, "Imperiale Politik und merkantiler Hintergrund," 28–29; Troebst, "Eine wichtige Quellenedition."

19 Kurc, *Sočinenie Kil'burgera*, 1–2, 17–18.

20 Kilburger stood in personal contact with De Rodes and Palmqvist. See Arne, "En svensk handelsspion," 140–141. Some of Kilburger's sources have been published and translated recently. See Baron (ed.), *The travels of Olearius*; Löfstrand et al. (eds.), *Zametki o Rossii*; Epstein, *Die Hof- und Zentralverwaltung im Moskauer Staat*; Pennington (ed.), *Grigorij Kotošixin*; Kotoshikhin, *Russia in the Reign of Aleksei Mikhailovich*. On the latter, see also: Maier, "Grigorij Kotošichin als Russischlehrer."

21 Hoffmann, *Ostsibirien und Nordpazifik*, 35–64.

22 Kilburger, "Kurzer Unterricht," 310.

23 Kilburger, "Kurzer Unterricht," 316–317. See also: Greiffenhagen, "Archangel als Handelsconcurrentin Revals," 163–165.

24 Kilburger, "Kurzer Unterricht," 310; Greiffenhagen, "Archangel als Handelsconcurrentin Revals," 165.

25 Kilburger, "Kurzer Unterricht," 340: "[…] In Wuchsne-Wolosok 75 Schritte von der Sna entspringet die Twertsa in einer sumpfichten Wiese und ergießet sich endlich bey der Stadt Tweer in die Wolga. (…) Wenn dannenher hier ein Durchschnitt sollte gemachet werden, würde man die ladogische See und folglich auch die Ostsee mit der kaspischen vereinigen."

26 Kilburger supposed that "(…) wenn die Russen so curiös wären als andre Europäer, daß eine Seefahrt aus dem Fluß Oby nach China und Ostindien ohnfehlbar sollte können erfunden werden." See Kilburger, "Kurzer Unterricht," 314.

27 Kilburger, "Kurzer Unterricht," 313–320; Arne, "En svensk handelsspion," 146–147.

28 Benz, *Leibniz und Peter der Grosse*, 41–42.

29 Benz, *Leibniz und Peter der Grosse*, 48:

> [Leibniz] hat die Bedeutung Rußlands als einer eurasischen Einheit entdeckt; er hat seine Anschauungen vom Russischen Reich nicht an den üblichen, höchst unzulänglichen Vorstellungen vom europäischen Rußland geformt, sondern hat die Bedeutung der Tatsache erkannt, daß das europäische Rußland nur der Kopf und das Vorwerk eines gewaltigen und wahrhaft unbegrenzte Möglichkeiten in sich schließenden eurasischen Gesamtreiches ist, das sich von Polen bis an die Westgrenze Chinas, im Norden bis an die Westgrenze Amerikas erstreckt.

30 In 2003, Kappeler coined the term in: Kappeler, "Južnyj i vostočnyj *frontir*," 55. In 2014, the journal *Ab Imperio* started the publication of a history course with the title 'A new imperial history of Northern Eurasia' (*Ru.* Novaja imperskaja istorija Severnoj Evrazii). This course was published in two volumes in 2017 (Gerasimov, Mogil'ner, and Glebov, *Novaja imperskaja istorija*). For an introduction, see [s.n.], "Političeskaja ėkologija." Perhaps this 'new' history is understood best as an attempt to deal with post-Soviet space. Curiously, the choice and use of the term 'northern Eurasia' is not discussed in what essentially remains a course in Russian history.

31 Cajander, *Beiträge zur Kenntnis*.

32 Von Hagen, "Empires, borderlands, diasporas," 454.

33 About the founders of Eurasianism in the 1920s, see Bassin, "'Classical' Eurasianism"; Glebov, "A life with imperial dreams"; Bassin, Glebov, and Laruelle (eds.), *Between Europe and Asia*. The contemporary Eurasian movement led by the controversial Aleksandr Gelyevich Dugin echoes that of the 'original' movement of the 1920s and will therefore not be treated separately. For an introductory survey, see Laruelle, "Aleksandr Dugin." The Eurasianist movement, which emerged in the immediate aftermath of the Bolshevik revolution and the end of the First World War, propagated the "physical unity of Eurasia" and went ways to contrast it with Europe and the European threat of the "standardizing civilization of modern Europe." It underlined Russia's distinctive character: Russia was neither European nor Asian (Glebov, "A life with imperial dreams," 299–329). To this end, the Eurasianist movement pointed towards the distinctive impact of the 'Turanians' on the emergence of the Russian state and culture and interpreted the 'Europeanizing reforms' of Peter the Great and his successors as the colonization by European(ised) elites of the Eurasian peoples. The term 'Turanian' is used here to contrast with the equally controversial but much more widespread term 'Aryan.' Remarkably, Oskar Halecki uses the Eurasianist argument to distinguish (East Central) Europe from Russia:

> Der grundlegende Gegensatz zu Europa und die Bedeutung des 'turanischen' Elementes werden [durch die Eurasische Schule] besonders betont, während der Unterschied zwischen dem europäischen und dem asiatischen Teil des Gesamtreiches völlig verschwindet. Daraus ergibt sich die naheliegende Schlußfolgerung, daß die Ostgrenze der europäischen Gemeinschaft in Vergangenheit und Gegenwart stets die Westgrenze Rußlands ist.
>
> (Halecki, *Europa*, 78–79)

Such claims result from the sheer neglect of Eurasia's borderlands and border basins, a biased view of Russian history and unwarranted claims of cultural descent and adherence.

34 About the distinction, though formulated in slightly different terms and with a less precise geographical demarcation of its constituent parts, see Christian, 'Inner Eurasia'; Christian, 'Silk roads or Steppe roads.'

35 Anderson and O'Dowd, 'Borders, border regions and territoriality,' 594. In the linguistic school of Lotman and others (known as the Tartu School), the term border (*Ru.* granica) is used to mark the semiotic difference between the internal world of the individual, the self, and the outside world of the other. See Lotman, *Semiosfera*, 257–268.
36 The terms border, boundary and frontier have a variety of meanings and uses, which make proper use of these terms hardly self-evident. In the present context, it is hoped that some significant functional distinctions have been made clear, even if this has led to oversimplifying the range of different meanings attached to these terms in different languages and scientific contexts. More extensively on the issue, see Anderson and O'Dowd, "Borders, border regions and territoriality," 603 note 1.
37 Anderson and O'Dowd, "Borders, border regions and territoriality," 594.
38 Paasi, "Regional transformation," 198.
39 Konrad, "Toward a theory of borders in motion," 1 and 3–6.
40 Konrad, "Toward a theory of borders in motion," 3 and 8. In this context, Konrad warns against the ‚territorial trap,' i.e. "(…) the trap of seeing the border line rather than viewing the dynamic interaction of which the border line is but one component (…)", which "(…) has rendered the simple border line durable and the complex motion surrounding it hazy if not superfluous."
41 Konrad, "Toward a theory of borders in motion," 1.
42 Konrad, "Toward a theory of borders in motion," 4–5.
43 Konrad, "Toward a theory of borders in motion," 6.
44 See, for example: Anderson and van Wincoop, "Gravity with gravitas"; Schulze and Wolf, "On the origins of border effects."
45 See, for example: Halecki, *Borderlands of western civilization*; Brower and Lazzerini (eds.), *Russia's orient*; Rieber, *The struggle*; Kappeler, "Rußlands *Frontier.*" An extended version of the latter was published as: Kappeler, "Južnyj i vostočnyj *frontir* Rossii."
46 LeDonne, *The grand strategy*, 15–37.
47 Rieber, *The struggle.*
48 The 'weak' version understands the history of globalization as a long-term process of "(…) increasing interconnectedness between people across vast spaces (…)." See Osterhammel, "Globalizations," 93; Osterhammel and Petterson, *Globalization*, 1–5.
49 Osterhammel and Petterson, *Globalization*, 21. For a recent critique, see Wimmler and Weber, "Contructing Atlantic Peripheries," 4–14.
50 Jones, *Das Wunder Europa*, 84–85, 142, 170.
51 Jones, *Das Wunder Europa*, XXXIX and 17. See also Table 12.1 and 266.
52 Hajnal, "European marriage patterns."
53 Jones, *Das Wunder Europa*, 273.
54 Cf. Jones, *Das Wunder Europa*, 3–4.
55 Gunn, *First globalization*, 7.
56 Gunn, *First globalization*, 11–13.
57 See, e.g. Chapter 3 on "The development and establishment of worldwide connections until 1750" in Osterhammel and Petterson, *Globalization*, 31–56.
58 Osterhammel and Petterson, *Globalization*, 43–44.
59 Scammell, *The world encompassed.*
60 The term 'ghost acreage' was first coined by Borgström in his *The hungry planet* (1965) to describe a method for estimating the area of land abroad, that is employed to produce goods for the home-country. Later, the method was applied by Eric Jones in *The European Miracle* (1981) and Kenneth Pomeranz in *The great divergence* (2000).

61 North, *Geschichte der Ostsee*, 16. The historical study of borderlands receives much attention from scholars all over the world. Excellent starting points for getting acquainted with the literature include: Lee and North (eds.), *Globalizing borderlands studies* and Opilowska, Kurcz, and Roose (eds.), *Advances*.
62 Halecki, "The historical role"; Halecki, *Borderlands of western civilization*, 3–11. In the 1940s and 1950s, Halecki defined East Central Europe on several occasions as "a convenient common name for the whole group of smaller countries between [Germany and Russia] (...)" (See Halecki, "The historical role," 9) and as "a wide isthmus" between the Baltic, Black and Adriatic Seas (See Halecki, *Borderlands*, 6), meaning that East Central Europe comprises a part of Europe stretching from present-day Finland to Greece via the Baltic States, Poland and Hungary between Italy, Germany, Sweden, Russia and Turkey. Making clear that Russia is not a part of East Central Europe, Halecki wrote in 1957: "Heute muß es klar sein, daß alle Ostseeländer, einschließlich der an der Ostküste gelegenen, ein wesentlicher Bestandteil jeder *echten* (my cursivation – W.S.) atlantischen Gemeinschaft sind." (See Halecki, *Europa*, 58) and he specifies further on that "(...) die Ostgrenze der europäischen Gemeinschaft stets die Westgrenze Rußlands ist." (Halecki, *Europa*, 79).
63 Zernack, *Nordosteuropa*, 9–21.
64 Kirby, *The Baltic world*.
65 For an extensive review of the concept, see Tuchtenhagen, "The best (and the worst)"; Lehti, "Mapping the study"; Troebst, "Klaus Zernack."
66 Tuchtenhagen, "The best (and the worst)."
67 Zernack, *Osteuropa*, 51–59; Zernack, *Nordosteuropa*, 9–21. Zernack underlines the innovative character of his attempt to link the Baltic Sea with Northeastern Europe: "Der Versuch, das Ostseegebiet aus seiner historischen Verknüpfung mit Osteuropa als eine (...) eigenständige Teilregion der osteuropäischen Geschichte, nämlich Nordosteuropa, zu begründen, stößt in Neuland vor und sieht sich daher vor besondere Schwierigkeiten gestellt." (Zernack, *Osteuropa*, 51–52).
68 Zernack, *Osteuropa*, 53: "(...) Berührungsfeld von skandinavischen mit hansischen und von baltisch- und slavisch-autochtoner mit deutsch-kolonialer Faktoren."
69 Zernack, *Osteuropa*, 53.
70 Zernack, *Nordosteuropa*, 9–21 there 9.
71 Zernack, *Osteuropa*, 53; Zernack, *Nordosteuropa*, 11; Zernack, "Das Zeitalter der nordischen Kriege," 77. According to Tuchtenhagen, Zernack seems to have expanded his views beyond the 'early modern period' at a later stage. See Tuchtenhagen, "The best (and the worst)," 363.
72 Zernack, *Osteuropa*, 32.
73 Zernack, *Nordosteuropa*, 10:

> Gewiß ist Ostsee ein treffsicherer Bezug, denn es handelt sich um den historischen Umkreis derjenigen Länder, die ein wesentliches historisches Gepräge von ihrer Lage an der Ostsee erfahren haben. Doch auf der einen Seite macht auch bei diesen Ländern die Ostseelage nicht alles aus, und andererseits ist '-raum' im Deutschen ein ungut klingendes Grundwort, zumindest haftet ihm etwas Bürokratisches an. (...) Nordosteuropa entspricht in der Wortbildungsweise den anderen Regionalbegriffen wenigstens des östlichen Europa (...), aber weist inhaltlich zugleich auf das Übergangsproblem zwischen Osteuropa und Nordeuropa/Skandinavien hin.

74 Zernack, *Nordosteuropa*, 10.
75 Tuchtenhagen, "The best (and the worst)," 367.
76 Tuchtenhagen "The best (and the worst)," 364.
77 Rönnbäck, "New and old peripheries."

78 Rönnbäck, "New and old peripheries," 390.
79 Unfortunately, neither of these issues is dealt with in a separate article devoted to the source: Rönnbäck, "The Sound Toll Chamber"; Rönnbäck, "Balancing the Baltic trade."
80 Rönnbäck, "New and old peripheries," 393.
81 Rönnbäck, "New and old peripheries," 378.
82 Rönnbäck, "New and old peripheries," 377. Prussia is absent in Rönnbäck's description.
83 Rönnbäck, "New and old peripheries," 377; Pomeranz, *The great divergence*, 253–263.
84 Rönnbäck, "New and old peripheries," 377.
85 Rönnbäck, "New and old peripheries," 377.
86 Rönnbäck, "New and old peripheries," 386–387.

References

[s.n.]. "Političeskaja Ėkologija. Formirovanie regiona severnoj Evrazii." *Ab Imperio* 1 (2014): 249–290.

Anderson, James; O'Dowd, Liam. "Borders, border regions and territoriality. Contradictory meanings, changing significance." *Regional Studies* 33, 7 (1999): 593–604.

Anderson, James E.; Wincoop, Eric van. "Gravity with gravitas. A solution to the border puzzle." *The American Economic Review* 93, 1 (2003): 170–192.

Antognazza, Maria Rosa. *Leibniz. An intellectual biography.* Cambridge 2011 (reprint 2009).

Ariew, Roger. "G.W. Leibniz. Life and works." In *The Cambridge companion to Leibniz*, edited by Nicholas Jolley, 18–42. Cambridge 1995.

Arne, T.J. "En svensk handelsspion i Ryssland på 1600–talet." In *Det stora Svitjod. Essayer om gångna tiders svensk-ryska kulturförbindelser*, edited by T.J. Arne, 134–151. Stockholm 1917.

Baron, Samuel H. (ed.). *The travels of Olearius in seventeenth-century Russia.* Translated and edited by Samuel. H. Baron. Stanford 1967.

Bassin, Mark. "'Classical' Eurasianism and the geopolitics of Russian identity." *Ab Imperio* 2 (2003): 257–266.

Bassin, Mark; Glebov, Sergey; Laruelle, Marlene (eds.). *Between Europe and Asia. The origins, theories and legacies of Russian Eurasianism.* Pittsburgh 2015.

Benz, Ernst. *Leibniz und Peter der Grosse. Der Beitrag Leibnizens zur russischen Kultur, Religions- und Wirtschaftspolitik seiner Zeit.* Berlin 1947.

Borgström, Georg. *The hungry planet. The modern world at the edge of famine.* New York 1965.

Brower, Daniel L.; Lazzerini, Edward J. (eds.). *Russia's orient. Imperial borderlands and peoples.* Bloomington a.o. 1997.

Cajander, Aimo Kaarlo. *Beiträge zur Kenntnis der Vegetation der Alluvionen des nördlichen Eurasiens.* Helsingfors 1903.

Christian, David. "Inner Eurasia as a unit of world history." *Journal of World History* 5, 2 (1994): 173–211.

Christian, David. "Silk roads or Steppe roads. The silk roads in world history." *Journal of World History* 11, 1 (2000): 1–26.

Epstein, Fritz T. *Die Hof- und Zentralverwaltung im Moskauer Staat und die Bedeutung von G.K.Kotošichins zeitgenössischem Werk „Über Russland unter der Herrschaft des Zaren Aleksej Michajlovič" für die russische Verwaltungsgeschichte.* Hamburg 1978.

Fischer, Kuno. *Gottfried Wilhelm Leibniz. Leben, Werke und Lehre, Herausgegeben und eingeleitet von Thomas Sören Hoffmann*. Wiesbaden 2009.

Gerasimov, Il'ja Vladimirovič (ed.). *Novaja imperskaja istorija Severnoj Evrazii (2 vols.)*. Kazan' 2017.

Glebov, Sergei. "A life with imperial dreams. Petr Nikolaevich Savitsky, Eurasianism, and the invention of 'structuralist' geography." *Ab Imperio* 2 (2005): 299–329.

Greiffenhagen, Walter. "Archangel als Handelsconcurrentin Revals im 17. Jahrhundert." *Beiträge zur Kunde Esth-, Liv- und Kurlands* 4 (1894): 162–181.

Groh, Dieter. *Russland und das Selbstverständnis Europas. Ein Beitrag zur europäischen Geistesgeschichte*. Neuwied 1961.

Guerrier, W. *Leibniz in seinen Beziehungen zu Russland und Peter dem Grossen. Eine geschichtliche Darstellung dieses Verhältnisses nebst den darauf bezüglichen Briefen und Denkschriften*. St. Petersburg / Leipzig 1873.

Guhrauer, Gottschalk Eduard. *Gottfried Wilhelm Freiherr von Leibniz. Eine Biographie*. Hildesheim 1966 (reprint Breslau 1842).

Gunn, Geoffrey C. *First globalization. The Eurasian exchange 1500–1800*. Lanham 2003.

Guzevič, Dmitrij Ju; Guzevič, Irina D. *Pervoe evropejskoe putešestvie carja Petra. Analitičeskaja bibliografija za tri stoletija, 1697–2006*. Sankt-Peterburg 2008.

Guzevič, Dmitrij Ju; Guzevič, Irina D. *Velikoe Posol'stvo*. Sankt-Peterburg 2003.

Hajnal, John. "European marriage patterns in perspective." In *Population in history. Essays in historical demography*, edited by D.V. Glass and D.E. Eversley, 101–143. Chicago 1965.

Halecki, Oskar. *Borderlands of western civilization. A history of East Central Europe*. New York 1952.

Halecki, Oskar. *Europa. Grenzen und Gliederung seiner Geschichte*. Darmstadt 1957.

Halecki, Oskar. "The historical role of Central-Eastern Europe." *Annals of the American Academy of Political and Social Sciences* 232 (1944): 9–18.

Heinekamp, Albert (ed.). *Leibniz-Bibliographie. Band 2: Die Literatur über Leibniz 1981–1990*. Frankfurt am Main 1996.

Heinekamp, Albert (ed.). *Leibniz-Bibliographie. Die Literatur über Leibniz bis 1980 (2. neu bearbeitete Auflage)*. Frankfurt am Main 1984.

Hoffmann, Peter. *Ostsibirien und Nordpazifik in der zweiten Hälfte des 18. Jahrhunderts. Die Diskussion um die Ausdehnung Asiens*. Frankfurt am Main 2013.

Jazykov, D. "Opisanie puti iz Moskvy v Stokgol'm i Tobol'sk, v polovine XVII stoletija. Dopolnenie k Kil'burgerovu izvestiju o russkoj torgovli." *Severnyj archiv* janvar' (1823): 169–187.

Jones, Eric L. *The European miracle. Environments, economies and geopolitics in the history of Europe and Asia*. Third Edition. Cambridge 2003 (first edition 1981).

Jones, Eric L. *Das Wunder Europa. Umwelt, Wirtschaft und Geopolitik in der Geschichte Europas und Asiens*. Tübingen 2012.

Kappeler, Andreas. "Južnyj i vostočnyj *frontir* Rossii v XVI – XVIII vekach." *Ab Imperio* 1 (2003): 47–64.

Kappeler, Andreas. "Rußlands *Frontier* in der Frühen Neuzeit." In *Frieden und Krieg in der Frühen Neuzeit. Die europäische Staatenordnung und die außeneuropäische Welt*, edited by Ronald G. Asch, Wulf Eckart Voß, and Martin Wrede, 599–613. München 2001.

Kilburger, Johann Philipp. "Kurzer Unterricht von dem rußischen Handel, wie selbiger mit aus- und eingehender Waaren 1674 durch ganz Rußland getrieben worden." In *Magazin für die neue Historie und Geographie 3*, edited by Anton Friedrich Büsching, 245–341. Hamburg 1769.

Kirby, David. *Northern Europe in the early modern period. The Baltic world, 1492–1772.* London / New York 1990.

Konrad, Victor. "Toward a theory of borders in motion." *Journal of Borderlands Studies* 30, 1 (2015): 1–17.

Kotoshikhin, Grigorii Karpovich. *Russia in the Reign of Aleksei Mikhailovich.* Translated by Benjamin Phillip Uroff / Edited by Marshall Poe. De Gruyter 2014.

Kurc, B.G. *Sočinenie Kil'burgera o russkoj torgovle v carstvovanie Alekseja Michajloviča.* Kiev 1915.

Laruelle, Marlene. "Aleksandr Dugin. A Russian version of the European radical right?" In *Kennan Institute Occasional Papers* 294, 2006.

LeDonne, John P. *The grand strategy of the Russian Empire, 1650–1831.* New York 2004.

Lee, John W.I.; North, Michael (eds.). *Globalizing borderlands studies in Europe and North America.* Lincoln & London 2016.

Lehti, Marko. "Mapping the study of the Baltic Sea area. From Nation-centric to multinational history." *Journal of Baltic Studies* 33, 4 (2002): 431–446.

Leibniz, Gottfried Wilhelm. *Novissima Sinica Historiam Nostri Temporis Illustratura In quibus De Christianismo publica nunc primum autoritate propogato missa in Europam relatio exhibetur, deque favore scientiarum Europaearum ac moribus gentis et ipsius praesertim Monarchae, tum et de bello Sinensium cum Moscis ac pace constituta, multa hactenus ignota explicantur.* [s.l.] 1697.

Leibniz, Gottfried Wilhelm. *Sämtliche Schriften und Briefe. In eight series.* Berlin 1923.

Li, Wenchao; Poser, Hans (eds.). *Das Neueste über China.* Stuttgart 2000.

Löfstrand, Elisabeth; Kovalenko, Gennadij; Naylor, Martin (eds.). *Zametki o Rossii sdelannye Èrikom Pal'mkvistom v 1674 godu. Några observationer angående Ryssland, sammanfattade av Erik Palmquist år 1674. Some observations concerning Russia, summarised by Erik Palmquist in 1674.* Moskva 2012.

Lotman, Ju. M. *Semiosfera. Kul'tura i vzryv / Vnutri mysljaščich mirov / Stat'i i issledovanija, zametki.* Sankt-Peterburg 2004.

Maier, Ingrid. "Grigorij Kotošichin als Russischlehrer für zukünftige Übersetzer der Schwedischen Krone?" *Zeitschrift für Slawistik* 59, 4 (2014): 552–583.

Massie, Robert K. *Peter the Great. The compelling story of the man who created modern Russia, founded St Petersburg and made his country part of Europe.* London 2012.

Müller, Kurt (ed.). *Leibniz-Bibliographie. Die Literatur über Leibniz.* Frankfurt am Main 1967.

Müller, Kurt; Kronert, G. *Leben und Werk von Gottfried Wilhelm Leibniz. Eine Chronik.* Frankfurt am Main 1969.

Nesselrath, Hans-Günther; Reinbothe, Hermann. *Das neueste von China. Novissima Sinica.* Köln 1979.

North, Michael. *Geschichte der Ostsee. Handel und Kulturen.* München 2011.

Nyström, Per. "Mercatura Ruthenica." *Scandia: Tidskrift för historisk Forskning* 10, 2 (1937): 239–296.

Opilowska, Elzbieta; Kurcz, Zbigniew; Roose, Jochen (eds.). *Advances in European borderlands studies.* Baden-Baden 2017.

Osterhammel, Jürgen. *Die Entzauberung Asiens. Europa und die asiatischen Reiche im 18. Jahrhundert.* München 2010.

Osterhammel, Jürgen. "Globalizations." In *The Oxford handbook of world history*, edited by Jerry H. Bentley, 89–104. Oxford 2011.

Osterhammel, Jürgen; Petterson Niels P. *Globalization. A short history.* Princeton 2005.

Paasi, Anssi. "Regional transformation in the European context. Notes on regions, boundaries and identity." *Space & Polity* 6, 2 (2002): 197–201.

Pennington, Anne Elizabeth (ed.). *Grigorij Kotošixin: O Rossii V Carstvovanie Alekseja Mixajloviča. Text and commentary.* Oxford / New York 1980.

Pomeranz, Kenneth. *The great divergence. China, Europe and the making of the modern world economy.* Princeton and Oxford 2000.

Ravier, Émile. *Bibliographie des Œuvres de Leibniz.* Paris 1937.

Reinhard, Wolfgang. *Die Unterwerfung der Welt. Globalgeschichte der europäischen Expansion 1415–2015.* München 2016.

Richter, Liselotte. *Leibniz und sein Russlandbild.* Berlin 1946.

Rieber, Alfred J. *The struggle for the Eurasian borderlands. From the rise of early modern empires to the end of the First World War.* Cambridge 2014.

Roll, Christine. "Barbaren? *Tabula rasa*? Wie Leibniz sein neues Wissen über Russland auf den Begriff brachte. Eine Studie über die Bedeutung der Vernetzung gelehrter Korrespondenzen für die Ermöglichung aufgeklärter Diskurse." In *Umwelt und Weltgestaltung: Leibniz' politisches Denken in seiner Zeit*, edited by Friedrich Biederbeck, Irene Dingel, and Wenchao Li, 307–358. Göttingen 2014.

Rönnbäck, Klas. "Balancing the Baltic trade. Colonial commodities in the trade on the Baltic, 1773–1856." *Scandinavian Economic History Review* 58, 3 (2010): 188–202.

Rönnbäck, Klas. "New and old peripheries. Britain, the Baltic and the Americas in the great divergence." *Journal of Global History* 5, 3 (2010): 373–394.

Rönnbäck, Klas. "The Sound Toll Chamber Commodity Records. Estimating the reliability of a potential source to international trade history." *International Journal of Maritime History* 22, 1 (2010): 229–238.

Scammell, Geoffrey V. *The world encompassed. The first European maritime empires, ca. 800–1650.* Berkeley / Los Angeles 1981.

Schmidt (genannt Fiseldek), Christoff. "Kilburger's Unterricht vom russischen Handel, aus einer wolfenbüttelischen Handschrift berichtigt und ergänzt." In *Zur Geschichte und Litteratur. Aus den Schätzen der herzoglichen Bibliothek zu Wolfenbüttel* 5, edited by Gotthold Ephraim Lessing and Johann Joachim Eschenburg, 155–182. Braunschweig 1781.

Schulze, Max-Stephan; Wolf, Nikolaus. "On the origins of border effects. Insights from the Habsburg Empire." *Journal of Economic Geography* 9 (2009): 117–136.

Tavernier, Roger. *Russia and the low countries. An international bibliography, 1500–2000.* Groningen 2006.

Troebst, Stefan. "Eine wichtige Quellenedition der russischen Geschichte des 17. Jahrhunderts." *Quaestio Rossica* 4, 1 (2016): 281–286.

Troebst, Stefan. "Klaus Zernack als Nordosteuropahistoriker." *Zeitschrift für Ostmitteleuropa-Forschung* 50, 4 (2001): 572–586.

Tuchtenhagen, Ralph. "The best (and the worst) of several worlds. The shifting historiographical concept of Northeastern Europe." *European Review of History / Revue européenne d'histoire* 10, 2 (2003): 361–374.

Von Hagen, Mark. "Empires, borderlands, diasporas. Eurasia as anti-paradigm for the post-Soviet era." *American Historical Review* 109 (2004): 445–468.

Widmaier, Rita. *Leibniz korrespondiert mit China. Der Briefwechsel mit den Jesuitenmissionaren (1689–1714).* Frankfurt am Main 1990.

Wimmler, Jutta; Weber, Klaus. "Constructing Atlantic Peripheries: A critical view of the historiography." In *Globalized Peripheries. Central Europe and the Atlantic World, 1680–1860*, edited by Jutta Wimmler and Klaus Weber, 1–18. Woodbridge 2020.

Witsen, Nicolaes. *NOORD en OOST TARTARYE, OFTE BONDIG ONTWERP Van eenige dier LANDEN en VOLKEN, Welke voormaels bekent zijn geweest. Beneffens verscheide tot noch toe onbekende, en meest nooit voorheen beschreve Tartersche en Nabuurige Gewesten, Landstreeken, Steden, Rivieren, en Plaetzen, in de NOORDER en OOSTERLYKSE GEDEELTE VAN ASIA en EUROPA, Zoo buiten en binnen de Rivieren Tanais en Oby, als omtrent de Kaspische, Indische-Ooster, en Zwarte Zee gelegen; gelijk de Landschappen Niuche, Dauria, Jesso, Moegalia, Kalmakkia, Tangut, Usbek, en Noorder Persie, Turkestan, Georgia, Mengrelia, Cirkassia, Crim, Astakkia, Altin, Tingoesia, Siberia, Samojedia, en andere aen hunne TZAERSCHE MAJESTEITEN KROON gehoorende, Heerschappyen: Verdeeld in twee Stukken, Met der zelver Land-kaerten: mitsgaders, onderscheidene Afbeeldingen van Steden, Drachten, enz. Zedert naeuwkeurig onderzoek van veele Jaren, en eigen ondervindinge ontworpen, beschreven, geteekent, en in 't licht gegeven*. Amsterdam 1705 (second edition).

Zernack, Klaus. "Das Zeitalter der nordischen Kriege als frühneuzeitlicher Geschichtsepoche." *Zeitschrift für historische Forschung* 1 (1974): 54–79.

Zernack, Klaus. "Imperiale Politik und merkantiler Hintergrund. Ein Dokument der schwedischen Rußlandpolitik im 17. Jahrhundert." In *Russland – Deutschland – Amerika / Russia – Germany – America. Festschrift für Fritz T. Epstein zum 80. Geburtstag*, edited by Alexander Fischer, Günter Moltmann, and Klaus Schwabe, 23–36. Wiesbaden 1978.

Zernack, Klaus. *Nordosteuropa. Skizzen und Beiträge zu einer Geschichte der Ostseeländer*. Lüneburg 1993.

Zernack, Klaus. *Osteuropa. Eine Einführung in seine Geschichte*. München 1977.

3 The emergence of the Baltic as a privileged outlet for North Eurasian trade, 1670–1721

Introduction

The exploratory analysis of the first chapter has made clear that, more than anything, the last *Hansetag* of 1669 had a symbolic meaning. It marked the final collapse of a system that had dominated Baltic trade for centuries; the cities-members of the Hanseatic League, of which only nine were present in 1669, had to give in to the novel system of commercial exchange, which the Dutch and English had introduced to the Baltic since the sixteenth century.[1] At the last *Hansetag* of 1669, the remaining members of the League recognized that their traditional system of trade had become obsolete,[2] and that 'Dutch primacy,' as Jonathan Israel pinpointed it,[3] was now uncontested. When Lübeck invited the cities-members of the Hanseatic League in 1668, most other European nations envied the Dutch for their dominance in commercial affairs, England had just fought a second war with the Dutch Republic (1665–1667), and France made plans to send its military to occupy the Dutch Republic and take over its commerce. The Baltic served as 'backwaters' of the Dutch Republic.[4] In fact, for the Dutch Republic "[r]elations of a political nature with Sweden, Poland-Lithuania, the Elector of Brandenburg and the Czar of Muscovy were still of minor importance compared to relations with Denmark, which controlled the Sound and the two Belts."[5]

Around the mid-seventeenth century, the growing discontent with the commercial dominance of the Dutch led to the First Anglo-Dutch War (1652–1654),[6] and the subsequent opposition of Denmark and the Dutch Republic against England and Sweden in the Baltic.[7] The constellation was anything but straightforward: "(...) on finding that the Dutch intended to side with Denmark, the English Government decided to send a fleet to help Sweden. It was almost as disadvantageous for England as for the Netherlands that the Baltic should become a Swedish lake, but it would be even worse for it to pass into the power of the Dutch and Danes."[8] During the Second Northern War (1655–1660),[9] a battle of power between Muscovite and Swedish forces fought for the most part on Polish-Lithuanian territory,[10] Dutch fleets were active in the Baltic to secure the Republic's commerce in Danzig (1656)[11] and through the Sound (1658).[12] The primacy of the Dutch in these conflicts and the consolidation of Sweden as a regional power in the Baltic had a decisive impact on the role of the Baltic for North Eurasian trade in the remainder of the seventeenth century. With regard to the latter, the tax-free status, which was obtained for Swedish ships passing through the Danish Sound in 1645, provided an important impulse for the development of a Swedish mercantile fleet in the second half of the seventeenth century.[13] After the treaties of Copenhagen (1660), Oliva (1660), and Kardis (1661), which confirmed Sweden's territorial dominance, the Baltic gradually turned into an area where the interests of the Dutch Republic, France, England, Sweden, Muscovy, Poland-Lithuania, and (Brandenburg-)Prussia collided. Their international diplomacy and military actions, on the one hand, and domestic and foreign economic policies, on the other, provoked a paradigmatic shift in international politics and trade. The impact of policy-making at 'state' level on the structure of international commerce increased. It had become a widely spread understanding that international commerce was to serve national interests. In the Baltic and North-West Europe, the shift towards the pursuit of 'national' interests (rather than the network-based pursuit of commercial gains of the Hanseatic League) went hand in hand with the (forceful) implementation of mercantilist policies (see Section "Threats to Dutch primacy in the Baltic"). In the meantime, the North Eurasian mainland turned into an area of conflicting commercial interests as well (see Section "North Eurasia as transit zone for Asian goods"), which culminated in warfare between Sweden and an anti-Swedish coalition led by Muscovy at the turn of the eighteenth century and paved the way for the enforcement of new terms of trade (see Section "War and national interests").

Threats to Dutch primacy in the Baltic

Navigation laws

In the 1650s and 1660s, the British issued a set of Navigation Ordinances and Laws, which were designed to restrict the participation of Dutch masters in British trade, on the one hand, and to secure essential supplies by reinforcing them to be carried on British ships, on the other.[14] For trade through the Danish Sound, the Act of 1660, which succeeded the original Act of 1651, and the Act of 1662, which contained additional regulations for imports from the Netherlands or Germany, were the most important.[15] The 1660 Act stated, "European products might be imported in any ship from any place, except that certain enumerated articles must be brought in an English ship or, if alien duties were paid, in a ship of the country producing them."[16] The list of commodities thus affected by the Navigation Acts reveals that trade through the Danish Sound was an object of special attention for various interest groups negotiating their content in parliament. In particular, the Turkey, Muscovy (Russia), and Eastland companies, which were active in the Baltic, Muscovy, and the Levant, managed to receive protection from foreign competition by means of the Act of 1660; almost all commodities carried from these areas were now subjected to the novel regulations.[17] Besides Muscovite and Turkish goods, grain, hemp, flax, masts, pitch, potash, tar, and timber or boards all had to be imported in English-owned ships, or ships of the country of growth, production or manufacture of the enumerated goods. Additional payments were due on imports in other than English-built ships, and the importation from the Netherlands or Germany of flax, hemp, pitch, potash, tar, and timber was forbidden altogether.[18]

Much like the British, France, and Sweden openly disliked and envied the predominance of the Dutch mercantile and fishing fleets (not to forget their naval power). In 1667, the French Minister of Finance Jean-Baptiste Colbert (1619–1683) issued the second, even more restrictive version of his 1664 customs tariff,[19] which served purposes quite similar to the British Navigation Laws. Colbert strived for excluding foreign – and above all – Dutch ships from French harbours by means of additional taxes for merchandise entering French ports under a foreign flag.[20] Additionally, as a measure against the Dutch predominance in the carrying trade between the French Atlantic coast, Norway, and the Baltic – which essentially consisted of the exchange of salt and wine for grain, timber, hemp, and flax – the *Compagnie des Pyrénées* and the *Compagnie du Nord* were established.[21] The *Compagnie des Pyrénées* would tap from an alternative source of timber for naval construction that was not controlled by the Dutch.[22] The *Compagnie du Nord* would construct and operate its own ships in the traffic between France and the Baltic/Norway to take over maritime transport services from the Dutch.[23] Obviously, such measures contrasted sharply with the Dutch concept of *mare liberum*.[24]

A few years after Colbert's second tariff, the French merchant and economist Jacques Savary (1622–1690) published an influential manual for merchants, known best under its abbreviated title *Le parfait négociant* (1672). Many chapters in this merchant's manual provide detailed instructions about the institutions and *usances* of trade across Europe and in the entire world. Amidst these lengthy treatises, a very short chapter of only six pages stands out: *Que les Francois peuvent faire le commerce sur la Mer Baltique et en Moscovie avec autant et plus d'avantage que les Hollandois.*[25] This concise statement, which follows longer descriptive accounts of trade with the North, the Baltic, and Arkhangelsk, expresses an undeniable shift in the political attitude towards Baltic commercial exchange under Colbert. Until recently, Savary argued, the Dutch had completely dominated Baltic commercial exchange, but now the time has come to take over and do better. An anti-Dutch offensive was declared. In 1672, a year commonly described as 'year of disaster' (*Nl.* rampjaar) in Dutch historiography, both England and France attacked the Dutch Republic.[26] That year, the estimated total tonnage of trade through the Danish Sound was 201,327 tonnes, which was 47.8% lower than in 1671 and 52.8% lower than in 1670.[27]

As soon as war broke out in 1672, 'new' competitors emerged in the Baltic waters, determined to rule out Dutch competition. Most importantly, the diminished tonnage transported by Dutch carriers led to the intensification of tax-free Swedish shipping through the Sound. Moreover, Denmark and (much less so) Brandenburg-Prussia also experienced a net increase in the tonnage of Baltic traffic in the first half of the 1670s. The estimated total tonnage of Swedish tax-free shipping reached a first peak in 1674.[28] Nevertheless, the Dutch share remained considerable; neither its transport services nor its commercial system could be replaced easily with alternative carriers or routes. The result was a general, but only temporary decline of trade through the Danish Sound. The recovery of Dutch transport and trade in the wake of the Treaty of Westminster (February 1674) was as sudden as its decline a few years earlier. However, commercial exchange with the Baltic remained unstable, because of the ongoing Dutch War with France (1672–1678),[29] on the one hand, and the outbreak of the Scania War (1674–1679),[30] on the other. In 1675, the total tonnage of Dutch trade through the Sound stagnated roughly at the same level as the previous year, whereas the tonnage carried by English masters almost quadrupled[31] and 'Baltic turnover' at English ports almost doubled.[32]

Until 1676, the Dutch maritime transport sector was unable to restore its former dominance. In 1676, the tonnage of England's Baltic traffic was almost as large as that of the Dutch Republic and it seems that, insofar as competition with the Dutch is concerned, the Navigation Acts did have a positive impact on English shipping in the Baltic.[33] Such relations were unprecedented in the recent history of trade through the Danish Sound. Despite its recovery (in absolute terms), the share of the Dutch maritime transport sector in Baltic commercial exchange reached its low in 1676, when 'only' 39.3% of all Baltic traffic was executed by Dutch masters.[34] At the same time, the estimated total tonnages carried by Sweden, Denmark, and Brandenburg declined significantly under the impact of the Scania War. Between 1676 and 1679, Swedish shipping through the Danish Sound almost completely stopped. Temporary upswings in 1675 and 1677 notwithstanding, the volume of Danish traffic diminished to about 25%–50% of its pre-1675 volume in 1676, 1678, and 1679. At the end of the decade, the Dutch share in Baltic commercial exchange was back at the level of 1670: almost 80% of all Baltic traffic lied in the hands of Dutch masters and the Dutch Republic's share in the estimated total tonnage of Baltic commercial exchange was back at about 70%–75%.

During the relatively peaceful years after the peace treaties of Nijmegen (1678–1679), Fontainebleau (1679), and Saint-Germain-en-Laye (1679), the Dutch Republic almost completely regained its previous strength. At the same time, Sweden experienced its breakthrough in Baltic commercial exchange, not at the least thanks to its tax freedom in the Sound, whereas English and Scottish trade through the Danish Sound declined (see Table 3.1). The estimated tonnage of English and Scottish transport and trade through the Danish Sound reached its peak in 1676, but then started to decline all the way through the Exclusion Crisis (1679–1681). The downward spiral intensified further after the death of Charles II (1630–1685). In 1688, the internal political and religious turmoil, which James II (1633–1701) had inherited from

Table 3.1 Five-year averages of the estimated tonnage of (registered) exports and imports, 1670–1719

	Export							
	Departure				*Destination*			
	SW	*% SW*	*DK*	*% DK*	*NL*	*% NL*	*UK*	*% UK*
1670–1674	64,258	*28.2*	7,746	*3.9*	147,428	*58.8*	14,477	*6.2*
1675–1679	77,412	*32.0*	3,998	*1.7*	163,656	*65.1*	32,206	*13.6*
1680–1684	138,904	*31.8*	5,093	*1.2*	316,415	*72.5*	25,083	*5.8*
1685–1689	135,504	*36.1*	8,215	*2.2*	282,455	*74.4*	17,215	*4.5*
1690–1694	157,810	*48.1*	9,452	*2.9*	254,896	*75.0*	18,634	*5.7*
1695–1699	115,288	*40.9*	7,184	*2.9*	211,951	*74.1*	28,134	*10.6*
1700–1704	80,554	*39.6*	5,780	*2.9*	152,928	*73.5*	25,764	*12.6*
1705–1709	33,826	*18.1*	4,697	*2.6*	129,228	*71.3*	18,128	*10.3*
1710–1714	46,917	*23.3*	3,277	*1.7*	160,760	*76.9*	23,306	*11.7*
1715–1719	37,560	*35.5*	2,156	*2.4*	75,211	*71.1*	19,184	*19.0*
	Import							
	Departure				*Destination*			
	NL	*% NL*	*UK*	*% UK*	*SW*	*% SW*	*DK*	*% DK*
1670–1674	20,228	*26.5*	5,854	*8.1*	24,198	*32.2*	6,978	*9.9*
1675–1679	25,832	*27.8*	11,097	*12.5*	28,639	*31.0*	7,448	*8.1*
1680–1684	26,681	*26.1*	9,987	*9.6*	35,913	*35.0*	9,276	*8.9*
1685–1689	25,432	*25.8*	6,725	*7.2*	34,801	*33.7*	12,192	*12.3*
1690–1694	35,370	*36.2*	7,761	*8.2*	38,735	*40.4*	20,387	*20.9*
1695–1699	31,933	*27.8*	11,008	*10.0*	44,772	*39.1*	23,863	*21.2*
1700–1704	31,608	*34.0*	10,517	*11.2*	31,635	*34.6*	12,115	*12.8*
1705–1709	21,411	*26.5*	9,083	*11.1*	32,966	*39.9*	10,297	*12.6*
1710–1714	24,979	*35.6*	12,524	*17.8*	17,558	*25.2*	4,597	*6.7*
1715–1719	23,766	*26.1*	15,204	*17.1*	23,949	*26.8*	4,887	*5.7*
	Transport							
	NL	*% NL*	*UK*	*% UK*	*SW*	*% SW*	*DK*	*% DK*
1670–1674	172,037	*51.1*	10,951	*3.0*	57,298	*20.6*	18,354	*7.0*
1675–1679	190,006	*54.7*	74,069	*22.5*	2,396	*0.7*	16,864	*5.1*
1680–1684	364,523	*67.7*	43,292	*8.1*	32,042	*5.9*	19,797	*3.7*
1685–1689	332,058	*68.1*	27,029	*5.5*	41,318	*8.5*	33,325	*7.0*
1690–1694	192,557	*45.1*	15,981	*3.8*	114,722	*26.1*	66,557	*15.0*
1695–1699	204,441	*48.7*	23,456	*5.7*	85,795	*23.1*	42,552	*11.3*
1700–1704	170,865	*55.3*	24,217	*7.7*	60,731	*21.1*	21,289	*7.1*
1705–1709	131,656	*49.9*	10,005	*3.8*	74,168	*28.1*	25,756	*9.9*
1710–1714	193,763	*69.6*	37,067	*12.9*	2,806	*1.2*	5,019	*1.9*
1715–1719	121,104	*60.3*	44,422	*23.5*	846	*0.5*	4,560	*2.5*

Source: *Tetradas* [VSWG-JDA], 3_EI and 4_T.
Note: Exports and imports from Sweden (SW), Denmark (DK), the Dutch Republic (NL), and England and Scotland (UK) through the Danish Sound, and (registered) tonnage carried by Swedish, Danish, Dutch, and English or Scottish masters.
Legenda: Five-year averages.

Charles II, culminated in the Glorious Revolution and the breakthrough of a novel, secular form of state politics.[35] A union of English parliamentarians, which had sought the support of the Dutch Stadtholder Willem III of Orange (1650–1702), defeated James II and ended any further attempts to establish Catholicism in the Kingdom.[36]

England and the Dutch Republic established a personal union. Consequently, after 1688, England's previous attempts to position itself as a competitor of the Dutch Republic in international commerce now were embedded in a different, more complex institutional framework. One of the immediate effects of this novel environment of English trade through the Danish Sound seems to have been another reduction of the volume of its turnover and transport services after the outbreak of the War of the Grand Alliance, or Nine Years' War in 1689 (see Table 3.1).

In the meantime, the estimated total tonnage of trade through the Danish Sound reached a peak in the late 1680s. Decline set in with the outbreak of the Nine Years' War and, two brief upswings in 1693/94 and 1697/99 notwithstanding would continue throughout the first decades of the eighteenth century.[37] The total tonnage of trade through the Danish Sound diminished strongly at the start (1689–1691) and the end of the war (1696–1697). However, when the first signs of a bad harvest became apparent in various French regions in 1691 and 1692, causing distress and fear among French soldiers and ordinary people alike,[38] the estimated tonnage of exports from grain-producing areas such as Ducal Prussia, Poland-Lithuania, and Courland started to rise. In the same period, Sweden abandoned most of its export restrictions for grain from its Baltic provinces.[39] Following a disastrous harvest in almost all of France in 1693, the tonnages exported from these areas increased dramatically.[40] The 1693 famine provided an excellent opportunity for Scandinavian and Baltic maritime transporters, who were approached by local commercial agents and diplomats, most importantly consul Bonrepaus in Copenhagen, to deliver large quantities of grain to the French government.[41] Denmark and – even more so – Sweden benefited greatly from this phase of the war of the 'multiconfessional' Grand Alliance against France, not at the least thanks to their tax freedom in the Danish Sound and the treaties of armed neutrality, which they had signed in 1691 and 1693.[42] The more modest maritime transport sectors of Courland and Poland-Lithuania also experienced significant growth, which – at least in part – resulted from the (virtual) migration of Dutch (and perhaps English) shipmasters to ports in the Baltic.[43] Consequently, the share of Dutch masters in Baltic traffic dropped to about 60%, whereas that of Baltic masters started to rise rapidly and reached a peak in the 1690s (see Table 3.1). In 1696, trade through the Danish Sound experienced its strongest decline since the 'year of disaster' 1672, which was probably due to a series of bad harvests in the grain-producing parts of the Baltic.[44] Dutch masters transported less than half of the volume of goods compared to the previous year and so did Danish, Prussian, Hanseatic, and Polish masters. The only significant exceptions to the general decline of Baltic commercial exchange in 1696 were England and Scotland, whose transport and turnover grew, both in absolute terms and – more impressively – relative to other political entities.[45]

Stormaktstiden

Sweden reached the apogee of its power in the 1690s,[46] and this is reflected in the increasing tonnages of Swedish exports from the Baltic, especially after the Scania War (1675–1679) (see Table 3.1). Throughout the 1690s, Swedish tonnage exported through the Danish Sound exceeded that of the traditional bulk supplier, Poland-Lithuania (exporting, in particular, via Danzig). Although Sweden's tax freedom in the Danish Sound makes it hard to reconstruct the composition of its exports from the Baltic, it is clear that Sweden's "eastern Baltic provinces," i.e. the territories of Livonia, Estonia, and Ingria, supplied a significant part of Sweden's estimated tonnage exported through the Sound.

The estimated tonnage of Swedish exports from ports in the Baltic experienced an almost uninterrupted increase between 1672 and 1694. Exports rose from 43,295 tonnes in 1672 to 193,261 tonnes in 1693 (including estimated tax-free exports).[47] During the same period, Sweden's share in the estimated total tonnage of exports from the Baltic rose from about 20% to almost 50%. The share of Swedish tax-free exports through the Sound increased strongly during this period and flourished, in particular, during the first phase of the Nine Years' War (1689–1697). Even so, it is unlikely that the Sound toll registers have captured all of Sweden's exports from ports in the Baltic during this period.[48]

Riga and Reval, the two major ports in the Swedish eastern Baltic provinces, served as the main outlets for the grain produced on large Livonian, Estonian, and Lithuanian estates. Riga was by far the most important port in Sweden's eastern Baltic provinces, and its significance for the Swedish Empire went well beyond the regional level. In fact, soon after its conquest in 1621, Riga became "the cornerstone of Sweden's Baltic empire."[49] Together with Reval, Riga accounted for more than 84% of all registered rye exports from Sweden through the Danish Sound between 1670 and 1700.[50] During the same period, Stettin, then part of Swedish Pomerania, maintained a share of 5.7% in rye exports, whereas the contribution of other ports in the Swedish Baltic provinces, like Arensburg (Kuressaare), Pernau (Pärnu), Narva, or Nyen was limited.[51]

Riga also served as the main Swedish port for the exportation of hemp, flax, and hemp- and flaxseed.[52] Pernau, Narva, and Nyen, on the other hand, held a significant share in Sweden's timber exports through the Danish Sound. Grown in the vast Muscovite hinterland of these ports, hemp(seed), flax(seed), and timber constituted a vital part of Swedish-Russian transit trade in the second half of the seventeenth century. Quite differently, various clusters of ports on the Swedish mainland (Stockholm, Norrköping, Kalmar, and Västervik), in the Gulf of Finland (Vyborg), and on the island of Gotland dominated the exportation of iron, tar, and pitch.[53] Stockholm had an overwhelming share of 88.2% in (registered) iron exports from Sweden.[54] Tar and pitch exports were divided almost equally among Stockholm and nearby Trångsund, on the one hand, and the northeastern shores of the Gulf of Finland, with Vyborg, Nyen, and Narva, on the other.[55]

Thus, regardless of its inevitable inaccuracies, available estimates for the years between 1670 and 1700 underline the importance of the Swedish ports in the eastern Baltic provinces (in particular, Riga, Pernau, Reval, Narva, and Nyen) for the exportation of grain from Lithuanian, Livonian, and Estonian estates, as well as for the exportation of products of Russian transit trade, such as hemp, flax, pitch, tar, and timber. Moreover, these estimates confirm the significance of Stockholm and its immediate surroundings in the exportation of Swedish iron and of the northeastern part of the Swedish realm for the production and exportation of tar and pitch. Finally, the statistics of trade through the Danish Sound reveal the increasing competition between Sweden and Poland-Lithuania in the exportation of foodstuffs and raw materials, on the one hand, but it reveals changes in the bilateral commodity flows from Sweden and Poland-Lithuania to the Dutch Republic and England towards the end of the seventeenth century as well.[56] Raw materials exports became particularly important towards the end of the seventeenth century and turned into an object of England's growing interest in Baltic affairs.[57]

Mercantilism in the Baltic

The open battle against the commercial dominance of the Dutch extended to France and Northern Europe. Sweden's striving for *dominium maris baltici*, which was the cornerstone of its establishment as a great power in the second half of the seventeenth century,[58] entailed the breakthrough of mercantilist thought in other parts of the Baltic realm, most importantly in Brandenburg-Prussia, Courland, and the Holy Roman Empire.[59] Around the mid-1670s, the Elector of Brandenburg and Duke of Prussia, Frederick William (1620–1688), had started to develop an internationally oriented mercantilist policy, which foresaw the establishment of a Prussian mercantile fleet, Brandenburg's participation in overseas (colonial) trade, and the exploitation of Livonia, the claims on which had been given up 'for eternity' by Poland-Lithuania in the 1660 Treaty of Oliva.[60] A decade earlier, in 1665, Brandenburg had signed a commercial treaty with England.[61] The impact of Frederick William's mercantilist policies on the Brandenburg-Prussian economy is hard to assess as they were implemented at two different levels of government. On the one hand, there is the level of single German territorial states, which strived for expansion and wanted to increase their political and economic power. Among them, Brandenburg-Prussia occupied a peculiar position. It consisted of several dispersed territories, of which the most significant was Ducal Prussia, a fief of the Kingdom of Poland located outside of the Holy Roman Empire. Ducal Prussia had been a constituent part of the House Brandenburg since the establishment of a personal union in 1618. Frederick William found in Ducal Prussia an ideal territory for strengthening his realm's international position. In Ducal Prussia, he wanted to lay the foundation for an independent European policy, which was no longer restricted by the Holy Roman Empire.[62] On the other hand, there is the level of the Holy Roman Empire itself, where, after the end of the Thirty Years' War (1618–1648), a particular kind of imperial mercantilism seems to have emerged, in which "[t]he empire became an entity in a mercantilist sense (…)."[63] The Emperor represented the Holy Roman Empire and took decisions that affected the Empire as a whole.[64] In 1673, the Emperor Leopold I (1640–1705) signed a treaty with Spain and the Dutch Republic; in 1681, a treaty of association with the Dutch Republic, Sweden, and Spain; in 1688, the Emperor issued the famous imperial *avocatoria* prohibiting French imports to the Empire; and in 1701, he reached an agreement with the maritime powers in the war against France. In these cases, the Empire came to the fore as a single entity. However, whereas Ingomar Bog traces an emerging imperial mercantilism or *Reichsmerkantilismus* in the increasing efforts of the Holy Roman Empire to strengthen its economic and political power by regulating and redirecting trade flows, newer research follows the early criticism of Bog's viewpoint, and shows itself less convinced.[65] It argues that *Reichsmerkantilismus* did not exist in the form that Bog had described,[66] and that the successes of cameralist policies in German territories were visible only in some domains of economic policy-making, including infrastructural development.[67] In fact, the Holy Roman Empire encountered numerous problems trying to sustain its 'unity' and around 1715 the era of imperial mercantilism ended: "From that time onwards (…), it was no longer possible to enforce a unified trade policy from Vienna against the divergent commercial interests of the different constituent principalities of the Empire."[68]

Regardless of its final assessment, the efforts to establish some sort of *Reichsmerkantilismus* significantly influenced economic policy-making in the Holy Roman Empire. Much like its French and British counterparts, measures were taken to limit foreign dominance in the Holy Roman Empire's commerce.[69] The rapid rise of the Dutch Republic was observed with a combination of envy and admiration.[70] Conscious of the advantages of the maritime powers and acknowledging that the Holy Roman Empire would not be able to obtain a share in overseas (colonial) trade without the maritime powers' assistance, efforts were made to obtain a share in colonial trade by means of purchasing Guyana from the Dutch West India Company in 1664.[71] The latter would remain responsible for the transportation of goods from the colony.[72] Although the so-called Bavarian project of 1664 failed, a renewed attempt in 1669 resulted in a contract with the Dutch West India Company regarding a piece of coastline between the Amazon and Orinoco rivers, which became a fief of the Duke of Hanau.[73] However, due a variety of factors, a colony was never realized and the project was given up in 1672.

Overall, the impact of mercantilist policies in the German States on trade through the Danish Sound seems to have been limited. Many projects started, but only few of them were carried through. The tonnage estimates of trade through the Danish Sound confirm the limited contribution of the German States in the Baltic; commodity flows through the Danish Sound were restricted to grain and timber exports from Königsberg as well as some irregular grain exports from Mecklenburg.[74]

Sweden's isolation and Muscovy's awakening

During the final decades of the seventeenth century, the economic motives of the proponents of the quest for North Eurasian trade became more and more obvious. States became preoccupied with securing access to resources for their own benefit, and tried to prevent others from doing the same. Political and economic tension had already increased during the Nine Years' War and reached a peak in the wake of the Treaty of Rijswijk (1697). In the course of the Nine Years' War, Sweden developed a bond with France, insisted on making reprisals on England and the Dutch Republic, and cultivated anti-Danish sentiments.[75] Sweden's attitude worried the maritime powers, which in return, from 1694 onwards, tried to improve their relations with Denmark. In December 1696, in return for Dutch and English subsidies, Denmark prohibited trade with France, excluded French privateers from its ports and stopped its opposition against the Anglo-Dutch personal union. Moreover, in the Treaty of Rijswijk, Denmark gave up its previous claims on the sovereignty over Hamburg.[76] However, one important issue remained unsettled: the 'old' Holstein-Gottorf question. In 1689, a treaty signed in Altona confirmed the territorial claims and sovereignty of the Duke of Holstein-Gottorf. Neither Denmark nor Sweden accepted these claims and contested them on several occasions.[77]

In 1697, France assumed that control over the Swedish throne would consolidate the existing balance of power in the Baltic and provide an opportunity for France to restore its *barrière de l'Est*. This political concept was originally directed against the Habsburg Empire, but it also had a Baltic and – in particular – anti-Muscovite component.[78] Of crucial importance were the French efforts to contain and check Muscovy's territorial advances through the establishment of close political ties with Sweden, Brandenburg-Prussia, and Poland-Lithuania.[79] However, France's diplomatic actions were unsuccessful: in Sweden, Charles XII was installed; in Poland-Lithuania, the Saxon King August II was elected King of Poland. Alongside the old and recurring issue of Holstein-Gottorf, August II's election thus added yet another enduring issue to the precarious balance of power in the Baltic: the Livonian Issue, in which internal affairs and foreign policy matters coincided. Since 1629, Livonia had been an autonomous, but military weak province in the Swedish empire, which would be unable to defend itself in case of war. The incorporation of Livonia in the Swedish Empire was contested both by the Livonian (and Estonian) nobility. After 1694, their political autonomy within the Swedish Empire was completely abolished and the nobles were forced to participate in the defence of the Swedish Empire by means of the so-called *Güterreduktion*, an estate tax to serve the growing needs of the Swedish army. These internal issues obtained an international dimension after the election of August II to the Polish throne, since the regulations of the *pacta conventa* obliged the newly elected King to employ his proper (Saxon) forces to reconquer the provinces that had been taken away from Poland.[80] August II was well aware of the economic benefits, which such territorial expansion could bring.[81] He was not alone. Muscovy also had a 'latent tradition of claims on Livonia,' in which economic motives played a significant role.[82]

In the wake of the Treaty of Rijswijk, the Holstein question and the Livonian issue became an integral part of diplomatic negotiations aimed at isolating Sweden. Denmark initiated these negotiations and received the support of Saxony and Muscovy. Denmark used the Holstein question to test the reliability of the guarantors of the Treaty of Altona (1689) – before all Sweden, England and the Dutch Republic – and hoped to discredit Sweden. At that time, however, the Western European guarantors of the Treaty of Altona were preoccupied with the Spanish Succession, wanted to avoid warfare, and therefore stuck to the regulations of Altona.[83] Moreover, the Western European (maritime) powers tried to end the war of the Holy League against the Ottoman Empire, again with the Spanish Succession in mind. On the latter issue, the diplomatic efforts of the maritime powers collided with the interests of Saxony and Muscovy. Saxony hoped to conquer the river Vltava (*Ger.* Moldau) and, like Denmark, felt restricted by the diplomatic requests of the Western European powers. Logically then, Saxony supported Denmark's claims with regard to the Duchy of Holstein-Gottorf and, in the summer of 1698, agreed to form an offensive alliance with Muscovy against Sweden.

Muscovy was not inclined to end the war with the Ottoman Empire. It pursued the conquest of the strategic port of Kerch, located at the narrow strait between the Black Sea and the Sea of Azov.[84] Without Kerch, Muscovy's earlier conquests in the Sea of Azov would hardly be effective.[85] This, in turn, was a development watched anxiously by the British. England was worried about the Russian conquest of Azov in 1696, and feared that Russia's southern expansion would lead to a reorientation of trade routes away from the Baltic towards the Black Sea. This possibility was perceived as a threat to England's trade and shipping: the Baltic ports were significant suppliers of *naval stores*, which were produced largely in the Muscovite hinterland of the then Swedish ports in the eastern Baltic. These naval stores were of crucial importance for England's commercial development.[86] A reorientation towards the Black Sea would make them more accessible to competing powers, such as Spain and – more importantly – France. As a result, England's on-going concerns about its dependence on the Baltic market for naval stores, which had been "a standing aim of England's commercial and colonial policy [during the whole of the 17th century and for some time afterwards] (...)"[87] obtained an additional dimension after the Russian conquest of Azov. Naval stores seem to have dominated the English minds at the turn of the eighteenth century. In the context of Russia's advances on the Black Sea coast and the threat of losing its preferential access to naval stores from North Eurasia, England intensified the exploration of new supply routes from its North American colonies and from Ireland, but it was quickly realized that most of these supplies were of inferior quality.[88]

Besides the Holstein question and the Livonian issue in the Baltic, and the Muscovite conquests in the Black Sea area, there was yet a fourth unsettled issue that caused significant tension during the closing years of the seventeenth century. That issue was the establishment of a *linea communicationis* between Brandenburg and Ducal Prussia, in which the ports of Danzig and Elbing played a pivotal role.[89] Since the acquisition of East Pomerania by the Prince-elector (*Ger.* Kurfürst) of Brandenburg in the wake of the Peace of Westphalia and the sovereignty granted to Ducal (East) Prussia in 1657, the establishment of a territorial link between Brandenburg and Ducal Prussia, which had been united by a personal union since 1618, continuously occupied the minds of its rulers. Until the end of the seventeenth century, however, Brandenburg-Prussia's efforts remained unsuccessful. Even after the struggles of 1698–1699, the port of Elbing, which Prussia had longed for since 1657, remained Polish.[90]

North Eurasia as transit zone for Asian goods

The trans-Caspian route

Among the North Eurasian resources, Asian goods played a peculiar role. They bring the final – and certainly the biggest – actor in the quest for North Eurasian trade into play: Muscovy, the Empire of the Tsars, which inspired Leibniz in developing his worldview. This section reviews Muscovy's role in the transit of Asian goods from Persia (Safavid Iran), India, and China to Western Europe in the seventeenth century, explains how Muscovy's role was contested by the Swedes, and how the transit of Asian goods gained the interest of other political entities as well since the second half of the seventeenth century. Thus, another dimension is added to the quest for North Eurasian trade, which looks well beyond its western border basins, but maintains a most intimate link with them at the same time.

After a very long pre-history of intermittent trade, the commercial relations between Safavid Iran and Muscovy obtained a regular character for the first time after the Muscovite conquest of Astrakhan in 1556. About half a century later, Shah Abbas I (1587–1629) shifted his attention towards the emerging maritime powers of that time, England, the Dutch Republic, and their East India Companies, to establish maritime trade through the Persian Gulf.[91] Weakened by the loss of access to the Baltic Sea after the Livonian Wars (1558–1584), and the internal turmoil during the Time of Troubles (1598–1613),[92] the Muscovite state was of little official interest to Safavid Iran. Nevertheless, Muscovy continued to host one of three transit routes for Iranian commodities to Europe: the 'ancient' Anatolian land route to the Black Sea, the 'novel' Persian Gulf route and the Caspian route to Moscow via Astrakhan and the Volga.[93]

In the broader context of a general rise of European interest in Central Asia in the first half of the seventeenth century, European powers across the North Sea and the Baltic became increasingly aware of the prospects of a profitable transit trade of Persian, Indian, and Chinese commodities via Muscovy and initiated travels, exploratory and diplomatic missions to Muscovy and Siberia.[94] The Polish and Austrian missions were guided at least partly by political concerns and were "(...) intent on shifting the [Ottoman] military pressure from their own borders to those of Iran."[95] The Ottoman Empire continued to be a major factor of influence in the southern borderlands of North Eurasia. Under the reign of Tsar Aleksey Mikhailovich (1629–1676), Muscovy increased its efforts to isolate the Ottoman Empire. In the Truce of Andrusovo, signed 1667, Poland-Lithuania and Muscovy agreed to join forces against the Ottomans.[96] The treaty also included commercial incentives for Polish merchants, who received transit rights through Russia.[97] In the same year, a commercial treaty of the Muscovite state with the Armenian traders of New Julfa (a suburb of Isfahan)[98] marked the beginning of a new era in Muscovite-Iranian trade. Although the transit rights and privileges granted in the 1667 treaties seem to contrast sharply with the protectionist measures issued roughly at the same time in the Muscovite Commercial Treaty of 1667,[99] both express the main goals of Muscovite policy at that time: the protection of its relatively inexperienced merchant community against foreign competition, the search for allies against the Ottoman Empire, and the desire to benefit from the changing patterns of international trade under the impact of Europe's overseas expansion.[100] Trade regulations were issued to increase the active participation of Russian merchants in Muscovy's domestic, foreign, and transit trade,[101] limit the freedom of foreign merchants to trade in the Russian interior, and stimulate foreign trade via a limited number of *gateways*: Arkhangelsk, Vologda, Moscow, Smolensk, and Astrakhan.[102] Numerous exceptions notwithstanding,[103] foreign merchants were not allowed to trade in the Russian interior and were thus bounded to the named gateways for executing their business.[104]

The goal of the 1667 agreement with the Armenian Company in New Julfa was to redirect Persian raw silk exports from Aleppo and Smyrna in the Levant to Astrakhan, Moscow, and Arkhangelsk.[105] Tired of frequent disturbances on the routes through Ottoman territories and the negative impact on the Levant trade of the enduring issues between the Republic of Venice and the Ottoman Empire, the Armenians of New Julfa were themselves inclined to use the transit route through Muscovy.[106] Although their business venture seems to have been rather unsuccessful at first,[107] not at the least because of the disturbances caused by Stepan Razin's uprising (1668–1672), Muscovy persisted in diverting Persian commodity flows towards its territory. Between 1673 and 1676, Muscovy made significant concessions to its own merchants, who complained about the competition from the New Julfan merchants.[108] In 1673, most Armenian transit rights were suspended,[109] to be restored as early as 1676. Afterwards, the transit trade of Iranian commodities through Muscovy intensified rapidly.[110]

Well aware of the potential profits from participation in Muscovy's transit trade of Persian goods, the Swedish government gradually made its commercial policies towards Muscovy less restrictive. As a result, two important changes occurred in the structure of the transit trade with Persian goods through Muscovy in the last quarter of the seventeenth century. By the mid-1680s, Armenian merchants started to prefer the shorter route to the Baltic via Novgorod over the much longer northern route to Arkhangelsk on the White Sea.[111] Naturally, the Swedes, who saw an opportunity to benefit from the Armenian transit trade, welcomed their preference for the Baltic route.[112] In 1686, after protracted Swedish and Dutch negotiations at the Muscovite court, Armenian merchants received the right to transfer their goods from Astrakhan to Arkhangelsk or Novgorod, and Sweden granted them the right to establish a trading house in Narva. Additionally, it provided tax cuts for the export of Persian goods to Amsterdam via Narva. The *Derivation* of the Persian (silk) trade from Arkhangelsk to Swedish ports in the Baltic was a success. Whereas Narva and Nyen, on the one hand, and Arkhangelsk, on the other, had served more or less separate hinterlands before, the competition between them became stronger towards the end of the seventeenth century.[113]

The shift towards the Baltic of the transit of Persian goods, which had been initiated by Sweden, attracted other regional powers as well, and culminated in the establishment of trade relations between Courland and Iran in 1696,[114] and Brandenburg-Prussia and Muscovy in 1697. As early as 1689, the Elector of Brandenburg, Frederick III (1657–1713), had signed three important treaties, which allowed his subjects to conduct trade at Arkhangelsk, Pskov, and Smolensk.[115] These declarations would constitute the basis for all future commercial agreements between Russia and Prussia.[116] In 1697, anticipating the changes at hand in the precarious balance of power in the Baltic Sea area in the closing years of the seventeenth century (see Section "Threats to Dutch primacy in the Baltic" of this chapter), the Elector (and later King) of Brandenburg-Prussia and Tsar Peter negotiated a new treaty of alliance during the latter's (incognito) stay in Königsberg. The Elector's expectations reveal full acknowledgement of Muscovy's strategic role in Asian exchange. The *Traité verbal d'alliance* of 31 May 1697 granted Prussian merchants passage to Arkhangelsk, Novgorod, Pskov, and Moscow as well as to Astrakhan, Persia, and China upon payment of the usual taxes.[117] Similarly, Russian subject were free to trade in Prussian cities.[118]

Land routes to the Khanates, India, and China

After its incorporation into Muscovy around the mid-sixteenth century, Astrakhan emerged as "(…) the principal crossroads where merchants from Russia, Iran, Central Asia and India met and exchanged their wares."[119] Towards the end of the seventeenth century, Astrakhan gained importance as an *entrepôt* not only for Persian trade but also for transit trade with India and the Khanates.[120] Although the first Muscovite initiatives to establish commercial relations with India and the Khanates date back to the mid-seventeenth century, it was Peter the Great, who increased Muscovy's involvement in Central Asian affairs and organized several embassies and expeditions to explore the vast, largely unknown, dangerous and hardly accessible landmasses of Central Asia. The goals of the embassies and expeditions ranged from establishing profitable trade relations to military exploration and outright conquest.[121] The Khanates of Khiva and Bukhara constituted areas of primary interest. Through them, Persia and India would become accessible for Muscovite commerce. The interest was mutual: throughout the seventeenth century, 8 embassies went from Muscovy to Central Asia and 41 in the other direction.[122] Muscovy was guided by the prospect of obtaining access to copper, lead, ores, raw silk, cotton textiles, wool, dyes, fruits, and spices. Most of these commodities had been in the firm hands of competing Western European overseas enterprises, which were active in the area from their settlements along the coast of the Red Sea and the Persian Gulf. Moreover, rumours that plentiful of gold may be found along the rivers Amu Darya and Syr Darya in the Khanates of Khiva and Bukhara drew Muscovy to the area.[123] It was perceived that, upon taking control of the Caspian Sea and the Khanates, Muscovy would be able to obtain a large stake in Asian commerce. In Donnelly's words, Tsar Peter the Great dreamed of nothing less than "(…) shifting the bulk of Asian trade from the sea routes around Africa and via the Levant to a new route through Muscovy."[124] Although for the most part Muscovy's policies towards the Khanates and India were unsuccessful during Peter the Great's reign, they bear witness to a *grand scheme* for (re-)directing trade towards the Baltic ports. A crucial role in this *grand scheme* was attributed to the Volga and the Caspian Sea, which "(…) seemed to be the key to Transcaucasia, Persia, Central Asia and even India."[125] From 1713 onwards, having been informed about the remnants of the river Amu Darya, which used to mouth into the Caspian Sea, Peter the Great sent out several expeditions hoping to find a way to restore the ancient course of this river and establish water connections with the Khanates and perhaps even with India. Neither of these aims was realized – in the former case because the instability of the Khanates obstructed the development of commercial relations; in the latter case simply because no water connection to India was there to be found.[126]

Whereas the search for the land route to India and international interest in the borderlands between North and South Eurasia would revive only in the nineteenth century (see Chapter 6), the development of the fairs of Makaryev and Irbit, which became *de facto* gateways to Siberia and China, was of more immediate significance for North Eurasian trade. Pushed forward by several embassies and exploratory missions, as well as by ongoing border disputes, Muscovy and China institutionalized their commercial and political relations in the groundbreaking Treaty of Nerchinsk in 1689. Among other things, this treaty foresaw the establishment of trading posts on both sides of the Russo-Chinese border, in Kyakhta and May-Ma-Chen.[127] Although Muscovy had to accept the loss of control over the strategic Amur basin in the treaty regulations, the expectations of commercial benefit from the institutionalization of Russo-Chinese commercial relations prevailed.[128] In practice, however, the establishment of a flourishing regular trade with China turned out to be anything but smooth. Despite enduring efforts to remain neutral, Russia became deeply involved in a regional conflict between Manchus and Dzungars in the late seventeenth century, which put severe pressure on Russo-Chinese diplomatic relations.[129] Moreover, the first state caravan (*Ru.* kazennyj karavan) heading for Beijing departed only in 1699,[130] and illicit trade continued to be significant.[131] Although three more state caravans were sent in 1705, 1711 and 1713,[132] these problems would only be overcome – at least partly – after the death of the Kangxi Emperor in 1722,[133] and after several more Russian diplomatic missions had been sent to Beijing in the late 1710s and early 1720s.[134] The famous missions of Lev Vasilyevich Izmailov (1685–1738), Lorenz Lange (c. 1690–1752), and Sava Lukich Vladislavich-Raguzinsky (1669–1738) to the Chinese court in 1719, 1721–1722, and 1723–1724 gradually paved the way for renewed Russo-Chinese commercial relations.[135] But even so, no state caravans were admitted to Chinese territory for several years in a row,[136] and the state of Russo-Chinese trade remained cumbersome.[137] It would take until 1727 for Russo-Chinese commercial relations to consolidate in the famous Treaty of Kyakhta.[138]

Perceived versus real significance

Leibniz' worldview was exemplary for the perception of the changing role of Muscovy in transit trade from Persia, India, and China to Western Europe. During the closing decades of the seventeenth century, all parties involved in commercial exchange with the Baltic engaged in diplomatic efforts to come to terms with Muscovy about the organization of transit trade with Persia, India, and China. Even though Western Europe's share in overland trade with Persia, India, and China through Muscovy may not have been quite large, it was *perceived* as very significant. On the one hand, Muscovy's advances in (Central) Asia were observed closely by the maritime powers (the Dutch Republic and England), since it was *perceived* that Muscovy's control over the Khanates might lead to a reorientation of Persian and Indian trade in favour of Muscovy. On the other hand, towards the end of the seventeenth century, Muscovy's efforts to expand towards the Black Sea coast alarmed

England. The latter feared that the much-needed *naval stores* (hemp, flax, timber, iron), which it acquired via ports in the Baltic and the White Sea, would now be exported from the Black Sea, might potentially come under French and Spanish control, and would thus pose a threat to the European balance of power (see Section "Threats to Dutch primacy in the Baltic" of this chapter).

The transit of commodities from Central Russia, Safavid Iran (Persia), or China to Western Europe was the almost exclusive domain of Sweden and Muscovy in the seventeenth century.[139] Their relation had a long and troublesome history, during which the rationale of each party changed several times. The transit of Asian goods through Muscovy was a matter of ongoing concern and prolonged diplomatic efforts. Due to its crucial geographical position, Muscovy played a primary role in the pursuit of gains expected from the transit trade with Asia. The term *Derivationspolitik* captures the aims of Sweden's transit policy. Their ultimate goal was to divert commodity flows from the Russian hinterland, including flows that originated in Siberia, Persia or China, to Sweden's ports in the Baltic, rather than seeing them transferred to Arkhangelsk on the White Sea coast. Besides Sweden, several other (less powerful) parties tried to secure a position in this transit trade, or tried to attract it to one (or more) of its ports. The Swedes tried to increase their benefits from transit trade with the Russian interior and take over the distribution of goods from foreign carriers. The Russians tried to increase their grasp on foreign and transit trade by means of a contradictory combination of restrictions, prohibitions, and privileges. However, for as long as Sweden controlled the strategically vital ports in the eastern Baltic, such as Riga, Narva, Nyen, and Vyborg, the White Sea port of Arkhangelsk continued to serve as Muscovy's only direct 'Window on Europe.'[140] Ultimately, the contradictions between the mercantilist systems of the Swedes and the Russians boosted the conflict potential of the Baltic as a border basin of North Eurasia, and paved the way for a long period of warfare in the Baltic between 1700 and 1721.

War and national interests

A regional conflict

The Great Northern War started early in 1700, when Saxony attacked Livonia and threatened to occupy Riga, while – almost at the same time – Denmark entered the Holstein territories of the Duke of Gottorf and started an open war with Sweden.[141] Both Saxony and Denmark had proceeded without a declaration of war.[142] Sweden reacted fiercely and, concerned about their commercial interests, England and the Dutch Republic intervened, when the Swedish navy prepared an attack on Copenhagen. On 8 August 1700, Denmark adhered to the Treaty of Travendal, which – among other things – stipulated that Denmark had to acknowledge Holstein's sovereignty.

The treaty was signed by England, the Dutch Republic, France, and – with some delay – Sweden, which obliged itself to leaving Danish territory. On the very same day, Russia signed the Peace of Constantinople, which put an end to the war with the Ottoman Empire and liberated the Russian troops for waging war against Sweden. Less than two weeks later, before Russia could be informed about the Treaty of Travendal, Russia declared war on Sweden, attacked Ingria and swiftly moved on to Narva.[143] Saxony's fears of a resurgence of Russia's 'latent interest' in Livonia now led to a complex international power game. August II used the death of Charles II of Spain on 1 November 1700 as an opportunity to join forces with France against the Habsburg Emperor, with the prospect of occupying Silesia and establishing a 'land bridge' between Saxony and Poland. Alarmed by the possible economic consequences, England, the Dutch Republic, Denmark, Hanover, and the Emperor reconstituted the 'Grand Alliance' (The Hague, 7 September 1701) to prevent France and Saxony from executing these plans.[144] In the meantime, Russia had asked Brandenburg-Prussia to take military action against Sweden in accordance with the 1697 treaty of alliance (see Section "North Eurasia as transit zone for Asian goods" of this chapter),[145] but Frederick William preferred to wait and tried to remain neutral.[146] In fact, in 1701, he formally joined the Grand Alliance.[147] The alliance had a dual effect on the state of war in Europe during the first decade of the eighteenth century. On the one hand, it forced Saxony to keep its bond with Russia, even though it was anxious about Russia's plans with Livonia; on the other, it helped to preserve a clear distinction between issues related to the Spanish Succession and the attack on Sweden's *dominium maris baltici*.

After the brief opening episode during which the maritime powers intervened, the war against Sweden turned into a regional conflict. However, its impact on the trade with Western European nations can hardly be overestimated. The Baltic's most vital commercial areas – Sweden's eastern Baltic provinces and Poland-Lithuania – were severely affected by warfare between Sweden, Saxony and Russia. In reaction to the Saxon and Russian attacks on Sweden's eastern Baltic provinces, and first of all Livonia, Sweden showed its military strength and beat its enemies in Narva in November 1700 and Riga in July 1701. Charles XII (1682–1718), the Swedish King, forced the Saxon army out of Livonia and occupied Courland, leaving his dominions in Ingria without proper defence. Charles XII's decision to move further south into Poland in 1702 not only had a major impact on the volume and structure of Baltic commercial exchange in the years to come, it also shaped the conditions for Russia's consolidation on the northeastern shores of the Baltic Sea and the foundation of St. Petersburg in May 1703.[148] The war against Sweden had become a war of Sweden against the personal union of Saxony and Poland, which unfolded on Polish territory until 1705.

Sweden's presence in Poland-Lithuania had far-reaching consequences. Quickly, the Polish nobility was divided into two camps: the Confederation of Sandomierz, which took the side of August II and was supported by Russia, and the Confederation of Warsaw, which leaned towards Sweden and supported (though not wholeheartedly) the coronation of Stanisław Leszczyński (1677–1766), chosen by Charles XII, as the new King of Poland in September 1705.[149] Saxony was weakened and defeated once more by the Swedish army in February 1706. This was the sign for Charles XII to follow August II into Saxony. On 24 September 1706, August II was forced to sign the Treaty of Altranstädt, in which he resigned from the Polish throne and gave up all anti-Swedish alliances. England, the Dutch Republic, and Brandenburg-Prussia guaranteed the Treaty of Altranstädt and August's resignation from the Polish throne.[150] However, Sweden's residency in Altranstädt would turn out to be just a brief interlude before the war against Sweden would take another dramatic turn.

In the meantime, Brandenburg-Prussia had seen a good opportunity for pursuing its own goal of establishing a *linea communicationis* between Brandenburg and Ducal (eastern) Prussia, but hesitated to use military force and become actively involved in the war in Poland. Initially, in 1701, Frederick I (1657–1713), who had crowned himself King in Prussia that year, confirmed his neutral position by adhering to the Grand Alliance of The Hague. Frederick I hoped to find sufficient support in Poland for his plans to establish an overland connection between the *disjecta membra* of Brandenburg-Prussia, but the diplomatic efforts of the Berlin court were hardly successful: Sweden, Saxony, Russia, and the various Polish parties all had their own objections towards Frederick I's plans. Even alternative solutions, such as a return to the previous 'Equivalence'-plan of his father, which foresaw giving up the stipulations of the *Tractatus Elbingae redditae* in return for a small land corridor between East Pomerania and the Vistula, were explored but never realized. Overall, it became clear to Frederick I that he would not be able to make progress unless he gave up his neutrality as well as his support to Poland-Lithuania.[151]

Russia re-entered the stage in the course of 1707, when the Swedish army left Saxony and started to move towards Moscow. In January 1708, Charles XII reached the Russian-Lithuanian border around Grodno, Vilna, and Minsk, but rather than attacking Russia through the centre, he decided to move south first, hoping to benefit from better supplies for his army as well as from the support of the Ukrainian *hetman* Ivan Mazepa (1639–1709). However, the latter chose the Swedish side only in October 1708 and by that time the Russian army had already hit the Swedish army in the heart with a successful attack on its supply chain near Mohylew (*Ru.* Mogilëv).[152] The uppercut followed on 27 June 1709 in the famous Battle of Poltava, when the Russians defeated the Swedish and Cossack armies, weakened by hunger, sickness, and cold. Mazepa and Charles XII managed to flee to Moldavia; most of the Swedish army was captured.[153] In October 1709, Denmark, Saxony, and Russia revived their original alliance of 1700, but now Peter I had become its driving force.

Remarkably, it was a brief episode of war against the Ottoman Empire, which would exert a major influence on the continuation of the war against

Sweden, and on the actions of the revived alliance. Rather unexpectedly, after the Battle of the Prut (1711), Peter I signed a truce and peace treaty with the Ottomans. Russia's subsequent withdrawal from the shores of the Black Sea gave a decisive impulse to the emergence of the Baltic as an area of vested interest in North Eurasia. Russia consolidated and significantly expanded its earlier gains in the Baltic after the capitulations of Riga, Pernau, and Reval in 1710 and the annexations of parts of the Finnish coast and the islands of Åland between 1710 and 1714.[154] Significantly, Peter I guaranteed existing privileges in the newly conquered territories and thus secured their support.[155] Further west, Great Britain, the Dutch Republic, and Austria enforced the neutrality of Northern Germany in reaction to the resurrection of the alliance of Denmark, Saxony, and Russia.[156] The maritime powers were still concerned about the 'tranquillity of the North' and the Emperor wanted to avoid warfare in his territories.[157] The opposite happened. In 1711, Brandenburg-Prussia joined the triple alliance against Sweden, the next year Russian troops entered the territory of the Holy Roman Empire and besieged Stralsund.[158] In the meantime, Russia's interests extended to Mecklenburg, where Peter I hoped to gain a strong foothold in anticipation of the construction of a canal between the Elbe and Wismar and the latter's development as commercial gateway between the North and Baltic Seas.[159] Charles XII, who had received the right to return to his dominions in the wake of the Russo-Turkish treaty of 1711, reacted with the blockade of the ports in the (former) Swedish Baltic provinces, a privateering ordinance to disturb maritime shipping in the Baltic and his return to the stage in Stralsund in November 1714.[160]

Postponed by the preoccupation of the Western European powers with the Spanish Succession, the conflict between Sweden and Russia flared up in 1715. The former's decline and the latter's rise obliged the Western European powers to reconsider their 'Baltic policies.' The British played a particular role. Their long-standing commercial and naval interests made active involvement in 'Baltic affairs' inevitable. Shortly after the foundation of St. Petersburg, Charles Whitworth (1675–1725) had been sent to Russia to negotiate a "closer union of friendship in view of mutual commercial and industrial advantages, and for the welfare of English subjects."[161] In 1708, three years after his arrival in Russia, it was clear that Whitworth's mission had failed. Despite enduring attempts, no commercial agreement was signed and the English became convinced that "(...) the chief design of the Russians in seeming to further treaty proposals was not to promote commerce, but rather to draw the English into some sort of political alliance, a prospect which England could not tolerate."[162] During the following years, the political relations between Russia and England deteriorated further, not at the least because of conflicting political and commercial interests in the border basins of North Eurasia. Whereas Great Britain tried to secure commercial privileges in Russia, which the tsar was willing to grant such privileges only "(...) upon specific reciprocal concessions from London in the diplomatic sphere."[163] Peter the Great demanded British support for his endeavours against the Swedes in the Baltic and the Ottomans in the Black Sea. Moreover, after the Battle of Poltava (1709), Great Britain's worries about the Russian expansion in the Baltic at the cost of its allied maritime power Sweden aggravated. England had concluded a treaty of mutual assistance with Sweden in 1700; the Treaty of Travendal mentioned earlier, which the Swedes now used to appeal for British aid in the ongoing war with Russia and its allies. Finally, the British and Dutch alike anxiously observed the take-off of Russian commercial shipbuilding in Azov (Black Sea) and Arkhangelsk (White Sea).[164] In this way, "[t]he double-faced English policy of seeking commercial privileges on one hand and opposing Russia politically and diplomatically on the other was not likely to further British hopes of securing a commercial treaty at St. Petersburg."[165]

The combination of the impressive advances of Peter I and the disturbances caused to maritime trade made a reaction from the side of the Western European powers inevitable. Great Britain watched Russian as well as Swedish territorial claims and advances anxiously, and outlined its international diplomacy accordingly. Despite enduring political differences, the British resumed their treaty negotiations with Russia in 1714, when Withworth's successor George Mackenzie arrived in St. Petersburg.[166] British interests in North Eurasian *naval stores* were too high to watch the balance of power in the Baltic change without intervening.[167] Great Britain and the Dutch Republic restricted themselves to providing convoys for their merchant fleets on their way to various destinations in the White Sea and the Baltic.[168] Both refrained from getting involved in naval action, despite recurrent requests from the side of Denmark and Prussia to assist in attacking the Swedish fleet at Karlskrona.[169] The convoys were needed to "force access for [British and Dutch] traders to the Baltic ports under blockade by Charles XII, and to protect them from the Swedish privateers."[170]

In October 1715, Great Britain had joined the anti-Swedish coalition guided by the Russian ambassador in London (1709–1711) and The Hague (1711–1718), Boris Ivanovich Kurakin. The anti-Swedish alliance's accompanying treaty of Greifswald (October 1715) foresaw the guarantee to Hanover of the former Swedish Duchies of Bremen and Verden, on the one hand, and to Muscovy of part of the former Swedish eastern Baltic provinces (Ingria, Karelia, and Estonia), on the other. The former meant that Great Britain, which formed a personal union with the Electorate of Hanover since 1714, would gain control over the main gateways to the German States: the mouths of Weser and Elbe.[171] The latter would establish Russia firmly on the shores of the Baltic Sea, but without the possibility to monopolize Baltic trade. Both George I (1660–1727) and Peter I welcomed the treaty as a great means to further their mutual interests.[172] However, as Chance pointed out, "[n]ot yet was it realized how formidable a bird of prey was hatched from the Muscovite egg."[173] A dramatic shift occurred already in the next year, when Great Britain left the anti-Swedish coalition to pursue a policy of containment with regard to Russia.

Commercial interests at stake

Alarmed by Russia's rapid westward expansion, the occupation of Mecklenburg and the far-reaching plans to establish an *entrepôt* for Russian trade in Wismar in 1716,[174] the British changed their tactics. In the wake of the marriage of Karl Leopold (1678–1747), Duke of Mecklenburg-Schwerin, and Peter the Great's niece Katarina Ivanovna (1691–1733) in 1716, suspicion and fear towards the Russian advances had become widespread.[175] In this context, the German historian Gustav von Droysen (1808–1884) cites a French memoir, which, not without exaggeration, expresses these fears: "(...) Russia already has the trade to China, the Black Sea and the Caspian Sea; soon, it will also gain total control over Baltic trade."[176]

Great Britain became involved in concerted military action with the Danes in the summer of 1716. A coalition of Great Britain, Austria, and France emerged in late 1716. The Dutch Republic joined the coalition in January 1717. In the meantime, British and Dutch commercial treaty negotiations with Russia continued.[177] Though neither Mackenzie, nor his successor Admiral Norris,[178] who was sent to St. Petersburg in 1718, could conclude the negotiations with the Russians successfully, the British rationale for pursuing a commercial treaty is noteworthy. In an amendment to the proposed treaty, the British requested permission for their subjects to trade in Kazan and Astrakhan on the Volga.[179] An internal British instruction specified that "the trade to Casan and Astracan (...) [was] very essential and must be insisted on."[180] British commercial interests were not limited to the Baltic; they had a much broader scope, comprising both the North Eurasian hinterland of the Baltic ports and North Eurasia itself as a transit route for Central Asian goods.

Russia's relations with its allies of the first hour, Denmark and Saxony, worsened rapidly in the autumn of 1716. Saxony's support for Russia was lost, when it became clear to August II that Russia used its military presence in Poland-Lithuania to enforce political decisions and 'reforms' in the Commonwealth.[181] Although August II (again) officially ruled over Poland, Russia's military presence profoundly limited his actual influence. Russo-Danish relations were troubled by the failed landing on Scania, which Russia, Denmark, and Prussia had planned in 1715, but which Peter I had abandoned at the last minute.[182] Only France and Prussia now (officially) maintained good relations with Russia. Prussia's relations with Russia had improved after the coronation of Frederick William I (1688–1740) in 1713 and resulted in the treaty of Schwedt, signed on the 6 October 1713, the Russo-Prussian treaty of alliance of St. Petersburg in June 1714, and a treaty of mutual military support in the fall of 1715.[183] In the same year, Prussia had occupied part of Swedish Pomerania including the port of Stettin;[184] Denmark occupied the rest of Swedish Pomerania, causing significant friction between Denmark and Prussia.[185] After long negotiations between the three parties,[186] Russia, France, and Prussia signed a rather weak treaty of friendship and trade in Amsterdam in August 1717.[187]

Although the treaty of Amsterdam was unsuccessful from a political point of view, it symbolized a cautious departure from the previous *barrière de l'est* in the wake of the new international political constellation that had emerged after the Battle of Poltava and the end of the War of Spanish Succession.[188] Neither party, however, was satisfied with the treaty. Russia wanted France to abandon Sweden and take its side instead, but France refused to commit to an alliance with Russia and forced the latter to accept a harmless (not to say meaningless) treaty of friendship. Moreover, Russia did not receive any French guarantees for its territorial gains in the Baltic.[189] France made clear that it wanted to stay out of the conflict in the Baltic as much as possible, but it was cautious not to destroy its relations with Russia and Prussia. Great Britain, however, was now urged to play a more active role in the conflict. Bearing in mind its enduring concerns with Baltic commercial exchange and well aware of its precarious dependency of raw materials from the Russian interior, George I now sought to contain Russia's expansion in the Baltic, without giving up on his ambition to sign a commercial treaty with the Tsar.[190] The goal of the Treaty of Vienna (January 1719) was to put an end to Russia's occupation of Polish territory and defend Danzig and Elbing against Russia and Prussia.[191] Whereas George I achieved these goals and managed to force Russia and Sweden into signing a bilateral peace treaty in Nystadt (30 August 1721), he could not prevent Poland-Lithuania from becoming fully dependent on Russia.[192]

This chapter has shown that, insofar as trade through the Danish Sound is concerned, 1697 – and perhaps even the start of the Nine Years' War in 1688 – marked the beginning of a long phase of stagnation and decline. In this sense, the year 1697 turned out to be a milestone in the political economy of trade through the Danish Sound. By that time, Sweden's expansionist attitude and policies towards its Baltic provinces, fed by domestic concerns as well as by commercial interests in transit trade with Muscovy, had already led to the sustained interest in the easternmost part of the Baltic Sea of merchants from the Dutch Republic and England. The introduction of mercantilist economic policies in France, Brandenburg-Prussia, the Holy Roman Empire, and Sweden; the increasingly self-conscious Muscovite policies; the establishment of a personal union between England and the Dutch Republic; and the growing antagonisms between England and France turned the Baltic into an area of political and economic significance at the European level.

Around 1700, the Baltic no longer served as the 'backwaters' of the Dutch and their commercial system, but had become the arena of processes of state-building and power politics, which were firmly embedded in the emerging economic and state sciences. The emergence of the Baltic as an area of vested interest in European commerce was determined by the eagerness to break Dutch 'maritime' dominance as well as by increasing British interests in North Eurasian trade. Moreover, the roles of Sweden and Muscovy as adversaries in a long-standing struggle for North Eurasian markets exerted a decisive influence on the political economy of Baltic trade at the turn of the century. The underlying mercantilist concerns coincided with an upsurge of commercial interest in Central Asia by Europe's leading economic powers, the search for relevant alliances, and the acknowledgement of Muscovy's strategic role in Western Europe's trade with Central Russia, Persia, and China.

Remarkably, the significance attached to a number of issues in international commerce in the late seventeenth and early eighteenth centuries greatly exceeded their (potential) monetary value. However, precisely these issues and the different ways in which their protagonists dealt with them provide valuable insights about the larger context of novel commercial opportunities. The initial perception of 'new' commercial opportunities, 'new' trade routes, and 'new' areas of trade in the increasingly competitive and information-driven international environment of the late seventeenth century marked the start of a radically new phase in the political economy of Baltic trade. The Baltic no longer was a 'lake' of regional importance; it had become a border basin of North Eurasia and the scene of conflicting national interests at a European scale.

Notes

1 Häpke, "Der Untergang der hansischen Vormachtstellung"; Spading, "Zu den Ursachen"; Schildhauer, "Reformation im Ostseeraum"; Lloyd, *England and the German Hanse*; Jenks, *England, die Hanse und Preußen*; Van Tielhof, "Der Getreidehandel der Danziger Kaufleute"; Jenks, "Die Distributionsrevolution." Several authors have placed the discussion about the decline of the Hanse and the rise of the Dutch and English in the context of lack of innovation (Ger. *innovatorischer Rückstand*) in the Hanseatic economy. See, e.g.: Jenks, "War die Hanse kreditfeindlich?"; Pitz, "Steigende und fallende Tendenzen," 60–77; Denzel, "Kommerzielle Innovationen," 67–99 there 72.

2 The perception of the decline and abolition of the traditional Hanse has been discussed recently in: Ressel, "Die zeitgenössische Perzeption."

3 Israel, *Dutch primacy in world trade*.

4 Of course, English and Scottish trade with the Baltic was of some significance as well, but compared to the near-monopoly of the Dutch commercial system, it was of secondary importance. For a general survey, see North, *Geschichte der Ostsee*, 149–153.

5 Tjaden, "The Dutch," 61.

6 Ballhausen, *Der erste Englisch-Holländische Seekrieg*, 3–699.

7 Anderson, *Naval wars*, 71–103; Frost, *The Northern wars*, Chapter 7; Oakley, *War and peace in the Baltic*, Chapter 6.

8 Anderson, *Naval wars*, 87.

9 Tjaden, "The Dutch," 89.

10 Frost, *After the Deluge*.

11 Tjaden, "The Dutch," 91.

12 Ballhausen, *Seekrieg*, 709–750; Tjaden, "The Dutch," 92.

13 Åström, "The English navigation laws," 12.

14 For details, see Harper, *Navigation laws*, 387–414.

15 Åström, "The English navigation laws," 3.

16 Harper, *Navigation laws*, 53 and 404.

17 Harper, *Navigation laws*, 54. Interestingly, in the Navigation Law of 1660, specific requirements were issued for the British timber trade with Muscovy, which was carried out via Arkhangelsk for the most part:

> Be it enacted by the aforesaid that no goods or commodities of the growth, production, or manufacture of Muscovy, or of the countries, dominions, territories to the Great Duke or Emperor of Muscovy or Russia belonging, as also that no sort of masts, timber or boards etc be imported into England Ireland or Wales or Berwick upon Tweed in any ship or ships, vessel or vessels whatsoever, but in such as do really and without fraud belong to the people thereof or to some of them, as the true owners or proprietors thereof, and whereof the masters and threefourths of the mariners at least are English; except only in such foreign ships as are of the build of that country or place of which the said goods are the growth, production or manufacture respectively etc.
> (see Pearson, *England's timber trade*, 18–19)

18 Harper, *Navigation laws*, 405–406; Åström, "The English navigation laws," 3–8.
19 Clément (ed.), *Lettres, instructions et mémoires*, Vol. II.1, CXXVII:

> La déclaration de 1667 inaugura un régime tout différent. Le tarif de 1664 était précédé d'un long exposé des motifs de la réforme intérieure; en 1667, Colbert, en le bouleversant complétement, se borne à dire que „l'établissement de diverses manufactures dans le royaume en ayant notablement changé le prix, il avoit fait procéder à une nouvelle taxe sur l'entrée et la sortie d'aucunes marchandises.

20 Clément (ed.), *Lettres, instructions et mémoires, II.1*, CXXVIII–CXXIX.
21 The idea for establishing a 'Compagnie de Commerce du Nord' was formulated for the first time in 1663, but only after Potemkin's mission to France in 1667–1668, the plans were executed. The company was founded in July 1669. See Grönebaum, *Frankreich in Ost- und Nordeuropa*, 46–52; 54–56. Among other things, the French requested free passage through Muscovy to Persia and other Asian countries, but Muscovy denied.
22 Clément (ed.), *Lettres, instructions et mémoires, II.1*, CLX–CLXXXVIII.
23 Boissonade and Charliat, "Colbert et la Compagnie"; Clément (ed.), *Lettres, instructions et mémoires, II.1*, CLX–CLXXXVIII; Clément (ed.), *Lettres, instructions et mémoires, II.2*, 800–802: Édit portant establissement d'une compagnie de commerce pour le Nord.
24 Steinberg, *The social construction of the ocean*, 89–98.
25 Savary, *Le parfait negociant*, II: 108; also mentioned in Grönebaum, *Frankreich in Ost- und Nordeuropa*, 61.
26 Roorda, *Het rampjaar 1672*.
27 *Tetradas* [VSWG-JDA], 1_Turnover: *Estimated total turnover.* The figures given here include an estimate of Swedish tax-free shipping. For details, see Scheltjens, "Tetradas."
28 *Tetradas* [VSWG-JDA], 1_Turnover: *Estimated total turnover.*
29 Harding, *Seapower and naval warfare*, 96.
30 Zernack, *Schwedisch-russische Beziehungen*, 57–99; Frost, *The Northern wars*, Chapter 8.
31 *Tetradas* [VSWG-JDA], 4_T: *Transport services by countries (areas).*
32 *Tetradas* [VSWG-JDA], 5_BIE: *United Kingdom.*
33 Harper, *Navigation laws*, 315–317.
34 *Tetradas* [VSWG-JDA], 4_T: *Transport services by countries (areas).*
35 Kampmann, "Ein großes Bündnis," 31; Onnekink, *The last war of religion*, 69–88; Pincus, *1688*.
36 Harding, *Seapower and naval warfare*, 115–120.
37 *Tetradas* [VSWG-JDA], 1_Turnover: *Estimated total turnover.*
38 Berger, "Pontchartrain," 38.
39 Soom, *Der baltische Getreidehandel.*

40 In particular, see *Tetradas* [VSWG-JDA], 6_BTR: *Exports from Poland-Lithuania to France.*
41 Berger, "Pontchartrain," 51–53.
42 Early in 1691, Denmark and Sweden had been driven into each other's arms after unsuccessful offensive treaty negotiations with England and the Dutch Republic. On May 9, 1691, Denmark and Sweden signed a "treaty for the protection of their commerce according to the laws of nations, neutrality and treaties," which has been pinpointed as the first 'Armed Neutrality.' As soon as the treaty was signed, the Dutch "hastened to ease matters by patching up a convention with Denmark, since Sweden would not come to terms," but disagreements over Danish passports and annoyance with the conduct of Danish shipmasters and privateers from Zeeland continued to trouble Dutch-Danish relations. English negotiations with Denmark were equally unsuccessful and in March 1693, Denmark and Sweden signed an "extended treaty." This treaty as well was signed despite the obvious enmity between both northern powers: "it was due merely to a coincidence of commercial interests." See Lane, "The relations," 168–172.
43 See Ufkes, "Nederlandse schippers"; Bromley, "The North Sea in wartime." For the merchant fleet of Danzig and its composition in the latter part of the seventeenth century, see also: Groth, "Wykazy gdańskich statków"; Groth, "Hauptprobleme der danziger Schiffahrt." On 'virtual' migration, see Scheltjens, *Dutch deltas*, Chapter 4.
44 Liiv, *Die wirtschaftliche Lage*, 173–174; Neumann and Lindgrén, "The great famines."
45 *Tetradas* [VSWG-JDA], 4_T: *Transport services by countries (areas)*; 5_BIE: *United Kingdom.*
46 Lane, "The relations," 177.
47 *Tetradas* [VSWG-JDA], 1_Turnover: *Estimated total turnover*; 5_BIE: *Sweden.*
48 Besides the obvious inaccuracies of estimating tax-free shipping, part of Sweden's export trade did not leave the Baltic. Variable quantities of grain produced in these provinces were exported to the Swedish mainland (mostly Stockholm), especially in times of crop failure, or when the needs of the Swedish army had to be met urgently. Likewise, about one quarter of all registered Swedish iron bar production went from Stockholm to various destinations in the Baltic. See Boëthius and Heckscher, *Svensk Handelsstatistik*, 746.
49 Attman, *Swedish aspirations*, 12.
50 The history of the port of Riga in the seventeenth century has received significant scholarly attention, but for the most part the port's development remains isolated from the broader context of Swedish trade through the Danish Sound. For introductory surveys, see Harder-Gersdorff, "Riga als handelsmetropole"; Kotilaine, "Riga's trade"; Kotilaine, "The significance"; Kotljarchuk, "Riga and commercial aspects."
51 *Tetradas* [VSWG-JDA], 8_CIES_Bex_FS: *Rye.*
52 *Tetradas* [VSWG-JDA], 8_CIES_Bex_RM: *Hemp, Flax, Hempseed, Flaxseed.*
53 *Tetradas* [VSWG-JDA], 8_CIES_Bex_RM: *Iron.*
54 *Tetradas* [VSWG-JDA], 8_CIES_Bex_RM: *Iron.*
55 *Tetradas* [VSWG-JDA], 8_CIES_Bex_RM: *Pitch, Tar, "Tar and Pitch."*
56 *Tetradas* [VSWG-JDA], 6_BTR: *Poland-Lithuania to the Netherlands, Poland-Lithuania to the United Kingdom, Sweden to the Netherlands, Sweden to the United Kingdom.*
57 This is also visible in the data on Muscovite imports and exports via Swedish ports in the Baltic, compiled in: Pijrimjaė, "Sostav, ob"em i raspredelenie." For a descriptive analysis of imports to Narva from 1661 to 1700, see Pijrimjae, "Torgovye otnošenija."

58 Sweden's history in the seventeenth century is commonly described as the era of Sweden as a 'great power' (*Sw.* Stormaktstiden). For introductory surveys on the character of this era, see Zernack, "Schweden als europäische Großmacht"; Roberts, *The Swedish imperial experience*; Attman, *Swedish aspirations*; and Troebst, "Debating the mercantile background."

59 The role of mercantilist policies in the Polish-Lithuanian Commonwealth remains less clear, because the different and far-reaching interests and privileges of magnate families and towns (such as Danzig) prevented state-level policies from being effective, if at all they could be implemented.

60 Zernack, *Schwedisch-russische Beziehungen*, 41; Szultka, "Handel morski i porty Brandenburgii-Prus," 186–195, and the literature cited there.

61 Bog, *Der Reichsmerkantilismus*, 14.

62 Dietrich, 'Der preußische Staat,' 4.

63 Bog, *Der Reichsmerkantilismus*, 30.

64 Bog, *Der Reichsmerkantilismus*, 32.

65 North, *Deutsche Wirtschaftsgeschichte*, 183.

66 Dietrich, 'Der preußische Staat,' 3–4; North, *Deutsche Wirtschaftsgeschichte*, 183.

67 North, *Deutsche Wirtschaftsgeschichte*, 183–184.

68 Bog, *Der Reichsmerkantilismus*, 1.

69 Bog, *Der Reichsmerkantilismus*, 15–18.

70 Bog, *Der Reichsmerkantilismus*, 8–9.

71 Bog, *Der Reichsmerkantilismus*, 13–14.

72 Böhret, *Virtuelle Tagzettel*, 19–20: "Ich bin überzeugt, dass wir durch eine überseeische Kolonie große Vorteile bekommen werden: Rohstoffe, Kolonialwaren, Gold und wir können mit Kapitalanlagen gute Zinserträge erwarten. Das alles bei überschaubaren Investitionen, zumal die Seetransporte von der Westindischen Kompagnie übernommen warden."

73 Bog, *Der Reichsmerkantilismus*, 14.

74 *Tetradas* [VSWG-JDA], 7_PIES_Königsberg: *Exports of foodstuffs, Exports of raw materials*; 3_EI_Bex: *Countries (areas) of departure of exports.*

75 Lane, "The relations," 177.

76 Lane, "The relations," 181–184.

77 Oakley, *War and peace in the Baltic*, 107; Kellenbenz, "Die Herzogtümer," 201–416.

78 Zernack, "Der große nordische Krieg," 160–161.

79 Grönebaum, *Frankreich in Ost- und Nordeuropa*, 67–114; Zernack, "Der große nordische Krieg," 159. In line with this strategy of containment, France established 'friendly,' though not formalized relations with the Ottoman Empire, not only to the annoyance of Muscovy, but of most European powers as well (in particular, the Habsburg Empire and England). Alarmed by France's course of action as well as by its increasing influence on Baltic affairs, Muscovy was encouraged to establish a front against the Ottoman Empire by joining the Holy League and by signing a perpetual peace with Poland-Lithuania in 1686.

80 Zernack, "Der große nordische Krieg," 162–163. Zernack remains cautious to see a direct causal relationship between internal Livonian affairs and the outbreak of the Great Northern War:

> Gewiß dürfen die deutlichen Anzeichen des Loyalitätskonflikts der baltischen Ritterschaften gegenüber der schwedischen Krone nicht überschätzt werden, was ihre kausale Verknüpfung mit der Entfesselung des Nordischen Krieges angeht. In seinem außenpolitischen Vorgehen blieb der ständepolitische Sprecher der [livonischen] Ritterschaften, Johann Reinhold von Patkul, ein Einzelgänger, wenn auch ein diplomatisch sehr erfolgreicher. Denn immerhin

> hat er mit seiner persönlichen Diplomatie die Brücke von dem livländischen Verfassungskonflikt – und damit der Strukturkrise des schwedischen Ostseereiches – zur Politik der anti-schwedischen Koalitionsbildung unter denjenigen Mächten geschlagen, die an der Revision der Machtverhältnisse in Nordosteuropa das lebhafteste Interesse zu zeigen begannen.
>
> (Zernack, "Der große nordische Krieg," 162)

81 Zernack, "Der große nordische Krieg," 167–168; Forberger, "Zur wirtschaftsgeschichtlichen Neueinschätzung," 208–253.
82 Zernack, "Der große nordische Krieg," 163.
83 Zernack, "Der große nordische Krieg," 163–166; Hassinger, *Brandenburg-Preußen*, 40.
84 Zernack, "Der große nordische Krieg," 164–165.
85 Oreškova, *Russko-tureckie otnošenija*, 29.
86 Pearson, *England's timber trade*, Chapter 2.
87 Åström, *From Stockholm to St. Petersburg*, 15.
88 Reading, *The Anglo-Russian commercial treaty*, 1938: 18–32; Åström, *From Stockholm to St. Petersburg*, 16–19. See also: Albion, *Forests and sea power*; Adler, *England's Versorgung mit Schiffsbaumaterialien*; Knight, "New England forests"; Malone, "England and the Baltic naval stores trade."
89 Hassinger, *Brandenburg-Preußen*, 11–30 and 33–34.
90 Oakley, *War and peace in the Baltic*, 110.
91 Matthee, "Anti-Ottoman politics," 742; 747.
92 Oakley, *War and peace in the Baltic*, 27–53.
93 Matthee, "Anti-Ottoman politics," 747. The Anatolian and Caspian routes had been in use for centuries.
94 See, e.g.: Schade, *Die Niederlande und Russland*; Van Amelsfoort, "De diplomatieke betrekkingen"; Matthee, "Anti-Ottoman politics," 750; Kellenbenz, "Der russische Transithandel," 481–498; Sohrabi, "Early Swedish travelers to Persia," 631–637; Troebst, "Rußland als 'Magazin der Handlung zwischen Asien und Europa'?"; Troebst, "Die Kaspi-Volga-Ostseeroute"; Troebst, "Narva, Libau oder Danzig?"; Troebst, "Narva und der Außenhandel Persiens"; Troebst, "Russia and the Safavid Empire"; Troebst, "Armenian Merchants in seventeenth-century North-Eastern Europe"; Mattiesen, "Die Versuche zur Erschließung"; Hoffmann, *Ostsibirien*, 55–59.
95 Matthee, "Anti-Ottoman politics," 750.
96 Lewitter, "The Russo-Polish treaty of 1686," 5–9; Matthee, "Anti-Ottoman politics," 751.
97 Matthee, "Anti-Ottoman politics," 751.
98 McCabe, *The Shah's silk for Europe's silver*; Aslanian, *From the Indian Ocean to the Mediterranean*.
99 PSZ, I, 408.
100 Donnelly, "Peter the Great and Central Asia," 206; Matthee, "Anti-Ottoman politics," 750.
101 Kotilaine, "Competing claims," 280–281.
102 PSZ, I, 408.
103 Amburger, "Zur Geschichte des Großhandels"; Baron, "Who were the gosti?"; Baron, "The fate of the gosti."
104 PSZ, I, 408.
105 Troebst, "Isfahan – Moskau – Amsterdam." See also: *Armjano-russkie otnošenija v XVII veke*, 31–41; 45–64; PSZ, I, 409 and 410.
106 Matthee, "Anti-Ottoman politics," 751–752.
107 *Armjano-Russkie otnošenija*, 90–91.
108 *Armjano-Russkie otnošenija*, 129–142.

109 PSZ, I, 539.
110 Carswell, "The Armenians in the East-West trade"; Curtin, *Cross-cultural trade in world history*, 191–196. The routes and business practices of Armenian merchants in the late seventeenth century are documented in: Kévonian, "Marchands arméniens au XVIIe siècle," 199–244.
111 Matthee, "Anti-Ottoman politics," 754.
112 Documentary evidence for the first decades of the eighteenth century indicates that Arkhangelsk continued to have some relevance during the first decades of the eighteenth century, when the Baltic route was interrupted because of the war against Sweden. See *Armjano-russkie otnošenija v pervoj treti XVIII veka, II.1*, 7–8, 15–16, 18–19, 21–22, 28–30, 42–53; PSZ, IV, 2192; PSZ, VII, 5086.
113 Zevakin, "Persidskij vopros"; Kellenbenz, "Der russische Transithandel," 492–493; Kotilaine, "Competing claims," 281–283; 299–302; Troebst, "Narva, Libau oder Danzig?"; Troebst, "Narva und der Außenhandel Persiens."
114 Gulbenkian, "Philippe de Zagly." The treaty of Courland with Persia was shortlived. After Herzog Casimir's death in 1698, it was not renewed. See Kellenbenz, "Der russische Transithandel," 494.
115 Martens, *Receuil des traités et conventions V*, 28–38.
116 Martens, *Receuil des traités et conventions V*, 31.
117 Martens, *Receuil des traités et conventions V*, 43:

> (...) considérant qu'il a plu à Dieu et à la nature de faire en sorte que les terres de Sa Majesté le Tzar, plus que toute autre, produisent les précieuses peaux d'animaux qu'on emploie comme fourrures, et comme par contre on ne trouve que dans la principauté électorale de Prusse la pierre d'ambre fort estimée en Perse, en Chine et autres contrées orientales, qu'un traité de commerce sur l'échange des objets de commerce ci-dessus mentionnés soit conclu entre les deux souverains.

118 Martens, *Receuil des traités et conventions V*, 45–50.
119 Matthee, "Anti-Ottoman politics," 742.
120 Matthee, "Anti-Ottoman politics," 753.
121 Donnelly, "Peter the Great and Central Asia," 203–204; 210.
122 Donnelly, "Peter the Great and Central Asia," 205; *Materialy po istorii Turkmen i Turkmenii, II*, 329–330.
123 Donnelly, "Peter the Great and Central Asia," 207; Lystsov, *Persidskij pochod Petra I*, 16.
124 Donnelly, "Peter the Great and Central Asia," 208. See also: PSZ, V, 2994.
125 Donnelly, "Peter the Great and Central Asia," 207.
126 Donnelly, "Peter the Great and Central Asia," 209–214.
127 Korsak, *Istoriko-statističeskoe obozrenie*, 12–14; 17. About the establishment and early development of Russo-Chinese trade relations, see O'Brien, *Russia under two tsars*, 105–124; Foust, *Muscovite and Mandarin*; Hill-Paulus, *Nikolaj Gavrilovič Spatharij*; Wanner, "First Russian-Chinese diplomatic relations"; Wanner, "The Russian-Chinese trade in Kyakhta."
128 Korsak, *Istoriko-statističeskoe obozrenie*, 19.
129 Foust, *Muscovite and Mandarin*, 15–17.
130 Korsak, *Istoriko-statističeskoe obozrenie*, 20.
131 Foust, *Muscovite and Mandarin*, 14.
132 Korsak, *Istoriko-statističeskoe obozrenie*, 21–23.
133 Foust, *Muscovite and Mandarin*, 17.
134 Korsak, *Istoriko-statističeskoe obozrenie*, 24–27; Foust, *Muscovite and Mandarin*, 18–23.
135 Reports and journals documenting these diplomatic missions have rapidly found their way in historiography: *Journal de la Résidence du sieur Lange*; Pallas, *Tagebuch*

zwoer Reysen; Korsak, *Istoriko-statističeskoe obozrenie*, 24–25; Foust, *Muscovite and Mandarin*, 18–20, 26–30.

136 Foust, *Muscovite and Mandarin*, 20.
137 Foust, *Muscovite and Mandarin*, 15–23.
138 Foust, *Muscovite and Mandarin*, 44–52.
139 Kotilaine, "Competing claims"; Kotilaine, *Russia's foreign trade and economic expansion*; Soom, *Die Politik Schwedens*, 72–73, 191, 233–236; Troebst, *Handelskontrolle – "Derivation" – Eindammung*; Troebst, 'Stockholm und Riga.'
140 Cf. Kotilaine, *Russia's foreign trade and economic expansion*.
141 Zernack, "Der große nordische Krieg," 168.
142 Lewitter, "Russia, Poland and the Baltic," 3; Zernack, "Der große nordische Krieg," 168–169.
143 Zernack, "Der große nordische Krieg," 169–171.
144 Zernack, "Der große nordische Krieg," 170.
145 Martens, *Receuil des traités et conventions V*, 51–52.
146 Hassinger, *Brandenburg-Preußen*, 42; Martens, *Receuil des traités et conventions V*, 54–56.
147 Hassinger, *Brandenburg-Preußen*, 59.
148 See Zernack, "Der große nordische Krieg," 172–173:

> Zum einen ermöglichte die militärische Verteidigungsschwäche der Baltischen Provinzen dem Zaren ziemlich unbehindert ein territoriales Glacis für seine Kriegsziele an der Ostsee aufzubauen. Für Karl [Charles XII – W.S.] hatte die strategische Südwendung hingegen eine jahrelange Bindung an den polnischen Kriegsschauplatz zur Folge.

149 Zernack, "Der große nordische Krieg," 177.
150 Zernack, "Der große nordische Krieg," 178; Kretzschmar, "Der Friedensschluß von Altranstädt 1706/07."
151 Hassinger, *Brandenburg-Preußen*, 59–86.
152 Zernack, "Der große nordische Krieg," 180.
153 Zernack, "Der große nordische Krieg," 180–181.
154 Zernack, "Der große nordische Krieg," 181–187.
155 Zernack, "Der große nordische Krieg," 183:

> An diesem Ausgreifen über die russischen Voraussetzungen und Grundlagen und der bewußten Aufnahme intakter ostmitteleuropäischer Strukturen in den Reichsverband sollte die 'überrussische Absicht' in Peters Imperiumskonzept aller Welt vor Augen geführt warden. Die deutsch-baltischen Stände der Ostseeprovinzen konnten auf diese Weise sehr rasch für eine russische Reichsloyalität gewonnen werden, (…).

156 Zernack, 'Der große nordische Krieg,' 186; The so-called Neutrality Convention of 1710 provided that "the German Provinces of Sweden would neither be invaded nor used by the Swedes as bases for attack" (See Chance, "The Northern policy," 81).
157 Chance, "The Northern policy," 82.
158 Zernack, "Der große nordische Krieg," 186.
159 See extensively in: Mediger, *Mecklenburg, Rußland und England-Hanover.* A competing plan (the 'Bassewitscher Projekt') was proposed by Karl Friedrich, the Duke of Holstein, in 1714, but the Tsar stuck to Mecklenburg. See Zernack, "Der große nordische Krieg," 186–187.
160 Zernack, "Der große nordische Krieg," 184–185 and 188.
161 Reading, *The Anglo-Russian commercial treaty*, 63.
162 Reading, *The Anglo-Russian commercial treaty*, 65.
163 Reading, *The Anglo-Russian commercial treaty*, 68.

164 Reading, *The Anglo-Russian commercial treaty*, 65–68 and 75.
165 Reading, *The Anglo-Russian commercial treaty*, 68.
166 Reading, *The Anglo-Russian commercial treaty*, 74.
167 Indeed, as Reading has pointed out,

> English policy was intimately associated with this idea of the northern balance of power. Ever prepared to view with alarm any too-absolute domination of the Baltic by any one power, English policy hinged upon keeping that sea open so that the trade in the essential naval stores might continue unimpaired.
> (see Reading, *The Anglo-Russian commercial treaty*, 75)

168 Chance, "The Baltic expedition," 447–450; Chance, "The Northern question in 1716," 693–700.
169 Chance, "The Baltic expedition," 450–454.
170 Chance, "The Baltic expedition," 443.
171 Chance, "The Baltic expedition," 459–461.
172 Chance, "The Northern policy," 90, 93.
173 Chance, "The Northern policy," 90.
174 Hassinger, *Brandenburg-Preußen*, Chapters 3–5; Reading, *The Anglo-Russian commercial treaty*, 85–86.
175 McKay, "The struggle for control," 367–368; Chance, "The Northern policy," 93; Chance, "The Northern question in 1717," 33–34.
176 Droysen, *Geschichte der preussischen Politik*, IV, ii, 193 and "Le commerce de la mer baltique, autrefois libre à toutes les nations, crie de nos jours vengeance de se voir réduite à la seule discrétion du Zaar." (see Droysen, *Geschichte der preussischen Politik*, IV, ii, 193, footnote 1).
177 McKay, "The struggle for control," 368–369.
178 Reading, *The Anglo-Russian commercial treaty*, 87.
179 Chance, "The Northern question in 1716," 701.
180 Chance, "The Northern question in 1716," 701 note 74.
181 Zernack, "Der große nordische Krieg," 189.
182 Zernack, "Der große nordische Krieg," 189.
183 PSZ, V, 2816.
184 Rachel, *Die Handels-, Zoll- und Akzisepolitik*, 549.
185 Rachel, *Die Handels-, Zoll- und Akzisepolitik*, 553–554.
186 Vasil'ev, *Rußland und Frankreich*, 69–75.
187 Martens, *Receuil des traités et conventions V*, 157–167.
188 Massie, *Peter der Große*, 541; Vasil'ev, *Rußland und Frankreich*, 14–23.
189 Vasil'ev, *Rußland und Frankreich*, 91–107.
190 Chance, "The Northern question in 1718."
191 Lewitter, "Poland, Russia and the treaty of Vienna."
192 Zernack, "Der große nordische Krieg," 198–201.

References

Adler, G. *England's Versorgung mit Schiffsbaumaterialien aus Englischen und Amerikanischen Quellen vornehmlich im 17. Jahrhundert*. Stuttgart 1929.

Albion, Robert Greenhalgh. *Forests and sea power. The timber problem of the Royal Navy 1652–1862*. Cambridge 1926.

Amburger, Erik. "Zur Geschichte des Großhandels in Rußland. Die gosti." *Vierteljahrschrift für Sozial- und Wirtschaftsgeschichte* 46, 2 (1959): 248–261.

Anderson, R.C. *Naval wars in the Baltic during the sailing-ship epoch, 1522–1850*. London 1910.

Aslanian, Sebouh David. *From the Indian Ocean to the Mediterranean. The global trade networks of Armenian merchants from New Julfa.* Berkeley 2011.
Åström, Sven-Erik. *From Stockholm to St. Petersburg. Commercial factors in the political relations between England and Sweden, 1675–1700.* Helsinki 1962.
Åström, Sven-Erik. "The English navigation laws and the Baltic trade." *Scandinavian Economic History Review* 8, 1 (1960): 3–18.
Attman, Artur. *Swedish aspirations and the Russian market during the seventeenth century.* Göteborg 1985.
Ballhausen, Carl. *Der erste Englisch-Holländische Seekrieg 1652–1654 sowie der Schwedisch-Holländische Seekrieg 1658–1659.* Den Haag 1923.
Baron, Samuel H. "The fate of the *gosti* in the reign of Peter the Great." *Cahiers du monde russe et soviétique* 14, 4 (1973): 488–512.
Baron, Samuel H. "Who were the gosti?" *California Slavic Studies* 7 (1973): 1–40.
Berger, Patrice. "Pontchartrain and the grain trade during the famine of 1693." *The Journal of Modern History* 48, 4 (1976): 37–86.
Boëthius, Bertil; Heckscher, Eli F. *Svensk Handelsstatistik 1637–1737 / Swedish statistics of foreign trade 1637–1737.* Stockholm 1938.
Bog, Ingomar. *Der Reichsmerkantilismus. Studien zur Wirtschaftspolitik des Heiligen Römischen Reiches im 17. und 18. Jahrhundert.* Stuttgart 1959.
Böhret, Carl. *Virtuelle Tagzettel des Universalgelehrten und Politikberaters Johann Joachim Becher (1635–1682).* Speyer 2011.
Boissonade, P.; Charliat, P. "Colbert et la Compagnie de Commerce du Nord." *Revue d'histoire économique et sociale* 17, 2 (1929): 156–204.
Bromley, J.S. "The North Sea in wartime (1688–1713)." *Bijdragen en Mededelingen betreffende de geschiedenis der Nederlanden* 92 (1997): 270–299.
Carswell, John. "The Armenians in the East-West trade through Persia in the XVIIth century." In *Sociétés et compagnies de commerce en Orient et dans l'Océan Indien*, edited by Michel Mollat, 481–486. Paris 1971.
Chance, J.F. "The Baltic expedition and Northern treaties of 1715." *The English Historical Review* 17, 67 (1902): 443–465.
Chance, J.F. "The Northern policy of George I. to 1716." *Transactions of the Royal Historical Society, New Series* 20 (1906): 79–107.
Chance, J.F. "The Northern question in 1716." *The English Historical Review* 18, 72 (1903): 676–704.
Chance, J.F. "The Northern question in 1717." *The English Historical Review* 20, 77 (1905): 33–60.
Chance, J.F. "The Northern question in 1718." *The English Historical Review* 21, 83 (1906): 460–492.
Clément, Pierre (ed.). *Lettres, instructions et mémoires de Colbert, Tome II.1: Finances, impôts, monnaies.* Paris 1863.
Clément, Pierre (ed.). *Lettres, instructions et mémoires de Colbert, Tome II.2: Industrie, Commerce.* Paris 1863.
Curtin, Philip D. *Cross-cultural trade in world history.* Cambridge 1984.
Denzel, Markus A. "Kommerzielle Innovationen für den Hanseraum? Ein Beitrag zum Strukturwandel des internationalen Handels des 15. und 16. Jahrhunderts." In *Hansischer Handel im Strukturwandel vom 15. zum 16. Jahrhundert. Tagung des Hansischen Geschichtsvereins 2014 in Lübeck*, edited by R. Hammel-Kiesow and S. Selzer, 67–99. Köln / Weimar / Wien 2016.

Dietrich, Richard. "Der preußische Staat und seine Landesteile in den politischen Testamenten der Hohenzollern." In *Expansion und Integration. Zur Eingliederung neugewonnener Gebiete in den preußischen Staat*, edited by Peter Baumgart. Köln / Wien 1984.

Donnelly, Alton S. "Peter the Great and Central Asia." *Canadian Slavonic Papers / Revue Canadienne des Slavistes* 17, 2/3 (1975): 202–217.

Droysen, Johann Gustav. *Geschichte der preussischen Politik, IV. Theil*. Leipzig 1867.

Eekman, Thomas. "Seven years with Peter the Great: the Dutchman Jacob de Bie's observations." In *Peter the Great and the West. New perspectives*, edited by Lindsay Hughes, 207–224. London 2001.

Forberger, Rudolf. "Zur wirtschaftsgeschichtlichen Neueinschätzung der sächsisch-polnischen Union." In *Um die polnische Krone. Sachsen und Polen während des nordischen Krieges, 1700–1721*, edited by Johannes Kalisch and Józef Gierowski, 208–253. Berlin 1962.

Foust, Clifford M. *Muscovite and Mandarin. Russia's trade with China and its setting 1727–1805*. Chapel Hill 1969.

Frost, Robert I. *After the Deluge. Poland-Lithuania and the Second Northern War*. Cambridge 1993.

Frost, Robert I. *The northern wars. War, state and society in northeastern Europe, 1558–1721*. London 2000.

Grönebaum, Ferdinand. *Frankreich in Ost- und Nordeuropa. Die Französisch-Russischen Beziehungen von 1648–1689*. Wiesbaden 1968.

Groth, Andrzej. "Hauptprobleme der danziger Schiffahrt in der 2. Hälfte des 17. Jahrhunderts." *Studia Maritima* 4 (1975): 109–134.

Groth, Andrzej. "Wykazy gdańskich statków eksploatowanych w latach 1660–1697." *Zapiski Historyczne* 9 (1975): 85–120.

Gulbenkian, R. "Philippe de Zagly, marchand arménien de Julfa et l'établissement du commerce persan en Courland en 1696." *Revue des Études arméniennes* 7 (1970): 361–399.

Häpke, Rudolf. "Der Untergang der hansischen Vormachtstellung in der Ostsee (1531–1544)." *Hansische Geschichtsblätter* 18 (1912): 85–119.

Harder-Gersdorff, Elisabeth. "Riga als Handelsmetropole des Ostseeraums in der Frühen Neuzeit (16.–18. Jahrhundert)." In *Riga und der Ostseeraum. Von der Gründung 1201 bis in die Frühe Neuzeit*, edited by Ilgvars Misans and Horst Wernicke, 261–294. Marburg 2005.

Harding, Richard. *Seapower and naval warfare, 1650–1830*. London / New York 1999.

Harper, Lawrence Averell. *The English navigation laws. A seventeenth-century experiment in social engineering*. New York 1939.

Hassinger, Ernst. *Brandenburg-Preußen, Schweden und Russland, 1700–1713*. München 1953.

Hassinger, Herbert. "Die erste Wiener orientalische Handelskompagnie, 1667–1683." *Vierteljahrschrift für Sozial- und Wirtschaftsgeschichte* 35, 1 (1942): 1–53.

Hill-Paulus, Beate. *Nikolaj Gavrilovič Saptharij (1636–1708) und seine Gesandtschaft nach China*. Hamburg 1978.

Hoffmann, Peter. *Ostsibirien und Nordpazifik in der zweiten Hälfte des 18. Jahrhunderts. Die Diskussion um die Ausdehnung Asiens*. Frankfurt am Main 2013.

Ioannisjan, Ašot (ed.). *Armjano-russkie otnošenija v pervoj treti XVIII veka. Tom II, čast' 1*. Erevan 1964.

Israel, Jonathan I. *Dutch primacy in world trade, 1585–1740.* Oxford 1989.

Jenks, Stuart. "Die Distributionsrevolution des 15. Jahrhunderts." *Hansische Geschichtsblätter* 132 (2014): 47–78.

Jenks, Stuart. *England, die Hanse und Preußen. Handel und Diplomatie, 1377–1474.* Köln / Wien 1992.

Jenks, Stuart. "War die Hanse kreditfeindlich?" *Vierteljahrschrift für Sozial- und Wirtschaftsgeschichte* 69 (1982): 305–338.

Journal de la Résidence du sieur Lange, agent de sa Majesté Impériale de la Grande Russie à la Cour de la Chine; dans les années 1721 & 1722. Leyde 1726.

Kampmann, Christoph. "Ein großes Bündnis der katholischen Dynastien 1688? Neue Perspektiven auf die Entstehung des Neunjährigen Krieges und der Glorious Revolution." *Historische Zeitschrift* 294 (2012): 31–58.

Kellenbenz, Hermann. "Der russische Transithandel mit dem Orient im 17. und zu Beginn des 18. Jahrhunderts." *Jahrbücher für Geschichte Osteuropas, Neue Folge* 12, 4 (1965): 481–498.

Kellenbenz, Hermann. "Die Herzogtümer vom Kopenhagener Frieden bis zur Wiedervereinigung Schleswigs, 1660–1721." *Geschichte Schleswig-Holsteins* V (1960): 201–416.

Kévonian, Kéram. "Marchands arméniens au XVIIe siècle. A propos d'un livre arménien publié à Amsterdam en 1699." *Cahiers du monde russe et soviétique* 16, 2 (1975): 199–244.

Knight, R.G.B. "New England forests and British seapower: Albion revisited." *The American Neptune* 46, 4 (1986): 221–229.

Korsak, A. *Istoriko-statističeskoe obozrenie torgovych snošenij Rosii s Kitaem.* Kazan' 1857.

Kotilaine, Jarmo T. "Competing claims. Russian foreign trade via Arkhangelsk and the Eastern Baltic ports in the 17th century." *Kritika. Explorations in Russian and Eurasian History* 4, 2 (2003): 279–311.

Kotilaine, Jarmo T. "Riga's trade with its Muscovite hinterland in the seventeenth century." *Journal of Baltic Studies* 30, 2 (1999): 129–161.

Kotilaine, Jarmo T. *Russia's foreign trade and economic expansion in the seventeenth century. Windows on the world.* Leiden 2005.

Kotilaine, Jarmo T. "The significance of Russian transit trade for the Swedish Eastern Baltic ports in the seventeenth century." *Zeitschrift fur Ostmitteleuropa-Forschung* 49, 4 (2000): 556–589.

Kotljarchuk, Andrej. "Riga and commercial aspects of the Lithuanian-Swedish relationship during the seventeenth century." In *The dynamics of economic culture in the North Sea and Baltic region*, edited by Hanno Brand and Leos Müller, 240–249. Hilversum 2007.

Kretzschmar, Hellmut. "Der Friedensschluß von Altranstädt 1706/07." In *Um die polnische Krone. Sachsen und Polen während des nordischen Krieges, 1700–1721*, edited by J. Kalisch and J. Gierowski, 161–183. Berlin 1962.

Lane, M. "The relations between England and the Northern Powers, 1689–1697. Part I. Denmark." *Transactions of the Royal Historical Society* 5 (1911): 157–191.

Lewitter, L.R. "Poland, Russia and the treaty of Vienna of 5 January 1719." *The Historical Journal* 13, 1 (1970): 3–30.

Lewitter, L.R. "Russia, Poland and the Baltic, 1697–1721." *The Historical Journal* 11, 1 (1968): 3–34.

Lewitter, L.R. "The Russo-Polish treaty of 1686 and its antecendents." *The Polish Review* 9, 3 (1964): 5–29.

Liiv, Otto. *Die wirtschaftliche Lage des estnischen Gebietes am Ausgang des XVII. Jahrhunderts. 1. Allgemeiner Überblick, Getreideproduktion und Getreidehandel.* Tartu 1935.

Lloyd, Terence Henry. *England and the German Hanse 1157–1611. A study of their trade and commercial diplomacy.* Cambridge 1991.

Lystsov, Vikentij Pavlovič. *Persidskij pochod Petra I, 1722–1723.* Moskva 1951.

Malone, Joseph J. "England and the Baltic naval stores trade in the seventeenth and eighteenth centuries." *The Mariner's Mirror* 58, 4 (1972): 375–395.

Martens, Friedrich Fromhold. *Sobranie traktatov i konvencij zaključennych Rossieju s inostrannymi deržavami / Receuil des Traités et Conventions, conclus par la Russie avec les Puissances Etrangères.* 15 volumes. Sankt Petersburg 1874–1909.

Massie, Robert K. *Peter the Great. The compelling story of the man who created modern Russia, founded St Petersburg and made his country part of Europe.* London 2012.

Materialy po istorii Turkmen i Turkmenii, II. 1938–1939.

Matthee, Rudi. "Anti-Ottoman politics and transit rights. The seventeenth-century trade in silks between Safavid Iran and Muscovy." *Cahiers du monde russe* 35, 4 (1994): 739–761.

Mattiesen, Heinz. "Die Versuche zur Erschließung eines Handelsweges Danzig-Kurland-Moskau-Asien, besonders für Seide, 1640–1655." *Jahrbücher für Geschichte Osteuropas* 3, 4 (1938): 533–567.

McCabe, Ina Baghdiantz. *The Shah's silk for Europe's silver. The Eurasian trade of the Julfa Armenians in Safavid Iran.* Atlanta 1993.

McKay, Derek. "The struggle for control of George I's Northern Policy, 1718–1719." *The Journal of Modern History* 45, 3 (1973): 367–386.

Mediger, Walther. *Mecklenburg, Rußland und England-Hannover, 1706–1721. Ein Beitrag zur Geschichte des nordischen Krieges.* Hildesheim 1967.

Neumann, J.; Lindgrén, S. "Great historical events that were significantly affected by the weather: 4, The great famines in Finland and Estonia, 1695–1697." *Bulletin of the American Meteorological Society* 60, 7 (1979): 775–787.

North, Michael. *Deutsche Wirtschaftsgeschichte. Ein Jahrtausend im Überblick.* Second Edition. München 2005.

North, Michael. *Geschichte der Ostsee. Handel und Kulturen.* München 2011.

Oakley, Stewart P. *War and peace in the Baltic, 1560–1790.* London / New York 1993.

O'Brien, Bickford. *Russia under two tsars 1682–1689. The Regency of Sophia Alekseevna.* Berkeley / Los Angeles 1952.

Onnekink, David. *War and religion after Westphalia 1648–1713.* Farnham 2009.

Oreškova, S.F. *Russko-tureckie otnošenija v načale XVIII v.* Moskva 1971.

Osterhammel, Jürgen. *Die Entzauberung Asiens. Europa und die asiatischen Reiche im 18. Jahrhundert.* München 2010.

Pallas. *Tagebuch zwoer Reysen, welche in den Jahren 1727, 1728 und 1736 von Kjachta und Zuruchaitu durch die Mongoley nach Peking gethan worden von Lorenz Lange, ehemaligem Ruß. Kays. Kanzleyrath. Nebst einer geographisch-historischen Beschreibung der Stadt Peking. Mit Kupfern.* Leipzig 1781.

Parsamjan, V.A. (ed.). *Armjano-russkie otnosenija v XVII veke.* Erevan 1953.

Pearson, C.W. *England's timber trade in the last of the 17th and first of the 18th century, more especially with the Baltic Sea.* Göttingen 1869.

Pijrimjaė, Ch.A. "Sostav, ob"em i raspredelenie russkogo vyvoza 1661–1700 gg. čerez švedskie vladenija v Pribaltike na primere torgovli g. Narvy." *Skandinavskij Sbornik* 5 (1962): 34–97.

Pijrimjaė, Ch.A. "Torgovye otnošenija Rossii so Šveciej i drugimi stranami Evropy po materialam Narvskogo vvoza v 1661–1700 gg." *Skandinavskij Sbornik* 7 (1963): 44–86.

Pincus, Steven. *1688. The first modern revolution*. New Haven / London 2009.

Pitz, Ernst. "Steigende und fallende Tendenzen in Politik und Wirtschaftsleben der Hanse im 16. Jahrhundert." *Hansische Geschichtsblätter* 102 (1984): 39–77.

PSZ: *Polnoe Sobranie Zakonov Rossijskoj Imperii, poveleniem Gosudarja Imperatora Nikolaja Pavloviča sostavlennoe*. 45 volumes. Sankt Petersburg 1830.

Rachel, Hugo. *Die Handels-, Zoll-, und Akzisepolitik Preußens, Band 2 (2), 1713–1740. Aktenstücke und Beilagen*. Berlin 1922.

Reading, Douglas K. *The Anglo-Russian commercial treaty of 1734*. New Haven / London / Oxford 1938.

Ressel, Magnus. "Die zeitgenössische Perzeption des Niedergangs der Hansekontore in den 'Hanseatica' (1674) des Danziger Syndikus Wenzel Mittendorp." *Hansische Geschichtsblätter* 132 (2014): 79–103.

Roberts, Michael. *The Swedish imperial experience*. Cambridge 1979.

Roorda, Daniel Jeen. *Het rampjaar 1672*. Bussum 1971.

Savary, Jacques. *Le parfait negociant, ou Instruction generale pour ce qui regarde le commerce de toute sorte de marchandises, tant de France que des pays estrangers*. Paris 1675.

Schade, Hans. *Die Niederlande und Russland. Handel und Aufnahme diplomatischer Kontakte zu Anfang des 17. Jahrhunderts*. Frankfurt am Main 1992.

Scheltjens, Werner. *Dutch Deltas. Emergence, functions and structure of the Low Countries' maritime transport system, ca. 1300–1850*. Leiden / Boston 2015.

Schildhauer, Johannes. "Reformation im Ostseeraum und beginnender Kampf um das Dominium maris Baltici im 16. Jahrhundert." In *Der Ost- und Nordseeraum. Politik — Ideologie — Kultur vom 12. bis zum 17. Jahrhundert*, edited by Konrad Fritze, Eckhard Müller-Mertens and Johannes Schildhauer, 19–35. Weimar 1986.

Sohrabi, Bahram. "Early Swedish travelers to Persia." *Iranian Studies* 38, 4 (2005): 631–660.

Soom, Arnold. *Der baltische Getreidehandel im 17. Jahrhundert*. Stockholm 1961.

Soom, Arnold. *Die Politik Schwedens bezüglich des Russischen Transithandels über die estnischen Städte in den Jahren 1636–1656*. Tartu 1940.

Spading, Klaus. "Zu den Ursachen für das Eindringen der Holländer in das hansische Zwischenhandelsmonopol im 15. Jahrhundert." In *Neue hansische Studien* 17, edited by Konrad Fritze, Eckhard Müller-Mertens, Johannes Schildhauer and Erhard Voigt, 227–242. Berlin 1970.

Steinberg, Philip E. *The social construction of the ocean*. Cambridge 2001.

Szultka, Szymon. "Handel morski i porty Brandenburgii-Prus w drugiej połowie XVII I XVIII wieku." *Studia Maritima* 28 (2015): 185–227.

Tetradas [VSWG-JDA]: *Tetradas: Tonnage estimates of trade through the Danish Sound, 1670–1856 (Replication data and selected statistics). Version: 1*. VSWG – Journal of Social and Economic History. Dataset, edited by Werner Scheltjens. https://journaldata.zbw.eu/dataset/tetradas

Tjaden, Anja. "The Dutch in the Baltic, 1544–1721." In *In quest of trade and security. The Baltic in power politics 1500–1990, volume I: 1500–1890*, edited by Göran Rystad, Klaus-R. Böhme, and Wilhelm L. Carlgren, 61–136. Stockholm 1994.

Troebst, Stefan. "Armenian Merchants in seventeenth-century North-Eastern Europe." *Mitropa. Jahresheft des GWZO* (2015), 14–17.

Troebst, Stefan. "Debating the mercantile background to early modern Swedish empire-building. Michael Roberts vs Artur Attman." *European History Quarterly* 24, 4 (1994): 495–509.

Troebst, Stefan. "Die Kaspi-Volga-Ostseeroute in der Handelspolitik Karl XI. Die schwedischen Persien-Mission von Ludvig Fabritius 1679–1700." *Forschungen zur Osteuropäischen Geschichte* 54 (1998): 127–204.

Troebst, Stefan. *Handelskontrolle – "Derivation" – Eindammung: schwedische Moskaupolitik 1617–1661.* Wiesbaden 1997.

Troebst, Stefan. "Isafahan – Moskau – Amsterdam. Zur Entstehungsgeschichte des Moskauischen Transitprivilegs für die Armenische Handelskompagnie in Persien (1666–1676)." *Jahrbuch für die Geschichte Osteuropas* 41, 2 (1993): 179–209.

Troebst, Stefan. "Narva, Libau oder Danzig? Die Volga-Kaspi-Ostseeroute im Außenhandel des frühneuzeitlichen Ostmitteleuropa." In *Fernhandel und Handelspolitik der baltischen Städte in der Hansezeit. Beiträge zur Erforschung mittelalterlicher und frühneuzeitlicher Handelsbeziehungen und –wege im europäischen Rahmen*, edited by Norbert Angermann and Paul Kaegben, 339–353. Lüneburg 2001.

Troebst, Stefan. "Narva und der Außenhandel Persiens im 17. Jahrhundert. Zum merkantilen Hintergrund schwedischer Großmachtpolitik." In *Die schwedischen Ostseeprovinzen Estland und Livland im 16.–18. Jahrhundert*, edited by Aleksander Loit and Helmut Piirimäe, 161–170. Uppsala 1993.

Troebst, Stefan. "Rußland als „Magazin der Handlung zwischen Asien und Europa"? Die Frage des Orienthandels bei der schwedischen Moskaugesandtschaft 1673/74." *Forschungen zur osteuropäischen Geschichte* 58 (2001): 287–300.

Troebst, Stefan. "Russia and the Safavid Empire." In *Iran and the world in the Safavid age*, edited by Willem Floor and Edmund Herzig, 253–258. London a.o. 2012.

Troebst, Stefan. "Stockholm und Riga als "Handelsconcurrentinnen" Archangelsk? Zum merkantilen Hintergrund schwedischer Großmachtpolitik 1650–1700." *Forschungen zur osteuropaischen Geschichte* 48 (1993): 259–294.

Ufkes, Tonko. "Nederlandse schippers op Danziger and Stockholmse handels-schepen, 1670–1700." *Tijdschrift voor zeegeschiedenis* 15 (1996): 25–51.

Van Amelsfoort, P.E.H. "De diplomatieke betrekkingen tussen de Republiek en Rusland 1614–1665." *Spiegel Historiael* 17, 5 (1982): 261–265.

Van Koningsbrugge, Hans. "Van Kwaad tot Erger: de verslechterende Nederlands-Russische relaties 1711–1718." In *Noord- en Zuid-Nederlanders in Rusland 1703–2003*, edited by Emmanuel Waegemans and Hans Van Koningsbrugge, 3–30. Groningen 2004.

Van Tielhof, Milja. "Der Getreidehandel der Danziger Kaufleute in Amsterdam um die Mitte des 16. Jahrhunderts." *Hansische Geschichtsblätter* 113 (1995): 93–110.

Vasil'ev, Matvej. *Russland und Frankreich von der Thronbesteigung Peters des Grossen bis zum Vertrage von Amsterdam.* [s.l.] 1902.

Wanner, Michal. "First Russian-Chinese diplomatic relations and business relationship 1689–1728." *Prague Papers on the History of International Relations* 17, 2 (2013): 66–76.

Wanner, Michal. "The Russian-Chinese trade in Kyakhta, its organisation and commodity structure, 1727–1861." *Prague Papers on the History of International Relations* 18, 2 (2014): 35–49.

Zernack, Klaus. "Der große nordische Krieg." In *Nordosteuropa. Skizzen und Beiträge zu einer Geschichte der Ostseeländer*, 157–202. Lüneburg 1993.

Zernack, Klaus. "Schweden als europäische Großmacht der frühen Neuzeit." *Historische Zeitschrift* 232 (1981): 327–357.
Zernack, Klaus. *Studien zu den schwedisch-russischen Beziehungen in der 2. Hälfte des 17. Jahrhunderts. Teil I: Die diplomatischen Beziehungen zwischen Schweden und Moskau von 1675 bis 1689.* Gießen 1958.
Zevakin, E.S. "Persidskij vopros v russko-evropejskich otnošenijach XVII v." *Istoričeskie zapiski* 8 (1940): 129–162.

4 The consolidation of the Baltic's special role in North Eurasian trade, 1703–1766

Introduction

The foundation of St. Petersburg, the attempts of the European powers to contain and check Russia's advances in the Baltic, the (commercial) treaty negotiations of the Western European powers with Peter the Great during the final phase of the Great Northern War, and the confirmation of Brandenburg-Prussia's territorial expansion in 1720 (Treaty of Stockholm) heralded the consolidation of the Baltic as an area of vested interest in North Eurasia. Russia now controlled several ports in the Baltic, of which St. Petersburg, the Empire's brand-new capital since 1712, would become by far the most important in the course of one generation. Brandenburg-Prussia had managed to extend its coastline, which now included Stettin at the mouth of the river Oder, and since 1701, Brandenburg and Ducal (or East) Prussia were bound together in a personal union under the leadership of the King *in* Prussia. Sweden was thrown back almost entirely to its mainland. It had only a few possessions left on the southern Baltic Sea coast in Swedish Pomerania and had lost its tax-free status in the Danish Sound. Poland-Lithuania had become a protectorate of the Russian Tsar. Even though it officially maintained its independence and continued to be ruled by August II, King of Saxony, it was clear that Poland-Lithuania was no longer in a position to pursue an autonomous foreign policy. Along the coast of the North Sea, the territorial and dynastic changes that had occurred during the Spanish War of Succession and the Great Northern War were at least as significant. In 1714, a union of Hanover and Great Britain under King George I replaced the personal union between the Dutch Republic and England. The former Spanish Netherlands were now ruled by the Habsburg dynasty and were renamed Austrian Netherlands, providing the Habsburg Empire, alongside Trieste on the Adriatic coast, with much-wanted access to the North Sea. Occasional warfare notwithstanding, in particular, during the Polish War of Succession (1733–1736), the Russo-Swedish War (1741–1743), and the War of the Austrian Succession (1740–1748), the Baltic Sea basin became a relatively peaceful environment for trade after the Russo-Swedish Treaty of Nystadt (1721).

Despite the disturbances of the Great Northern War and the complex international constellation that arose during the Seven Years' War (1756–1763), continuity seems to have prevailed in trade through the Danish Sound between 1670 and 1769. Although Great Britain and the Russian Empire found themselves in opposite camps during the Seven Years' War, this hardly hampered their commerce. On the contrary, it was very much in the interests of Russia to secure neutrality in the Baltic – if not for commercial reasons, then at least for the supply of its troops. Russia pursued this policy of neutrality together with Sweden, Denmark, and Poland-Lithuania, which resulted in the famous declaration of the freedom of Baltic commerce (13 March 1758) and the St. Petersburg neutrality convention (9 March 1759).[1]

Throughout the century from 1670 to 1769, ports in the eastern Baltic area – from the Vistula to the Neva (*east* in Table 4.1) – supplied more than

Table 4.1 Grain, raw materials, and manufactures exports through the Danish Sound, 1670–1856

		Departure				*Destination*			
	Total	*South*	*East*	*Scan*	*Rest*	*atl*	*nsea*	*uk*	*Rest*
Grain									
1670–1719	144,966	4	92	3	1	3	91	1	5
1720–1769	126,500	6	91	3	0	5	84	3	8
1770–1809	240,839	15	78	7	0	10	50	20	20
1810–1839	296,931	34	59	7	0	5	41	34	20
1840–1856	429,441	41	47	12	0	1	28	61	9
Raw materials									
1670–1719	47,938	3	66	29	2	5	64	23	8
1720–1769	143,468	5	68	27	0	14	54	29	3
1770–1809	286,080	4	75	21	0	14	26	50	10
1810–1839	318,729	3	74	24	0	10	20	55	15
1840–1856	474,100	2	71	27	0	11	20	59	11
Manufactures									
1670–1719	1,124	0	99	0	1	3	20	59	19
1720–1769	5,321	1	98	1	0	3	27	68	2
1770–1809	6,845	1	94	5	0	16	14	54	17
1810–1839	5,423	1	92	7	0	9	13	16	62
1840–1856	3,939	1	92	6	0	4	19	15	62

Source: Tetradas [VSWG-JDA], 2_C_Bex: Commodity categories.
Note: total = annual average of total estimated tonnage exported per period (in tonnes); south = percentage share of ports in the southern Baltic area (between Lübeck and the Oder) in annual average exports per period; east = percentage share of ports in the southern Baltic area (from the Vistula to the Neva) in annual average exports per period; scan = percentage share of ports in Denmark, Sweden and Finland in annual average exports per period; rest = percentage share of other ports; atl = European Atlantic coast; nsea = North-West Europe (except UK); UK = United Kingdom.

90% on average of all grain exported through the Danish Sound. Almost the entire amount was sent to ports in the North Sea (*nsea* in Table 4.1), most importantly to Amsterdam.[2] However, compared to the 1670–1719 period, the share in the supply of 'Baltic grain' of other destinations in the Atlantic (*atl* in Table 4.1), Great Britain (*uk*) or elsewhere (*rest*) increased from 9% to 16% on average during the decades from 1720 to 1769. Although this is not a massive increase, it confirms that the former Dutch quasi-monopoly in trade through the Danish Sound was no longer self-evident. A look ahead into the decades after 1770 shows that this increase may be seen as an early sign of upcoming fundamental changes in the geography of the North Eurasian grain trade through the Danish Sound.

The same might be said of exports of raw materials and manufactures through the Danish Sound, albeit with one important distinction. Whereas the annual average tonnage of grain exports hardly changed and even declined somewhat from the first (144,966 tonnes) to the second period (126,500 tonnes), that of raw materials exported through the Danish Sound towards destinations along the coasts of the North Sea and the Atlantic tripled, from 47,938 tonnes in 1670–1719 to 143,468 tonnes in 1720–1769. The increase in the exportation of manufactures was even stronger and grew from 1,124 tonnes in 1670–1719 to 5,321 tonnes in 1720–1769. The estimated tonnage of manufactures exported through the Danish Sound almost quintupled after the Great Northern War, but compared to foodstuffs and raw materials it remained small. At the same time, the shares of the supply areas in the Baltic of raw materials and manufactured goods hardly changed: two-thirds of all raw materials and almost all manufactures were exported from ports in the eastern Baltic area. Ports in the North Sea basin gradually declined as destinations of raw materials exported from the Baltic (from 64% in 1670–1719 to 54% in 1720–1769). At the same time, the delivery of manufactured goods to ports in Great Britain increased (from 59% in 1670–1719 to 68% in 1720–1769). Bearing in mind that the average tonnage of raw materials exported through the Danish Sound between 1720 and 1769 exceeded that of grain exports, the increasing shares of ports along the Atlantic coast and in Great Britain as destinations of these raw materials indicate the emergence of novel patterns of distribution. After the Great Northern War, the Baltic became more than just the 'granary of Europe,' and it certainly became more than just the 'backwaters of the Dutch.' Other commercial and political forces – most importantly Great Britain – advanced in trade through the Danish Sound and started to change its character.

The rise of the British in some sectors of trade through the Danish Sound, most prominently in the exportation of *naval stores* from Russia, went hand in hand with the increasing power and rise to supremacy of the British Navy. In the meantime, the decline of the Dutch commercial system continued. Even though it is premature to speak of the collapse of the Dutch commercial system, as several scholars have duly noted in their critique of Jonathan Israel's standard work on 'Dutch primacy' in world trade, it must be clear that *strictu sensu* the time of Dutch predominance in the Baltic was indeed over by 1740.[3] Although the Dutch continued their trade with a number of ports in the Baltic, and maintained a major share in grain exports through the Danish Sound for decades to come,[4] their stake in the strategically more important trades with *naval stores* and manufactures declined.[5] Moreover, they had missed the opportunity to institutionalize their commercial relations with Russia, and many Russia-based merchants of Dutch descent hesitated for too long before moving their business to St. Petersburg (see below). Thus, insofar as trade through the Danish Sound is concerned, one might even conclude that there was not as much competition and rivalry between Great Britain and the Dutch Republic as historiography assumes. Rather, in the Baltic two complementary commercial systems existed one next to the other around the mid-eighteenth century.

On the one hand, there was the increasingly outdated system of intermediate trade, which the Dutch had developed in the sixteenth century. This system consisted essentially of the exportation of grain and (later) raw materials from the Baltic and the importation, either direct or via Amsterdam, of southern European and colonial (overseas) products, such as salt, wine, fruits, spices, coffee, and sugar. On the other hand, there was the increasingly powerful and demanding British system of commercial exploitation, which had experienced its breakthrough in the wake of the Acts of Navigation, and had become a powerful factor in trade through the Danish Sound since the turn of the eighteenth century (see Chapter 3). Except for re-exports of commodities from its own colonies, British commerce with the Baltic was not based primarily on intermediate trade. With the aim of getting hold of the North Eurasian raw materials that could only be exported in sufficient quantities from ports in the Baltic, more and more British bottoms were employed to sail through the Danish Sound between Great Britain and – most importantly – Russia. The driving forces of British demand were the domestic economy and the navy. In sharp contrast to the Dutch, Britain's interest in 'Baltic trade' strongly intertwined with considerations of economic and naval power. Britain needed the North Eurasian raw materials, and after 1780 also its grain (see Chapter 5), to fuel its nascent industrial production and further its naval power.

This chapter deals with the consolidation of the Baltic as an area of vested interest in North Eurasian trade. It traces the main directions of the quest for North Eurasian trade, which had started at the turn of the eighteenth century, and describes their impact on trade through the Danish Sound. The quest unfolded primarily in the Russian government's enduring efforts to create the appropriate circumstances for newly founded St. Petersburg to become the Russian Empire's 'New Amsterdam.'[6] Three axes may be discerned in the Russian policies. First, interventionist mercantilist policies reshaped the position of Arkhangelsk in the Russian trade system, re-established the former Swedish ports in the Gulf of Finland, and aimed at the development of infrastructure in the Russian mainland (see Section "The creation of 'New

Amsterdam'"). The second set of policy measures addressed the establishment of a commercial infrastructure for improving the connections between North Eurasia and the Baltic (see Section "(Re-)directing North Eurasian commodity flows"). The third policy axis shaped Russia's international commercial exchange (see Section "British advances in North Eurasian trade"). The commercial treaty of Great Britain and the Russian Empire in 1734, on the one hand, and the related British efforts to revitalize transit trade to Persia via the Russian Empire in 1740–1741, on the other, were groundbreaking events in the consolidation of the Baltic as the preferred borderland of North Eurasia. These events bore witness of a double interest in Russia as supplier of raw materials and market for British manufactures. They were embedded in far-reaching British commercial ambitions, which, according to Reading, "(…) stopped at nothing less than making [Russia] (…) a very profitable satellite of England's economic stellar system."[7]

The creation of 'New Amsterdam'

As a direct consequence of ongoing warfare in the Baltic during the first two decades of the eighteenth century, trade at Arkhangelsk flourished in an unprecedented way.[8] The annual turnover at Arkhangelsk rose from 1.5 million roubles in 1704 to 2.3 million roubles in 1717.[9] In 1716, 89 Dutch ships registered in Amsterdam to join the early and late convoys destined to Arkhangelsk. This was perhaps the highest number of Dutch ships calling at the White Sea port during the entire eighteenth century.[10] However, even before turning into the Empire's new capital in 1712, the first signs of commercial and political interests vested in St. Petersburg rather than Arkhangelsk already appeared in the dealings with the Armenian merchants of New Julfa, who specialized in the silk trade to Western Europe. In 1708, Armenian merchants obtained the right to travel to St. Petersburg or Narva and continue their journey to Western Europe from there, even on Swedish ships. In this way, they could avoid the longer route via Arkhangelsk during the ongoing Russo-Swedish War in the Baltic.[11] In 1711, the contractual agreement between the Armenian merchants and Peter I was renewed.[12] The Armenians benefited from a new set of privileges in the Persian transit trade, granted to them after the Russian defeat against the Ottoman Empire in 1711 (see Chapter 3). A few years later, in 1719, the privileges were abolished and the Armenians had to comply with the general regulations for foreign trade, because – despite extensive privileges – they continued exporting silk from Persia via Turkey rather than Russia.[13] Even though little serial data is available about the values traded using the transit routes through Muscovy/Russia, the mere fact that Peter I would promote St. Petersburg as a transit hub just a few years after its foundation, and would allow Armenian merchants to use Swedish ships to fulfil their transport needs, shows the breadth and depth which the quest for North Eurasian trade had already obtained at that time. Peter's focus lay on the Baltic, and a shift of commercial interaction from the

White Sea to the Baltic was necessary for this focus to obtain a sustainable character. Far-reaching measures were taken to provoke the long-awaited shift from the White Sea to the Baltic, and to St. Petersburg, in particular. These measures included the incorporation of the ports in Sweden's former eastern Baltic provinces – most importantly Riga, Reval, Narva, Nyen, and Vyborg – in the Russian Empire,[14] and a series of tariffs and regulations, which redesigned the hinterlands of Russia's Baltic ports and Arkhangelsk.

Whereas the dealings with the Armenians still had a somewhat episodic character, an *ukaz* issued in November 1713 would mark the starting point of a long series of laws and regulations promoting St. Petersburg at the cost of Arkhangelsk.[15] Between 1714 and 1720, several attempts were made to limit exports from Arkhangelsk in favour of St. Petersburg, whereas merchants in Narva retained their right to carry out trade according to previous Swedish regulations until 1718.[16] In 1714, it was determined that ¼ of all *iufti* (*Ger.* Juchten) produced in Russia had to be transported to St. Petersburg, that merchants had the choice to export hemp from Arkhangelsk or St. Petersburg, and that other exports had to be carried out via Arkhangelsk.[17] The same *ukaz* stated that equal quantities of all goods had to be exported from Arkhangelsk and St. Petersburg in 1715.[18] In the following years, the distribution of goods between Arkhangelsk and St. Petersburg would be subject to continuous alterations, all of them in favour of St. Petersburg.[19] In November 1717, Tsar Peter the Great published a new arrangement for 1718: ⅔ of all goods destined for exportation would have to be shipped via St. Petersburg and only ⅓ via Arkhangelsk. Merchants from Novgorod and Pskov reacted to the new regulations with a request to allow them to abandon the Arkhangelsk route: because of the proximity of St. Petersburg, they no longer saw the need to use it. As this request answered perfectly to the wishes of Peter the Great, it comes as no surprise that they were immediately granted permission. Merchants of Kargopol, on the other hand, who argued that the distance to St. Petersburg was much larger and asked permission to continue sending their goods to Arkhangelsk, received a negative answer from the Senate.[20]

British and Dutch merchants reacted quite differently to the take-off of St. Petersburg in the 1710s. Forced by the new regulations directed against Arkhangelsk, most English merchants left the White Sea port rather quickly in the 1710s,[21] whereas their Dutch competitors seem to have been more reluctant to abandon their business in the North in favour of the new capital on the Neva.[22] The Dutch merchant colony and its representatives at the Russian court issued several complaints about the restrictive policies towards the commerce of Arkhangelsk – without being successful.[23] The British seem to have taken the move to St. Petersburg for granted; they were much faster to establish their trade at the new port, and even contributed to developing policy measures for hampering trade at Arkhangelsk.[24]

From 1718 and until the introduction of a new customs tariff in 1724, trade regulations in Narva underwent some fundamental changes, which were all inspired by Peter the Great's wish to make St. Petersburg the Russian Empire's main port. On the one hand, the growth of trade via Narva continued to be a matter of concern; on the other, measures were taken to avoid trade in St. Petersburg to be disturbed by Narva.[25] A 1718 *ukaz* stated that foreign merchants were obliged to import flax, hemp and *iufti* to Narva, while they also had to make their ships available to local merchants for the exportation of goods abroad. The aim was to stimulate trade through Narva, but these regulations could not compete with the more profitable measures that were applied to St. Petersburg. In 1720, Russian merchants sending goods coming from the country's interior to St. Petersburg were to pay a 3% tax as opposed to 5% if they went elsewhere. If the goods transported to St. Petersburg were exported, the Russian merchants were exempted from paying these 3% as well.[26] This measure served the double goal of stimulating both the development of a Russian merchant community and the port of St. Petersburg.

Statistics of Russian foreign trade are scarce during most of the eighteenth century. Nevertheless, a compilation of scattered data about the volume and value of imports and exports from Arkhangelsk and St. Petersburg underlines the profound impact of the intervention in the distribution patterns and commodity flows from the Russian interior towards its maritime borders immediately after the Great Northern War. Compared to the average of 1717–1719, the exported tonnage and value of all major items from St. Petersburg – except grain, the export of which would be forbidden until 1762[27] – rose significantly, whereas the registered values of exports from Arkhangelsk experienced a strong decline (see Table 4.2).[28] The *hausse* of the Arkhangelsk trade was over. Commodities that, until then, would have to be shipped via Arkhangelsk could now also be handled in Russia's Baltic ports. Nevertheless, Arkhangelsk would retain, albeit at a more modest level than before, a significant function in the Russian commercial system throughout the eighteenth century and part of the nineteenth century. Arkhangelsk became a port of secondary importance, after St. Petersburg and Riga. However, in times

Table 4.2 Comparison of exports from Arkhangelsk and St. Petersburg, 1717–1719; 1726

	Arkhangelsk		*St. Petersburg*	
	1717–1719	*1726*	*1717–1719*	*1726*
Hemp and flax (in pood)	545,321	808	157,224	552,978
Tallow (in pood)	122,666	24,051	7,252	25,094
Iron (in pood)	35,285		2,000	55,149
Juchten (in pood)	164,137	2,872	6,175	169,137
Linen fabrics (in arshine)	2,278,819	718,986	672,500	9,600,307
Persian silk (in pood)				2,192

Source: Semenov, *Izuchenie istoricheskikh svedenii*, II (3), 21; 23–24.
Note: Annual average for the years 1717–1719 and 1726. Linen fabrics in 1717–1719 also comprised 577 pieces of sail from Arkhangelsk and 541 from St. Petersburg. Linen fabrics in 1726 also comprised 7,747 pieces of sail from St. Petersburg. 1 pood = 16.38 kg; 1 arshine = 0.71 m.

of war – during the Continental Blockade or in the wake of the November Uprising in Poland 1830 – or in times of excessive demand – during the grain crisis after the Tambora eruption of 1816 or during the potato famine – the port still offered a highly appreciated alternative for the Russian Empire's more vulnerable Baltic (and later also Black Sea) ports (see Figure 4.1).

Whereas the early measures to promote the port of St. Petersburg had an ad hoc character, after the Treaty of Nystadt (1721), structural and more efficient measures were taken. A groundbreaking *ukaz* of November 26, 1721 literally redesigned the hinterlands of Russia's maritime ports and created considerable comparative advantages for the port of St. Petersburg.[29] From 1721 onwards, only goods originating in Pskov and its district could be transported to Narva for export.[30] Goods originating near Gzhatsk and closer to Velikiye Luki had to be sent to St. Petersburg instead of Riga; Riga's hinterland was restricted to West Russia and Ukraine.[31] The hinterland of Arkhangelsk was limited to the districts along the Northern Dvina insofar as they had an immediate connection with the White Sea port.[32] Export goods that were transported previously to the Yug or other rivers, or to Vologda via the winter route, now had to be transported to St. Petersburg instead. In 1722, merchants of Pskov obtained the freedom to send their goods to Narva or St. Petersburg according to their needs,[33] which subjected Narva once more to severe competition from St. Petersburg. In the same year, Narva was put under the rule of the governor of St. Petersburg[34] after which both St.

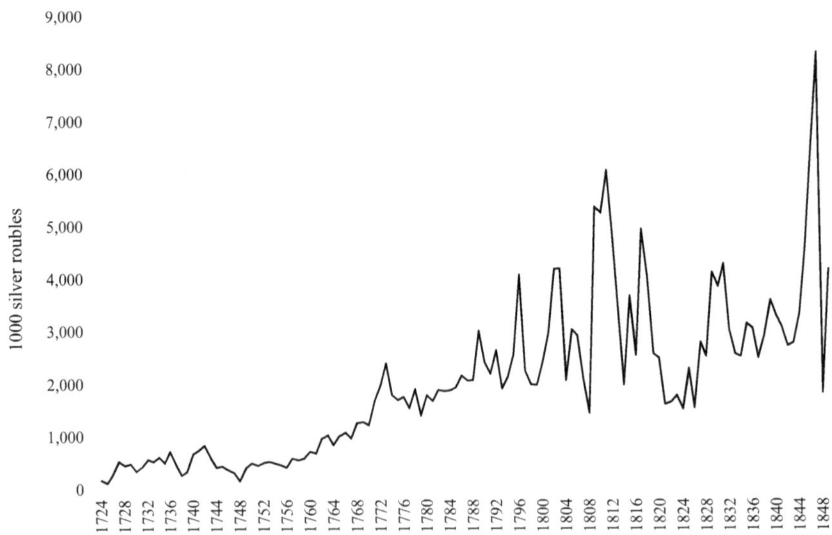

Figure 4.1 Estimated value of foreign trade at Arkhangelsk, 1724–1849.

Note: Only exports in 1724 and 1725. In silver rubles. Conversion to silver rubles based on Denzel, *Handbook*, 359.

Sources: 1724–1818 from Kozlov, *Archangel'skaja gubernija*, tables inserted between pages 218 and 219; 1819–1849 from *Gosudarstvennaja vnešnjaja torgovlja*.

Petersburg and Narva obtained a tax advantage of 2% and 1% as opposed to other ports in the Baltic Sea.[35]

Next to reshaping the hinterlands of Russian ports in the Gulf of Finland and Arkhangelsk, the customs tariff of 1724 was important for the further development of foreign trade with Russia in the eighteenth century. The 1724 customs tariff applied to the import and export of commodities via St. Petersburg, Vyborg, Narva, Arkhangelsk and Kola.[36] According to the new tariff, an additional 25% was levied on all exports from Arkhangelsk, on top of the 5% export duty that also applied to the exports from the other ports mentioned in the 1724 tariff regulation.[37] The 1724 customs tariff strengthened St. Petersburg's exceptional position, whereas the position of Riga, Reval and some smaller former Swedish ports was sustained by the fact that the 1724 tariff did not apply to them.[38] Together with the foundation of textile manufactures around St. Petersburg and the further development of the iron industry in the Ural Mountains,[39] the accelerated diffusion of the Dutch fine-blade sawmill technology in the eastern part of the Gulf of Finland shaped the respective roles of St. Petersburg, Arkhangelsk, Narva, and Vyborg in Russia's foreign trade.[40] Narva, Vyborg and to some extent St. Petersburg became ports for the exportation of timber.[41] St. Petersburg would become Russia's main gateway to Europe for exports of commodities originating from the Russian interior, while it would also serve as the main gateway to the Russian interior for imports of valuable goods from Europe and its colonies.[42] In 1731 earlier restrictive rules were replaced with a more differentiated tariff, which foresaw the reduction of internal tolls in St. Petersburg from 5% to 3%, and the increase of the same tax in Arkhangelsk from 5% to 7%.[43] Smaller changes notwithstanding, the unequal tax treatment of St. Petersburg and Arkhangelsk would be abolished only in 1762.[44] Moreover, the highest import tax was reduced from 75% to 20% and the categorization of commodities in different tax rates was designed to stimulate industrial development in the Russian mainland. In the meantime, the Russian textile industry was privatized after the death of Peter the Great, but no new manufactures were established during the next three decades.[45]

(Re-)directing North Eurasian commodity flows

Whereas the previous section has shed light on the tax and customs policy measures, which were taken to stimulate the reorientation of North Eurasian commodity flows to Russian ports in the Baltic rather than to Arkhangelsk, this section discusses the far-reaching efforts to support these measures with infrastructural improvements in the Russia-controlled mainland of North Eurasia. Moreover, this section underlines the breadth and depth of commodity flows in North Eurasia based on a review of Russian tax registers for the year 1764. Although the description of these measures and the survey of the origins and directions of commodity flows through North Eurasia are succinct, they substantiate how the development of St. Petersburg took place within a broad context of commercial regulations aimed at promoting the distribution of commodities across all of North Eurasia.

On 17 January 1701, Peter the Great issued an *ukaz* prohibiting 'Greek' merchants and inhabitants of cities in southern Russia (*Ru.* malorossijskie goroda) to travel to Moscow, the fairs of the Svensky Monastery, or other fairs, and trade among themselves. They were informed that a fair would take place in Azov,[46] a settlement conquered during the Muscovite war with the Ottoman Empire (1683–1699). The *ukaz* stipulated that the fair of the Svensky Monastery was to take place for the last time in 1701, and that the monastery would be compensated for its abolition. Russian merchants were required to go to Azov instead,[47] whereas Poles were to go to Smolensk to carry out their trade with Russian merchants. Ten years later, on 25 June 1711, the fair of the Svensky Monastery was restored in the wake of the Russian capitulation after the Battle of the Prut.[48] Peter the Great's first attempt to establish a window on Europe in Azov turned out to be unsuccessful. From now on, the Tsar focused entirely on the Baltic Sea, where Russian troops started to play the upper hand and managed to consolidate crucial positions in the wake of Sweden's defeat at Poltava (1709) (see Section "War and national interests" of Chapter 3). Poltava marked the start of the rapid introduction of economic, administrative, and infrastructural reforms in the nascent Russian Empire. Most significant were the foundation of the Senate in 1711 and the declaration of St. Petersburg, Peter's 'New Amsterdam,' as the Russian Empire's new capital in 1712.[49] The Russian Empire's centre of power moved towards the Neva estuary.

Soon after its foundation, the first efforts were made to connect the new capital to its immense Russian hinterland, by means of canals and land routes between St. Petersburg and Moscow.[50] Even before the end of the Great Northern War and the consolidation of the Russian Empire's conquests along the shores of the Baltic Sea, several infrastructural projects were initiated in the Russian mainland, with the goal of disclosing and expanding the hinterland of St. Petersburg.[51] During the Great Northern War, efforts to establish a Baltic fleet had already resulted in the foundation of a number of ship wharfs and supporting industries near the new capital: shipbuilding and timber production, weaponry, metallurgy, iron, and textile industries.[52] The stimulating effect of these industries on Russian exports can hardly be overestimated. The development of shipbuilding provided an important impulse for the timber producing industry. In addition to state-controlled ship building wharfs, a number of regional centres for the production of timber arose in the first decades of the eighteenth century. In 1706, the first fine-blade sawmill was put into use in the area around Arkhangelsk, soon followed by sawmills in Narva and in the surroundings of Novgorod, along the Syas river and near Vyshny Volochyok, both located along waterways leading directly to St. Petersburg.[53] The iron industry of the Olonets Region (north of Lake Onega) and in the Ural Mountains,[54] at that time organized and controlled by the government, developed quickly in the first decades of the eighteenth century. Despite its large distance to the Baltic, the production supplies in the Ural appeared to be profitable and of good quality. Transportation from the Ural Mountains to the Russian capital posed several problems. Originally, there was no direct water connection between the two regions. In 1709, a canal was dug between the Tsna and the Tvertsa rivers, close to Vyshny Volochyok. From 1710 onwards, iron could be transported over water to St. Petersburg, but even then, transportation was time-consuming and difficult, especially on Lake Ladoga.[55] A canal avoiding the dangers of the lake was planned.

Construction works on the Ladoga-Canal started in 1713 and were finished in 1728.[56] In addition to these construction works, places for loading and unloading goods (*Ru.* pristan') were established at strategic places within the system of waterways, for example, in Gzhatsk.[57] Moreover, new regulations outlined the use of roads for sending goods to the newly acquired Baltic ports of the Russian Empire,[58] or to the newly defined Polish border.[59] Similar regulations for the routes to Siberia had been issued in the closing decade of the seventeenth century,[60] and were confirmed in the mid-eighteenth century.[61] One of the first initiatives with regard to improving the connections between the two capitals of the Russian Empire involved the reconstruction of the road from St. Petersburg to the river Volkhov, and the construction of a new road from the river Volkhov to Moscow.[62] In the late 1720s, the construction of another new road between St. Petersburg and Shlisselburg was initiated.[63]

By the end of the 1720s, most of the produce of the Ural mines went by waterway to St. Petersburg.[64] For the commercial networks that carried out this trade, the Makaryev fair was perfectly located on the left bank of the Volga, in reach of the water connections from the Moscow region (via the Kolomna and Oka rivers), the East (via the Kama and its adjacent rivers) and the South (downstream the Volga). The foundation of St. Petersburg entailed the rise of the fair of Makaryev as the Russian Empire biggest fair,[65] and administrative measures supported the fair's development as a hub of transport and trade routes from all corners of North Eurasia. The important Magistrate's Ordinance of 1721 (*Ru.* Ustav Glavnogo Magistrata) commissioned to increase the number of fairs in the Russian Empire, most importantly in places that could be accessed over water.[66] The schedule of the different fairs was discussed with the Department of Commerce and other governmental institutions. In addition to the establishment of fairs to increase government income and support internal commerce, the foundation of stock exchanges (*Ru.* birža) in large ports and inland cities was promoted.[67] From 1729, the fairs of Makaryev, the Svensky Monastery and Krolevets were scheduled in such order, that Russian merchants would have the time to meet and execute business with their Greek and Polish counterparts at the fair of the Svensky Monastery. To make that possible, the Makaryev fair, as before, took place from 29 June until 8 July, but the start of the fair of Krolevets was delayed from 1 to 15 September. In this way, Russian merchants could move from the Makaryev fair to the fair of the Svensky Monastery first, and afterwards to the fair of Krolevets.[68] A few years later, the dates of the fairs of Makaryev, the Svensky Monastery and Krolevets were adapted again. Based on a report of the Department of Commerce, an *ukaz* was issued, which stipulated that, from 1735 onwards, the Makaryev fair would start on June 20, the fair of the Svensky Monastery on August 15 and the fair of Krolevets not until mid-September.[69] Government involvement in the foundation and organization of fairs in the Russian Empire continued in the 1730s. The *ukaz* of 9 June 1730 outlined plans to establish fairs in Smolensk and Toropets as well as roads and toll stations across the Polish border (Sevsk, Bryansk, Kursk; Smolensk, Toropets) which served the same goal.[70] In this context, the favourable international salt trade of Smolensk, where salt from Perm and Staraya Russa was sold, is mentioned. In 1731, the foundation of a fair in Kyiv for the trade with "Silesian and other German horses" was issued by *ukaz*.[71]

At the end of the 1740s, the starting dates of the fairs of Makaryev, the Svensky Monastery and Krolevets, which apparently were the most important points of contact of Muscovites with foreign merchants, were changed again. This time the changes were more radical. From now on, the Makaryev fair started on July 1, the fair of the Svensky Monastery on 1 September and the Krolevets fair was delayed until 15 October (in 1757 moved back to 1 September).[72] This schedule enabled Russian merchants to participate in all three fairs.[73] Although these adaptations may be interpreted as evidence of the importance attached to fairs in the Russian Empire, they also show the rather limited number of places of intraregional importance in the Russian mainland. Besides the well-known fairs of Irbit in Siberia and Makaryev on the Volga, only the fairs of Krolevets and the Svensky Monastery in South Russia, Smolensk in West Russia and Yekaterinburg in the Urals reached beyond their own regions.[74]

The interventionist commercial policies of the Russian Empire, the infrastructural development and – last but not least – the British influence, which was consolidated in the Anglo-Russian commercial treaty of 1734 (see the next section), paved the way for the next step in the creation of a North Eurasian system of commercial exchange: the abolition of internal tolls and the establishment of an encompassing network of local and regional markets and fairs. A first breakthrough in the establishment of a nation-wide network of fairs occurred in 1755, when the previous system of internal tolls of the Russian Empire was abolished in favour of a comparatively modern and innovative system of toll collection at the Empire's ports and borders.[75] The customs regulations of 1757 (*Ru.* Tamožennyj Ustav) must have had significant impact on the Russian Empire's internal commerce: the number of regular markets rose from 627 in the 1750s to 1630 in the 1760s.[76] The abolition of the internal tolls coincided with an attempt of the Russian government to obtain a better insight in the structure of its import, export and transit trades. The surviving customs registers provide a unique opportunity to establish the main directions of commodities flows in the Russian Empire around the mid-1760s.[77] Besides St. Petersburg, the toll stations of Arkhangelsk, Riga, Nezhin, Dobryansk, and Vasylkiv were of particular importance.

According to the 1764 customs statistics, the most significant commodities exported from St. Petersburg were brought there from Siberia, Central Russia, various river ports along the Volga, the western territories between Kharkiv, Moscow, St. Petersburg and the Russo-Lithuanian border, as well as some places in North-West Russia between St. Petersburg and Arkhangelsk (mostly *iufti* and flax). Very small quantities of green tea, raw silk from Persia and even some Indian and Chinese fine woven silks were exported from St. Petersburg as well.[78] These export items leave little doubt about the impact of the foundation of St. Petersburg and the construction of the Canal of Vyshny Volochyok on the distribution and exportation of North Eurasian commodities via the new capital on the Neva embankment.

Hemp was produced primarily in the central provinces (*Ru.* gubernii) of Chernigov, Kursk, Oryol, Tula, and Tambov; flax was produced for the most part in the western, north-western and central provinces of Vologda, Yaroslavl, Vladimir, Novgorod, Pskov, Livonia, Courland, Vilna, and Vitebsk. The different production areas also explain why – at least until the late 1830s – hemp was exported for the most part from St. Petersburg and flax for the most part from Riga. About 80% of the flax exported from Riga arrived there by land route from the surrounding areas; only one-fifth of Riga's flax imports from its hinterland arrived by means of the Western Dvina and its adjacent rivers. St. Petersburg was the second-largest flax exporter in the Russian Empire, but the largest hemp-exporter. Flax exported from the Russian capital arrived there by water from Pskov and Novgorod. Hemp was collected at different kays (*Ru.* pristani) along the Upper Volga, such as the *pristani* of Gzhatsk, Rzhev, and Zubtsov. The latter served as the point of departure for hemp gathered from the provinces of Kaluga, Tula, Oryol, and Kursk. Hemp and flax were also exported from the Prussian ports of Memel and Königsberg, who bought these products in the provinces of Courland, Vilna, Mohylew, and Chernigov, and competed with both St. Petersburg and Riga.[79]

Although tallow was produced in areas located closer to the Black Sea coast than to St. Petersburg, the connections to the latter were better and therefore, tallow was sent all the way to North-West Russia for exportation, incurring high transportation costs and long delivery times. A major part of the Russian tallow production was sent to St. Petersburg from the *pristani* of Morshansk and Kazan, where the produce of the provinces of Tambov, Saratov, Kazan, Simbirsk, Penza, and Nizhny Novgorod was collected. Additionally, a significant part of the annual tallow exports was brought to St. Petersburg via the Upper Volga from the provinces of Kursk, Oryol, Tula, Kaluga, Kharkiv, Moscow, Kolomna, and Voronezh.[80]

Chinese goods entered the North Eurasian system of commercial exchange mostly via Kyakhta and were transported to Central Russia via a complex system of rivers and overland routes.[81] Remarkably, some of the

Chinese goods that were imported to the Russian Empire, were exported subsequently to the Polish-Lithuanian Commonwealth via the toll stations of Vasylkiv, Dobryansk, and Nezhin. The latter was an important market place on the left bank of the Dnepr (the so-called *Levoberež'e*), which had become part of the Russian Empire in 1654. The goods exported via the toll station of Nezhin almost exclusively originated from Moscow and went in two major directions: either to the so-called 'Turkish lands' or to Danzig. The merchants active on these routes were predominantly of 'Greek' origin; they almost exclusively carried furs.[82] The pattern of commercial exchange relations captured by the registers of the toll station of Vasylkiv was somewhat more complex: goods were exported from Kyiv, Moscow, Romny, Nezhin, and Kharkiv in the direction of, among other places, Berdichiv, Brody, Jassy, Warsaw, and several small Polish villages. At the toll station of Dobryansk goods passed, which came from the Southern Russian fairs of Nezhin, Romny, Poltava, or Krolevets and went in the direction of Danzig, Mohylew, Breslau, or smaller villages near the toll station itself.[83] The total value of exports of Chinese goods via the toll stations of Vasylkiv, Dobryansk, and the Shelegovskaya and Boyevskaya frontier posts (see below), was 77,684 roubles, or just under 1% of total exports from the Russian Empire in 1764. Notwithstanding their limited value, there are good reasons for including them in this section on North Eurasian commodity flows. First, their registered value at customs belies their perceived significance. Second, with a value at customs of just below 1% of total exports, it is remarkable that these goods at all found their way into the customs registers. The least we can assume is that they were considered important commodities in Russia's foreign trade. Finally, we have no real way of knowing how 'representative' the year 1764 was for the transit trade with Chinese goods through the Russian Empire. Therefore, their inclusion seems to be the only right thing to do.

The largest quantities of Chinese goods were exported from Vasylkiv and Dobryansk, two toll stations that were strongly connected to the commodity flows passing through Nezhin. The 1764 toll registers of Dobryansk reveal that small quantities of damasks (*kitajki*) in different colours were sent from Nezhin to Danzig and Zelva, a White Russian place on the way to Grodno, and from Borzna, east of Nezhin, to Bogdaniec, which could refer to a Polish settlement on the Warthe, located west of Landsberg, or in the vicinity of Białystok.[84] Furthermore, some high-quality Chinese green tea (*džulan*) was exported from Nezhin to Danzig via Dobryansk.[85] Exports of Chinese goods to Poland-Lithuania via the toll station of Vasylkiv, located south of Kyiv, not only served a different region, they were of a different magnitude as well.[86] Chinese goods had a 45% share in the total value of exports from Vasylkiv in 1764, which clearly indicates that this toll station was located on a specialist route between China and the southernmost parts of Poland-Lithuania. The variety of Chinese goods exported via Vasylkiv was similar to that of Dobryansk and included different kinds of *kitajki*. For the most part, they went from Nezhin, Kyiv, and Romny through Vasylkiv to Brody and Berdichiv. Similarly, green (*džulan*) and other tea was sent from Kyiv and Nezhin to Brody and Berdichiv.

Chinese goods were also exported to Poland-Lithuania from Central rather than South Russia via the frontier posts (Ru. *zastava*) and toll stations of the Shelegovskaya *zastava* (Shelegovka) near Smolensk and the Boyevskaya *zastava* near Vitebsk.[87] The latter was a relatively small toll station through which Chinese goods were exported from Moscow and Toropets to Nevel, Velizh, Vitebsk, and Shklov, an important fair on the river Dnepr in the Mohylew district. Besides the obligatory *kitajki*, green tea was transferred via Boyevskaya as well, leading to a 40%-share of Chinese goods in the total value at customs of its exports. At Shelegovka, the share of Chinese goods in the value of exports to Poland-Lithuania was even greater than in Vasylkiv (see above), but the volume was only half as large. Chinese goods constituted more than 60% of the total export value at Shelegovka. *Kitajki* dominated the exports, but in contrast to the South Russian toll stations, the share of Chinese tea was much larger. Chinese goods came in via Moscow, Smolensk, and Toropets and left Shelegovka mostly for Shklov. Finally, small quantities of Chinese goods were also exported to Central Asia via Astrakhan and to Western Europe via St. Petersburg.[88]

With easier access to the data, much more could be said about the commodity flows entering, exiting, and traversing North Eurasia. But even the succinct survey above should have made clear that North Eurasian commodity flows were confined neither to the immediate hinterland of Russia's Baltic ports nor to European Russia alone. A significant part originated in the vast Siberian territories east of the Ural Mountains; a much smaller, but perhaps not less significant part went in transit through Russia from Persia, Central Asia, and China. Again, it seems that the perceived significance of these flows must have been higher than what the actual registered values at customs suggest. Logically then, both Russia's role as predominant political and economic actor in North Eurasia and the economic interests of foreign parties eager to obtain North Eurasian products had an important impact on the course of international relations after the 1721 Treaty of Nystadt.

British advances in North Eurasian trade

Friction and rapprochement

In 1720, the rupture of Anglo-Russian diplomatic relations was the inevitable result of the previous decades of double-faced British diplomacy (see Chapter 3). The sources of friction between Russia and Great Britain were large: besides Sweden, interests conflicted with regard to Mecklenburg and Schleswig-Holstein as well.[89] Despite the diplomatic crisis between Great Britain and Russia at the end of the Great Northern War (in 1720–1721), governmental decrees issued at the time repeatedly pointed out the freedom of British trade with Russia.[90] Anglo-Russian trade was affected partially. British imports from Russia continued, whereas British exports to Russia experienced a marked decline in the years following the Treaty of Nystadt (1721). At least in part, this decline was caused by the fact that the British started to pay in currency for the naval stores exported from Russian ports in the Baltic.[91] Moreover, Prussian competition in woollen cloth deliveries to Russia and the restoration of Armenian privileges in the trans-Russian Persian trade also affected British imports to Russia negatively.[92] Prussian woollen cloth supplies to Russia increased under the impulse of a plan to develop Russo-Prussian trade by means of the foundation of a "Russian Company" in Berlin.[93] This company was founded after Prussian merchants had managed to obtain a contract for the delivery of soldier's cloth to Russia in 1724.[94] Armenian transit trade through Russia collapsed during the Russo-Persian war (1722–1725) and led to a temporary reorientation of commodity flows to British-controlled ports in the Persian Gulf.[95] After the Russo-Persian war, a new *ukaz* regarding the Armenian company was issued, which granted a tax reduction on silk and other Persian goods imported by the Armenians of New Julfa via Astrakhan.'[96] The Russo-Persian treaty of 1732 consolidated the Armenians' special treatment, and the latter regained their former predominance in the trans-Russian Persian trade. Moreover, the treaty of Rasht foresaw the free passage of Russian merchants to Persia and their transit to India, but it is unlikely that these privileges could make up for the loss of the southern coast of the Caspian Sea to Persia.[97]

The prohibitive customs tariff of 1724, which highly taxed the raw materials export from the Russian interior and stipulated that customs were to be paid in hard currency, marked the start of a decade of attempts to negotiate better conditions for British trade with Russia.[98] In February 1726, a British demand to lower the taxes on raw materials exports and exempt them from paying duties in hard currency was partially met.[99] In the meantime, after the death of Peter the Great (1725), suspicion arose among the British that Russia may plan an invasion in northern Germany in the summer of 1726. For the tenth time in 14 years, the British sent a fleet to the Baltic in order to safeguard its commercial interests.[100] The naval expedition of 1727 was paralleled by changes on the throne in Great Britain as well as in Russia and led to a reversal in British policy and diplomacy.[101] Russia now expressed its interest in active cooperation with Great Britain and issued several declarations concerning the freedom of British commerce.[102] Britain welcomed this policy change. Not only had "most of the existing basis for Anglo-Russian hostility disappeared" after the death of George I and Catherine I, Great Britain had come to terms with the fact that it would be "[u]nable to force back the Russians into their former international position (…)."[103] Moreover, Great Britain was well aware of the increasing competition from the side of Prussia and Austria. The Austro-Russian offensive and defensive alliance of 1726 and the Russo-Prussian defensive alliance of the same year had alarmed Great Britain.[104]

The 1726 alliance included three Austrian *desiderata*, which underline how the Baltic had become an integral part of concerns with global trade and commodity flows. Besides an arrangement favouring the Silesian textile-manufacturing sector as supplier for the Russian army rather than its British and Prussian counterpart,[105] Austria wished to obtain a dispensation for the Ostend Company to trade with China and Persia through Russia.[106] The latter collided strongly with British interests in Russia and provided an impetus for the reconciliation of Anglo-Russian relations in the closing years of the 1720s. Probably, it also played a role in the re-establishment of Anglo-Austrian friendship through the British guarantee of the Pragmatic Sanction in 1730–1731, which led to the dissolution of the Ostend Company and thus annulled this particular threat.

Great Britain had no intention to be pushed out of the lucrative woollen cloth market by Prussia and used the dynastic changes of 1727 to intensify its treaty negotiations with Russia. In 1728, Prussia promised, "to give Muscovy a free port in Pomerania for the importation of Muscovite raw materials, if only the military cloth contracts were drawn up with the Berlin Company for a reasonable period."[107] Great Britain reacted quickly with the re-opening of its consulate in St. Petersburg, after which the Berlin Company decided to establish an office in St. Petersburg as well.[108] The competition of Prussia and Great Britain for the Russian cloth market increased further. Between 1730 and 1734, they both supplied woollen cloth to Russia, which refused to sign formal contracts before delivery of the cloth.[109]

From about 1730 onwards, the British treaty negotiations with Russia went into their final phase.[110] Although Russia's repeated requests for British concessions in political affairs (e.g. during the Polish Succession in 1733) caused considerable delay,[111] the Anglo-Russian treaty of friendship and commerce was finally signed in December 1734.[112] The *traité d'amitié et de commerce*[113] was the result of long negotiations between the Russian Empire and Great Britain, in which the latter refused to sign a treaty of alliance, arguing that a treaty of commerce would be more beneficial to both parties.[114] Significantly, throughout the drafts and negotiations, Great Britain threatened to move their business to the American colonies unless Russia would refrain from making its political ambitions part of the deal.[115] A 1732 British memorandum about the needs of English trade in Russia expressed a similar threat.[116] Under item 14, greatly exaggerating the actual position of British trade with Russia and obviously mistaking trade at St. Petersburg or 'Russian trade,' the memorandum states that

> (...) British trade (...) [in Russia] was equal to all other branches of trade combined, and yet the British had the mortification of seeing another country preferred; Russia yearly bought great quantities of soldiers' cloth from [Prussia], while the English had similar goods lying on their hands. This cloth, which could be provided cheaper and better by England than any other nation, ought to be bought from England. Otherwise, this nation would unavoidably have to procure its naval stores from its own plantations.[117]

Only threats from the part of Great Britain to start producing 'Russian' goods in its North American territories led to the finalization of the negotiations for an Anglo-Russian commercial treaty.[118]

The Anglo-Russian commercial treaty

The treaty stipulated freedom of navigation and commerce between Great Britain and Russia.[119] Both nations agreed to treat each other as 'most favoured nation.' Among other things, the treaty contained articles solving the issues of Prussian competition and the Persian transit trade.[120] The freedom of navigation and commerce extended not only to ships and other means of transportation anywhere in both countries, but also to raw materials and finished goods, including Asian goods.[121] British merchants obtained the right to transit goods to and from Persia via Russia upon payment of a 3% ad valorem duty, like the Armenians,[122] and on the condition of hiring Russian transport services at a fair price for executing the transit of the goods through the Russian interior.[123] Moreover, British subjects were allowed to pay customs in roubles at a fixed exchange rate of 1.25 roubles per thaler (*Ru.* efimok). Besides being advantageous for British merchants compared to their competitors who were obliged to settle their customs duties in hard currency, the fixed exchange rate carried the promise of future profits in case the rouble would decline against the *efimok*, but was beneficial for the Russian treasury at least for as long as it was higher than the actual exchange rate.[124] Finally, Great Britain obtained a number of tax benefits for its imports to Russia: 2% per arshine on soldiers' cloth (*Ru.* soldatskoe sukno), which finally gave British merchants a competitive advantage over Prussia,[125] 2% per arshine on *drap de la Comté de York* (known in Russia as *kostroži*), 1% per arshine on *flanelle large*, and 0.75% per arshine on *flanelle étroite*.[126] Since Russia signed no further commercial treaties within any Western European countries after 1734, Great Britain found itself in a comfortable position to consolidate its vital Russian connection.

Two aspects of the British transit rights for commerce with Persia require further attention. On the one hand, British interests were by no means limited to Persia alone, but spread to all of Central Asia. This becomes clear in the participation of British members of the Russia Company in commercial missions to Orenburg and the Khanates in the early 1730s.[127] On the other, the efforts of the British Russia Company to obtain transit rights to Persia took place in the context of an enduring battle between British monopolist companies and proponents of freedom of trade. The internal struggle between the large British monopolist companies active in the 'Eastern trade' predated the Anglo-Russian commercial treaty, but obtained new vigour in the wake of its conclusion. According to opponents of the treaty, the entire content of Article VIII was illegal and conflicted with both the Navigation Act of 1660 and the privileges granted to the Levant Company and the EIC.[128] Apparently, the British government regarded the Persian transit trade through Russia as "(...) sufficiently important first to secure it by treaty from St. Petersburg and then to settle the legal issue afterward."[129] This explains why the rights granted by the Anglo-Russian commercial treaty of 1734 could not be exploited immediately by British merchants: a necessary change in British regulations was blocked by the British Levant Company, which feared to lose its monopoly on Persian silk exports via Turkey to the British Russia Company.[130] In June 1741, after initial travels and negotiations in Persia by the illustrious John Elton,[131] the Russia Company obtained legal rights to trade in Persia from British parliament, despite protests from the Turkey Company.[132] At the same time, British merchants in Russia had obtained several additional rights and privileges, such as the right of shipbuilding in Kazan on the Volga and a number of privileges for passage and cargo handling in St. Petersburg, Astrakhan, Saratov, and Tsaritsyn.[133] In 1741, the Russian Collegium of Commerce even considered granting British merchants a privilege to export Persian and Russian commodities via Azov and Ochakiv on the Black Sea coast.[134] From then on, British transit trade with Persia via the Russian Empire rapidly pushed Russian trade with Persia out of the market.[135] Starting 1742, the British even had their own ships sailing the Caspian Sea between the Persian coast and Astrakhan.[136]

Within a few years' time, the Anglo-Russian commercial treaty and a 1738 prohibition on cloth deliveries from Prussia and the Russian Empire contributed to the collapse of the Berlin Company.[137] Moreover, unaccustomed to foreign competition, the Armenian transit trade through Russia was shaken badly by the extensive British transit rights. Protests from Armenian and Russian merchants against British competition became louder and soon they resorted to "political intrigue and a thousand and one subterfuges to weaken the British position."[138] John Elton's actions annoyed Russian and Armenian merchants, who accused him of contraband and – more seriously – of secretly developing Persian military power on the Caspian Sea.[139] When Elton started to cause too much trouble, Britain sent Jonas Hanway (...) to Persia "in an effort to settle the increasing dissension between English and Russians there and more especially to dissuade Elton from his hare-brained military employment under the Shah."[140] Hanway's mission was unsuccessful. Elton continued his business with the Shah and the Russian government finally decided to abrogate Article VIII on 13 December 1746.[141] As it had been the case with the Armenian merchants in 1673, enduring Russian complaints – in combination with worsening diplomatic relations with Persia[142] – led to the prohibition of British transit trade with Persia in 1746 and the annulment of the corresponding article in the Anglo-Russian commercial treaty.[143] The remainder of the treaty remained intact, but with the abrogation of Article VIII; the "promising development of an important British cotton trade with northern China via Russia was lost,"[144] and the Armenians could regain control of trans-Caspian commerce.[145] Even so, Britain retained significant advantages in all aspects of Russia's foreign trade. British merchants received beneficial treatment from the Russian government, became involved in Russian state business,[146] and some established textile and tow manufactures, sugar refineries and timber mills on Russian soil. They prepared British overseas goods (sugar) for consumption in the Russian Empire and processed Russia's resources to meet Britain's incessant demand for naval stores.[147]

French reaction

Despite its failure in trans-Russian Persian trade, Britain's advantages in Russia's foreign trade hardly remained uncontested. France waited for an opportunity to break its long-standing rival's increasingly strong position in Russia's foreign trade. With the outbreak of the Seven Years' War and the expectations attached to Russia's anticipated gains in the Black Sea, the time seemed ripe for France to try and reverse the existing order of North Eurasian trade. The international political constellation was complex. In 1756, Great Britain was at war with France in its overseas territories, when the Prussian King Fredrick II entered Saxony with his troops on his way to attack his long-standing rival Austria.[148] Russia took the opportunity that arose from the Prussian attack on Saxony and Austria to react in accordance with the 1746 (renewed) defensive alliance with the latter, which foresaw a Russian response in the case of Prussian aggression. At the end of 1756, Russia joined the neutrality convention and defensive alliance of Versailles,[149] which itself was the result of a diplomatic revolution and *renversement des alliances* earlier that year. The former archenemies France and Habsburg now allied against Great Britain and Prussia. The latter parties had signed a treaty of guarantee in the convention of Westminster in January 1756. The guarantee was meant to avoid warfare on the European continent, but instead, it provoked the emergence of a new bond of France, Austria and Russia in the course of 1756. Russia's own intentions went far beyond the mere adherence to the principles of neutrality and the defence of Austrian territories. The (secret) protocols of the conference of the Russian Imperial Court in 1756, which were published 1912,[150] provide a detailed insight into the underlying goals of Russian diplomacy around the mid-1750s.

The main reasons of the Russian Empire for reacting against the Prussian aggression in Saxony lied in the prospect of strategic territorial gains during the war. First, Russia wanted to break the growing power of the Prussian King. According to Maksim Yuryevich Anisimov, Russia had already started its preparations for war against Prussia in 1753.[151] Second, Russia anticipated an exchange of territories with Poland-Lithuania: Courland would become Russian and Poland-Lithuania would receive East Prussia in exchange.[152] This plan, of course, was based on the assumption that Russia would be able to occupy and retain East Prussia during its anti-Prussian military actions. Reality turned out to be quite different. The Russians applied military force in the Baltic to occupy East Prussia in 1758 and would govern it until 1762.[153] They also made several unsuccessful attempts to occupy Danzig and Kolberg.[154] Eventually, although Russia had already negotiated with Austria to keep East Prussia rather than return it to Poland-Lithuania,[155] the Russian troops withdrew.[156] Third, Russia expected to gain access to the Black Sea and planned to incorporate Ukrainian territories into the Empire. This, in turn, would bring the Russian Empire in a good position to strengthen the anti-Turkish coalition, on the one hand, and to redirect commodity flows from the Baltic to the Black Sea, on the other. Finally yet importantly, the secret protocol forecasted that, after having gained access to the Black Sea, Russia would be able to take control of almost the entire Levant trade.[157]

It is the latter point, in particular, in which France saw an opportunity to weaken Britain's commercial dominance in Russia. Even a partial redirection of commodity flows from ports in the Baltic to ports on the Black Sea coast would set free France's significant locational advantages. The boost of French diplomatic activity at the courts of Constantinople and St. Petersburg hardly comes as a surprise. Le Duc de Choiseul, the head of French foreign policy from 1758 until 1770, argued that Russia should be convinced to enter into a defensive alliance against Britain first, before a commercial treaty would seal the deal and break Britain's commercial dominance in Russia.[158] Russia itself also had high expectations of its anticipated territorial gains in the southern part of the Empire. In fact, Russia had never given up previous claims on the coast of the Sea of Azov and the Black Sea (see Chapter 3). It continued to develop ideas about commerce via the Black Sea throughout the first half of the eighteenth century.[159] The war of Austria and Russia against the Ottoman Empire and the related treaty negotiations at the congress of Nemirov (1737)[160] made clear to the French consul in Constantinople that one of the economic reasons for this war was to regain access to the north-eastern corner of the Sea of Azov.[161] In the end, the congress of Nemirov was unsuccessful and the peace treaty of Belgrade (1739) left Russia's position in the Black Sea almost unchanged. Although the Porte maintained its rule of the Black Sea and the Sea of Azov, Russia was allowed to re-establish its civilian presence in Azov and Taganrog and navigate the Black Sea using Ottoman ships.[162] During the 30 years that followed the peace treaty of Belgrade, the Russian Empire strengthened its presence in the territories near the Black Sea, promoted their colonization, militarized the region, and thus prepared its 'crushing victory' and the fundamental turn in the regional balance of power, which would occur during the war with the Ottoman Empire between 1768 and 1774 (see Chapter 5).[163]

In the mid-1740s, the Russian residents in Constantinople, Aleksey Andreevich Veshnyakov (1700–1745) and Adrian Ivanovich Neplyuyev (1712–1750) elaborated far-reaching plans for the development of Russian trade via the Black Sea.[164] Interestingly, they received instructions to approach the Italian States first and point out the benefits of direct trade with Russia via the Black Sea to them: It would give the Italians the opportunity to bypass the intermediacy of British and Dutch merchants.[165] Moreover, it was assumed that the establishment of Black Sea trade would incline the British Levant company to avoid the Mediterranean (and the Barbary pirates), and move to the Baltic instead for conducting transit trade with Persia via Russia.[166] Neplyuyev's more pragmatic plans included, among other things, the construction of ports in Taganrog and Cherkassk.[167] However, as long as the Ottoman Porte refused to let ships with foreign flags pass through the Bosporus, all of these plans and ideas were doomed to remain unrealized.[168]

Even so, however, these very plans show the ongoing Russian concern with the grand direction of North Eurasian commodity flows. In 1757, the Russian envoy in Constantinople, Obreskov, was – again – asked to negotiate free passage through the Bosporus for the Russian merchant fleet.[169] This attempt was backed by the foundation of a privileged company for Russia's Black Sea trade at the mouth of the river Temernik, near present-day Rostov-on-Don.[170] Parallel to the foundation of this company, commercial treaty negotiations were started with France and the Republic of Venice.[171] In 1760, Étienne François, le Duc de Choiseul (1719–1785) submitted a proposal for the establishment of a French company for the Russian trade, which would buy in Russia "(…) Ukrainian tobacco, hemp and flax, [i.e.] those goods that the French are forced to buy from their enemies even in wartime (…)."[172] Although the Black Sea company of Temernik was unsuccessful and therefore dissolved in 1762,[173] it bears witness of Russia's intentions with regard to the Black Sea as well as the international trading activities between Cossacks, Russians, Ottomans and Greeks, which already took place in southern Russia prior to the groundbreaking Treaty of Küçük Kajnarca in 1774 (see Chapter 5).

In the meantime, since 1757, Great Britain and Russia had started to negotiate the renewal of their 1734 commercial treaty. The debates between both parties lasted for about ten years, overlapped with Russia's involvement in the Seven Years' War (which hardly affected Anglo-Russian trade),[174] and showed the increasing self-consciousness of the Russian Empire in matters concerning their international trade.[175] In light of the Seven Years' War and the threat of disturbance of trade through the Danish Sound, the Russian Empire wanted to decrease its dependence on British ships, and preferred to use Swedish and Danish ships to supply its troops in Prussia. This, of course, collided with British interests, as Russia's proposals came nowhere near the British search to extend its existing advantages and ignored the British desire to put the famous article about transit trade back on the table.[176] Only when the 1764 Prusso-Russian treaty revived British fears of being eclipsed by Prussian (Silesian) woollen cloth imports to Russia, as had happened in the 1720s, the treaty negotiations went into their final phase. Russia showed its good will by replacing some of the ancient privileges of Riga merchants (against which Britain had occasionally complained) with a new commercial regulation (*Ger.* Handels-Ordnung) and made some concessions to British merchants active in the timber and iron trades.[177] Britain, in turn, had to accept that – again – transit rights for Asian goods would not make it into the treaty.[178] A new Anglo-Russian commercial treaty was finally signed in 1766.

This chapter has shown that the development of transport infrastructure in the Russian interior, the wide-ranging efforts to promote St. Petersburg as a new gateway to North Eurasia at the expense of Arkhangelsk, and the promotion of industrial development in North-West and Central Russia as well as in the Ural Mountains, led to the emergence of new patterns of distribution and trade in North Eurasia. First of all, the shift of foreign trade from the coast of the White Sea to the Baltic forced Russian and foreign merchants alike to restructure their business. As a result, St. Petersburg could assume a leading role in Russia's foreign trade within a remarkably short period. Second, the former Swedish ports in the Baltic obtained different roles under Russian rule. These changes affected Baltic trade as a whole and strengthened the complementarity of ports in the Baltic in the first half of the eighteenth century. Although some ports dealt with similar commodities, regional specialization prevailed. The latter, in turn, affected the structure of the import and export trade of the main proponents of Baltic commercial exchange: the Dutch Republic and Great Britain. Rather than being competitors, their involvement in Baltic commercial exchange had distinct characteristics.

Although the significance of the infrastructural developments initiated after the foundation of St. Petersburg should not be underestimated, construction works and plans to create an infrastructure of land routes, rivers, and canals were developed almost exclusively with the 'two capitals' in mind. The enduring efforts to establish and sustain the centrality of St. Petersburg as the main gateway of Russia's foreign trade produced mixed results. On the one hand, the new capital of the Russian Empire was indeed connected to a wide hinterland stretching all the way to the Russo-Chinese border in Kyakhta. On the other, there were only few alternatives for the transportation of goods to St. Petersburg; insofar as water transportation was concerned, the system of waterways connecting St. Petersburg to the Volga river basin via the canal of Vyshny Volochyok did not have an alternative.

Further evidence for the enduring role and consolidation of the Baltic as an area of vested interest was found in the reversing alliances that marked the beginning and end of the Seven Years' War (1756–1763), in the long diplomatic negotiations about East Prussia, which had been occupied by the Russian army shortly after the outbreak of the war, and in the different meanings attached to the concept of 'neutrality' by the belligerents. The latter, in particular, marked the dawn of a new era in Baltic commercial exchange that would last until the early nineteenth century. The main proponents of the French-Indian War (1754–1763) and the Seven Years' War also acquired the biggest gains. Great Britain established itself as the leading overseas economic power, confirmed its status as the strongest navy of the world and benefited from rapidly increasing revenues from foreign trade, whereas on the continent, Prussia secured its earlier territorial gains in Central Europe and became one of the leading powers in European politics. After the Seven Years' War, a new international constellation determined the structure of Baltic commercial exchange for the remainder of the century.

Notes

1 For more information about the 1758 declaration and 1759 convention, see Anisimov, *Semiletnjaja vojna*, 49; 326–339. On the legal concept of neutrality and its development during the eighteenth century and – in particular – during the Seven Years' War, see Kulsrud, *Maritime neutrality to 1780*; Helfman, "Neutrality"; Helfman, "Commerce on trial."
2 *Tetradas* [VSWG-JDA], 8_CIES_Bex_FS: *Barley, Oats, Rye, Wheat*; 7_PIES_Amsterdam: *Exports of foodstuffs.*
3 Israel, *Dutch primacy in world trade*; and the discussion in volume 106 of the Low Countries Historical review: Van Zanden, "Een fraaie synthese"; Noordegraaf, "Vooruit en achteruit"; Israel, "The 'new history'."
4 *Tetradas* [VSWG-JDA], 8_CIES_Bex_FS: *Barley, Oats, Rye, Wheat.*
5 *Tetradas* [VSWG-JDA], 5_BIE: *Netherlands, United Kingdom.*
6 Visually by far the most attractive elaboration of the metaphor is: Gorbatenko, *Novyj Amsterdam.*
7 Reading, *The Anglo-Russian commercial treaty*, 39–40.
8 Veluwenkamp, *Archangel*; Repin, "Ot diskriminacii k fritrederstvu," 228–249; Čulkov, *Istoričeskoe opisanie rossijskoj kommercii*, I (2), 107; Repin, "Izmenenie," 175–192; Repin, "Učastie kupečestva," 177–199. An account of Russian exports from Arkhangelsk in the early eighteenth century can be found in: De Buck, "De Russische uitvoer uit Archangel," 136–142.
9 Repin, "Izmenenie," 175–192; Repin, "Ot diskriminacii k fritrederstvu," 228–249.
10 Scheltjens, "The influence of spatial change."
11 *Armjano-russkie otnošenija*, II (1), 28–30; PSZ, IV, 2192; 2356; 2490; 2609.
12 *Armjano-russkie otnošenija*, II (1), 42–53.
13 PSZ, V, 3385.
14 Semenov, *Izuchenie istoricheskikh svedenii*, II (3), 21.
15 Čulkov, *Istoričeskoe opisanie rossijskoj kommercii*, I (2), 55–56. From a Dutch rather than a North Eurasian perspective, the following overview of the changing laws and regulations has been described previously in: Scheltjens, *De invloed*, 133–137 and 155–156.
16 Čulkov, *Istoričeskoe opisanie rossijskoj kommercii*, V (2), 100–103; 109; 111–112.
17 Repin, "Izmenenie," 181; Čulkov, *Istoričeskoe opisanie rossijskoj kommercii*, I (2), 46.
18 Repin, "Izmenenie," 181; PSZ, V, 2784.
19 Čulkov, *Istoričeskoe opisanie rossijskoj kommercii*, I (2), 61; Repin, "Izmenenie," 181; PSZ, V, 3051, 3115, 3268.
20 Repin, "Ot diskriminacii k fritrederstvu," 231; Čulkov, *Istoričeskoe opisanie rossijskoj kommercii*, I (2), 107.
21 Demkin, *Britanskoe kupečestvo*, 13–15; 17–18. The actual number of merchants and issues of identiying them are subject of ongoing debate in Russian historiography, see Demkin, *Britanskoe kupečestvo*, 15; Zacharov, *Zapadnoevropejskie kupcy*, 100–130.
22 An overview is given in: Veluwenkamp, "Dutch merchants"; Zacharov, *Zapadnoevropejskie kupcy*, 130–142.
23 Hovinga, "In dienst van de Republiek"; Eekman, "Seven years with Peter the Great"; Van Koningsbrugge, "Van kwaad tot erger."
24 Demkin, *Britanskoe kupečestvo*, 33–34.
25 Čulkov, *Istoričeskoe opisanie rossijskoj kommercii*, V (2), 132.
26 Čulkov, *Istoričeskoe opisanie rossijskoj kommercii*, V (2), 117–118.
27 PSZ, XVI, 11630.
28 Semenov, *Izuchenie istoricheskikh svedenii*, II (3), 21–31.

29 PSZ, VI, 3860; Repin, "Ot diskriminacii k fritrederstvu," 231; Čulkov, *Istoričeskoe opisanie rossijskoj kommercii*, I (2), 103–105.
30 Čulkov, *Istoričeskoe opisanie rossijskoj kommercii*, V (2), 118.
31 Čulkov, *Istoričeskoe opisanie rossijskoj kommercii*, V (2), 174; PSZ, VI, 3860; Repin, "Ot diskriminacii k fritrederstvu," 231; Semenov, *Izuchenie istoricheskikh svedenii*, I, 58–59.
32 The location of the provinces is described as follows: "... Provincii, kotorye prilegli (...) k vodjanomu chodu Dviny *bez perevolok zemleju*." This literally means that no passages over land (barrages) were allowed during transportation of goods to Arkhangelsk.
33 Čulkov, *Istoričeskoe opisanie rossijskoj kommercii*, V (2), 118–119.
34 Čulkov, *Istoričeskoe opisanie rossijskoj kommercii*, V (2), 123–124.
35 Semenov, *Izuchenie istoricheskikh svedenii*, I, 58.
36 *Tarif sanktpeterburgskogo, vyborgskogo, narvskogo, archangelogorodskogo, kol'skogo portov*, 47–81.
37 Repin, "Ot diskriminacii k fritrederstvu," 231–232; Čulkov, *Istoričeskoe opisanie rossijskoj kommercii*, I (2), 108–109; V (2), 129–132.
38 Demkin, *Britanskoe kupečestvo*, 19.
39 Matley, "Defense manufactures of St. Petersburg," 418–423.
40 Åström, *From tar to timber*; Åström, "Technology and timber exports," 1–14.
41 *Tetradas* [VSWG-JDA], 8_CIES_Bex_RM: *Balks, Boards, Deals, Staves*; 7_PIES_Narva: *Exports of raw materials*; 7_PIES_StPetersburg: *Exports of raw materials*; 7_PIES_Vyborg: *Exports of raw materials.*
42 Demkin, *Vnešnjaja torgovlja. Vedomost' ob importe.*
43 Čulkov, *Istoričeskoe opisanie rossijskoj kommercii*, I (2), 127–128; V (2), 180–183; Repin, "Ot diskriminacii k fritrederstvu," 234–235; Nekrasov, *Rol' Rossii*, 23–24.
44 Repin, "Ot diskriminacii k fritrederstvu," 238–239.
45 Wallace, "Entrepreneurship," 8–9.
46 PSZ, IV, 1826.
47 PSZ, IV, 1840.
48 PSZ, IV, 2387; V, 3086.
49 Petrov, *Istorija Sankt-Peterburga*, 57.
50 PSZ, IV, 2312; IX, 6372. See also: Stuckenberg, *Beschreibung*.
51 For a detailed survey of these efforts and their impact on the connectivity of the port of St. Petersburg with its hinterland, see Jones, "Getting the goods to St. Petersburg," 413–433.
52 Blackwell, *The beginnings*, Chapter 1; Matley, "Defense manufactures of St. Petersburg," 411–426; Kahan, "Entrepreneurship in the early development of iron manufactories," 395–422; Wallace, "Entrepreneurship and the Russian textile industry," 1–25.
53 Matley, "Defense manufactures of St. Petersburg," 415–416.
54 Kahan, "Entrepreneurship in the early development of iron manufactories," 401.
55 Matley, "Defense manufactures of St. Petersburg," 420–423; Jones, "Getting the goods."
56 PSZ, V, 3228.
57 PSZ, XI, 8313, 8316, 8398, 8521.
58 PSZ, VI, 3860; X, 7631; XI, 8036, 8115, 8181. As with other efforts to 'modernize' Russia, Sweden served as an example for the construction of roads as well. See PSZ, VII, 4568.
59 PSZ, VIII, 5573.
60 PSZ, III, 1518, 1594, 1665.
61 PSZ, XIV, 10302; XV, 11073.

62 PSZ, VI, 3484; 4025.
63 PSZ, VIII, 6145; 6199; XVII, 12579.
64 Matley, "Defense manufactures of St. Petersburg," 411–426.
65 [s.n.], *Polnaja istorija Nižegorodskoj jarmarki*, 22.
66 In slightly different wording, the following information about the development of markets and fairs in North Eurasia has been published previously in: Scheltjens, "North-Eurasian fairs."
67 PSZ, VI, 3708, chapters XVII and XVIII.
68 PSZ, VIII, 5306.
69 PSZ, IX, 6583, 6964.
70 PSZ, VIII, 5573.
71 PSZ, VIII, 5773.
72 PSZ, XIV, 10695.
73 PSZ, XIII, 9609, 9663, 9958.
74 Mironov, *Vnutrennij rynok*, 62.
75 PSZ, XIV, 10486.
76 At the same time, however, the total number of fairs in the Russian Empire increased to 627 in the 1750s, but for the most part these so-called fairs were in fact just regular markets of local and regional importance. See Mironov, *Vnutrennij rynok*, 62.
77 Rossijskij Gosudarstvennyj Archiv Drevnich Aktov (Russian State Archive of Ancient Documents – further RGADA), F. 277 (Manufaktur-Kollegija), Op. 3, Dela 619–631. For a short description of this archive, see Scheltjens, 'Russia: 1758–1766.' Of this collection, only the customs registers of St. Petersburg for the year 1764 have been published in print: Demkin, *Vnešnjaja torgovlja. Vedomost' ob importe*; Demkin, *Vnešnjaja torgovlja. Vedomost' ob ėksporte*. For a descriptive account of the commodities of Anglo-Russian trade, which constituted a major part of Russia's foreign trade, see Demkin, *Britanskoe kupečestvo*, 46–94.
78 Demkin, *Vnešnjaja torgovlja. Vedomost' ob ėksporte*, 112–113.
79 Nebolsin, *Statističeskoe obozrenie*, II, 7–12.
80 Nebolsin, *Statističeskoe obozrenie*, II, 114–115.
81 Heller, "Der russisch-chinesische Handel in Kjachta," 515–536.
82 RGADA, F. 277, Op. 3, Delo 626, f. 452–466.
83 RGADA, F. 277, Op. 3, Delo 626, f. 414–425.
84 RGADA, F. 277, Op. 3, Delo 626, f. 416.
85 RGADA, F. 277, Op. 3, Delo 626, f. 423.
86 RGADA, F. 277, Op. 3, Delo 626, f. 376–410.
87 RGADA, F. 277, Op. 3, Delo 626, f. 362–373; 468–478.
88 In 1764, no cotton and silk manufactures were exported from Arkhangelsk. The only 'Chinese good' exported from Arkhangelsk in 1764 was tea, but its quantity was negligible: one pood and 12 pounds, worth 75 roubles and 50 kopecks. From the port of Riga, six *kitajki* were exported. From St. Petersburg 81 pood of green tea with a total value of 4,071 roubles and 87 kopecks were exported to London (28 pood), Lübeck (24 pood), Amsterdam (nine pood), Stettin (seven pood) and other ports on the Baltic and North Seas. See RGADA, F. 277, Op. 3, Delo 626; Demkin, *Vnešnjaja torgovlja. Vedomost' ob ėksporte*, 112.
89 Peter the Great wanted to exploit his dynastic influence in Holstein to reunite the Duchies under the Duke of Holstein, who was married to Peter's daughter Anna. This, in turn, would improve Russia's position towards Denmark and create opportunities to

> (...) apply effective pressure upon Denmark through Holstein toward a reduction of the sound-duty upon Russian merchandise. At the same time, Great

Britain had signed a secret agreement with Denmark about Schleswig, in which it had promised to return Schleswig to Denmark in return for having purchased Bremen and Verden from the Danes.

(Reading, *The Anglo-Russian commercial treaty*, 91–92)

90 Demkin, *Britanskoe kupečestvo*, 18; Reading, *The Anglo-Russian commercial treaty*, 41.
91 Reading, *The Anglo-Russian commercial treaty*, 90–91.
92 Reading, *The Anglo-Russian commercial treaty*, 91; Erkinger, *Die armenische Diaspora*, 80–82.
93 Reading, *The Anglo-Russian commercial treaty*, 273–279.
94 Hinrichs, *Die Wollindustrie in Preußen*, 213–216.
95 Reading, *The Anglo-Russian commercial treaty*, 228.
96 PSZ, VII, 5086.
97 Reading, *The Anglo-Russian commercial treaty*, 228–229; Nekrasov, *Rol' Rossii*, 80–81.
98 Described *in extenso* in: Reading, *The Anglo-Russian commercial treaty*, 60–155; Demkin, *Russko-britanskie torgovye otnošenija*, 4–5; 14–21; Demkin, *Britanskoe kupečestvo*, 18–19.
99 Demkin, *Britanskoe kupečestvo*, 19.
100 Nekrasov, *Rol' Rossii*, 62–64.
101 Reading, *The Anglo-Russian commercial treaty*, 92–94.
102 Nekrasov, *Rol' Rossii*, 72–73 and 141–142; Martens, *Receuil des traités et conventions IX (X)*, 45–62.
103 Reading, *The Anglo-Russian commercial treaty*, 94–98. See also: Nekrasov, *Rol' Rossii*, 153–156.
104 Nekrasov, *Rol' Rossii*, 46–47; Reading, *The Anglo-Russian commercial treaty*, 94–95; 108. The Austro-Russian alliance

(...) was so well founded upon hard fact and reason that it was to survive the Franco-Austrian rapprochement of 1756, the aggrandizement of Prussia, and all the other revolutions of European politics; even the partitions of Poland, which first threatened to dissolve it, only ended by strengthening and confirming it.

(Reading, *The Anglo-Russian commercial treaty*, 108)

105 Droysen, *Geschichte der preussischen Politik*, IV (2), 195.
106 Reading, *The Anglo-Russian commercial treaty*, 95.
107 Reading, *The Anglo-Russian commercial treaty*, 283.
108 Reading, *The Anglo-Russian commercial treaty*, 283–284.
109 Reading, *The Anglo-Russian commercial treaty*, 286–288.
110 Demkin, *Britanskoe kupečestvo*, 20–22; Demkin, *Russko-britanskie torgovye otnošenija*, 22–30.
111 Reading, *The Anglo-Russian commercial treaty*, 102–103; 125–155.
112 Demkin, *Britanskoe kupečestvo*, 20.
113 Martens, *Receuil des traités et conventions IX (X)*, 62–89.
114 Martens, *Receuil des traités et conventions IX (X)*, 71.
115 Reading, *The Anglo-Russian commercial treaty*, 145:

Generally, Walpole said, the present situation was very unfavorable for a political union with Russia in that the Polish affair had already disturbed the North and the king must wait until this was settled. If the Russians kept on insisting upon this political alliance as a condition of the treaty, England would have to turn to her American colonies for her naval supplies.

116 Reading, *The Anglo-Russian commercial treaty*, 117.

117 Reading, *The Anglo-Russian commercial treaty*, 119.
118 Martens, *Receuil des traités et conventions IX (X)*, 71–72.
119 Martens, *Receuil des traités et conventions IX (X)*, 74.
120 Treaty text: Reading, *The Anglo-Russian commercial treaty*, 302–320. Article VIII reads as follows:

> On est convenu que les sujets de la Grande Bretagne puissant apporter dans la Russie toutes sortes d'effets ou marchandises et les transporter au travers des Etats de la Russie par le plus court et le plus convenable chemin en Perse, payant trois pour cent en rixdalers *ad valorem*, pour le droit et transit des dites marchandises et pas d'avantage sous quelque prétexte que ce soit. Néanmoins les marchands anglais seront obligés de s'accommoder avec les sujets russes touchant les frais du transport tant par eau que par terre, et de leur donner pour cela un prix raisonnable, et des orders les plus précis seront donnés pour que les marchands anglais trouvent toute l'expédition et facilité sur la route, pareillement qu'ils puissant apporter toutes sortes d'effets et marchandises de Perse, et les transporter au travers de la Russie avec la même liberté et ainsance, payant seulement trois pour cent en rixdalers *ad valorem*, pour le droit et transit, comptant les rixdalers de la manière qu'il est d'usage dans les douanes russiennes (...).

See Reading, *The Anglo-Russian commercial treaty*, 305–306.
121 Martens, *Receuil des traités et conventions IX (X)*, 74–78.
122 Demkin, *Britanskoe kupečestvo*, 36–37.
123 Martens, *Receuil des traités et conventions IX (X)*, 78.
124 Demkin, *Britanskoe kupečestvo*, 20.
125 Previously British merchants had been filing complaints about the fact that Russia would not buy *drap de soldat* from Great Britain, buying them from Prussia instead. See Martens, *Receuil des traités et conventions IX (X)*, 66–67.
126 Martens, *Receuil des traités et conventions IX (X)*, 88.
127 Demkin, *Britanskoe kupečestvo*, 37–38.
128 Reading, *The Anglo-Russian commercial treaty*, 237–238.
129 Reading, *The Anglo-Russian commercial treaty*, 239.
130 Demkin, *Britanskoe kupečestvo*, 21–22.
131 About John Elton, see Demkin, *Britanskoe kupečestvo*, 37–41; Reading, *The Anglo-Russian commercial treaty*, 239–242.
132 Reading, *The Anglo-Russian commercial treaty*, 245–246; Demkin, *Britanskoe kupečestvo*, 22, 38–39.
133 Reading, *The Anglo-Russian commercial treaty*, 248–249.
134 Demkin, *Britanskoe kupečestvo*, 37–38.
135 Demkin, *Britanskoe kupečestvo*, 50–51.
136 Demkin, *Britanskoe kupečestvo*, 39.
137 Reading, *The Anglo-Russian commercial treaty*, 290–291.
138 Reading, *The Anglo-Russian commercial treaty*, 250.
139 Reading, *The Anglo-Russian commercial treaty*, 250–253.
140 Reading, *The Anglo-Russian commercial treaty*, 253–254.
141 Reading, *The Anglo-Russian commercial treaty*, 256.
142 Demkin, *Britanskoe kupečestvo*, 40.
143 Demkin, *Britanskoe kupečestvo*, 22.
144 Reading, *The Anglo-Russian commercial treaty*, 257.
145 Reading, *The Anglo-Russian commercial treaty*, 257–258.
146 Demkin, *Britanskoe kupečestvo*, 114–146.
147 Demkin, *Britanskoe kupečestvo*, 147–184. An example of British interest is naval stores is described in: Clendenning, "William Gomm."

148 Anisimov, *Semiletnjaja vojna*, 96.
149 Anisimov, *Semiletnjaja vojna*, 32–33; 97.
150 *Protokoly konferencii.*
151 Anisimov, *Semiletnjaja vojna*, 97–98.
152 Anisimov, *Semiletnjaja vojna*, 127–133.
153 Anisimov, *Semiletnjaja vojna*, 134, 144; LeDonne, *The grand strategy*, 89–92.
154 Anisimov, *Semiletnjaja vojna*, 170, 179–181.
155 This was agreed upon in the context of a new Austro-Russian treaty that replaced the previous treaty of 1746. See Anisimov, *Semiletnjaja vojna*, 231; Martens, *Receuil des traités et conventions IX (X)*, 203–259.
156 Anisimov, *Semiletnjaja vojna*, 223–227.
157 Anisimov, *Semiletnjaja vojna*, 33; *Protokoly konferencii*, 54.
158 Anisimov, *Semiletnjaja vojna*, 178–183.
159 Uljanickij, *Dardanelly*, 52–75.
160 Sacke, "Adel und Bürgertum," 820; Nekrasov, *Rol' Rossii*, 74–81.
161 Uljanickij, *Dardanelly*, 38; Nekrasov, *Rol' Rossii*, 258–260; Tertecel, "The Russian-Ottoman peace treaty," 225.
162 Tertecel, "The Russian-Ottoman peace treaty," 228–229; Robinson, *Straits*, 10–11; Sanin, "Problema Černomorskich prolivov," 45–49.
163 Tertecel, "The Russian-Ottoman peace treaty," 229–230.
164 Described in detail in Uljanickij, *Dardanelly*, 71ff. See also: Sanin, "Problema Černomorskich prolivov," 52.
165 Uljanickij, *Dardanelly*, 72.
166 Uljanickij, *Dardanelly*, 72–73.
167 Uljanickij, *Dardanelly*, 76–77.
168 Schnakenbourg, "Genèse d'un nouveau commerce," 3–4.
169 Sacke, "Adel und Bürgertum," 820; Anisimov, *Semiletnjaja vojna*, 343, 350.
170 Sacke, "Adel und Bürgertum," 820–821. Scarce statistics of the turnover at Temernik are found in: Storch, *Historisch-statistisches Gemälde – Supplementband*, 32.
171 Bilici, *La politique française en Mer Noire*; Uljanickij, *Dardanelly*, 84–87; Sacke, "Adel und Bürgertum," 820.
172 Anisimov, *Semiletnjaja vojna*, 240, 287–288.
173 Storch, *Supplementband*, 32.
174 Clendenning, "The Anglo-Russian trade treaty," 478.
175 Clendenning, "The economic awakening."
176 Clendenning, "The Anglo-Russian trade treaty," 481–483.
177 Clendenning, "The Anglo-Russian trade treaty," 503–507.
178 Demkin, *Britanskoe kupečestvo*, 23–24.

References

[s.n.]. *Polnaja istorija Nižegorodskoj jarmarki, prežde byvšej Makar'evskoj.* Moskva 1833.

Anisimov, Maksim Jur'evič. *Semiletnjaja vojna i rossijskaja diplomatija v 1756–1763 gg.* Moskva 2014.

Åström, Sven-Erik. *From tar to timber. Studies in Northeast European forest exploitation and foreign trade, 1660–1860.* Helsinki 1988.

Åström, Sven-Erik. "Technology and timber exports from the Gulf of Finland, 1661–1740." *Scandinavian Economic History Review* 23, 1 (1975): 1–14.

Bilici, Faruk. *La politique française en Mer Noire, 1747–1789. Vicissitudes d'une implantation.* Paris 1992.

Blackwell, William L. *The beginnings of Russian industrialization, 1800–1860*. Princeton 1968.

Buck, Piet de. "De Russische uitvoer uit Archangel naar Amsterdam in het begin van de achttiende eeuw (1703 en 1709)." *Economisch- en Sociaal-Historisch Jaarboek* 51 (1988): 126–193.

Clendenning, P.H. "The economic awakening of Russia in the eighteenth century." *Journal of European Economic History* 14, 3 (1985): 443–471.

Clendenning, P.H. "William Gomm. A case study of the foreign entrepreneur in eighteenth century Russia." *Journal of European Economic History* 6, 3 (1997): 533–548.

Clendenning, Philip. "The Anglo-Russian trade treaty of 1766 – An example of eighteenth-century power group interests." *Journal of European Economic History* 19, 3 (1990): 475–520.

Čulkov Michail Dmitrievič. *Istoričeskoe opisanie rossijskoj kommercii pri vsech portach i granicach ot drevnich vremjan do nyne nastojaščego i vsech preimuščestvennych uzakonenij po onoj gosudarja imperatora Petra Velikogo i nyne blagopolučno carstvujuščej gosudaryni imperatricy Ekateriny Velikija, sočinennoe Michajlom Čulkovym*. Sankt-Peterburg 1781–1787.

Demkin, A.V. *Britanskoe kupečestvo v Rossii XVIII veka*. Moskva 1998.

Demkin, A.V. (ed.). *Russko-britanskoe torgovye otnošenija v XVIII veke. Sbornik dokumentov*. Moskva 1994.

Demkin, A.V. *Vnešnjaja torgovlja Rossii čerez peterburgskij port. 1764 god. Vedomost' ob ėksporte rossijskich tovarov*. Moskva 1996.

Demkin, A.V. *Vnešnjaja torgovlja Rossii čerez peterburgskij port. 1764 god. Vedomost' ob importe inostrannych tovarov*. Moskva 1996.

Denzel, Markus A. *Handbook of world exchange rates, 1590–1914*. Farnham 2010.

Droysen, Johann Gustav. *Geschichte der preussischen Politik, IV. Theil*. Leipzig 1867.

Eekman, Thomas. "Seven Years with Peter the Great: the Dutchman Jacob de Bie's observations." In *Peter the Great and the West. New perspectives*, edited by Lindsay Hughes, 207–224. London 2001.

Erkinger, Tamara. *Die armenische Diaspora im vorrevolutionären Russland* (Diplomarbeit Unversität Wien). Wien 2010.

Gorbatenko, Sergey / Gorbatenko, Sergej. *Novyj Amsterdam. Sankt-Peterburg i architekturnye obrazy Niderlandov / New Amsterdam. St. Petersburg and architectural images of the Netherlands*. Sankt-Peterburg / Saint Petersburg 2003.

Gosudarstvennaja vnešnjaja torgovlja v raznych ee vidach za … god. Sankt-Peterburg 1812–1862.

Helfman, Tara. "Commerce on trial. Neutral rights and private warfare in the Seven Years' War." In *Trade and war. The neutrality of commerce in the inter-state system*, edited by Koen Stapelbroek, 14–41. Helsinki 2011.

Helfman, Tara. "Neutrality, the law of nations and the natural law tradition. A study of the Seven Years' War." *The Yale Journal of International Law* 30 (2005): 549–586.

Heller, Klaus. "Der russisch-chinesische Handel in Kjachta: Eine Besonderheit in den außenwirtschaftlichen Beziehungen Rußlands im 18. und 19. Jahrhundert." *Jahrbücher für Geschichte Osteuropas, Neue Folge* 29, 4 (1981): 515–536.

Hinrichs, Carl. *Die Wollindustrie in Preußen unter Friedrich Wilhelm I. Darstellung und Aktenbeilagen*. Berlin 1933.

Hovinga, Vincent. "In dienst van de Republiek: het mislukte residentschap van Jacob de Bie (1711–1718)." In *Van de Vierpotige Leeuw en de Tweekoppige Adelaar:*

Studies over Nederlands-Russische Relaties, edited by Hans Van Koningsbrugge and Emmanuel Waegemans, 17–37. Groningen 2002.

Ioannisjan, Ašot (ed.). *Armjano-russkie otnošenija v pervoj treti XVIII veka. Tom II, čast' 1.* Erevan 1964.

Israel, Jonathan I. *Dutch primacy in world trade, 1585–1740.* Oxford 1989.

Israel, Jonathan I. "The 'new history' versus 'traditional history' in interpreting Dutch world trade primacy." *Bijdragen en Mededelingen betreffende de Geschiedenis der Nederlanden* 106, 3 (1991): 469–479.

Jones, Robert E. "Getting the goods to St. Petersburg: Water transport from the interior 1703–1811." *Slavic Review* 43, 3 (1984): 413–433.

Kahan, Arcadius. "Entrepreneurship in the early development of iron manufacturing in Russia." *Economic Development and Cultural Change* 10, 4 (1962): 395–422.

Kozlov, N. *Archangel'skaja Gubernija* (= Materialy dlja Geografii i statistiki Rossii, 1). Sankt-Peterburg 1865.

Kulsrud, Carl J. *Maritime neutrality to 1780. A history of the main principles governing neutrality and belligerency to 1780.* Boston 1936.

LeDonne, John P. *The grand strategy of the Russian Empire, 1650–1831.* New York 2004.

Martens, Friedrich Fromhold. *Sobranie traktatov i konvencij zaključennych Rossieju s inostrannymi deržavami / Receuil des Traités et Conventions, conclus par la Russie avec les Puissances Etrangères.* 15 volumes. Sankt Petersburg 1874–1909.

Matley, Ian M. "Defense manufactures of St. Petersburg 1703–1730." *Geographical Review* 71, 4 (1981): 411–426.

Mironov, Boris N. *Vnutrennij rynok Rossii vo vtoroj polovine XVIII – pervoj polovine XIX v.* Leningrad 1981.

Nebolsin, Grigorij. *Statističeskoe obozrenie vnešnej torgovli Rossii.* Sankt-Peterburg 1850.

Nekrasov, Georgij Aleksandrovič. *Rol' Rossii v evropejskoj meždunarodnoj politike 1725–1739 gg.* Moskva 1976.

Noordegraaf, Leo. "Vooruit en achteruit in de handelsgeschiedenis van de Republiek." *Bijdragen en Mededelingen betreffende de Geschiedenis der Nederlanden* 106, 3 (1991): 458–468.

Petrov, Pavel Nikolaevič. *Istorija Sankt-Peterburga s osnovanija goroda do vvedenija v dejstvie vybornogo gorodskogo upravlenija po učreždenijam o gubernijach, 1703–1782.* Moskva 2004 (reprint Sankt-Peterburg 1885).

PSZ: *Polnoe Sobranie Zakonov Rossijskoj Imperii, poveleniem Gosudarja Imperatora Nikolaja Pavloviča sostavlennoe.* 45 volumes. Sankt Petersburg 1830.

Protokoly konferencii pri vysočajšem dvore. Tom I: 14 Marta 1756 – 13 Marta 1757 (= Sbornik imperatorskogo istoričestkogo obščestva, 136). Sankt-Peterburg 1912.

Reading, Douglas K. *The Anglo-Russian commercial treaty of 1734.* New Haven / London / Oxford 1938.

Repin, Nikolaj Nikolaevič. "Izmenenie ob"ema i struktury ėksporta Archangel'skogo i Peterburgskogo portov v pervoj polovine XVIII v." In *Promyšlennost' i torgovlja Rossii XVII–XVIII vv.: sbornik statej*, 175–192. Moskva 1983.

Repin, Nikolaj Nikolaevič. "Ot diskriminacii k fritrederstvu, Pravitel'stvennaja reglamentacija torgovli čerez Archangel'sk v 20–60-e gody XVIII v. i ee rezul'tat." In *Archangel'sk v XVIII veke / Arkhangelsk in the XVIII century*, edited by Ju.N. Bespjatych, 228–249. Sankt-Peterburg 1997.

Repin, Nikolaj Nikolaevič. "Učastie kupečestva Evropejskogo Severa vo vnešnej torgovli čerez Archangel'sk v pervoj četverti XVIII veka." *Materialy po istorii Evropejskogo Severa SSSR. Severnyj archeologičeskij sbornik* 3 (1973): 177–199.

RGADA: Rossijskij Gosudarstvennyj Archiv Drevnich Aktov (Russian State Archive of Ancient Documents further RGADA), F. 277 (Manufaktur-Kollegija), Op. 3, Dela 619–631.

Robinson, Walter. *Straits of the Dardanelles and the Bosphorus. The right of way under international law.* London 1878.

Sacke, Georg. "Adel und Bürgertum in der Regierungszeit Katharinas II von Russland." *Revue belge de philologie et d'histoire* 17, 3–4 (1938): 815–852.

Sanin, G.A. "Problema Černomorskich prolivov vo vnešnej politike Rossii XVIII v." In *Rossija i Černomorskie prolivy (XVIII–XX stoletija)*, edited by L.N. Nežinskij and A.V. Ignat'ev, 43–81. Moskva 1999.

Scheltjens, Werner. *De invloed van ruimtelijke verandering op operationele strategieën in de vroeg-moderne Nederlandse scheepvaart. Een case-study over de Nederlandse scheepvaart in de Finse Golf en op Archangel, 1703–1740.* Groningen 2009.

Scheltjens, Werner. "North-Eurasian fairs from the Late Middle Ages to the nineteenth century." In *Europäische Messegeschichte. 9.–19. Jahrhundert*, edited by Markus A. Denzel, 325–352. Köln / Weimar / Wien 2018.

Scheltjens, Werner. "Russia: 1758–1766." In *Eighteenth-century international trade statistics: Sources and methods (special issue of the Revue de l'OFCE 140)*, edited by Loïc Charles and Guillaume Daudin, 343–344. Paris 2015.

Scheltjens, Werner. "The influence of spatial change on operational strategies in early modern Dutch shipping. A case study of Dutch shipping in the Gulf of Finland and Archangel, 1703–1740." *International Journal of Maritime History* 23, 1 (2011): 115–147.

Schnakenbourg, Eric. "Genèse d'un nouveau commerce. La France et l'ouverture du marché russe par la mer Noire dans la seconde moitié du XVIIIe siècle." *Cahiers de la Méditerranée* 83 (2011): 309–325.

Semenov A. *Izuchenie istoricheskikh svedenii o rossijskoy vneshney torgovle i promyshlennosti s poloviny XVII-go stoletiya po 1858 god (3 parts bound in 2 vols).* Newtonville 1977 (reprint 1859).

Storch, Heinrich von. *Historisch-statistisches Gemälde des Russischen Reichs am Ende des achtzehnten Jahrhunderts.* Leipzig 1797–1803.

Stuckenberg, J.Ch. *Beschreibung aller, im Russischen Reiche gegrabenen oder projectirten, schiff- und flossbaren Kanaele, in historisch-statistisch-technischer Beziehung, nach den vollständigsten und zuverlässigsten Quellen verfasst, und von der Kaiserlichen Sankt-Petersburgischen Akademie der Wissenschaften eines Demidowschen Preises gewürdigt. Mit einer Karte.* St. Petersburg 1841.

Tarif sanktpeterburgskogo, vyborgskogo, narvskogo, archangelogorodskogo, kol'skogo portov, 1724.

Tertecel, Adrian. "The Russian-Ottoman peace treaty of Belgrade (1739) and its consequences." In *Enjeux politiques, économiques et militaires en mer noire (XIVe–XXIe siècles). Études à la mémoire de Mihail Guboglu*, edited by Faruk Bilibi, Ionel Cândea, and Anca Popescu, 125–140. Braïla 2007.

Tetradas [VSWG-JDA]: *Tetradas: Tonnage estimates of trade through the Danish Sound, 1670–1856 (Replication data and selected statistics). Version: 1.* VSWG – Journal of Social and Economic History. Dataset, edited by Werner Scheltjens. https://journaldata.zbw.eu/dataset/tetradas

Uljanickij, Vladimir. *Dardanelly, Bosfor, i Černoe More v XVIII veke*. Moskva 1883.
Van Koningsbrugge, Hans. "Van Kwaad tot Erger: de verslechterende Nederlands-Russische relaties 1711–1718." In *Noord- en Zuid-Nederlanders in Rusland 1703–2003*, edited by Emmanuel Waegemans and Hans Van Koningsbrugge, 3–30. Groningen 2004.
Van Zanden, Jan Luiten. "Een fraaie synthese op een wankele basis. Discussie over J.I. Israel, *Dutch primacy in world trade*." *Bijdragen en mededelingen betreffende de Geschiedenis der Nederlanden* 106, 3 (1991): 451–457.
Veluwenkamp Jan Willem. "Dutch merchants in St. Petersburg in the eighteenth century." *Tijdschrift voor Skandinavistiek* 16 (1995): 235–291.
Veluwenkamp, Jan Willem. *Archangel. Nederlandse ondernemers in Rusland, 1550–1785*. Amsterdam 2000.
Wallace, Daniel. "Entrepreneurship and the Russian textile industry: From Peter the Great to Catherine the Great." *Russian Review* 54, 1 (1995): 1–25.
Zacharov, Viktor Nikolaevič. / Zakharov, Viktor Nikolaevich. *Zapadnoevropejskie kupcy v rossijskoj torgovle XVIII veka / West-European merchants in Russian trade of the 18th century*. Moskva 2005.

5 The culmination of conflicting commercial and political interests in North Eurasian trade, 1764–1814

Introduction

Between 1764 and 1805, the estimated total tonnage of trade through the Danish Sound rose from just over 600,000 to more than one million tonnes, which corresponds to an average annual increase of 1.7%. Two major phases can be discerned within this long period of growth. During the second half of the 1760s, the rise that had started more than a decade earlier continued. From the late 1760s until the early 1780s, the estimated tonnage of Baltic commercial exchange stabilized at 700,000–850,000 tonnes annually, with noticeable declines only in 1771, 1776, and 1781–1782. The following year, 1783, however, marked a new record high: 1,121,892 tonnes of goods were registered in the Danish Sound.[1] Although the end of the Fourth Anglo-Dutch War (1781–1783) might have stimulated turnover in the Danish Sound, it is more likely that the sudden upswing was caused by the Laki Eruption of 1783, which resulted in floods, draughts, and bad harvests in parts of Europe throughout the 1780s. After the Laki Eruption, the annual estimated tonnage of trade through the Danish Sound became more volatile. Strong upswings in 1792, 1796, 1802, and 1805 alternated with sudden declines in 1786–1788, 1795, and 1799–1801. Exports, in particular, obtained a more and more irregular and unpredictable character.[2] In the end, the estimated total tonnage of trade through the Danish Sound in 1783 was almost identical to that of 1805. Yet precisely during this very period, the main features of the geographical and commodity structure of trade through the Danish Sound changed dramatically.

The closing section of the previous chapter already provided a first look into the changes, which the structure of North Eurasian trade through the Danish Sound would undergo during the final third of the eighteenth century and has pointed towards the pivotal roles played by Great Britain, France, Prussia, and Russia. This chapter addresses the political-economic background of the 'novel' commercial relations that took the upper hand during the last decades of the eighteenth century. The chapter examines how Anglo-Russian trade, which had been identified as a prime mover of change in the preceding chapter, developed further after the Seven Years' War (1756–1763). It does so against the background of groundbreaking territorial developments in the borderlands of the Black Sea and the Baltic as well as on the American continent, and the breakthrough of British industrialization with its obvious impact on British interests in foreign trade.

This chapter contextualizes the exponential growth of British trade through the Danish Sound in the latter part of the eighteenth century (see Section "Britain's rise to absolute dominance"). Then, it addresses regime changes in North Eurasia's western border basins, focusing, in particular, on Russia's southern expansion towards the Black Sea and on the first partition of Poland-Lithuania in the Baltic realm (see Section "Regime changes in North Eurasia's border basins"). The last section shows that the tensions and dependencies between Great Britain, France, Russia, and Prussia reached a peak in the decade from 1795 until 1805. The resulting insecurities gave an important impetus to the British search for alternative supplies of raw materials, on the one hand, and ended in the temporary collapse of trade through the Danish Sound during the Continental Blockade, on the other (see Section "Relocation, repression and collapse").

Britain's rise to absolute dominance

The estimated tonnage of Anglo-Russian trade through the Danish Sound in eighteenth century grew from an annual average of 1,919 tonnes in 1713–1717, i.e. during the Great Northern War, to an annual average of 182,281 tonnes in the years prior to the Continental Blockade (1803–1807). Trade peaked between 1793 and 1797, when almost 200,000 tonnes of goods were shipped annually between Great Britain and Russia's Baltic ports. Whereas at the start of the eighteenth century, Anglo-Russian trade accounted for about 5% of total tonnage declared at the Danish customs offices in the Sound, its share flirted with and even exceeded the 20% mark at the end of the eighteenth century. From then on, the total tonnage of Anglo-Russian trade started to decline somewhat, probably under the impact of the French Wars (1793–1813). British imports from Russia were responsible for most of the growth in the tonnage of Anglo-Russian trade (see Figure 5.1).[3] A first, very modest upswing in the tonnage of British imports from Russia occurred in the years immediately after the Great Northern War, but then the volume of Anglo-Russian trade roughly remained at the same level until the late 1740s. The Anglo-Russian commercial treaty of 1734 does not seem to have had an immediate positive impact on the tonnage of British imports from Russia (see Figure 5.1).

However, within 20 years after the conclusion of the Anglo-Russian trade treaty, the British share in total Russian exports to the West rose from about 40% to more than 58%, whereas the Russian share in total British imports from the Baltic rose from 21% to 36% during the same period (see Graph 1). Both these increasing shares indicate the strength and intensity of Anglo-Russian trade relations in the context of international trade through

Figure 5.1 British imports from Russia, 1720–1805.

Note: Five-year moving averages. In tonnes. TOT = total estimated tonnage of British imports from Russia; % RU (right axis) = share of Britain in total Russian exports to the West; % UK (right axis) = share of Russia in total British imports from the Baltic.

Source: Tetradas [VSWG-JDA], 6_BTR_Bex: Exports from Russia to the United Kingdom.

the Danish Sound. Tonnages started to increase rapidly in the 1740s, when British imports embarked upon a long series of growth, that was interrupted only briefly by the Seven Years' War (1756–1763) and stagnated for some time during the American War of Independence (1776–1783). Growth accelerated after the coronation of Catherine II (1729–1796) in 1762, and came to a halt only after her death.

British exports to Russia followed a slightly different and more irregular pattern, but here as well, the absence of immediate changes in the wake of the 1734 commercial treaty is clear (see Figure 5.2). The most significant growth spurts in British exports to Russia occurred between 1770 and 1776, on the one hand, and between 1789 and 1805, on the other. The reasons for the first period cannot be explained easily. The rise during the latter period was in line with a more general rise to dominance of British trade with the Baltic, and the substitution of French and southern European imports to the Baltic, which were usually carried by Dutch masters, with British imports to the Baltic.[4] As a result, with a share that exceeded 70% after 1800, Russia had become a major destination of British imports to the Baltic in the late eighteenth century.

In the final quarter of the eighteenth century, French salt imports through the Danish Sound, which were complemented with imports of Spanish, Portuguese, and Italian salt, were substituted almost entirely with British rock-salt imports from Liverpool.[5] Although the emergence of the Liverpool salt trade dates back to the seventeenth century, bulk exports of rock salt to the

Figure 5.2 British exports to Russia, 1720–1805.

Note: Five-year moving averages. In tonnes. Based on STRO. Legend: TOT = total estimated tonnage of British exports to Russia via the Danish Sound; % RU (right axis) = share of Britain in total Russian imports through the Danish Sound; % UK (right axis) = share of Russia in total British exports to the Baltic.

Source: Tetradas [VSWG-JDA], 6_BTR_Wim: Imports from the United Kingdom to Russia.

Baltic took off only around 1760. They relied on initial improvements to the transport infrastructure between the port of Liverpool and the saline district of Cheshire, and efficiency gains in the coal supply to the area and in rock-salt mining techniques.[6] Like the substitution of French and southern European salt imports to the Baltic with British imports, a similar geographical reorientation of imports of overseas goods took place.[7] French imports of overseas goods to the Baltic had taken off immediately after the Great Northern War. At first, sugar, coffee, and tobacco imported to the Baltic mostly arrived from Bordeaux. They were complemented with modest imports from Nantes from the 1750s onwards as well as from Le Havre de Grâce and La Rochelle from the late 1760s.[8] The estimated tonnage of these imports rose considerably between 1721 and 1756. French imports of overseas products to the Baltic came to a complete halt during the Seven Years' War, but resumed at a higher level in 1764. Between 1764 and 1792, the estimated tonnage of overseas products imported to the Baltic reached a peak of almost 10,000 tonnes in 1789, after which a rapid decline set in due to the disturbing impact of the French Revolutionary Wars.[9] Severely affected by the French Revolution, and, in particular, the revolt on the island of Saint-Domingue, which caused a complete interruption of sugar imports to Bordeaux,[10] almost no French imports of overseas products through the Danish Sound were executed between 1794 and 1803. In part, the changing role of Hamburg in the redistribution of French sugar to the Baltic might explain the decline of French imports of overseas products to the Baltic.[11] However, the estimated tonnage of sugar re-exports from Hamburg through the Danish Sound was too low to compensate for the overall decline in the volume of French imports to the Baltic during and after the French Wars.[12] More than others, Great Britain substituted French imports of overseas goods through the Danish Sound from the mid-1790s onwards.[13]

The further analysis of Anglo-Russian trade in the long eighteenth century places the trade in bar iron, hemp, flax, deals, balks and linen in a broad, international context. Historiography has outlined part of the long-term development of the international trade in these commodities in the eighteenth century. Most previous research has relied on Bang and Korst's *Tabeller over skibsfart* (see Chapter 1),[14] has produced and reproduced fragmentary numbers on a variety of topics related to British trade with Russia,[15] or has focused the long-term analysis of foreign merchant colonies in Anglo-Russian trade.[16] Only Herbert Kaplan has delivered a detailed quantitative account of the development of Anglo-Russian trade between 1762 and 1796 based on primary data from the British Public Record Office.[17] Kaplan collected most of his data from the reports sent from the St. Petersburg customs house to London.[18] The data from the St. Petersburg customs office allowed making a distinction between imports to Britain, in general, and those carried on British ships. For the sake of comparison, aggregated data on total British imports of a range of commodities was included as well. Although Kaplan does pay some attention to British exports to Russia, his predominant focus is on the importation into Great Britain of naval stores. In particular, Kaplan dealt with bar iron, hemp, flax, timber (mostly deals) as well as linen and some of the main types of Russia-produced cloth.

The absolute estimated average annual value of exports from St. Petersburg increased more than threefold between 1768 and 1793, but the share of Great Britain in it declined from 61.8% in the period 1768–1779 to 53.3% in 1783–1793. However, the estimated values are expressed in current roubles and do not account for inflation and price fluctuations. As a result, the actual growth or decline of British imports from St. Petersburg, in general, and of single commodities, in particular, remains unclear. Indeed, the more detailed picture that emerges from Kaplan's value estimates of British imports from St. Petersburg shows the growth of bar iron and linen imports alongside the decline of hemp and flax imports.[19] The estimated values of British imports from St. Petersburg show only just that. Bar iron is the only commodity for which Kaplan provides a comparison with imports from Sweden, at least for the time-period from 1764 until 1782. Even though St. Petersburg dwarfed all other Russian ports in terms of turnover, the value estimates do not inform us about the value share of Russia in total foreign imports to Great Britain or the British share in the value of total Russian foreign trade. Moreover, Kaplan's value estimates remain silent about the volume (tonnage) of other (non-Russian) British naval stores imports from the Baltic, or the volume (tonnage) and share of other naval stores exported through the Danish Sound, but not destined to Great Britain.

STRO helps placing the development of Anglo-Russian trade in the long eighteenth century in such broader context. Hence, compared to Kaplan's value estimates, the tonnage estimates based on STRO are available over longer periods and cover other countries of departure and destination as well, alongside Russia and Great Britain. Moreover, the comparability of tonnage estimates based on STRO with the tonnages calculated by Kaplan is much higher than that of value series in different currencies. The novel quantitative evidence places the history of Anglo-Russian trade in the long eighteenth century in a broader geographical context. It allows paying special attention to Sweden and Prussia as competitors of the Russian Empire, on the one hand, and of other destinations in Western Europe as competitors of Great Britain, on the other.

Great Britain dominated bar iron, hemp, flax, and linen exports through the Danish Sound, and Russia played a major role as their supplier. From the 1770s onwards, in particular, Russia supplied up to one half (iron, flax, linen) and even up to three quarters (hemp) of these commodities to Great Britain (see RU-UK in Table 5.1). The pattern of deals and balks, however, is rather surprising and points towards the emergence of highly specialized supply markets in the Baltic in the course of the century. The British demand for both deals and balks grew exponentially during this period and reached a peak between 1800 and 1806, when 75% of all deals and 80% of all balks exported through the Danish Sound were destined to Great Britain (see UK in Table 5.1). However, whereas Russia was a major source for deals, it only played a minor role in the supply of balks. The latter were supplied to Great Britain mostly from Prussia, especially since the 1760s. This is also the time when the Dutch lost their significance in the timber trade through the Danish Sound, as the declining shares of exports to the Dutch Republic and – from 1795 – the Batavian Republic clearly indicate (see NL in Table 5.1).

Despite British predominance, the rise of other destinations during the same period from ca. 1770 until 1806 is remarkable (see other in Table 5.1). Britain no longer had to share the Baltic market with a declining Dutch Republic. Other players now tried to push forward, not at the least encouraged by the Russian Empire, which itself was looking for ways to reduce its dependence on Great Britain. Besides France and the United States, the competing destinations of naval stores were usually smaller states in southern Europe, such as Portugal, Spain, Sicily, and Tuscany, who had signed commercial treaties with Russia in the 1780s.[20] They shared an interest in trying to limit and overcome British dominance in their foreign trade. Neither the increasing importance of Prussia, nor the (modest) emergence of competitors of Great Britain since the 1770s have been sufficiently acknowledged in previous research on Anglo-Russian trade in the eighteenth century. In the closing decades of the eighteenth century, attempts to bypass Great Britain in

Table 5.1 Naval stores in Anglo-Russian trade through the Danish Sound, 1690–1806

		1690–1699	*1700–1709*	*1710–1719*	*1720–1729*	*1730–1739*	*1740–1749*	*1750–1759*	*1760–1769*	*1770–1779*	*1780–1789*	*1790–1799*	*1800–1806*
Deals	UK	19	28	28	26	18	11	23	42	47	47	66	75
	RU-UK			*0*	*7*	*2*	*0*	*16*	*34*	*43*	*42*	*57*	*50*
	NL	61	40	39	41	52	51	43	26	21	17	10	7
	Other	20	33	33	33	30	38	35	31	32	36	23	18
Balks	UK	4	0	5	4	5	6	18	23	38	49	60	80
	RU-UK			*0*	*2*	*4*	*6*	*16*	*13*	*9*	*6*	*7*	*10*
	NL	3	5	3	1	2	2	5	9	11	10	7	6
	Other	94	94	92	95	94	92	76	68	51	41	32	14
(bar) Iron	UK	66	73	52	63	62	65	73	74	73	69	73	65
	RU-UK	*0*	*0*	*0*	*3*	*11*	*16*	*30*	*38*	*51*	*49*	*49*	*35*
	NL	9	13	41	26	13	0	0	7	7	4	3	2
	Other	25	14	7	11	25	35	27	19	20	27	24	34
Hemp	UK	31	38	44	45	54	60	59	57	55	57	73	74
	RU-UK			*10*	*39*	*52*	*58*	*57*	*55*	*54*	*56*	*73*	*72*
	NL	49	55	50	50	41	31	25	24	18	13	5	1
	Other	19	7	6	5	5	9	16	18	27	30	22	25
Flax	UK	62	62	69	65	64	58	57	55	55	50	58	60
	RU-UK			*7*	*33*	*44*	*40*	*44*	*44*	*51*	*45*	*56*	*54*
	NL	18	26	20	22	15	7	4	3	3	1	1	0
	Other	19	11	11	13	21	35	40	42	42	49	41	40
Linen	UK	67	75	75	71	70	74	67	69	63	61	66	53
	RU-UK			*9*	*42*	*29*	*26*	*27*	*32*	*38*	*41*	*56*	*47*
	NL	18	24	24	26	29	24	25	21	26	18	5	3
	Other	15	1	1	2	1	3	8	10	11	20	29	44

Source: *Tetradas* [VSWG-JDA], 8_CIES_Bex_MF: *Linen*; 8_CIES_Bex_RM: *Balks, Deals, Flax, Hemp, Iron*; 6_BTR_Bex: *Exports from Russia.*
Note: Percentage shares of the estimated tonnage of balks, deals, flax, hemp, iron, and linen exports from the Baltic to Britain (UK), the Dutch Republic (NL), and other destinations (other) as well as from Russia to Britain (RU-UK).

the establishment of foreign trade relations intensified, leading to increasing tension between Russia and Great Britain and the reorientation of part of British Baltic trade towards Prussia. The latter had the ambition of increasing its share in Baltic trade at the cost of Poland-Lithuania, on the one hand, and Russia, on the other.

Regime changes in North Eurasia's border basins

Partition and expansion

After the death of August III (1696–1763) and the end of the Saxon-Polish personal union in 1763, a combination of external and internal influences determined the future prospects of Poland-Lithuania. Internally, part of the ruling class of magnates was convinced of the need to take matters in their own hands, if Poland-Lithuania was to survive. Some of them, like the Czartoryski family,[21] tried to initiate a kind of state reforms, while others favoured cooperation with foreign states, but none of them shied away from putting their own economic goals on the political agenda. The magnates were roughly divided into two camps: pro-French magnates, like the influential Potocki family, could be found mostly in Poland proper, whereas pro-Russian magnates were found mostly in the Grand Duchy of Lithuania.[22] Although historiography tends to describe the magnates of Poland-Lithuania as inward looking and disinterested in foreign affairs, some of their strategies indicate towards the opposite. The 'weakness' of the state apparatus provided a fruitful basis for magnates to sustain and expand their power at the cost of societal development in the Commonwealth.[23] At the same time, Prussia and Russia extended their external political pressure on Poland-Lithuania in the immediate aftermath of the Seven Years' War, whereas Saxony, Austria and the Ottoman Empire played a secondary role.[24] Prussia had manifested itself as an ambitious military power with a keen eye on West Prussia and the port of Danzig.[25] Russia managed to exert an even stronger influence on Polish-Lithuanian affairs than ever before,[26] even though Poland-Lithuania had already been ruled for almost 50 years as a Russian protectorate.[27] Alliances between the European powers were restructured in the wake of the Seven Years' War, paving the way for the establishment of the so-called Northern System.[28]

On 31 March 1764, a defensive alliance with Prussia against Austria and a secret convention concerning the election of a Piast to the Polish throne were signed at St. Petersburg.[29] From then on, Prussia and Russia cooperated in their northern affairs.[30] Among other things, they agreed to introduce Stanisław August Poniatowski (1732–1798) – "(…) the polished, pliable, cosmopolitan nephew of the Russian-backed Czartoryski faction (…)"[31] – to the Polish-Lithuanian throne. In 1769, the defensive alliance of 1764 was renewed (second renewal 20 March 1777),[32] albeit with one significant difference. In the third secret article of the 1769 treaty of alliance, it was stated that

Prussia and Russia would jointly prevent Sweden from changing its constitution and disturbing the 'tranquillity' of the North.[33] The secret article also gave Prussia the right to enter Swedish Pomerania; a clause that Catherine II was concerned about at first, since it would give Prussia access to ports 'as good as Danzig,' but which she accepted later.[34] Russia and Prussia had their reasons for keeping an eye on Sweden: the Russo-Swedish War (1788–1790) would make clear that Sweden had not given up on *dominium maris baltici* yet. Compared to their Swedish policies, the Russian and Prussian plans with regard to Poland-Lithuania were more radical. Russia wanted to keep its protectorate weak and dependent, and continued to position it as an advance post of the Russian Empire; Prussia wanted to unite its scattered territories in Brandenburg and Ducal Prussia through the annexation of West Prussia and the port of Danzig.[35]

Britain's response to the Prussian and Russian plans was limited. In view of the diplomatic search for a successor to the Polish throne, the British Chancellor expressed the commercial interest of Great Britain in the Baltic, and the role of Russia and Poland-Lithuania therein, maintaining that "(...) it is in the British interest that the future King of Poland should be devoted to Russia, (...)."[36] Commerce continued to be Great Britain's primary concern, and a weak and dependent Polish King would provide the most suitable way to consolidate its interests. Shortly after the conclusion of the Russo-Prussian defensive alliance of 1764, the commercial treaty between Great Britain and Russia was – finally – renewed (1766),[37] and a commercial treaty between Great Britain and Prussia was signed.[38] While it refused to take a diplomatic position other than one that would align well with its commercial interests, Great Britain supported Russia's efforts to put Poniatowski on the Polish throne and thus tacitly accepted the dramatic future prospects of Poland-Lithuania as outlined by Prussia and Russia.[39] At the same time, it comes as no surprise that Great Britain turned out to be in an ideal position to benefit from the execution of their plans.

The first partition itself "came about mainly as a by-product of [other] events"[40] in the western border basins of North Eurasia, and more precisely of the Polish and Turkish issues in international politics. The suppression of the anti-Russian and anti-Poniatowski Confederation of Bar in Poland (1768) involved the participation of Cossacks, who did not shy away from crossing the border with the Ottoman Empire.[41] This, in turn, provoked anxiety in the Ottoman Empire, which, encouraged by France, declared war on Russia.[42] The latter achieved victory after victory in this war. Russia now threatened the Ottoman Empire, and brought Austria and Prussia into a complicated position:

> [Frederick the Great's] alliance with Russia of 1764, concluded on a one-sided basis for protection against Austria, (...) threatened to drag it into the conflict if Austria came to Turkey's defence. (...) Austria's dilemma was even worse. Russia's (...) prospective gains in the Black Sea and the Balkans endangered Austria strategically almost as much as they did the

> Turks, but an Austrian intervention to stop Russia would bring Prussia into the war and force Austria to fight the main battle in Germany, while freeing Russia to concentrate on the Turks.[43]

Attempting to limit the damages of Russia's expansionist course, Austria agreed to accept a Russo-Prussian scheme to partition Poland, but required compensation in the form of part of the territory of the Polish-Lithuanian Commonwealth, arguing that "(…) it was better to weaken Poland than to let the Ottoman Empire be destroyed (…)."[44] By agreeing to the partition of Poland-Lithuania, Austria avoided getting involved in a war with Russia, and Prussia avoided having to support Russia in a war against the Ottoman Empire and, probably, Austria.

The King of Prussia announced the first partition on 19 January 1773.[45] A wider international conflict was avoided, but the partition did not bring the anticipated benefits for the remaining part of Poland-Lithuania, nor did it settle the rivalry between Prussia and Austria. Rather, it continued to feed the Prussian desire for Danzig, and it gave Russia more freedom than ever before to pursue its southern expansion towards the Black Sea coast. By the year 1774, Russia had gained part of the northern Black Sea coast and had obtained the right to establish a fleet in the Black Sea. Relying on Prince Grigoriy Aleksandrovich Potemkin (1739–1791) to oversee the process, Catherine II almost immediately started with the incorporation of its newly acquired southern territories into the realm.[46] The Russian Empire now possessed the mouths of Bug, Dnepr and Don, but the Porte retained the strategic area around the fortress of Ochakiv (*Ru.* Očakov), and thus controlled the entrance to the ports of Nikolayev and Kherson, as well as the Danubian Principalities and Bessarabia.[47] The Crimea became independent territory under Russian protection, but the Sultan "retained spiritual suzerainty over its Muslim Tatar population."[48] In light of the numerous issues that remained unresolved in the famous Treaty of Küçük Kajnarca (see Section "Relocation, repression and collapse" of this chapter),[49] which Russia and the Ottoman Empire had signed in July 1774, the Russian annexation of the Crimea in 1783 does not come as a surprise. Equally predictable is the start of Russia's expansion in the Caucasus and the establishment of a protectorate over the eastern Georgian Kingdom of Kartli-Kakheti in the Treaty of Georgievsk in 1783.[50] Both the Crimea and the Caucasus played a strategic role in the protracted pursuit of a profitable trade with Asian goods through Russia. The establishment of control over the eastern part of the Kingdom of Georgia was a prelude to Russia's active struggle for power in Central Asia and its wish to destroy Persian influence, which would enter into its final phase in the Russo-Persian Wars (1804–1813 and 1826–1828).[51]

Novel commercial practices in the Baltic

Before the first partition, the predominance of Danzig and Königsberg as main outlets for foodstuffs (grain) and raw materials (timber) from

Poland-Lithuania was undisputed.[52] The highest quantities of grain were exported to the Dutch Republic (and most importantly to Amsterdam).[53] In 1767 and 1768, however, considerable quantities of grain were exported from Danzig and Königsberg to Great Britain. Further exports from Poland-Lithuania were executed via Riga, Libau, and – to some extent – Memel. In contrast to Danzig and Königsberg, these ports had a different commodity and geographical structure.

Although its raw materials exports also included masts and timber, Riga's most important export commodities were hemp and flax, which were grown in its extensive Lithuanian and (White-)Russian hinterlands. In 1762, as part of a set of groundbreaking commercial regulations, which annulled persisting differences in Russian customs regulations at the Empire's different ports, Riga (as well as St. Petersburg) had obtained certain rights to export grain.[54] Nevertheless, earlier commercial privileges based on Swedish traditions were still in force at the port of Riga, so some advantages over 'other' Russian ports persisted even after 1762.[55] The tonnage of Libau's exports was more modest and less differentiated: the Dutch Republic was by far the most important destination and grain exports were predominant.[56] Besides these ports, from 1764 onwards, the East Prussian port of Memel emerged as exporter of timber to the Dutch Republic and, more importantly, Great Britain. The growth of Memel was related directly to the decision of the Polish magnate family Radziwiłł to start exploiting the massive forestry resources of its lands and estates.[57] The magnitude of this decision would only become clear at a later stage (see below).

After the first partition, exports from Danzig plummeted.[58] For some time at least, the Dutch commercial system found an alternative for Danzig in the ports of Courland (before all Libau) and Riga. With a share of 86.3% of all exports from Courland, the Dutch almost monopolized exports from this area.[59] The biggest gains of Poland-Lithuania's loss of market share, however, went to Russia and, before all, Prussia. Both powers benefited from growing exports to the Dutch Republic and – especially – Great Britain, but also from increasing exports to France, Portugal, Spain, and the Mediterranean. The latter strived for independent commercial relations with the economic powers in the Baltic, were less and less reluctant to bypass the Dutch Republic and Great Britain in the organization of this trade, and often relied on neutral Scandinavian ships to avoid capture at sea.[60]

Only a few years after the first partition, novel commercial practices experienced their breakthrough in trade through the Danish Sound.[61] Restrictive Prussian commercial policies obstructed the traditional grain export route from Danzig to Amsterdam, which had dominated commercial relations between Poland-Lithuania and the Dutch Republic for almost two centuries. These obstructions entailed an immediate reaction from the part of the Dutch commercial system, which sought to replace its traditional outlet for Polish grain in Danzig with exports from Königsberg, Pillau, Libau, and Riga. Insofar as grain exports to the Dutch Republic between 1772 and 1775 are concerned, Riga and Libau seem to have benefited the most in the immediate aftermath of the first partition. The relocation of trade and transport relations from Danzig to other ports turned out to be quite a challenge: the reaction of Dutch merchants and carriers to the changing business environment in the eastern Baltic seems to have been anything but swift. On the contrary, insofar as the role of Dutch carriers on the traditional route between Danzig and Amsterdam is concerned, the decline of this route went hand in hand with a general decline of the maritime transport sector in Dutch regions specializing in this type of transport services.[62] The carriers seem to have been not nearly as flexible as is often assumed. The general decline of the Dutch maritime transport sector seems to have been caused at least in part to their being locked-in on a route that had become obstructed due to external circumstances. Quite differently, grain exports to Great Britain were executed from Danzig, as was noted before, but more importantly from Königsberg and Memel. British grain exports from Riga were less significant. Libau was insignificant. At the same time, raw materials exports shifted from Danzig and Königsberg (Pillau) before the first partition to Memel and Riga between 1772 and 1775. The strongest increase can be observed in the raw materials exports from Memel between 1772 and 1774 and from Riga in 1775.[63]

Commercial treaties with Poland-Lithuania

The bilateral commercial treaties that each of the partitioning powers signed with the remaining part of Poland-Lithuania in 1775 were decisive for the further development of the Commonwealth's international position.[64] This section focuses on the Prusso-Polish commercial treaty of 1775, which confirmed Poland-Lithuania's loss of access to the sea and arguably had the largest impact on its further development. The treaty institutionalized those aspects of the territorial changes of the first partition that were of immediate importance for Prussia's commercial interests in Poland-Lithuania. Even before the first partition, Frederick the Great (1712–1786) had already sent his financial advisor Franz Balthasar Schönberg von Brenckenhoff (1723–1780) to Poland in order to explore how these territories could be connected to Prussian possessions. Brenckenhoff's plan foresaw taking control of Poland's trade by means of a system of canals connecting Poland and Prussia. According to Brenckenhoff's report, this would drastically increase Prussia's tax income.[65]

Prussia pursued several goals at once in the Prusso-Polish commercial treaty.[66] It wanted to protect its domestic industries, harm Leipzig and promote Frankfurt (Oder) instead, take over Danzig's trade and combat smuggling. In short, the Prusso-Polish treaty was designed to import raw materials from Poland at the lowest possible rate, limit imports of other countries to Poland-Lithuania as much as possible, and take over the Polish grain export trade. Prussia established manufactures close to the Polish border, which were to replace imports from other countries. In Pomerania and Stettin 'English beer' breweries were established to replace actual British beer imports; imports of faience at Danzig were to be replaced by Prussian faience imports; imports of foreign textile manufactures via the fair of Leipzig and the land route through Bohemia, which allowed avoiding Prussian tolls, were to be replaced with Prussian products.[67]

Frederick's first strategy of taking over Poland's grain trade was to employ high taxes. Thus, during the first years after the partition and before the treaty was signed, Frederick decided to levy a 20% transit duty on grain to Danzig, which in reality turned out to be as high as 50%, and ordered to export grain to Silesia instead of Danzig. In the longer term, however, Prussian advisors concluded that if taking over the Polish grain trade at the expense of Danzig were to be successful, the commodity flows were to be diverted to Elbing and Stettin and Prussian capital would have to replace Polish and foreign merchant capital.[68] In Elbing, special benefits would have to be granted to merchants, whereas a necessary condition for diverting the Polish grain trade to Stettin would be the construction of a canal in Bydgoszcz, which had been planned by the Polish government in 1766, i.e. before the first partition,[69] but which was never realized. In the 1775 treaty, the transit duty for grain was fixed at 12% as opposed to 2% for goods imported to Prussia. A new regulation on the import of Polish grain to Silesia was issued, which was expanded later to include the Mark, Pomerania, West and East Prussia, Brandenburg, and all other Prussian provinces bordering Poland-Lithuania.[70] In the tariff of 24 May 1775, the official prices for grain, which were used to calculate taxes, were much higher than the actual prices; consequently, the actual duties were higher than the official 12%.[71] Moreover, in 1776, Frederick ordered to sell grain in Elbing and Stettin using the Berlin measure, which was 10% bigger than that of Warsaw, while the prices remained the same.[72] All these measures provoked a sharp decline in the price of grain after the first partition. Finally, transit to Prussia via Silesia was so costly that it was unsuccessful. The *Polnische Getreide-Handlungs-Societät*, which was established in 1776 to tackle this issue, did not bring relief and was dismantled soon.[73] Overall, the effects of the treaty on the Polish grain trade were chaos and disorder rather than a smooth and well-organized diversion and take-over by the Prussian authorities.

In a manner that proved to be quite similar to the Polish grain trade, the new Prussian regulations brought the Commonwealth's timber trade to ruin. In 1770, the so-called *Haupt-Nutzholz-Administration* (HNA) was established under the auspices of the Prussian Forest Department. In this way, a factual Prussian state monopoly on foreign timber exports was established. Then, the HNA did not pay the 50% transit duty for timber transported through Prussia, which was established 1737, then lowered, but restored to 50% in 1770. Again, the initial plan was to redirect timber flows from the Vistula to the Oder at the expense of Danzig; Frederick wanted to take the timber trade out of the hands of Danzig merchants and put it under the control of the HNA. The diversion of timber flows away from Danzig would take place via the Notetz and several canals to Elbing, Stettin, Swinemünde, or Hamburg. Alternatively, Lithuanian timber supplies could be exported from Memel, which would also harm Danzig. The centralization of timber exports in the hands of the HNA as well as the efforts to circumvent and obstruct Danzig brought the Polish timber exports to ruin. It became too costly and problematic for private merchants to engage in direct trade, and HNA's role as intermediary made timber costly as well. On top of that, a number of Prussian merchants who sought special privileges from the Prussian King put the entire system under pressure.[74]

The rise of Anglo-Prussian trade

In the meantime, Great Britain managed to strengthen its position in most of the eastern Baltic area. Danzig, Königsberg, Pillau, Memel, and occasionally Riga were used as outlets for foodstuffs exports to Great Britain during a number of consecutive years in the late 1770s (1777–1778) and the 1780s (1783–1785).[75] During these years, the volume of foodstuffs exports to Great Britain increased manifold but it returned to occasional, very small-scale exports afterwards. Foodstuffs exports from Great Britain were not regular yet; external supplies were needed only when domestic production proved to be insufficient.[76] During the same period, and especially in the latter part of the 1780s, raw materials exports boomed, particularly from Memel, where British presence was now well established, and from the traditional timber outlets in the Gulf of Finland (Vyborg and St. Petersburg).[77] For the most part, the growing volume of Prusso-British exports in 1776–1778 was due to the manifold increase in raw materials exports from Memel, in which the British developed a particular interest in the 1770s, not at the least as a means to replace 'failing' timber supplies from its former American colonies. From 1778, Great Britain had a consul in Memel, James Durno (1751–1807), a timber merchant, who acted as representative of both the Radziwiłł family and the British Court at the same time, thus effectively making himself *incontournable* insofar as Memel's timber exports to Great Britain were concerned.[78] It may be assumed that the British consul in Memel, with his close contacts to the Radziwiłł family, has exerted an important influence on the direction of commodity flows from the Lithuanian hinterland to Prussian rather than Russian ports.[79] Compared to the year 1786, Prussia's share in Lithuanian exports increased from 47.1% to 75.7%, whereas that of all of Lithuania's other neighbours (Poland, Russia and Courland) declined strongly. Poland's share went from 17.4% to a mere 6.6%; Russia's share went from 24.3% to 11.2%.[80] Margot Herzfeld was probably right to argue that the 1775 commercial treaty was more important for East Prussia than for the rest of the Prussian Crown lands. East Prussia did not have a large agriculture nor its own manufactures and was thus fully dependent on the trade with goods from the Kingdom of Poland and – even more importantly – the Grand Duchy of Lithuania.[81] However, Herzfeld only noticed the decline of Polish-East-Prussian trade at

Königsberg, arguing that Riga and Libau were now in a much better position to receive goods from the now Russian territories in Belarus and Lithuania,[82] but failed to take the rise of Memel into account. Indeed, Memel's rapid rise seems to have coincided with significant increases in the supply of timber to Great Britain as the industrialization of the country and the expansion of the British Navy were pacing up.

In the 1780s, the overall volume of naval stores exports from Russia to Great Britain had become so high, that the British government grew concerned about its dependence on the Russian Empire as their dominant supplier. Moreover, Great Britain was annoyed with the 1780 League of Armed Neutrality, by means of which the Russian Empire tried to position itself as a maritime power.[83] Especially in 1787, when the 1766 commercial treaty was not renewed, and Russia signed commercial treaties with France, Portugal, Spain, and Naples instead (see above), Britain's attitude towards Russia had started to become less friendly and more adverse.[84] This, in turn, supported the establishment of Memel as a supplier of timber to Great Britain. Other naval stores as well, like hemp and flax, were grown in the Lithuanian hinterlands of the Baltic ports, and were exported to Great Britain mostly via St. Petersburg and the Prussian port of Memel. Overall, Great Britain's weight in trade through the Danish Sound continued to grow at an ever-increasing pace in the decades after the first partition of Poland-Lithuania.

The Eastern Crisis

Great Britain's weight in 'Baltic affairs' became particularly apparent during the so-called Eastern Crisis of 1787–1791, a turbulent, multifaceted and rather complex episode in Central and East European history, which started with the outbreak of another Russo-Turkish War in August 1787.[85] The main protagonists of the Eastern Crisis, which unfolded on the southern Black Sea front and the northern Baltic front at the same time, were Great Britain, Prussia, and Poland, on the one hand, and Russia, Austria, and the Ottoman Empire, on the other. The Dutch Republic, which was allied to Prussia and Great Britain in the 1788 Triple Alliance, played a secondary role.[86] So did Sweden, which was allied to the Porte and planned an attack on the Russian Empire in 1788; and Danzig, which was defended by the Polish state, but did not consider itself Polish territory.[87] Even though existing historical surveys of the Eastern Crisis focus mostly on the international diplomacy of the various courts, it is clear that the exploitation of opportunities for diverting commodity flows was a primary concern on both fronts. On the southern front, the Russian Empire continued to be preoccupied with expanding its presence on the Black Sea coast. The cessation of the strategic fortress of Ochakiv played an essential role in the execution of these plans.[88] By means of a proposal to act jointly in the war against the Porte, Poland tried to achieve benefits of its own, not at the least access to a port on the Black Sea.[89] At the same time, Prussia still longed for the port of Danzig and the strategically located trading city of Thorn (*Pl.* Toruń) on the Vistula, but neither England nor Russia and Poland were ready to grant Prussia such territorial expansion. Even though the Russo-Prussian alliance officially continued to exist until 1788, it had lost its meaning in the early 1780s, when the League of Armed Neutrality was formed (1780),[90] and a Russo-Austrian treaty was signed (1781).[91] Later in the same decade, Russia guaranteed yet another treaty between Prussia and the city of Danzig, signed 20 March 1785, thanks to which Danzig could maintain its autonomous position in what remained of Poland-Lithuania, even though Prussia was openly dissatisfied.[92] By the end of the 1780s, the continued quarrels between the partitioning powers in the Baltic regarding the position of Danzig turned out to be decisive for the future of Polish-Lithuania.

The Prussian foreign minister, Ewald Friedrich Graf von Hertzberg (1725–1795), proposed an exchange of territory (*Ger.* Ländertausch), by which Austria would return Galicia to Poland as compensation for the loss of Danzig and Thorn to Prussia. Austria would be compensated with Moldavia and Walachia; and Russia would retain the Crimea and receive Ochakiv and Bessarabia on top. Hertzberg's plan met with Russian, Polish, and English opposition and failed.[93] However, the issue of Danzig was now – again – on Prussian, Russian, and British agendas. It had become clear to William Pitt the Younger (1759–1806), that Poland-Lithuania represented a viable alternative to the Russian Empire as supplier of naval stores.[94] Not surprisingly, James Durno instructed Pitt.[95] After the failure of Hertzberg's *Ländertausch*, Great Britain tried to convince Prussia and Poland to sign a commercial treaty, which would also establish Danzig as free port for British trade with Poland; afterwards an Anglo-Polish commercial treaty could be signed.[96] However, the Prusso-Polish alliance of 1790 did not solve the Danzig issue, and gradually Great Britain became convinced that a cessation of Danzig and Thorn to Prussia would be in their best interest.[97] Catherine II saw her own interests in the supply of naval stores to Great Britain endangered, and agitated fiercely against it in the public sphere.[98] On top of that, Catherine did not accept Pitt's plan to surrender Ochakiv and end the war with the Ottoman Empire.[99] Thereafter, the strategic positions of all major parties involved in the Eastern Crisis changed. Great Britain saw its hopes for signing a commercial treaty with Poland disappear after Prussia's opposition against the abolition of Danzig's staple rights,[100] and – out of fear for its Levant trade – decided to make a drastic change in its policy towards Russia and Turkey. Great Britain no longer disapproved of the cessation of Ochakiv by the Russian Empire.[101]

At the same time, a new *rapprochement* took place between Russia and Prussia, which endangered the position of Poland. The events would take their definitive turn after the official inauguration of the Polish constitution on 3 May 1791, which greatly upset Catherine II and made her decide to enter Poland in January 1792. Prussia was too involved in a war against France and could not come to assist Poland, even though the latter now offered to cede Danzig and Thorn to Prussia. When Russia proposed Prussia to undertake another partition of Poland, Prussia did not oppose against the idea.[102] In the second partition of 1793, Danzig finally became part of Prussia.[103] Again, British commercial interests in Poland prevailed and, some pro forma protests notwithstanding, Britain accepted the second partition of Poland-Lithuania.[104] By doing so, Britain achieved an important political goal as well: it now had two continental allies in the war against France: Prussia and Russia.[105] Two years later, Austria, Russia, and Prussia divided the remaining parts of Poland-Lithuania and its vassal state Courland.[106] Prussia and Russia now controlled most of the eastern coastline of the Baltic Sea including the main outlets for the produce of its vast North Eurasian hinterland to maritime destinations across all of Europe. Among them, Great Britain was predominant. All other European states envied British economic and naval power. In fact, in the closing decade of the eighteenth century, "(...) *Perfide Albion* [i.e. Great Britain – W.S.] came to occupy the same position in the popular imagination as its predecessor [i.e. the Dutch Republic – W.S.]; only it was regarded as still more dangerous owing to the great development of its industries and political power."[107]

The French Wars

In February 1793, Britain's main opponent on the European continent, France, embarked upon a "policy of economic strangulation," which would determine the course of international trade for the next 20 years.[108] During this period, which is often referred to as the time of the 'French Wars,' Great Britain and France went ways to restrict, hinder and blockade the antagonist's trade. Soon all of Europe was sucked into the end game of the mercantilist era. In the course of 1793, the Anglo-French commercial war was resumed after a short period of relief in the wake of the Treaty of Eden (1786),[109] and both Great Britain and France issued blockade and compulsory measures to harm the other nation's commercial exchange.[110] France issued far-reaching prohibitions of goods assumed to be of British origin (like sugar),[111] and in September 1793 it issued its own Navigation Act, which was an exact copy of the English 1651 Navigation Act.[112] In response, Britain developed the principle of a maritime blockade, which could take different forms. On the one hand, the British maritime blockade involved the actual blocking of the enemy's ports and coasts; on the other, it could take the form of a 'paper blockade' – that is a declaration "(...) that the [enemy's] ports (...) were *ipso facto* blockaded by virtue of their geographical position."[113]

The outbreak of the French Wars in 1793 also led to the prohibition of French imports to Russia.[114] This opened the gates for the further strengthening of British predominance in trade through the Danish Sound, even if Great Britain had to bear with competition from the side of southern European nations and the United States (see Section "Britain's rise to absolute dominance" of this chapter), and with the impact of Russia's new customs tariff of 1797. In the same year, the Anglo-Russian treaty of commerce was renewed.[115] Goal of the 1797 tariff was to promote the exportation of Russian manufactures, but it also contained a draconic 100% increase of duties on timber exports.[116] In response, British imports from Prussia now grew more rapidly than imports from Russia. In part, the growth of Anglo-Prussian trade was due to rapid increases in the British demand for wheat since the early 1790s;[117] in part, Prussian supplies of deals and – to some extent – linen also started to rise.[118] In the meantime, Sweden recovered somewhat from the Russian competition in bar iron exports to Great Britain. Due to a sudden decline of Russian bar iron exports through the Danish Sound after 1800, Sweden could catch up and even surpass Russia with average annual exports through the Danish Sound of just over 25,000 tonnes.[119] The latter changes were probably caused by the Russian customs tariff of 1797,[120] which replaced the more liberal 1782 customs tariff and had much in common with the 1793 import prohibitions. Perhaps the 1797 tariff is best understood as part of Russia's efforts to diminish its dependence on British trade. The large number of protectionist measures and outright prohibitions,[121] which characterized the short reign of Paul I (1754–1801), clearly point in that direction,[122] and so do the resumption of trade with the Batavian Republic (1797) and France (February 1801),[123] and the alliance with the Ottoman Empire of 1800.[124]

In the meantime, the French and British measures led to increasing pressure on neutral trade, especially in the wake of the Law of Nivôse (18 January 1798). The latter

> (…) laid down that the nationality of a vessel should be determined by its cargo, so that if any vessel was carrying goods of any kind coming from England or its possessions, no matter who was the owner, this fact alone should justify confiscation, not only of these goods, but also of the vessel itself and its entire cargo. Moreover, any vessel that had touched at a British port was forbidden to put in at any French port; and earlier it had already been made a practice to seize vessels bound for a British port.[125]

Such regulations, of which the Law of Nivôse probably was the most extreme, were counteracted by institutional changes in the organization of neutral trade. At the same time, they resulted in the French and – by extension – continental self-blockade.[126]

At the time of Napoleon Bonaparte (1769–1821)'s accession to power in 1799, international commerce was determined by British mercantilism in the maritime sphere, French anti-British counter-measures on the European continent, and the gathering of neutral third parties to withstand and circumvent the disturbances of the French and British commercial policies. In 1800, the neutral powers Denmark, Sweden, Russia, and Prussia gathered in the Second League of Armed Neutrality, which echoed the principles of its 1780 predecessor, but provided more guarantees against capture under blockade. The new League of Armed Neutrality was directed mostly against Britain, and morally and politically supported Napoleon. The political differences between Russia and Britain reached a peak in late 1800, when trade between the two countries was prohibited. Exports from Russia to Prussia were prohibited as well to avoid the further relocation of Anglo-Russian trade to Prussian ports.[127] These draconic measures were short-lived, and trade with the United Kingdom was resumed immediately after the first battle of Copenhagen and the violent death of Paul I in March 1801.[128] The 1797 tariff, however, remained in force.[129]

Although the success of the 1800 League of Armed Neutrality was short-lived, its legacy should not be underestimated. Napoleon adopted the principles of the League in his 1800 treaty with the United States, and the Anglo-Russian navigation convention of 1801, which was "the only result of the action of the neutrals," established that free ships should not make free goods and that war-ships rather than privateers should be allowed to survey convoyed trading vessels.[130] Although these regulations strengthened the power of neutrals, and showed that Great Britain and France alike seem to have been reluctant to cause a complete disruption of international maritime commerce, the commercial war was bound to continue. The Peace of Amiens (1802) brought little more than some temporary relief. With the blockades of the Mouth of the Elbe and Weser in Northern Germany, the Anglo-French commercial war soon reached a new level. The next year, in August 1804, "(...) all French ports on the Channel and the North Sea were declared under blockade."[131] Such declarations were issued for several reasons and were characterized by their manifest mercantilist background. First, blockades of enemy ports were meant "(...) to cut off all kinds of exports from the enemy to the neutrals, especially if they competed with those of the home country."[132] Moreover, they were aimed "(...) at getting rid of the excess of export goods in the home country and (...) at preventing the enemy from selling his products."[133] And finally, they were designated to

> place [enemy] imports of under the control of the naval power itself [i.e. Great Britain – W.S.], so that the country [i.e. Great Britain – W.S.] might thereby give preference, so far as possible, to its own products and those of its colonies, and also so that it might take over trade and navigation with the enemy mainland.[134]

In the autumn of 1805, the British blockade was annulled.[135] Until 1806, the total estimated tonnage of trade through the Danish Sound remained largely unaffected by the disturbances caused by the British and French in European waters and overseas. During the same period, however, the structure of trade through the Danish Sound underwent significant changes.

Whereas in 1764, 12,925 tonnes or about 9% of the total tonnage of Polish-Lithuanian exports through the Danish Sound were exported to Great Britain, the latter's share and absolute volume had more than tripled to 45,135 tonnes or 54.9% in 1783 (see Table 5.2). More than half of Poland-Lithuania's exports were now destined to Great Britain. On the one hand, it is clear

Table 5.2 Exports from the Baltic to Great Britain in 1764, 1783, and 1805

	Estimated tonnage of exports			*Exports from Poland-Lithuania*		
	TOT	*UK*	*% UK*	*TOT*	*UK*	*% UK*
1764	684,155	114,405	16.7	143,798	12,925	9.0
1783	1,121,892	319,471	28.5	82,291	45,135	54.9
1805	1,081,921	449,517	41.5			
	Exports from Prussia			*Exports from Russia*		
	TOT	*UK*	*% UK*	*TOT*	*UK*	*% UK*
1764	73,049	9,333	12.8	168,536	64,567	38.3
1783	262,903	117,838	44.8	303,734	104,508	34.4
1805	298,034	225,229	75.6	378,367	161,841	42.8

Source: Tetradas [VSWG-JDA], 3_EI_Bex: Countries (areas) of destination of exports.
Note: TOT = total; UK = exports to Great Britain (United Kingdom); % UK = share of British exports.

that the volume of exports from Poland-Lithuania had declined strongly between 1764 and 1783; on the other hand, the growing involvement of Great Britain in trade through the Danish Sound becomes apparent. The strong increase of exports from Poland-Lithuania to Great Britain reflects the latter's emergence as a net importer of grain since the early 1780s.[136] Moreover, Great Britain obtained a massive share in exports from Prussia through the Danish Sound between 1764 and 1805.[137] In 1764, Great Britain accounted for only 12.8% of total Prussian exports through the Danish Sound; 40 years later, Britain's share had risen to 75.6%; its tonnage had increased from 9,333 (1764) to 225,229 tonnes (1805) (see Table 5.2). The tonnage of Prussian exports even exceeded that of Russian exports to Great Britain. The Russian exports grew continuously in the second half of the eighteenth century, but at a slower pace than their Prussian counterparts did. After the Seven Years' War, the development of Anglo-Russian trade obtained a different character.

On the one hand, during the first years of the nineteenth century, the British wartime economy, with its great demand for North Eurasian naval stores and grain, contributed significantly to the rapid growth of Russia's foreign trade.[138] The estimated total value of Russia's foreign trade increased from 75.6 million silver roubles in 1798–1800 to 103.4 million silver roubles is 1805.[139] The annual average British share in the total estimated value of Russia's foreign trade was as high as 64% of exports from Russia and 29% of imports to Russia between 1794 and 1800;[140] a brief disturbance in 1800–1801 notwithstanding, it sustained the same allure during the first years of the nineteenth century. On the other hand, whereas Kaplan asserts that neither Britain nor Russia was successful in reducing their dependence on each other during the reign of Catherine II, the more encompassing view based on STRO and *Tetradas* indicates that the perceived British dependence on Russian naval stores may have been less of a problem than commonly assumed. The impact of the reorientation of British trade through the Danish Sound towards Prussian ports is undeniable. Britain's incessant search for alternative suppliers of naval stores leveraged its extensive network of consuls and representatives to find suppliers other than Russia, which it found most importantly in Prussia. Moreover, recent research has shown that throughout the eighteenth century the British made efforts to find alternative sources of supply for hemp, flax and timber across the globe.[141] This search was largely unsuccessful during most of the eighteenth century, not only in terms of the quantity of alternative supplies produced, but also in terms of their quality. On top of that, it was hampered further by American independence and the (temporary) loss of these former supply areas. The disturbances caused by the French Wars in European waters as well as across the Atlantic, intensified the search for alternative sources of naval sources and contributed significantly to the course of British trade with North Eurasia in the first half of the nineteenth century (see Chapter 6).

Relocation, repression, and collapse

After Küçük Kajnarca

Although the Baltic still was by far the most important outlet for Russia's foreign trade during the first years of the nineteenth century, the rapid growth of trade via ports in the Black Sea is remarkable. Early beginnings of this growth can be traced back to the period immediately following the Treaty of Küçük Kajnarca (1774).[142] Prior to the annexation of the Crimean Khanate (1783) and the take-off of commercial development organized by the government,[143] Russia's Black Sea trade was concentrated for the most part in Taganrog, an Ancient Greek settlement that was revived in the course of the Russo-Turkish War (1768–1774), and Kherson, which was (re-)established in 1778. French merchants, such as the famous Antoine-Ignace Anthoine, baron de Saint-Joseph (1749–1826), were quick to establish commercial relations with Russia in Kherson, but Austrian merchants as well rapidly acknowledged the prospects of the Treaty of Küçük Kajnarca. Years before the Austro-Russian commercial treaty of 1785, they had already established a company for the establishment of trade between the Danube and Kherson.[144] During this period, the Russian Empire signed commercial treaties with a number of states in the Mediterranean basin and southern Europe (see Section "Regime changes in North Eurasia's border basins" of this chapter). The Russian Empire and its southern and central European allies acknowledged the potential benefits of establishing 'new' commercial relations via the Black Sea. Regardless of the successes and failures of France and Austria's early attempts to establish trade via the ports of Kherson and Taganrog, it was obvious that the Treaty of Küçük Kajnarca was widely perceived as groundbreaking and significant for the future of European commercial relations.

More than anything else, the parties involved embraced the chance to boost their participation in the quest for North Eurasian trade.

Although the volumes traded were small, two aspects of their commercial development reveal how these ports affected the roles of the Baltic and the Black Sea as border basins of North Eurasia. On the one hand, Anthoine's descriptive account of the commodities traded at Kherson reveals a remarkable overlap with the export bundle of St. Petersburg in 1764, which has been described above (see Chapter 4).[145] On the other hand, the 1784 *ukaz* on the transit trade with Poland-Lithuania, which was issued to increase Polish exports to Kherson,[146] brought some relief for the Prussian obstruction of trade via Danzig and its attempts to redirect this trade to Elbing or Königsberg.[147] Postponed by the Russo-Turkish War (1787–1791), societal development in southern Russia, in general, and the development of trade via the Black Sea, in particular, came in full swing after the Treaty of Jassy (1792) and the foundation of the port of Odessa shortly thereafter.[148]

Between 1802 and 1806, the Black Sea already accounted for 9.6% of Russia's foreign trade, which was more than double the share of Russia's ports on the White Sea coast.[149] At the same time, the overland trade via the western land border of the Russian Empire did not undergo significant changes during the first years of the nineteenth century; its value (converted in silver roubles) even declined somewhat between 1802 and 1806. Besides the port of Taganrog, to which part of the iron exports from the Ural Mountains was diverted,[150] Odessa quickly became the leading Russian port on the Black Sea coast. Odessa's growth took off in 1803, when at least 150 new houses were built, urban and commercial infrastructure was developed, a bank was founded (1804), and merchants from Trieste, Venice, Livorno, Poland, and Greece migrated to the new port.[151] Odessa soon consolidated as gateway for southern Russian trade (see Table 5.3), and became another outlet for North Eurasian trade.

The rapid growth of Odessa and Taganrog during the first years of the nineteenth century was not only due to the opening of the Black Sea for foreign trade. Its development went hand in hand with the liberalization of grain exports from the Russian Empire in 1801 and the renewal of Russia's treaties with southern European states around 1798–1801.[152] Southern Russia (*Ru.* Novorossija) embarked upon an encompassing program of economic and societal development under the auspices of Armand-Emmanuel du Plessis, duc de Richelieu (1766–1822) in 1802, a French national who spent most of his active career in Russian government service until he was appointed Minister of Foreign Affairs under Louis XVIII (1755–1824) in 1815.[153] Richelieu supported the development of southern Russia, and the port of Odessa, in particular, with all possible means,[154] and attracted many French merchants to the port of Odessa.[155] In 1806, when France was at war with Russia, more than 1,000 French subjects lived in Odessa, despite the August 1805 rupture of diplomatic relations between France and Russia, which required French nationals to leave the country within ten days.[156] Even in times of

Table 5.3 Value of imports and exports at Taganrog, Odessa, Arkhangelsk, and St. Petersburg, 1782–1813

	Taganrog		*Odessa*		*Arkhangelsk*		*St. Petersburg*	
	Import	*Export*	*Import*	*Export*	*Import*	*Export*	*Import*	*Export*
1782	68	222.9			433	1,445	12,082	11,353
1783	78	187.6			431	1,425	11,557	9,998
1784	123	234.0			429	1,440	11,929	12,683
1785	160	308.9			404	1,523	9,804	13,228
1786	119	228.8			523	1,629	11,540	13,093
1787	141	78.8			427	1,631	15,098	15,604
1788					501	1,565	14,353	18,876
1789					826	2,178	14,103	19,943
1790					803	1,605	19,979	18,828
1791					658	1,523	20,447	16,301
1792	78	294.0			778	1,853	17,543	17,631
1793	111	303.9			328	1,580	10,352	16,868
1794	238	414.5			463	1,652	14,961	16,143
1795	194	466.6	43	25	580	1,974	16,229	22,396
1796	144	437.3	93	79	530	3,539	20,821	29,317
1797	300	512.4	130	79	449	1,794	14,137	23,689
1798	280	537.3	118	91	404	1,576	16,210	22,845
1799	334	724.5	304	111	301	1,674	12,636	25,001
1800	1,384	1218.4	265	288	175	2,231	11,334	21,369
1801	1,204	1015.5	502	520	320	2,630	17,260	22,297
1802	688	672.5	720	1,534	440	3,739	18,598	24,557
1803	990	1237.7			399	3,787	17,325	25,301
1804	1,928	1513.3		1,801	299	1,762	16,059	22,766
1805	1,966	2095.8		2,883	284	2,735	14,949	22,011
1806	1,645	1533.8		556	193	2,720	12,629	19,573
1807				181	316	1,739	9,737	15,558
1808				882	406	1,028	649	2,625
1809				770	2,298	3,056	2,245	8,802
1810				808	2,322	2,917	2,582	6,622
1811				2,045	3,669	2,379	6,751	10,517
1812				1,476	2,196	2,669	10,518	15,026
1813				2,233	1,399	1,924	20,315	13,904

Sources: Taganrog: *Sanktpeterburgskie kommerčeskie vedomosti*, 4 April 1807; Odessa: Herlihy, *Odessa*, 19; 39; Kozlov, *Archangel'skaja Gubernija*, tables inserted between pages 218 and 219; St. Petersburg: Cavalcanti, *Le relazioni commerciali*, 36–37.
Note: In '000 of silver rubles. Conversion to silver rubles based on Denzel, *Handbook*, 369.

war between Russia and France, Richelieu's influence at the Russian court was large. On condition of ceasing their correspondence with France, most French inhabitants of Odessa could stay; others decided to become Russian citizens, and some others left for Constantinople.[157] In this context, the development of transit trade via Odessa also contributed significantly to the city's growth during the first years of the nineteenth century.

The development of transit trade via Odessa was part of the Russian reaction to the disturbances caused by the French Wars. It was meant to increase the transit through Russia from one part of Europe to the other. Although this aspect of Russia's transit trade that was still in its infancy in the early nineteenth century, it would experience a remarkable upswing in 1807.[158] The Russian trade statistics of the years 1802–1807 show that most of the transit of European and Asian goods through the Russian Empire went in one direction: from Europe to Asia.[159] For the most part, the transit through the Russian Empire consisted of European textiles, furs (probably from overseas) and metal wares with China (via Kyakhta) and Central Asia as their final destination.[160] Smaller values were transported across the Russian Empire from Asia to Europe and from Asia to Asia. Odessa, as well as Taganrog and Feodosia,[161] played a special role in early nineteenth-century efforts to develop the transit of European and Asian goods to destinations on the European continent (in particular, to Prussia, Austria, Moldavia, and Walachia).[162]

The regulations for the transit trade via Odessa were published in March 1804, alongside stipulations about staple rights at the port.[163] In part, these regulations relied on a 1797 set of rules, but now the transit was made easier and more profitable.[164] Soon after, the directions of Odessa's transit trade were prescribed as well.[165] In light of the maritime blockade of the ports of Hamburg and Bremen (1803–1805), the development of the transit route from Odessa to Prussia and the Austrian Empire was promoted as a means to continue trade with the United Kingdom.[166] British textiles would be imported to Odessa and then distributed across the European continent via the toll stations of Radziwiłłów and Krinki. In return, Britain would be able to obtain its much-needed supplies of (Italian) silk and Silesian cloth via the port of Odessa as well.[167] Nikolai Petrovich Rumyantsev (1754–1826), the Russian minister of foreign affairs, followed three basic ideas with his economic policy measures: the reduction of imports through substitution with domestic production, the advancement of exports, and the spreading of transit trade. Rumyantsev's efforts to increase transit trade through Odessa and other Black Sea ports are significant for two reasons. They show the revival of old ideas about the establishment of direct commercial relations with India and Central Asia, in which Odessa would function as a gateway linking the West with the East, on the one hand, and awareness of the benefits of combining economic liberalist ideas with (moderate) protectionism, on the other.[168]

The strategic significance of the Black Sea for North Eurasian trade hardly went unnoticed in diplomatic circles. As early as September 1802, a Frenchmen called Émile Gaudin sent a note to Napoleon concerning the potential benefits for France of active involvement in the Black Sea and Levant trade as a means to compete with Britain and to strengthen the ties with Russia. Among other things, Gaudin suggested to open a trading route towards Anatolia, Izmir and Tehran, passing by Tbilisi, and to install commercial agents and trading houses in Kyiv, Moscow, Kazan, Astrakhan and northern Russia to compete with the British factors.[169] More evidence about the recognition of the strategic importance of the Black Sea as gateway for North Eurasian trade is found in the instructions for the new ambassador to Constantinople,

Guillaume Marie-Anne Brune (1764–1815), which were issued in September 1802 as well. The instructions show great awareness about the international scale and scope of the quest for North Eurasian trade, the anticipated benefits of trade with North Eurasian commodities via Russia's ports on the Black Sea coast, and the complementarity of the Baltic and the Black Sea as outlets for North Eurasian commodities. In particular, attention is drawn towards the rivers Dniester, Dnepr, Bug, Don, and Volga as arteries of North Eurasian trade.[170]

Based on these observations it becomes clear that the French anticipated the outcome of Russia's expansionist wars in the Caucasus. Indeed, the Russian Empire was on a course to strengthen its military and commercial position in the Black and Caspian Seas. Following Russia's occupation of Georgia in 1801,[171] Russia waged expansionist wars against Persia (1804–1813). A brief interlude in 1808 notwithstanding,[172] Russia also resumed war with the Ottoman Empire (1806–1812). In the wake of the Russian offensives against the Ottoman Empire and Persia, the latter concluded a strategic alliance with France (Treaty of Finkenstein, May 1807). However, as Paul W. Schroeder points out, this alliance was intended to put Persia on the map as a strategic British buffer in Central Asia. The treaty of Finkenstein was meant to make the British "take Persia seriously" and, eventually, to weaken and destroy the enduring Anglo-Russian alliance. Bearing in mind that Britain had strengthened its own position in India just a few years earlier, the first signs of an extension of the quest for North Eurasian trade towards the land border between North and South Eurasia become apparent for the first time.[173]

The Continental Blockade

The quest for North Eurasian trade reached its peak at the beginning of the 1806 sailing season. Britain renewed and extended its blockade of the North Sea, making a distinction between "(…) a strict blockade of the [North Sea] coast between the Mouth of the Seine and Ostend" and "(…) a less strict blockade of the rest of the coast between the Elbe and Brest."[174] Under certain conditions, neutral vessels were allowed to enter the ports of the outer section of the blockade. Napoleon reacted with a combination of repressive economic measures, which had to exclude Britain from all connections with the European mainland (and the North Sea coast, in particular) and the so-called 'continental self-blockade,' which foresaw nothing less than the closure of the French market to British industrial products and colonial goods of British origin.[175]

By the year 1806, Napoleon had already occupied large parts of continental Europe and withstood several coalition wars against France.[176] After the 'crushing of Prussia' at Jena and Auerstädt in October that year, Napoleon controlled part of the North Sea and Baltic coast from the Weser to the Vistula, alongside significant coastal strips in the Mediterranean. Nevertheless, the defeat of the French fleet in the infamous battle of Trafalgar one year earlier (21 October 1805) effectively got him stuck on the continent. Logically then, Napoleon's efforts and measures to 'destroy' the British enemy were now bound to affect the entire European continent. What this meant becomes clear in the regulations of the Berlin Decree issued 21 November 1806, in which many earlier prohibitions regarding the presence of British goods, subjects and vessels on the European continent were applied more vigorously than ever before.[177] Immediately after the Berlin Decree, British exports to the Continent were halted, causing an upsurge in marine insurance premiums.[178] In reaction to the Berlin Decree, Great Britain issued several Orders in Council, which hampered neutral shipping (7 January 1807), re-directed neutral trade to British ports and forbade direct intercourse between the enemy countries and other ports. Vessels sailing under the neutral flags of Mecklenburg, Oldenburg, Papenburg, or Kniphausen were declared "(...) lawful prize if they touched at an enemy port unless they were going from or coming to a British port" (19 August 1807).[179] In sum, international commerce was now determined by French self-blockade policies on the European continent directed against Great Britain, by British blockade policies directed against France's and its allies' exports, and by measures and counter-measures of neutrals, most importantly the United States, to defend their rights to trade.

Both the French and the neutrals (most importantly, the United States) reacted instantly to the regulations laid out in the British Ordinances. The Berlin Decree was largely ineffective, not at the least due to the corruption of the French officers responsible for enforcing its regulations. Napoleon acknowledged this and introduced more restrictive customs regulations and control systems, before issuing his famous Milan Decrees (23 November 1807 and 17 December 1807), which provided for the "(...) express and unrestricted extension of the System from the Continent to the sea, in so far as French privateers could make it effective there."[180] The Continental System now applied to neutral shipping as such. From then on, according to Eli Heckscher (1879–1952), "(...) there were no longer any neutrals[;] (...) they were either (...) Englishmen in disguise, or (...) accomplices of the English (...)."[181] In a failed attempt to induce the belligerents to make provisions for neutral American shipping and to put an end to their seizure,[182] the United States issued the Embargo Act (22 December 1807) and put into force the Non-importation Act (issued in 1806).[183] Thus, they established a self-blockade of their ports. This, in turn, led to the French Bayonne Decree (17 April 1808), which stated that all American vessels were to be seized under the assumption that, in reality, they were British vessels in disguise.[184]

In 1806, when the Continental System was unveiled and Napoleon successfully ended his campaign against the Holy Roman Empire, the estimated tonnage of Baltic commercial exchange was already halved. The decline continued in 1807 when only 334,884 tonnes were registered at the Sound. In 1808 and 1809, registered traffic through the Sound came to an almost complete stop: 10,365 tonnes were registered in 1808 and 32,142 tonnes in 1809.[185] However, the absence of registered traffic through the Danish Sound does not mean that North Eurasian trade *per se* collapsed. Warfare on the European continent and in overseas territories left belligerents and neutrals with three main ways to continue international trade: in disguise, with the help of licences, and via alternative routes. Smuggling – often via third countries – was a driving force for the establishment of new commercial routes. The use of licences issued by both British and French was a means to continue trade along 'traditional' lines.[186]

In the second half of 1807, under the impact of France's more restrictive customs regulations, British trade with the Continent stagnated. British textiles became scarce, prices and insurance premiums started to rise quickly.[187] The negative impact on Russia's foreign trade contributed to growing disappointment from the Russian side with Britain's 'insufficient' war efforts. The Russians complained about lack of British military and financial aid in the war against the Ottoman Empire; the British were annoyed with the fact that Russia continued its trade with France.[188] Tensions reached their peak when Russia changed sides after Napoleon and Alexander I's meeting at Tilsit (June 1807). The impact of this radical manoeuvre was felt immediately.

After Tilsit

Remarkably, Russia's adherence to the Continental System had already been outlined prior to the Tilsit meeting in an *ukaz* of January 1, 1807.[189] This ukaz has been described as a "(…) masterpiece in the application of the Continental system by Russia, which in fact hampered all foreign commerce for the benefit of Russians and Greeks, (…)."[190] Earlier historiography of the Napoleonic era has often pointed out that the ultimate goal of the treaty of Tilsit was the division of Europe in French and Russian spheres, and partitioning of the Ottoman Empire and the Black Sea according to the same principle. Although this explanation has been criticized for being overly simple,[191] in view of later events, it seems to have aligned quite well with Russia's self-perception as the main political and economic actor in North Eurasia. Russia applied the regulations of the Continental System more and more reluctantly since 1810,[192] when the defeat of Napoleon already heralded itself, and thus revealed its self-perception as the predominant North Eurasian power. According to the Russian scheme, the United Kingdom would be catered via the Baltic; Britain's rival France would be supplied via the Black Sea; and Russia itself would control both seas as well as the overland flows of Asian goods to Europe.

Regardless of these distant goals and anticipated benefits, Russia's adherence to Napoleon's Continental System had a devastating immediate impact on the prices of imported and exported goods,[193] and – consequently – on the value of Russia's foreign trade. The price of Russian export items, such as naval stores, iron and tallow, fell markedly – by 40% at least between 1804 and 1809 – and was aggravated by the rapid devaluation of the rouble (see

Table 5.4 Value of Russia's foreign trade via its western borderlands and border basins, 1802–1812

	Baltic	*White*	*Black*	*Land*
1802	57	3.8	3.6	13.2
1803	63.6	4.2	6.3	15.6
1804	57.3	2.1	7.2	11.7
1805	62.3	3.2	9.8	12.6
1806	55.6	3.2	6.1	10.9
1807	47.5	2.6	0.6	6.5
1808	10.6	1.7	5.1	18.9
1809	26	5.6	2.8	10.6
1810		>5.2	>1.9	9.6
1811				
1812	34.4	5.1	3.6	

Source: Zlotnikov, *Kontinental'naja blokada*, 11–12, 19; 293.
Note: In millions of silver roubles. Data for western land border (= Land in the table) in 1810 are incomplete.

Table 5.4). The price of imported commodities, however, rose strongly: Between 1804 and 1809, the price of one pood of sugar increased by 71.4% and that of one pood of cochineal by as much as 147.1%.[194] The strong decline in the value of Russia's foreign trade in 1808 is hardly surprising; after all, trade with its most important partner, the United Kingdom, was now forbidden. Russia had declared war on the United Kingdom and issued embargoes on British ships as early as October 1807, giving the British merchant fleet just enough time to leave Russian ports in the Baltic.[195] To make things worse, after the second British attack on Copenhagen, Denmark was occupied by the French,[196] the Danish Sound was 'closed,' and ships could only enter the Baltic if they had obtained an appropriate licence. Sweden now persisted as Great Britain's sole ally, and refused to become part of the Continental System.[197]

In 1808, in the wake of both the British and Americans' fierce reactions to the French Continental System and the French counteraction in the Milan decrees, new 'channels for trade' to the European continent were sought in Helgoland and Gothenburg, from where goods could be smuggled into Germany and the southern Baltic ports,[198] and in Spanish and Portuguese territories,[199] including Brazil,[200] where the Portuguese Royal family had found shelter just before Napoleon's invasion of Lisbon on 1 December 1808.[201] Russia as well tried to leverage these changes by means of the establishment of direct commercial relations with the Southern American states that had declared their independence. In 1810, Russia changed the 1798 commercial treaty with Portugal so that trade with Portugal would be forbidden, but trade with Brazil, Madeira and the Azores could continue.[202] The United States issued even stronger regulations for their trade with the United Kingdom and France in 1809,[203] which resulted in considerable increases of its trade with more or less neutral places, such as the Hanseatic Towns, Altona, Tönning in Schleswig, and probably Gothenburg.[204] Meanwhile, smuggling through Dutch and East Frisian ports to ports in the Baltic continued to flourish.[205]

In the Baltic itself, a regional military conflict between Russia and Sweden led to the annexation by Russia of the Grand Duchy of Finland (1809),[206] and Sweden's forced acceptance of the Treaty of Paris (January 1810), which foresaw the exclusion of British vessels and commodities (except salt) from Swedish ports.[207] On the coast of the North Sea, "(...) Napoleon became more and more convinced of the possibility of compelling obedience of the self-blockade beyond the limits of his own direct authority, (...)"[208] which stimulated him to incorporate Holland and "(...) the whole of the North Sea coast and the Holstein border up to the Baltic at the mouth of the Trave."[209] During the first years of the Continental Blockade, from 1807 until 1810, registered traffic through the Danish Sound was interrupted almost completely.[210] Nevertheless, as was mentioned before, trade continued, either in disguise, on different routes, and/or with licences. The commodity flows to and from North Eurasia during this period, show the complementarity of the different border basins and borderlands in the western part of North Eurasia. Scattered data shows that the closure of the Danish Sound immediately led to an upswing of import and export trade via the overland border, ports on the White Sea and, most significantly, the Black Sea (see Table 5.4).[211] During the first period, the shift from trade via Russia's border basins to trade via the western land border is undeniable. In 1808, when the crisis hit the Russia's foreign trade the hardest,[212] a remarkable upswing of trade via the western land border occurred (see Table 5.4).

Moreover, despite the ongoing Russo-Turkish War and the general decline of Russia's foreign trade since 1807, trade at the port of Odessa grew significantly between 1808 and 1810. Figures compiled by the French consul at Odessa indicate that the port played an essential role in the economic aspects of the Russo-Turkish War. In part, this growth was due to Odessa's role as the centre of supplies for the Russian army; in part, it resulted from the emergence of a new transit route via Odessa to the European continent.[213] Whereas, until 1807, the transit trade through Russia had been dominated by European manufactures sent through Russia to Asia (mostly China), the pattern changed drastically as trade through the Danish Sound was obstructed.[214] From 1807 on, a reversal of the transit trade through the Russian Empire occurred: its direction changed from 'Europe to Asia' before the blockade to 'Asia to Europe' during the blockade.[215] Two new routes emerged for the transit of goods from 'Asia to Europe.' On the first route, Asian goods were brought to Smyrna, were then transported overland to the border of the Sea of Marmara, from the port of Artak to the European border, and then further overland through Turkey and Illyria to Western Europe. The second route went from the Sea of Marmara to Odessa, and then overland through Austria to Western Europe.[216] The latter route experienced a remarkable upswing in 1808, but declined already the next year. In 1810, the decline continued due to new French regulations, which aimed at the reorientation of transit (with France as final destination) via the route through Illyria and Italy rather than via Odessa, Austria and Strasbourg.[217]

Rumyantsev was aware of the devastating effect of Russia's alliance with France, and tried to lower its impact by postponing decisions and making regulations less strict than what the French consul had prescribed. Prohibitions on the importation of British manufactured and overseas goods as well as on the entry of British ships in Russian ports were issued ten months after the treaty of Tilsit at the earliest.[218] Goods from Asia or Turkey, with whom Russia still had a lively Black Sea trade despite the ongoing war, as well as from Prussia, were exempt from the registration of the origin of goods with special labels.[219] This assured the continuation (and perhaps even expansion) of Russia's transit trade between Continental Europe and Asia via the Black Sea. Moreover, the Russian government found (secret) ways to continue trade with the United Kingdom, despite the prohibitions it had issued in the course of 1808, and seems to have played a double role with regard to its French ally.[220] In this context, it was quite clear that the Russian regulations for neutral shipping in 1809 and 1810 were employed as a means to 'neutralize' British ships.[221] Although the circumstances were far from ideal, trade with Britain could and – in fact – did continue. When a large number of 'neutral' ships arrived from Tenerife, Pernambuco and Brazil – as official documents would state – in July 1810, they could enter Russian ports in the Baltic and the White Sea, even though it was obvious that these ships and the goods they carried were in fact British.[222] Although the official practice of confiscating ships would continue until the end of 1810, ruining several Russian and German merchant houses in St. Petersburg and Riga,[223] Anglo-Russian trade was now hampered only by cumbersome 'official' procedures. Gradually, the control of neutral vessels became less strict and the breaches in the French-Russian union of Tilsit became stronger and stronger.

In 1810, trade was severely damaged by the Trianon Tariff (August 1810), the Fontainebleau decree (October 1810).[224] These novel decrees and regulations marked the start of the second period of the Continental Blockade, which lasted until 1814. In August 1810, Russia refused to introduce the new customs tariff of Trianon and with the 'order about neutral trade in 1811'[225] Russia put an end to its alliance with France,[226] started to intercept French ships in the Black Sea,[227] and at the same time, started to treat British shipping more and more favourably.[228] From 1810 until 1813, significant shares of Russia's foreign trade entered or left the Empire via the Western land border and ports on the White Sea rather than via its ports in the Baltic (see Table 5.4). For a short period, the relocation of foreign trade to the White Sea even entailed to the emergence of a peculiar transit route linking ports on the East Coast of the United States with Western Europe via Arkhangelsk and the western land border at Polangen (*Pl.* Połągą) and Radziwiłłów.[229] Although this particular transit route did not exist long,[230] the complementarity of the North Eurasian borderlands would remain a characteristic feature of North Eurasian trade on several occasions in the first half of the nineteenth century.

During the second phase of the Continental Blockade, three sides threatened the 'traditional' structure of North Eurasian trade. First, the disturbances caused by the Continental Blockade had reinforced the British search for alternative supplies of raw materials and posed a growing threat to North Eurasian trade.[231] Second, countries on the European continent took measures against the overwhelming commercial predominance of the United Kingdom and developed different ways to establish and strengthen domestic industries using prohibition and protection as their main tools. Thus, for example, the tonnage of most raw materials exports from Russia declined,[232] whereas that of several import items (especially sugar) increased drastically due to the intensification of transit trade through Russia, on the one hand, and the establishment of Russian sugar refineries during the Blockade, on the other.[233] Contrastingly, the importation of manufactured goods to Russia experienced a very strong decline as extensive measures were taken to strengthen and protect domestic textile production by means of the prohibitive customs tariff of 1811.[234] The Continental System fell apart rapidly when Napoleon embarked on his dramatic Russian campaign in 1812. By the time of his abdication in April 1814, the system was abolished.[235] As soon as trade through the Sound was resumed in late 1813, a swift return to pre-1806 volumes occurred.

The (temporary) loss of the North American market for British products provoked a significant increase in the exportation of naval stores (including iron) from North Eurasian ports in the Baltic and White Seas. Only North Eurasian supplies could meet the rapidly growing demands of the British Navy, both in terms of their quantity and the quality required for producing naval equipment. However, at the time when Great Britain's interest in the Baltic intensified, the latter's role as a border basin of North Eurasia was itself the subject of significant territorial changes. Great Britain's most significant trading partner in the Baltic, the Russian Empire, played a predominant role in these territorial changes. Russia finally recovered access to the Black Sea, on the one hand, and was one of the powers that partitioned Poland-Lithuania, on the other. In the meantime, the Dutch Republic was ruled out as a commercial power. Great Britain with its predominant naval and commercial fleet took over. However, Great Britain's self-perceived dependence on North Eurasian *naval stores* reached new levels as their demand exploded in the wake of the American War of Independence and, from the 1790s onwards, the French Wars. Furthermore, Prussia's economic policies in the annexed territories of Poland-Lithuania, and the battle against Danzig, in particular, provoked an important shift in commodity flows from the hinterland of the Baltic ports. Last but not least, Russia's gains on the Black Sea coast and its territorial advances in Poland-Lithuania gave Russia's self-confidence another boost and contributed to its increasingly adverse relationship towards Great Britain in the late 1780s. In turn, Great Britain tried to diminish its dependence on Russian naval stores, through reorientation towards Prussia and the intensification of its global search for alternative supplies. Although the attempts to procure alternative supplies of raw materials remained unsuccessful until the (early) nineteenth century, they bear witness of the fact that the quest for North Eurasian trade had become embedded firmly in considerations about political and economic power with a global scope. The threats to North Eurasian trade – British industrial power and production, Britain's search for alternative supplies of naval stores – were felt more clearly than ever before during the final stage of the Napoleonic system and would have a lasting impact on the further course of North Eurasian trade in the first half of the nineteenth century.

Notes

1 *Tetradas* [VSWG-JDA], 1_turnover: *Estimated total turnover.*
2 *Tetradas* [VSWG-JDA], 1_turnover: *Estimated total turnover.*
3 *Tetradas* [VSWG-JDA], 6_BTR_Bex: *Exports from Russia.*
4 Ryan, "The defense," 444–445; Scheltjens, "French imports," 152; 156–157.
5 Scheltjens, "French imports," 152.
6 Scheltjens, "French imports," 152; and also: Barker & Harris, *A Merseyside town*; Iredale, "John and Thomas Marshall"; Smithers, *Liverpool*; Poole, *The commerce.*
7 With slightly different wording, the rest of this paragraph has been published in Scheltjens, "French imports," 156.
8 *Tetradas* [VSWG-JDA], 8_CIES_Wim: *Sugar, Coffee, Tobacco, "SugarAndTobacco"*; 7_PIES_LeHavre: *Imports of foodstuffs.*
9 *Tetradas* [VSWG-JDA], 7_PIES_Bordeaux: *Imports of foodstuffs*; 8_CIES_Wim: *Sugar*; 5_BIE: *France.*
10 Crouzet, "War, blockade, and economic change"; Marzagalli, "Le négoce maritime."
11 dos Santos Arnold, "Atlantic Sugar and Central Europe."
12 *Tetradas* [VSWG-JDA], 7_PIES_Hamburg: *Import of foodstuffs*; 8_CIES_Wim: *Sugar.*
13 *Tetradas* [VSWG-JDA], 5_BIE: United Kingdom; 8_CIES_Wim: *Sugar.*
14 E.g. Åström, *From tar to timber.*
15 E.g. Hartley, *Russia*, 85–109. Hartley raises a number of relevant issues, but her account of Anglo-Russian trade is limited to a collection of rather loose points with regard to prices of commodities, the number of ships calling at Russian ports, and the quantities of some commodities exchanged. Remarkably, Hartley does not refer to Kaplan's work in her chapter on agriculture, industry and trade.
16 E.g. Zacharov, *Zapadnoevropejskie kupcy*, 92–130.
17 Therefore, it seemed worthwhile to have a closer look at the differences and similarities between Kaplan's data and my tonnage estimates of trade through the Danish Sound, at least insofar as they are comparable. The results are described in Scheltjens, "Tetradas."
18 Kaplan, *Russian overseas commerce.*
19 The growth of bar iron exports through the Danish Sound at the turn of the eighteenth century contrasts with the findings of Eklund, Evans and Rydén, who state that "(...) in the 1790s, (...) the prospects for Baltic iron [on the British market] darkened." They attribute large impact to Henry Cort's puddling process, patented in 1783, which provided "(...) an effective and expeditious way of using mineral coal to refine iron." Eklund, Evans and Rydén conclude that "[b]y the end of the Napoleonic Wars Russian iron had been entirely expelled from the British market whilst Swedish iron was restricted to niche markets

such as that for steel iron." This assessment finds little support in the tonnage estimates of iron exports through the Danish Sound during the first decades of the nineteenth century. See Eklund, Evans, and Rydén, 'From the Baltic to the Atlantic,' 213–214. Compare with: *Tetradas* [VSWG-JDA], 8_CIES_Bex:RM: *Iron*; 8_CIES_Bex_MF: *Iron staves.*

20 The commercial treaties of the mid-1780s were issued according to a number of basic principles, outlined during the preparation of the 1785 treaty of commerce with Austria. See Zlotnikov, *Kontinental'naja Blokada*, 81. The text of the treaties can be found in: PSZ, XXII, 16284, 16498, 16594. Furthermore, see Van Regermorter, "Commerce et politique"; Schop Soler, *Die spanisch-russischen Beziehungen*; Cavalcanti, *Le relazioni commerciale*, 123–150; Moreira, Martins, and Scheltjens, "Portuguese-Russian commercial relations," 74–77.

21 Lukowski, "Towards partition," 570–571.

22 Michalski, *Dyplomacja polska*, 487–490.

23 Schroeder, *The transformation of European politics*, 11–12.

24 Davies, *God's playground, I*, 516.

25 For a different point of view, see Schroeder, *The transformation of European politics*, 3: "Prussia survived the war, but barely, and the aggressive spirit of King Frederick the Great was broken by it."

26 Michalski, *Dyplomacja polska*, 484.

27 Davies, *God's playground, I*, 513.

28 Łojek, "British policy towards Russia," 3.

29 Martens, *Receuil des traités et conventions VI*, 1–32; Schroeder, *The transformation of European politics*, 13.

30 Łojek, "British policy towards Russia," 3.

31 Davies, *God's playground, I*, 516.

32 Martens, *Receuil des traités et conventions VI*, 48–64; 98.

33 Martens, *Receuil des traités et conventions VI*, 60.

34 Martens, *Receuil des traités et conventions VI*, 50.

35 Davies, *God's playground, I*, 515–516.

36 Martens, *Receuil des traités et conventions IX (X)*, 218.

37 Martens, *Receuil des traités et conventions IX (X)*, 203–259. Earlier in 1766, Great Britain had signed a treaty of friendship and commerce with Sweden, see Martens, *Receuil des traités et conventions IX (X)*, 75. The 1734 Anglo-Russian treaty had expired in 1755. Due to differences of opinion between British and Russian diplomats, which were inspired by Russia's high self-esteem and its growing self-confidence in political, military and commercial affairs, it took several years and a *Palace Revolution* before the treaty could finally be renewed in 1766. About this episode in Anglo-Russian diplomacy, see Clendenning, "The Anglo-Russian trade treaty."

38 Łojek, "The international crisis of 1791," 2.

39 Michael, *Englands Stellung.*

40 Schroeder, *The transformation of European politics*, 12–13.

41 About the Confederation of Bar, see Gierszewski, *The Polish-Lithuanian commonwealth*, 105–146.

42 Schroeder, *The transformation of European politics*, 12–13 and 35.

43 Schroeder, *The transformation of European politics*, 13.

44 Schroeder, *The transformation of European politics*, 16–17.

45 Martens, *Receuil des traités et conventions VI*, 64; 65–90; 90–98.

46 This process continues to attract scholarly attention. Valuable accounts include: Halm, *Österreich und Neurußland*, 19–66; Družinina, *Severnoe pričernomor'e*; Herlihy, *Russian grain*, 38–64; Ardeleanu, "The opening and development of the Black Sea."

47 Družinina, *Severnoe pričernomor'e*, 48–49.

48 Schroeder, *The transformation of European politics*, 22.

49 For an extensive, but rather one-sided account of the negotiations leading towards this treaty, see Družinina, *Kjučuk-Kajnardžijskij mir.*
50 Schroeder, *The transformation of European politics*, 22; Atkin, *Russia and Iran*, 30.
51 Atkin, *Russia and Iran*, 123–161.
52 *Tetradas* [VSWG-JDA], 2_C_Bex: *Itemized commodities*; 8_CIES_Bex_FS: *Barley, Oats, Rye, Wheat*; 8_CIES_Bex_RM: *Balks, Boards, Deals.*
53 *Tetradas* [VSWG-JDA], 8_CIES_Bex_FS: *Barley, Oats, Rye, Wheat*; 7_PIES_Amsterdam: *Exports of foodstuffs.*
54 PSZ, XVI, 11630.
55 Riga's special status was confirmed in the 1765 *Handels-Ordnung*, which stipulated, among other things:

> Den Pohlen, Litthauern und Curländern ist erlaubet ihre Landes-Producten wie zu Lande, so längst dem Düna-Strohm, zollfrey in Riga einzuführen, mit der ihnen zu ertheilenden Versicherung, daß ihre eingeführte Waaren, sie haben Nahmen wie sie wollen, nie sollen aufgehalten, noch die Ausschiffung derselben verboten werden (...).

See [s.n.], *Der Stadt Riga Handels-Ordnung*, 5.
56 *Tetradas* [VSWG-JDA], 7_PIES_Riga: *Exports of foodstuffs, Exports of raw materials*; 7_PIES_Memel: *Exports of foodstuffs, Exports of raw materials.*
57 Oddy, *European commerce*, 220.
58 *Tetradas* [VSWG-JDA], 7_PIES_Danzig: *Exports of foodstuffs, Exports of raw materials.*
59 See Scheltjens, "Die politische Ökonomie."
60 See Ressel, "Swedish Pomeranian shipping"; Müller, "Sweden's neutral trade"; Andersen and Voth, "Grapes of war," and the literature cited in these papers.
61 The historiography of the partitions is vast and varied. The most recent general introduction to the literature is: Krzoska, "Teilungserfahrung und Traditionsbildung." Furthermore, see Müller, *Die Teilungen*; Langer, "Die Beurteilung der Teilungen." The economic aspects of the partitions have received less scholarly attention, see Drozdowski, "Die Historiographie," 145-153; Topolski, "Reflections"; Topolski, "Poglądy"; Rostworowski, "Na drodze do pierwszego rozbioru"; Cieślak, "The Influence"; Biernat, "Wybrane problem." For recent additions with a focus on the Danish Sound toll registers as a source for observing changes in the structure of international shipping and trade in the wake of the partitions, see Kaps, *Desintegrationserscheinungen* (mimeo); Ressel, "The impact of the partitions"; Scheltjens, "Die krisenhaften Auswirkungen."
62 Scheltjens, *Dutch deltas*, Chapter 3.
63 Compare: *Tetradas* [VSWG-JDA], 7_PIES_Danzig: *Exports of raw materials*; 7_PIES_Königsberg: *Exports of raw materials*; 7_PIES_Memel: *Exports of raw materials*; 7_PIES_Riga: *Exports of raw materials.*
64 For the Prusso-Polish commercial treaty, see Wilder, *Traktat handlowy*; Herzfeld, "Der polnische Handelsvertrag." Wilder's study still is the most comprehensive study available on the subject. For the commercial regulations specified in a bilateral agreement between the Russian Empire and the Kingdom of Poland, see PSZ, XX, 14271. Herzfeld remarks that the Russo-Polish treaty, that was signed two weeks before the Prusso-Polish treaty, was carefully studied during the preparations for the latter. (See Herzfeld, "Der polnische Handelsvertrag," 71).
65 Wilder, *Traktat handlowy*, 170–171; 193; Bär, *Westpreußen unter Friedrich dem Großen, II*, 16.
66 The complex issue of relating and comparing the figures in STRO and *Tetradas* with Rolf Straubel's detailed analysis of the ports of Königsberg and Memel between 1763 and 1806/15 remains to be tackled in future research. See Straubel, *Die Handelsstädte.*
67 Wilder, *Traktat handlowy*, 178–179; 183–184.
68 Wilder, *Traktat handlowy*, 193–194.

69 Wilder, "Plan projekt budowy."
70 Wilder, *Traktat handlowy*, 195.
71 Wilder, *Traktat handlowy*, 184.
72 Wilder, *Traktat handlowy*, 196.
73 Wilder, *Traktat handlowy*, 196–200; Herzfeld, "Der polnische Handelsvertrag," 211–212.
74 Wilder, *Traktat handlowy*, 202–210.
75 *Tetradas* [VSWG-JDA], 7_PIES_Danzig: *Exports of foodstuffs*; 7_PIES_Königsberg: *Exports of foodstuffs*; 7_PIES_Memel: *Exports of foodstuffs*; 7_PIES_Riga: *Exports of foodstuffs*.
76 *Tetradas* [VSWG-JDA], 3_EI_Bex: *Countries (areas) of destination*; 8_CIES_Bex_FS: *Wheat*.
77 *Tetradas* [VSWG-JDA], 7_PIES_Memel: *Exports of raw materials*; 7_PIES_St-Petersburg: *Exports of raw materials*; 7_PIES_Vyborg: *Exports of raw materials*.
78 Libiszowska, "James Durno."
79 The study of the activities of James Durno, and his impact on British trade with Poland-Lithuania and the partitioning powers is a research desideratum, which could make an important contribution to the issue of the economic impact of the partitions. So far, historiography has treated this topic either in very general terms, or in the form of small-scale case-studies. An in-depth analysis of Durno's correspondence with the British and Prussian courts during the period of the partitions will shed a different light on the different opportunities to leverage the partitions.
80 Calculations based on values of exports from the Grand Duchy of Lithuania in 1786–1791. See Truska and Jasas, "Vnešnjaja torgovlja," 47.
81 Herzfeld, "Der polnische Handelsvertrag," 45–49.
82 Herzfeld, "Der polnische Handelsvertrag," 49.
83 Łojek, "British policy," 4; Hopf, *Danzig*, 103–170; Davey, "Securing the Sinews of sea power," 165–167; Kaplan, *Russian overseas commerce*, 113–131.
84 McKay and Scott, *The rise of the great powers*, 234–242; Łojek, "The international crisis of 1791," 23–36; Ehrman, *The British government*, 100–113.
85 For introductory surveys of the so-called 'Eastern Crisis,' see Schroeder, *The transformation of European politics*, 56–61 and 74–83; Łojek, "The international crisis of 1791"; Ehrman, *The British government*, 130–136. Only few historians have discussed the 'Eastern Crisis' from an economic perspective. Among them, most importantly: Gerhard, *England und der Aufstieg Russlands*, 275–308.
86 Ehrman, *The British government*, 117.
87 Hopf, *Danzig*, 138.
88 Webb, "Sea power."
89 Gerhard, *England und der Aufstieg Russlands*, 280–285; Klimesz, "Poland's trade." The opening of the Black Sea for Polish trade caused friction among the Polish magnates, giving the landowners of the southern part of Poland-Lithuania "(...) every cause to look kindly on their eastern protector" (see Lukowski, "Towards partition," 571).
90 Martens, *Receuil des traités et conventions VI*, 107–119.
91 Łojek, "British policy," 4.
92 Martens, *Receuil des traités et conventions VI*, 119–132.
93 Schroeder, *The transformation of European politics*, 60–61; Hopf, *Danzig*, 106–109.
94 Another sign of the increasing British interest in trade with Poland is the 1788 plan to create, with British assistance, a port in Polangen, on the small strip of land in Samogitia, which was actually still Polish at that time. See Wilder, "Projekt Franciska Piłsudskiego"; Misiuras, "The Šventoji project."
95 Ehrman, *The British government*, 113–119.

96 Ehrman, *The British government*, 111.
97 Hopf, *Danzig*, 121–133.
98 Gerhard, *England und der Aufstieg Russlands*, 319–320; Hopf, *Danzig*, 140–143. In the discussions that evolved around the British proposal to cede Danzig to Prussia and Russia's counter-reaction a large body of pamphlets and public statements was published, in which several Polish parties took position in favour of Great Britain or Russia, while others made alternative proposals. These publications have only scarcely been researched so far and are mostly referred to in the margin of the 4-year's Diet. A more extensive analysis of its participants, however, might shed light on the differences in economic reasoning between the various parties involved and the practical concerns used to support their arguments.
99 Schroeder, *The transformation of European politics*, 79.
100 Hopf, *Danzig*, 147.
101 Hopf, *Danzig*, 151; Schroeder, *The transformation of European politics*, 82.
102 Hopf, *Danzig*, 166.
103 Martens, *Receuil des traités et conventions VI*, 159–163.
104 Schroeder, *The transformation of European politics*, 124–125.
105 Schroeder, *The transformation of European politics*, 124.
106 Martens, *Receuil des traités et conventions VI*, 163–170.
107 Heckscher, *The continental system*, 28.
108 Heckscher, *The continental system*, 25 and 30–58.
109 For a short introduction to this treaty, see Henderson, "The Anglo-French commercial treaty"; Donaghay, "The exchange."
110 Heckscher, *The continental system*, 25 and 30–58.
111 Heckscher, *The continental system*, 25, 27.
112 Heckscher, *The continental system*, 27–28. The French Navigations Acts were issued 21 September 1793 and 18 October 1793.
113 Heckscher, *The continental system*, 31.
114 Zlotnikov, *Kontinental'naja blokada*, 49. The 1793 import prohibition was directed against revolutionary France, but also included a large number of other commodities. It also served to improve the exchange rate of the Russian rouble. See PSZ, XXIII, 16781, 17111, and *kniga tarifov*, III, obščee dopolnenie, 42–46.
115 Zlotnikov, *Kontinental'naja blokada*, 81.
116 Zlotnikov, *Kontinental'naja blokada*, 56–58.
117 *Tetradas* [VSWG-JDA], 6_BTR_Bex: *Exports from Prussia*; 8_CIES_Bex_FS: *Wheat.*
118 *Tetradas* [VSWG-JDA], 8_CIES_Bex_MF: *Linen*; 8_CIES_Bex_RM: *Deals.*
119 *Tetradas* [VSWG-JDA], 8_CIES_Bex_RM: *Iron*; 8_CIES_Bex_MF: *Iron staves*; 6_BTR_Bex: *Exports from Sweden, Exports from Russia.*
120 On the historiography of the 1797 tariff, see Zlotnikov, *Kontinental'naja blokada*, 49–55.
121 For example, the 1798 ban on timber exports, see Davey, "Securing the Sinews of sea power," 169.
122 For a summary overview of these measures, see Zlotnikov, *Kontinental'naja blokada*, 55–59.
123 Zlotnikov, *Kontinental'naja blokada*, 60–61.
124 Hösch, "Zar Paul I," 304. Hösch sees in Paul I's policy initiatives the contours of a novel foreign policy and self-perception of the Russian Empire, which comprised an active role in the Mediterranean (Malta, Ionian Islands) as well as a return to the 'old' idea of establishing a land route to India through the Russian Empire. See Hösch, "Zar Paul I," 308–314.
125 Heckscher, *The continental system*, 47.

126 Heckscher, *The continental system*, 50–51.
127 Zlotnikov, *Kontinental'naja blokada*, 60–61.
128 Zlotnikov, *Kontinental'naja blokada*, 88–91.
129 Zlotnikov, *Kontinental'naja blokada*, 62–71; 91–102; 117–128. Several proposals were made for a new tariff during the first years of Alexander's reign, but neither of them was successful.
130 Heckscher, *The continental system*, 78.
131 Heckscher, *The continental system*, 81.
132 Heckscher, *The continental system*, 37.
133 Heckscher, *The continental system*, 37.
134 Heckscher, *The continental system*, 37–38.
135 Heckscher, *The continental system*, 81–82.
136 *Tetradas* [VSWG-JDA], 8_CIES_Bex_FS: *Barley, Oats, Rye, Wheat.*
137 *Tetradas* [VSWG-JDA], 6_BTR_Bex: *Exports from Prussia.*
138 Zlotnikov, *Kontinental'naja blokada*, 24–29 and the quantitative survey of the main import and export items during the years 1802–1806 on pages 30–40 (exports: grain, hemp & flax, timber, iron, textiles) and 40–48 (imports: salt, dye stuffs, textiles).
139 Zlotnikov, *Kontinental'naja blokada*, 9.
140 Zlotnikov, *Kontinental'naja blokada*, 24.
141 Davey, "Securing the Sinews of sea power"; Mattingly, *Natural knowledge*, 17–44; 104–192; Borougerdi, *Cord of Empire*, 126–132; Crosby, *America, Russia, Hemp and Napoleon*.
142 Družinina, *Severnoe pričernomor'e*, 84–87.
143 Družinina, *Severnoe pričernomor'e*, 92.
144 Družinina, *Severnoe pričernomor'e*, 90; Halm, *Österreich und Neurußland*, 66–216; Halm, *Gründung und erstes Jahrzehnt*; Schnakenbourg, 'Genèse d'un nouveau commerce.'
145 Anthoine, *Essai historique*, 81–100.
146 PSZ, XXII, 16093.
147 Druzinina, *Severnoe pričernomor'e*, 89.
148 Druzinina, *Severnoe pričernomor'e*, 203–259.
149 Zlotnikov, *Kontinental'naja blokada*, 12.
150 Zlotnikov, *Kontinental'naja blokada*, 15; 19; 36–39.
151 Zlotnikov, *Kontinental'naja blokada*, 16; Herlihy, *Odessa*, 23–34.
152 Zlotnikov, *Kontinental'naja blokada*, 31–32. Remarkably, 1801 is the endpoint of Robert E. Jones' illuminating study on grain supplies to St. Petersburg. See Jones, *Bread upon the Waters*.
153 Bilici, "La France et la Mer Noire," 69–70; Herlihy, *Odessa*, 21–48.
154 In his 1813 memoir on Odessa, Richelieu reviews his achievements as administrator of southern Russia. He states that, under his administration, the city of Odessa had grown from 7–8,000 inhabitants in 1802 to 35,000 in 1813, whereas the value of commerce of all Russian Black Sea ports (including the Sea of Azov) had grown from 1.5 million roubles in 1796 to more than 45 million roubles in 1813. In 1813, Odessa accounted for more than half of this value. See Bilici, "La France et la Mer Noire," 69–70.
155 Bilici, "La France et la Mer Noire," 70.
156 Bilici, "La France et la Mer Noire," 73.
157 Bilici, "La France et la Mer Noire," 73.
158 Zlotnikov, *Kontinental'naja blokada*, 45.
159 *Gosudarstvennaja torgovlja 1802–1807.*
160 Zlotnikov, *Kontinental'naja blokada*, 46. See also: *Gosudarstvennaja torgovlja 1802–1807.*

161 Zlotnikov, *Kontinental'naja blokada*, 47; 116.
162 Zlotnikov, *Kontinental'naja blokada*, 117.
163 PSZ, XXVIII, 21196; 23572.
164 Zlotnikov, *Kontinental'naja blokada*, 47.
165 PSZ, XXVIII, 21530.
166 Zlotnikov, *Kontinental'naja blokada*, 47–48.
167 Zlotnikov, *Kontinental'naja blokada*, 47–48, based on an unpublished memorandum.
168 Zlotnikov, *Kontinental'naja blokada*, 47; 72–87.
169 Bilici, "La France et la Mer Noire," 57; Bilici's description is based on Driault, *La politique extérieure*, 359.
170 Bilici, "La France et la Mer Noire," 57. Both Gaudin's statement and Brune's instructions are included in a chapter devoted to the battle for the sea (*Fr.* La lutte pour la mer) in Driault's *La politique extérieure*, 339–376.
171 Schroeder, *The transformation*, 317.
172 Bilici, "La France et la Mer Noire," 68.
173 Schroeder, *The transformation of European politics*, 317–318.
174 Heckscher, *The continental system*, 81–82.
175 Heckscher, *The continental system*, 82–83.
176 Heckscher, *The continental system*, 88. The coalition wars are dealt with *in extenso* in: Schroeder, *The transformation of European politics*, 100–286.
177 Heckscher summarizes the fundamental regulations of the Berlin decree as follows:

> The fundamental regulations (…) [of the Berlin Decree] fall into four categories. First, the British Isles are formally declared in a state of blockade, and all trade or communication with them is prohibited (Articles 1 and 2). Secondly, the decree turns against all British subjects in territories occupied by the French; they are declared to be prisoners of war, and all property belonging to them to be fair prize (Articles 3 and 4). Thirdly, war is made on all British goods; all trade in them is prohibited and all goods belonging to England or coming from her factories or her colonies are declared to be fair prize, half of their value to be used to indemnify merchants for British captures (Articles 5 and 6). Fourthly and lastly, every vessel coming direct from ports of Great Britain or her colonies, or calling at them after the proclamation of the decree, is refused access to any port on the Continent (Article 7).

See Heckscher, *The continental system*, 90.
178 Heckscher, *The continental system*, 164–165.
179 Heckscher, *The continental system*, 114.
180 Heckscher, *The continental system*, 123–124; 166–167.
181 Heckscher, *The continental system*, 124–125; 171.
182 Frankel, 'The 1807–1809 embargo,' 291.
183 Heckscher, *The continental system*, 129–135.
184 Heckscher, *The continental system*, 135–136.
185 *Tetradas* [VSWG-JDA], 1_turnover: *Estimated total turnover.*
186 Ryan, "The defence of British trade"; Ryan, "Trade with the enemy."
187 Heckscher, *The continental system*, 169–170.
188 Schroeder, *The transformation of European politics*, 313; 317–320.
189 PSZ, XIX, 22418.
190 Bilici, "La France et la Mer Noire," 73.
191 Schroeder, *The transformation of European politics*, 320–321.
192 Schroeder, *The transformation of European politics*, 396.
193 Zlotnikov, *Kontinental'naja blokada*, 139–143.

194 Zlotnikov, *Kontinental'naja blokada*, 141–142.
195 Zlotnikov, *Kontinental'naja blokada*, 129–138.
196 Heckscher, *The continental system*, 122 and 168; Schroeder, *The transformation of European politics*, 327–331.
197 Heckscher, *The continental system*, 123.
198 Heckscher, *The continental system*, 178–180.
199 Hunter, "Wheat, War, and the American economy," 518–519.
200 Frankel, "The 1807–1809 embargo," 296.
201 Heckscher, *The continental system*, 174–175.
202 Bartley, "The inception," 228–229.
203 Heckscher, *The continental system*, 136–138.
204 Heckscher, *The continental system*, 180–183. In this context, Heckscher depicts the 'second Tönnig period,' which lasted from June until December 1809.
205 Heckscher, *The continental system*, 182.
206 Schroeder, *The transformation of European politics*, 334–335.
207 Heckscher, *The continental system*, 151.
208 Heckscher, *The continental system*, 151–152.
209 Heckscher, *The continental system*, 152.
210 *Tetradas* [VSWG-JDA], 1_turnover: *Estimated total turnover.*
211 The publication of foreign trade statistics of the Russian Empire was interrupted from 1808 until 1811. However, some information collected at the borders of the Russian Empire found its way to contemporary publications, which were processed by Zlotnikov in his work on the Continental Blockade in Russia. The latter's compilation of Russian foreign trade statistics between 1807 and 1812, as well as the resumed annual publication of tabular series of Russia's foreign trade from 1812 onwards, provide sufficient information for a brief assessment of the impact of the Continental Blockade on the directions of Russia's foreign and transit trade. See Zlotnikov, *Kontinental'naja blokada*, 290–302; *Gosudarstvennaja torgovlja.*
212 Zlotnikov, *Kontinental'naja blokada*, 302.
213 Bilici, *La politique française en Mer Noire*, 73–76.
214 Zlotnikov, *Kontinental'naja blokada*, 321–323.
215 Zlotnikov, *Kontinental'naja blokada*, 320.
216 Zlotnikov, *Kontinental'naja blokada*, 321.
217 Zlotnikov, *Kontinental'naja blokada*, 321–322.
218 Zlotnikov, *Kontinental'naja blokada*, 144–146.
219 Zlotnikov, *Kontinental'naja blokada*, 147.
220 Zlotnikov, *Kontinental'naja blokada*, 150–151.
221 Zlotnikov, *Kontinental'naja blokada*, 155–160.
222 Zlotnikov, *Kontinental'naja blokada*, 188–189.
223 Zlotnikov, *Kontinental'naja blokada*, 191.
224 Heckscher, *The continental system*, 153.
225 Zlotnikov, *Kontinental'naja blokada*, 246–253.
226 Heckscher, *The continental system*, 152; For a detailed description of French-Russian relations during the second period of the Continental Blockade, see Zlotnikov, *Kontinental'naja blokada*, 221–270.
227 Bilici, *La politique française en Mer Noire*, 79.
228 Heckscher, *The continental system*, 152–153; Zlotnikov, Kontinental'naja blokada, 246–253. According to Schroeder, the 'root cause' of the break of the Franco-Russian alliance was of a political rather than economic nature. It evolved around Napoleon's plan to restore the Polish state, which contrasted with Russia's search for international guarantees that this would never happen. See Schroeder, *The transformation*, 416–425.

229 Zlotnikov, *Kontinental'naja blokada*, 325–326.
230 Zlotnikov, *Kontinental'naja blokada*, 326.
231 Davey, "Securing the Sinews of sea power," 175–179.
232 Zlotnikov, *Kontinental'naja blokada*, 308–312.
233 Zlotnikov, *Kontinental'naja blokada*, 313–317; 322–326.
234 Zlotnikov, *Kontinental'naja blokada*, 227–246; 320.
235 Heckscher, *The continental system*, 154.

References

[s.n.]. *Der Stadt Riga Handels-Ordnung vom Jahr 1765*. Riga 1798.

Andersen, Dan H.; Voth, Hans-Joachim. "The grapes of war. Neutrality and mediterranean shipping under Danish flag, 1747–1807." *Scandinavian Economic History Review* 48 (2000): 5–27.

Anthoine, M. Baron de Saint-Joseph. *Essai historique sur le commerce et la navigation de la Mer-noire, ou Voyage et entreprises pour établir des rapports commerciaux et maritimes entre les ports de la Mer-Noire et ceux de la Méditerranée. Seconde édition*. Paris 1820.

Ardeleanu, Constantin. "The opening and development of the Black Sea for international trade and shipping (1774–1853)." *Euxeinos* 14 (2014): 30–52.

Åström, Sven-Erik. *From tar to timber. Studies in Northeast European forest exploitation and foreign trade, 1660–1860*. Helsinki 1988.

Atkin, Muriel. *Russia and Iran, 1780–1828*. Minneapolis 1980.

Bär, Max. *Westpreußen unter Friedrich dem Großen, II: Quellen*. Leipzig 1909.

Barker, Theodore Cardwell; Harris, John Raymond. *A Merseyside town in the Industrial Revolution. St. Helen's, 1750–1900*. Liverpool 1993.

Bartley, Russell H. "The inception of Russo-Brazilian relations (1808–1828)." *The Hispanic American Historical Review* 56, 2 (1976): 217–240.

Biernat, Czesław. "Wybrane problem handle Gdańska w okresie rozbiorów Polski." *Rocznik Gdański* 33 (1973): 5-21.

Bilici, Faruk. "La France et la Mer Noire sous le consulat et l'Empire: 'La porte du harem ouverte'." In *Méditerrannée, Moyen-Orient. Deux siècles de relations internationales. Recherches en hommage à Jacques Thobie*, edited by Walid Arbid, Salgur Kançal, Jean-David Mizrahi, and Samir Saul, 55–92. Paris 2003.

Bilici, Faruk. *La politique française en Mer Noire, 1747–1789. Vicissitudes d'une implantation*. Paris 1992.

Blackwell, William L. *The beginnings of Russian industrialization, 1800–1860*. Princeton 1968.

Borougerdi, Bradley J. *Cord of Empire, exotic intoxicant. Hemp and culture in the Atlantic World, 1600–1900* (PhD thesis, University of Texas at Arlington). Arlington 2014.

Cavalcanti, Maria Luisa. *Le relazioni commerciali tra il regno di Napoli e la Russia, 1777–1815. Fatti e teorie*. Genève 1979.

Cieślak, Edmund. "The Influence of the First Partition of Poland in the overseas trade of Gdańsk." In *From Dunkirk to Danzig: Shipping and trade in the North Sea and the Baltic, 1350–1850. Essays in Honour of J.A. Faber on the occasion of his retirement as Professor of Economic and Social History at the University of Amsterdam*, edited by W.G. Heeres et al., 203–215. Hilversum 1988.

Clendenning, Philip. "The Anglo-Russian trade treaty of 1766 – An example of eighteenth-century power group interests." *Journal of European Economic History* 19, 3 (1990): 475–520.

Crosby, Alfred. *America, Russia, Hemp and Napoleon. American trade with Russia and the Baltic, 1783–1812.* Cleveland 1965.
Crouzet, François. "War, blockade, and economic change in Europe, 1792–1815." *The Journal of Economic history* 24 (1964): 567–588.
Davey, James. "Securing the Sinews of sea power. British intervention in the Baltic, 1780–1815." *The International History Review* 33, 2 (2011): 161–184.
Davies, Norman. *God's playground. A history of Poland in two volumes. Vol. 1: The origins to 1795.* New York 1982.
Denzel, Markus A. *Handbook of world exchange rates, 1590–1914.* Farnham 2010.
Donaghay, Marie. "The exchange of products of the soil and industrial goods in the Anglo-French commercial treaty of 1786." *Journal of European Economic History* 2 (1990): 377–401.
dos Santos Arnold, Torsten. "Atlantic Sugar and Central Europe: Sugar importers in Hamburg and their trade with Bordeaux and Lisbon, 1733–1798." In *Globalized peripheries. Central Europe and the Atlantic World, 1680–1860*, edited by Jutta Wimmler and Klaus Weber, 99–116. Woodbridge 2020.
Driault, Édouard. *La politique extérieure du Premier Consul, 1800–1803.* Paris 1910.
Drozdowski, Marian. "Die Historiographie über die ökonomischen Folgen der Preussischen Annexionen für die polnischen Gebiete und den Hohenzollernstaat." *Polnische Weststudien* 5 (1986): 145-153.
Družinina, Elena Ioasafovna. *Kjučuk-Kajnardžijskij mir 1774 goda (ego podgotovka i zakljućenie).* Moskva 1955.
Družinina, Elena Ioasafovna. *Severnoe pričernomor'e v 1775–1800 gg.* Moskva 1959.
Ehrman, John. *The British government and commercial negotiations with Europe, 1783–1793.* Cambridge 1962.
Eklund, Asa; Evans, Chris; Rydén, Göran. "From the Baltic to the Atlantic. British merchants and the development of trade networks in the northern seas during the eighteenth century." In *Spinning the commercial web. International trade, merchants, and commercial cities, c. 1640–1939*, edited by Margrit Schulte Beerbühl and Jörg Vögele, 203–215. Frankfurt am Main 2004.
Frankel, Jeffrey A. "The 1807–1809 embargo against Britain." *The Journal of Economic History* 42, 2 (1982): 291–308.
Gerhard, Dietrich. *England und der Aufstieg Russlands. Zur Frage des Zusammenhanges der europäischen Staaten und ihres Ausgreifens in die außereuropäische Welt in Politik und Wirtschaft des 18. Jahrhunderts.* München 1933.
Gierszewski, Józef Andrzej. *The Polish-Lithuanian Commonwealth in the XVIIIth century. From anarchy to well-organised state.* Kraków 1996.
Gosudarstvennaja vnešnjaja torgovlja v raznych ee vidach za … god. Sankt-Peterburg 1812–1862.
Halm, Hans. *Gründung und erstes Jahrzehnt von Festung und Stadt Cherson.* Wiesbaden 1961.
Halm, Hans. *Österreich und Neurußland. Erster Band: Donauschiffahrt und –handel nach dem Südosten, 1718–1780.* Breslau 1943.
Hartley, Janet M. *Russia, 1762–1825. Military power, the state, and the people.* Westport / London 2008.
Heckscher, Eli F. *The continental system. An economic interpretation.* Oxford / New York 1922.
Henderson, W.O. "The Anglo-French commercial treaty of 1786." *The Economic History Review, New Series* 10, 1 (1957): 104–112.
Herlihy, Patricia. *Odessa. A history, 1794–1914.* Cambridge 1986.

Herlihy, Patricia; McGahey, Anne. *Russian grain and Mediterranean markets, 1774–1861.* University of Pennsylvania Dissertation. Philadelphia 1963.

Herzfeld, Margot. "Der polnische Handelsvertrag von 1775." *Forschungen zur Brandenburgischen und Preussischen Geschichte* 32 (1919): 57-107; 35 (1923): 45-82; 36 (1924): 210-220.

Hopf, Hans. "Danzig in der Vorgeschichte zur Zweiten Teilung Polens." *Zeitschrift des Westpreussischen Geschichtsvereins* 76 (1941): 103-170.

Hösch, Edgar. "Zar Paul I. (1796–1801) und die russische Mittelmeerpolitik am Ausgang des 18. Jahrhunderts." *Saeculum* 18, 3 (1968): 295–315.

Hunter, Brooke. "Wheat, War, and the American economy during the Age of Revolution." *The William and Mary Quarterly, Third Series* 62, 3 (2005): 505–526.

Iredale, D.A. "John and Thomas Marshall and the Society for improving the British salt trade. An example of trade regulation." *The Economic History Review, New Series* 20 (1967): 79–93.

Jones, Robert E. *Bread upon the waters. The St. Petersburg grain trade and the Russian economy, 1703–1811.* Pittsburgh 2013.

Kaplan, Herbert H. *Russian overseas commerce with Great Britain during the reign of Catherine II.* Philadelphia 1995.

Kaps, Klemens. *Desintegrationserscheinungen: Der Weichselhandel über Danzig (1772–1815)* (mimeo).

Klimesz, Henryk. "Poland's trade through the Black Sea in the eighteenth century." *The Polish Review* 15, 2 (1970): 55–80.

Kozlov, N. *Archangel'skaja Gubernija (= Materialy dlja Geografii i statistiki Rossii, 1).* Sankt-Peterburg 1865.

Krzoska, Markus. "Teilungserfahrungen und Traditionsbildung: Die Historiographie der Teilungen Polen-Litauens (1795-2011)." In *Die Teilungen Polen-Litauens: Inklusions- und Exklusionsmechanismen – Traditionsbildung – Vergleichsebenen*, edited by Hans-Jürgen Bömelburg, Andreas Gestrich and Helga Schnabel-Schüle, 37–104. Osnabrück 2013.

Langer, Dieter. "Die Beurteilung der Teilungen Polens in der polnischen Geschichtswissenschaft." *Jahrbücher für die Geschichte Osteuropas* 22 (1974): 580-592.

Libiszowska, Sofia. "James Durno i jego misja w Polsce." *Przegląd Historyczny* 1 (1973): 67-82.

Łojek, Jerzy. "British policy towards Russia, 1790-1791, and Polish affairs." *The Polish Review* 2 (1983): 3-17.

Łojek, Jerzy. "The International Crisis of 1791. Poland between the Triple Alliance and Russia." *East Central Europe* 2 (1975): 1-63.

Lukowski, Jerzy T. "Towards partition. Polish magnates and Russian intervention in Poland during the early reign of Stanisław August Poniatowski." *The Historical Journal* 28, 3 (1985): 557–574.

Martens, Friedrich Fromhold. *Sobranie traktatov i konvencij zaključennych Rossieju s inostrannymi deržavami / Receuil des Traités et Conventions, conclus par la Russie avec les Puissances Etrangères.* 15 volumes. Sankt Petersburg 1874–1909.

Marzagalli, Silvia. "Le négoce maritime et la rupture révolutionnaire. Un ancien débat revisité." *Annales historiques de la Révolution française* 2 (2008): 183–207.

Mattingly, Nick. *Natural knowledge and sea power. The cultivation of hemp in the British imperial world* (PhD thesis Southern Cross University). Lismore 2013.

McKay, Derek; Scott, Hamish M. *The rise of the great powers 1648–1815.* London / New York 1983.

Michael, Wolfgang. *Englands Stellung zur ersten Teilung Polens.* Hamburg / Leipzig 1890.

Michalski, Jerzy. "Dyplomacja polska w latach 1764–1795." In *Historia dyplomacji polskiej, Tom II*, edited by Zbigniew Wójcik, 483–692. Warszawa 1982.
Misiuras, Romuald. "The Šventoji project. 18th century plans for a Lithuanian Port." *Journal of Baltic Studies* 8 (1977): 28-50.
Moreira, Maria Cristina; Martins de Sousa, Rita; Scheltjens, Werner. "Commercial relations between Portugal and Russia. Neutrality, trade and finance." In *Small and medium powers in global history. Trade, conflicts, and neutrality from the 18th to the 20th centuries*, edited by Jari Eloranta, Eric Golson, Peter Hedberg, and Maria Cristina Moreira, 73–94. London / New York 2018.
Müller, Leos. "Sweden's neutral trade under Gustav III. The ideal of commercial independence under the predicament of political isolation." In *Trade and war. The neutrality of commerce in the inter-state system*, edited by Koen Stapelbroek, 144–160. Helsinki 2011.
Müller, Michael G. *Die Teilungen Polens 1772, 1793, 1795*. München 1984.
Oddy, J. Jepson. *European commerce, shewing new and secure channels of trade with the continent of Europe: detailing the produce, manufactures, and commerce, of Russia, Prussia, Sweden, Denmark, and Germany; as well as the trade of the rivers Elbe, Weser, and Ems; with a general view of the trade, navigation, produce, and manufactures, of the United Kingdom of Great Britain and Ireland; and its unexplored and improvable resources and interior wealth*. London 1805.
Poole, Braithwaite. *The commerce of Liverpool*. London / Liverpool 1854.
PSZ: *Polnoe Sobranie Zakonov Rossijskoj Imperii, poveleniem Gosudarja Imperatora Nikolaja Pavloviča sostavlennoe*. 45 volumes. Sankt Petersburg 1830.
Ressel, Magnus. "Swedish Pomeranian shipping in the Revolutionary Age (1776–1815)." *Forum navale: Sjöhistoriska Samfundets tidskrift* 68 (2012): 65–103.
Ressel, Magnus. "The impact of the partitions of Poland on the structure of Baltic trade." In *Early modern shipping and trade. Novel approaches using Sound Toll registers online*, edited by Jan Willem Veluwenkamp and Werner Scheltjens, 21–40. Leiden / Boston 2018.
Rostworowski, Emanuel. "Na drodze do pierwszego rozbioru. Fryderyk II wobec rozkładu przymierza francusko-austriackiego w latach 1769-1772." *Roczniki Historyczne* 18 (1949): 181-204.
Ryan, A.N. "The defence of British trade with the Baltic, 1808–1813." *The English Historical Review* 74, 292 (1959): 443–466.
Ryan, A.N. "Trade with the enemy in the Scandinavian and Baltic ports during the Napoleonic War. For and against." *Transactions of the Royal Historical Society, Fifth Series* 12 (1962): 123–140.
Sanktpeterburgskie kommerčeskie vedomosti, 4 April 1807.
Scheltjens, Werner. "Die krisenhaften Auswirkungen der Teilungen Polens auf die Struktur des Ostseehandels, 1772–1846." In *Wirtschaftskrisen als Wendepunkte. Ursachen, Folgen und historische Einordnungen vom Mittelalter bis zur Gegenwart*, edited by Dariusz Adamczyk and Stephan Lehnstaedt, 215–232. Osnabrück 2015.
Scheltjens, Werner. "Die politische Ökonomie der Teilungen Polens, oder der Ostseehandel neukonfiguriert." In *Ordnung und Chaos. Trends und Brüche in der Wirtschafts- und Sozialgeschichte*, edited by Günther Schulz, 29–51. Stuttgart 2019.
Scheltjens, Werner. *Dutch deltas. Emergence, functions and structure of the low countries' maritime transport system, ca. 1300–1850*. Leiden / Boston 2015.
Scheltjens, Werner. "French imports to the Baltic, 1670–1850: A quantitative analysis." In *Eighteenth-century international trade statistics: Sources and methods (Special Issue of the Revue de l'OFCE 140)*, edited by Loïc Charles and Guillaume Daudin, 137–173. Paris 2015.

Schnakenbourg, Eric. "Genèse d'un nouveau commerce. La France et l'ouverture du marché russe par la mer Noire dans la seconde moitié du XVIIIe siècle." *Cahiers de la Méditerranée* 83 (2011): 309–325.
Schop Soler, Ana M. *Die spanisch-russischen Beziehungen im 18. Jahrhundert*. Wiesbaden 1970.
Schremmer, Eckart. "Industrialisierung vor der Industrialisierung. Anmerkungen zu einem Konzept der Proto-Industrialisierung." *Geschichte und Gesellschaft* 6, 3 (1980): 420–448.
Schroeder, Paul W. *The transformation of European politics, 1763–1848*. Oxford 2003 (reprint 1994).
Smithers, Henry. *Liverpool, its commerce, statistics, and institutions, with a history of the cotton trade*. Liverpool 1825.
Straubel, Rolf. *Die Handelsstädte Königsberg und Memel in friderizianischer Zeit. Ein Beitrag zur Geschichte des ost- und gesamtpreußischen "Commerciums" sowie seiner sozialen Träger (1763–1806/15)*. Berlin 2003.
Tetradas [VSWG-JDA]: *Tetradas: Tonnage estimates of trade through the Danish Sound, 1670–1856 (Replication data and selected statistics). Version: 1.* VSWG – Journal of Social and Economic History. Dataset, edited by Werner Scheltjens. https://journaldata.zbw.eu/dataset/tetradas
Topolski, Jerzy. "Poglądy na rozbiory Polski." In *Stosunki polsko-niemieckie w historiografii, Vol. 1*, edited by Jerzy Krasuski, 410–515. Poznań 1974.
Topolski, Jerzy. "Reflections on the first partition of Poland (1772)." *Acta Poloniae Historica* 27 (1973): 89–104.
Truska, L.S.; Jasas, R.V. "Vnešnjaja torgovlja Velikogo Knjažestva Litovskogo v poslednie gody ego suščestvovanija (1785–1792)." *Lietuvos TSR Mokslų akademijos darbai, A serija / Trudy Akademii nauk Litovskoj SSR, Serija A* 32, 1 (1970): 23–52.
Van Regemorter, Jean-Louis. "Le mythe génois en Mer Noire. La France, la Russie et le commerce d'Asie par la route de Géorgie (1821–1831)." *Annales. Histoire, Sciences Sociales* 19, 3 (1964): 492–521.
Webb, Paul L.C. "Sea power in the Ochakov affair of 1791." *The International History Review* 2, 1 (1980): 13–33.
Wilder, Jan Antoni. "Plan projekt budowy kanalu Bydgoskiego." *Przegląd Bygoski* 4 (1936): 3-20.
Wilder, Jan Antoni. "Projekt Franciszka Piłsudskiego odbudowy portu pod Połągą." *Rocznik Gdański* 9, 10 (1935/36): 3-20.
Wilder, Jan Antoni. *Traktat handlowy polsko-pruski z roku 1775: gospodarcze znaczenie utraty dostępu do morza*. Warszawa 1937.
Zacharov, Viktor Nikolaevič / Zakharov, Viktor Nikolaevich. *Zapadnoevropejskie kupcy v rossijskoj torgovle XVIII veka / West-European merchants in Russian trade of the 18th century*. Moskva 2005.
Zlotnikov, Michail. *Kontinental'naja blokada i Rossija*. Moskva / Leningrad 1966.

6 The reconfiguration of North Eurasian trade in the first half of the nineteenth century

Introduction

When the later French Prime Minister of the restored Bourbon monarchy, Charles Maurice de Talleyrand-Périgord (1754–1838), handed Alexander I (1777–1825) the key to the city of Paris on 31 March 1814, the Tsar's political power had probably reached its zenith. The Russian Empire had defeated Napoleon after his disastrous siege of Moscow; it had consolidated its presence on the shores of the Black Sea, and, at the easternmost end of the Empire, had expanded along the shores of Alaska on the American continent. One century after Peter the Great, the threat of excessive Russian power again preoccupied the minds of the European leaders, who had gathered in Vienna to elaborate a framework for a peaceful Europe with many nations.[1] Neither the Russian Empire nor the Kingdom of Prussia could be circumvented during the groundbreaking negotiations taking place at the Congress of Vienna (1814–1815). The Russian Empire maintained its rule over Finland, which it had conquered from Sweden in 1809. More importantly, however, Alexander I wanted to take over the Duchy of Warsaw as well as some other former Polish territories to unite them with the Russian Empire, and Prussia wanted to occupy all of Saxony. Anxious about the consequences of these territorial claims, Austria and the United Kingdom signed a secret treaty in January 1815 to prevent Prussia and Russia from executing their plans, and were prepared to use military force if necessary. The Polish-Saxon crisis was settled in October 1815. The former Duchy of Warsaw was renamed Kingdom of Poland and came to be ruled by the Russian Tsar, who *as King* acted independently of Russia. The economically significant territories of the Province of Posen were handed over to Prussia and were renamed Grand Duchy of Posen. Cracow became a free city. Finally, Saxony was divided into two parts: one part was incorporated in the Kingdom of Prussia as Province of Saxony; the remainder became the Kingdom of Saxony. Bearing in mind that Prussia had also acquired Swedish Pomerania after an alteration to the 1814 Treaty of Kiel,[2] Prussia's territorial gains turned out to be no less significant than those of the Russian Empire. Although both continental powers booked significant gains, the United Kingdom ultimately checked the extent of their greed. The United Kingdom pursued – as it had done before – a cautious policy of non-intervention centred on its own economic goals. Aware of its dependence on the Russian Empire as well as on the Prussian alternative that had emerged for the first time in the latter decades of the eighteenth century (see Chapter 5), the United Kingdom supported Austria's opposition against the Russian claims on Polish territories. Similarly, the United Kingdom objected to Prussian claims on the Kingdom of Saxony. More than anything else, the British seem to have been concerned about losing access to vital Central and East European markets. The results of the Congress of Vienna changed the political map of Europe and provided the necessary conditions for the swift recovery of trade through the Danish Sound after the final defeat of Napoleon in Waterloo in late 1815. In the meantime, the peace treaties of Bucharest (1812) and Gulistan (1813) created the necessary conditions for the recovery of trade in the Black Sea, and across the Russo-Persian border in the Caspian Sea and the Caucasus.

This chapter places the quantitative development of North Eurasian trade since 1815 in the broader context of global competition between production areas of foodstuffs, raw materials and manufactures in Europe, across the Atlantic and East Asia. The first section deals with long-term changes in the supply and demand of foodstuffs and the impact of the opening of the Black Sea on the geography of their distribution from North Eurasia to Western Europe. The second section focuses on the impact of global competition and Russian economic policies on the North Eurasian trade with foodstuffs (grain) and raw materials (naval stores). Attention is paid to the impact of industrial modes of production in flour milling, the breakthrough of alternative supplies of (some) naval stores and the contribution of infrastructural developments. The third section highlights the gradual change of focus in international politics from the Baltic and the Black Sea towards the Central Asian borderlands of the Caucasus, the Caspian and the Khanates, which reinforces the decline of the Baltic as an area of special interest in international diplomatic and commercial relations. Analysing selected commodities of North Eurasian trade (grain, naval stores, other raw materials, and textiles), this chapter seeks to show that the United Kingdom's commercial dominance effectively turned the Baltic into their 'backwaters,' just as the Dutch had achieved two centuries earlier. In the meantime, the United Kingdom started to liberate itself from its previous dependence on the 'natural' advantages of North Eurasia, which had constituted the basis for British interest in North Eurasian trade and related 'Baltic affairs' since the late seventeenth century.

North Eurasia's border basins in transition

The Corn Laws and the deposit trade

Between 1670 and 1856, the 10-year average of grain exports through the Danish Sound rose from 179,215 to 405,393 tonnes.[3] This seemingly continuous growth hides significant changes in the composition of grain exports through the Danish Sound, the geographical patterns of their distribution to Western Europe, the regulations regarding grain imports to the United Kingdom and other European countries (i.e. the Corn Laws), the temporary impact of bad harvests and famine in parts of Europe, and finally, the impact of rising grain exports from the Black Sea. Together, these changes contributed to the reconfiguration of North Eurasian grain exports in the first half of the nineteenth century. Whereas rye had dominated grain exports from the Baltic for centuries, their share stagnated at the level reached around 1760, and started to decline after 1800, making way for rapidly increasing wheat, barley and – to some extent – oats exports.[4] Taking off in the 1770s, the share of wheat exports through the Danish Sound continued to rise in the first half of the nineteenth century. Significantly, throughout the entire period, the estimated tonnage and share of flour exports remained small.[5]

The changes in the demand for different types of grain went hand in hand with the emergence of Great Britain (from 1801: United Kingdom) as a net importer of North Eurasian grain from the second half of the eighteenth century. Between 1770 and 1809, this resulted in a 62% share of oats, a 39% share of wheat and a 21% share of barley exports through the Danish Sound.[6] Throughout the first half of the nineteenth century, the shares of oats, wheat, and barley continued to increase and were complemented with some flour exports. As a result, the United Kingdom reached shares in total grain exports through the Danish Sound, which were comparable to those of the Dutch Republic during the seventeenth and most of the eighteenth centuries. However, whereas rye exports had been a driving force of Dutch dominance in the Baltic, the United Kingdom hardly imported any rye, neither from the Baltic nor from elsewhere.[7]

The rise of the United Kingdom as the main source of demand for North Eurasian grain entailed the latter's dependence on the United Kingdom's general policy of limiting the importation of foreign grain, known as the Corn Laws. Introduced in 1815 and reorganized in 1828, the Corn Laws made the tax on grain imports reversely dependent on the average grain price in the United Kingdom: if the price was low, the tax was increased; if the price was high, the tax decreased.[8] Other Western European countries, like France, Belgium, and the Netherlands, but also Greece, adopted similar measures for grain taxation in the early 1830s, whereas the German Customs Union (*Ger.* Zollverein) and Scandinavia maintained a fixed rate tax on grain imports.[9] In general, the Corn Laws had a negative impact on North Eurasian grain exports.[10] Russian rye exports to the Netherlands, for example, declined by 72% between 1835 and 1842 compared to the period preceding the Corn Laws.[11] However, they were deactivated in times of crisis, and abolished during the famine of 1846–1847.[12] In addition to the Corn Laws, the Navigation Acts were still in place, granting tax advantages (*privileges*) for grain exports on vessels from the home country of the grain or from the destination of the grain. Grain exports from Russia could only be executed on Russian or British ships. Like in the United Kingdom, tax advantages for the domestic merchant fleet were in place in Naples, Genoa, France, the Netherlands, Sweden, and Denmark.[13]

The combination of the relative underdevelopment of the Russian merchant fleet with the unfavourable distance towards Russian ports and the negative impact of the Navigation Laws made it preferable to call at ports that *did* have a large merchant fleet and extensive grain storage facilities at their disposal.[14] This was the case in Scandinavian, Prussian and most Western Mediterranean ports. For the most part, Russian ships distributed grain only to these ports, since "[t]he great producing areas of the Baltic and later, South Russia, were too distant to be able to supply grain *quickly and directly* to *suddenly* [emphasis added] opened markets in Western Europe."[15] Free transit to Prussian ports for grain arriving from North Eurasia via the Memel and Vistula stimulated the rise of Prussian ports in grain exports to the United Kingdom, and made the storage of Russian grain in Prussian ports preferable.[16] The Baltic ports of Danzig and Stettin benefited the most from these changes, but the ongoing search for ports with a more advantageous location and better facilities still caused a relative decline of these Prussian ports compared to Hamburg.[17] According to Nebolsin, the rapid rise of Hamburg was directly related to the Corn Laws in the United Kingdom, because Hamburg offered a better infrastructure for price speculation, which – in the context of the Corn Laws – was very important.[18] Information transmission from Hamburg to the United Kingdom was faster than from Danzig or other ports in the Baltic, the information density was higher, the grain storage facilities were larger, and the merchant community was stronger. The availability and use of grain storage facilities for international commerce seems to have made a significant difference in the development of North Eurasian grain exports. Although such facilities were constructed throughout the Russian Empire since the early eighteenth century, most of the time they served only the local population.[19] Grain stored in these local facilities was exported only in exceptional circumstances, and the issue of insufficient storage facilities has been pointed out repeatedly in the historiography of Russia's foreign trade. Whereas in the course of the eighteenth century and during the first decades of the nineteenth century, large, export-oriented storage facilities were erected in Prussian, Swedish, and Danish ports in the Baltic, but also in Mediterranean ports like Marseille, Livorno, Trieste, Naples, and Genoa, Russian construction efforts remained of limited size and scope.[20] With the exception of Odessa and Riga, the size of grain storage facilities in Russian ports was limited. In Odessa, during the early development of its port infrastructure, grain storage facilities with a capacity of about 7,000 tonnes were constructed according the Prussian example. Similarly, Riga's grain storage facilities were said to be large and comparable to that of their Prussian neighbours.[21]

Structural changes in the grain trade through the Danish Sound

Compared to the earlier periods, a general decline in the share of eastern Baltic ports in grain exports through the Danish Sound occurred in the first half of the nineteenth century. The share of eastern Baltic ports in rye exports through the Sound between 1810 and 1856 declined from 93% to 76% (see Table 6.1). More severe was the declining share in barley, oats and wheat exports. Whereas the eastern Baltic ports had dominated these exports before the French Wars, they now had to face competition from Prussian ports in the southern Baltic, on the one hand, and Scandinavian (mostly Swedish) ports in the western Baltic, on the other. The development of flour exports shows a somewhat different pattern, which reflects the existence of (modest) flour production in a few areas in the southern Baltic and Scandinavia. Flour production was concentrated mostly in Copenhagen and, on a much smaller scale, in Danzig, St. Petersburg and Stettin before the French Wars.[22]

In the first half of the nineteenth century, the share of the latter as well as some Scandinavian ports increased, whereas Copenhagen almost completely disappeared as flour exporting port.[23] The share in barley exports of southern Baltic ports rose dramatically from 5% to 35% between 1810 and

Table 6.1 Geographical distribution of grain exports through the Danish Sound, 1670–1856

1670–1809	*Destinations*					*Departure (Baltic)*			
	Atl	*N.Sea*	*Scan*	*UK*	*Rest*	*East*	*South*	*West*	*Rest*
Barley	6	71	11	7	4	86	5	7	1
Rye	3	82	10	3	3	93	6	1	1
Oats	5	51	10	30	5	80	11	8	1
Wheat	9	71	1	13	5	90	5	1	4
Malt	0	21	74	1	4	8	56	34	3
Flour	1	21	7	1	70	22	14	66	1
Share	*5*	*76*	*9*	*7*	*4*	*89*	*7*	*3*	*2*
1810–1856	*Destinations*					*Departure (Baltic)*			
Barley	2	39	16	41	2	48	35	16	0
Rye	1	66	24	5	3	76	15	8	1
Oats	0	6	3	90	1	58	20	22	0
Wheat	6	20	2	69	3	57	39	1	4
Malt	0	4	94	0	2	1	65	34	0
Flour	0	23	12	45	21	61	26	13	0
Share	*3*	*34*	*11*	*49*	*3*	*60*	*30*	*8*	*2*

Source: *Tetradas* [VSWG-JDA], 8_CIES_Bex_FS: *Barley, Oats, Rye, Wheat.*
Note: Share = percentage share in total grain exports of the different areas of departure and destination during the specified periods. Legend: Atl = European Atlantic coast; N.Sea = ports on the North Sea coast; Scan = Scandinavian ports in the Baltic; UK = United Kingdom; East = Baltic ports from Vistula to Neva; South = southern Baltic ports from Lübeck up to the Oder; West = Scandinavian ports in the Baltic (Denmark, Finland, Sweden).

Table 6.2 Areas of departure of grain exports through the Danish Sound, 1810–1856

	1810–1839				*1840–1856*			
	East	*South*	*West*	*Rest*	*East*	*South*	*West*	*Rest*
Barley	60	33	7	0	31	39	29	1
Rye	84	12	4	0	64	19	16	1
Oats	75	20	5	0	32	20	47	1
Wheat	62	33	1	4	49	48	0	3
Malt	1	71	29	0	1	56	43	1
Flour	84	12	4	0	27	48	25	0
Share	*70*	*25*	*4*	*1*	*48*	*33*	*17*	*2*

Source: *Tetradas* [VSWG-JDA], 8_CIES_Bex_FS: *Barley, Oats, Rye, Wheat.*
Note: Share = percentage share in total grain exports of the different areas of departure during the designated periods. East = Baltic ports from Vistula to Neva; South = southern Baltic ports from Lübeck up to the Oder; West = Scandinavian ports in the Baltic (Denmark, Finland, Sweden).

1856. During the same period, the share of southern Baltic wheat exports grew even more strongly, from 5% to 39%. The rise of rye and oats exports from southern Baltic ports, on the contrary, was more modest: the former's share rose from 6% in 1670–1809 to 15% in 1810–1856; the latter's share from 11% in 1670–1809 to 20% in 1810–1856 (see Table 6.1). In short, the share in grain exports through the Sound of southern Baltic ports increased for all main types of grain, but was the strongest for barley and wheat. Scandinavian ports also increased their share in rye, barley, and oats exports, but the complete absence of any growth in the share of wheat exports through the Sound constitutes an important difference with their southern Baltic counterparts. Compared to the earlier period, rye exports from Scandinavian ports experienced an eightfold increase from 1% to 8%. Barley and oats exports more than doubled; the share of the former rose from 7% to 16%, that of the latter from 8% to 22% (see Table 6.2).

The pace of structural change in the composition and geographical origin of grain exports through the Danish Sound accelerated significantly after 1840 and reached a peak during the Crimean War (1853–1856) (see Table 6.2).[24] After 1840, the eastern Baltic ports lost their majority share in grain exports through the Sound; except for the Prussian ports of Danzig, Königsberg, and Memel, all of the eastern Baltic ports were part of the Russian Empire. Compared to the pre-Napoleonic period, the share in grain exports through the Danish Sound declined from 70% between 1810 and 1839 to 48% after 1840. Within a short period, the majority share of grain exported through the Danish Sound had shifted towards the southern and western Baltic coasts. The shift is even stronger for flour exports, even though their estimated tonnage remained small. Whereas in the 1810–1839 period, 84% of flour exports through the Sound came from the eastern Baltic ports and from

Danzig, in particular,[25] only a 27% share remained after 1840. Instead, the share of the southern Baltic area experienced a fourfold increase (from 12% to 48%) and Scandinavia's share rose to 25% (see Table 6.2).

The higher concentration of grain exports in the southern Baltic and Scandinavia and the shift towards the United Kingdom as the main destination of grain exported through the Danish Sound also had significant impact on the macrostructure of Russian grain exports. The demand-driven growth of wheat exports, and its finer types, in particular, entailed the rise of Russia's Black Sea trade. Shortly after the border regime changes of Küçük Kajnarca (1774) and Jassy (1792), the newly founded port of Odessa quickly became the most important node in novel international grain distribution networks with ties across the Mediterranean, the European Atlantic coast, and the United Kingdom (see Section "Relocation, repression and collapse" of Chapter 5).[26] The porto franco status, which was granted to the port of Odessa for a period of 30 years in 1819, and the Treaty of Adrianople (1829) provided the legal background for a major shift in the distribution of Russian grain.[27] However, neither the extensive efforts to develop the city, its hinterland and its commerce since the start of the nineteenth century,[28] nor Odessa's porto franco status, and the freedom of Russian commerce in the Black Sea since the Treaty of Adrianople resulted in the sustained growth of Black Sea trade during the first four decades of the nineteenth century. Temporary increases of grain exports in the wake of the Tambora eruption (1816) and the potato famine of the mid-1840s intertwined with severe crises caused by failing demand, bad harvests (especially in 1833–1835), and disturbances caused by warfare in the area. The latter was particularly important during the Greek War of Independence (1821–1824) and the Russo-Turkish War (1828–1829).[29]

The port of Odessa experienced its breakthrough as "the principal wheat exporting port of the Russian Empire"[30] only in the 1840s. By that time, the Russian Empire's role as 'granary of Europe' was already under threat. Prussian ports, as well as other producers in Western and Central Europe, offered a valuable and less volatile alternative for grain exports from the Russian Empire. Wheat exports from Odessa, however, seem to have been more volatile than Baltic wheat exports.[31] Moreover, barley, oats and rye exports were very small compared to exports of these commodities through the Danish Sound. Therefore, the breakthrough of the Black Sea grain trade in the first half of the nineteenth century, and the rise of Odessa, which is described often as particularly impressive, should probably be nuanced. The opening of the Black Sea did not lead to a complete alteration in the course of North Eurasian trade. Rather, a substitute for part of the 'traditional' grain supplies carried through the Danish Sound had emerged. In the second quarter of the nineteenth century, ports on the Black Sea coast exported 90% of the wheat grown in the Russian Empire. Only 6% was exported from Russian ports in the Baltic, 3% was exported overland to Western Europe and 1% went abroad from Arkhangelsk on the White Sea coast. Among the different types of wheat, which were exported from southern Russia via the Black

Sea ports, the soft *ozimaja-* and *girka*-types (*Fr.* blé tendre) were most valued in the United Kingdom.[32] Contrastingly, the hard *arnautka* (*Fr.* blé dur) was less in demand in the United Kingdom, but more popular in Italy and the Levant, because of its specific qualities for the production of flour and vermicelli. Three large grain-producing regions nourished wheat exports from southern Russian ports. Wheat exports from Odessa were delivered from the provinces of Podolsk, Volyn, Kyiv, Kherson and some districts in Bessarabia. Wheat exports from Taganrog, Rostov-on-the-Don, Mariupol, Berdyansk, Yevpatoriya, Feodosia, and Kerch arrived from Russia's southern provinces, the Caucasus, the lands of the Don and Black Sea Cossacks, and even from the lower Volga. Finally, a smaller proportion of wheat was exported from Bessarabia via Izmail on the Danube.[33] The structure of rye exports was different: 60% was exported from Russian Baltic ports, 16% overland, 12% from Arkhangelsk, and 12% from Odessa and other ports in the Black Sea. Oats exports were irregular and went abroad for the most part from the Russian Baltic ports or Arkhangelsk. Barley was exported mostly from Russia's Baltic ports. Maize was produced only in Bessarabia and southern Russia, but in relatively small quantities; exports went abroad mostly from Russia's Black Sea ports.[34]

Riga dominated grain exports from the Baltic. Next to St. Petersburg, Riga was the only Russian Baltic port that benefited from extensive water and overland connections to its hinterland. Grain from the provinces of Smolensk, Oryol, Tula, Vitebsk, Mohylew, Vilna (Vilnius), and Courland was transported to Riga via the Western Dvina and its adjacent rivers. Additionally, grain was brought to Riga overland. However, grain deliveries to Riga could only be executed during the first half of the year until mid-May. Orders had to be placed during winter or in the early spring. Later demand could only be met using Riga's grain storage supplies, which – compared to other Russian ports in the Baltic – were large and similar to Prussian facilities.[35] A small proportion of Russian grain exports was executed from Arkhangelsk. Its volume was subject to large fluctuations and depended on foreign demand for Russian grain. Most of the grain exported from Arkhangelsk was gathered at the regional centre of Velikiy Ustyug before further transportation to Arkhangelsk. The producers' reaction to increases in foreign demand was slow and subject to unfavourable climatic circumstances. Contracts were issued during winter and small boats delivered the grain to Arkhangelsk as soon as the sailing season started. When foreign demand suddenly increased, grain stored for local consumption was exported, because new harvests could not be delivered in time for exportation during the same sailing season.[36] Besides exports from Russian ports in the Black Sea, the Baltic and, the White Sea, grain was transported over water to the Prussian ports of Memel, Königsberg, Danzig, and Stettin from Russia's westernmost provinces. A smaller part was transported overland. The availability of extensive grain storage facilities seems to have given the former Prussian ports a significant advantage. Usually, grain could only be transported over water to Memel, Königsberg, and Danzig during spring; the latter part of the year was marked by low water levels, which made river transportation impossible. However, as grain could be stored in Prussian ports, exports could take off at the very beginning of the sailing season; on the contrary, they could also be delayed until prices were high.[37]

The enduring supply issues of the North Eurasian grain trade

Contemporaries observing the Russian grain trade in the first half of the nineteenth century had already concluded that the distance to western markets, slow and unreliable transportation, and the risks involved with speculation caused significant potential to remain unrealized.[38] The disadvantages of distance and climate become all the more apparent in the role of St. Petersburg in Russia's grain export trade in the first half of the nineteenth century. The Russian capital was the end station of grain produced in the 'Lower Provinces' (*Ru.* nizovye gubernii) along the Volga.[39] These grain-producing areas were connected to St. Petersburg via the canal system of Vyshny Volochyok since the early eighteenth century. Despite its advantages, this connection also served as a bottleneck in the transportation system from the Russian interior. The turn of the century marked an upswing of infrastructural works on the European continent, in particular, in Prussia and Russia. They pursued the development of water linkages between the basins of the Baltic and the Black Sea, on the one hand, and between the Russian interior and all three of its western border basins, on the other. The Black Sea and the Baltic were connected through the Ogiński and Berezina canals since the early nineteenth century. Around 1800, the construction in North-West and Central Russia of additional systems linking the Russian interior (i.e. the Volga river basin) to St. Petersburg started. By 1811, the Tikhvin, Mariya, and Syas canal systems were completed.[40]

Riverboat caravans characterized the transportation of grain (and other goods) from the lower provinces to the urban centres of the Russian Empire.[41] Hundreds of small riverboats gathered in the South to make their voyages upstream towards one of several commercial centres on the Volga, such as Saratov, Samara, Laishevo (at the mouth of the Kama), Kazan, Cheboksary, Vasilsursk (at the mouth of the Sura), Nizhny Novgorod (at the mouth of the Oka), and finally Rybinsk. At the latter station, an exchange market was established in 1811.[42] Most boats were unloaded here, since they could not go further upstream on the shallow waters of the Volga. At Rybinsk, part of the grain was sold and distributed to nearby cities and towns; most of it, however, was bought by merchants from St. Petersburg for domestic consumption and – sometimes – for exportation from St. Petersburg. On the way from Rybinsk to St. Petersburg, several other grain caravans joined the main caravan, which had been prepared in Rybinsk using different boats adapted to the shallow waters of the Upper Volga. Additionally, the winter road was used to transfer grain from the provinces of Tver, Moscow and Smolensk to

St. Petersburg and a less significant parallel north-western circuit between Novgorod and St. Petersburg was used as well to transport grain (mostly oats) to the Russian capital.[43]

The issue of time had an obvious impact on the competitiveness of Russian grain on increasingly global markets. Thus, if the navigation on the Volga started early enough, the grain could be transported via Rybinsk to St. Petersburg in the same year; if not, it had to be stored at Rybinsk until the next spring. When foreign demand for grain was high, a swift reaction was expected and grain supplies from the lower provinces across the Volga were required to arrive at St. Petersburg in the course of the sailing season. However, the available transport and storage infrastructure did not allow such reaction to short-term changes in foreign demand. Rapid exports from St. Petersburg were only possible insofar as a sufficient amount of grain was stored in Rybinsk, and even if that were the case, time constraints could prevent the grain from arriving at St. Petersburg before the end of the sailing season.[44] Often, grain had to stay *en route* during wintertime, which increased its price and caused significant losses. The large distances between the vital grain production areas and Russia's ports, the short sailing season, the interruptions caused by unloading and reloading several times along the way, the slow speed of the riverboat caravans and – finally – the lack of sufficient grain storage capacities at the port of St. Petersburg constituted a high-risk, uncertain business environment.

Only in exceptional circumstances, when clear signals of bad harvests and grain shortages justified buying up large quantities of grain in Rybinsk and further down the Volga, grain exports from St. Petersburg would experience a sudden upswing and for some time high volumes would leave the Russian capital. The famous 'potato famine' of the mid-1840s offered such opportunity and provoked a wave of speculation in the Russian grain trade. The prospects of the profitable exportation of grain to Western Europe seduced many merchants into employing their capital for buying up excessive volumes of grain. In 1847, the effects of speculation in the grain trade reached unprecedented levels, at least insofar as exports through the Danish Sound are concerned. Compared to the previous year 1846, the value of Russian grain exports from the Baltic had more than tripled and even exceeded that of 1839, which was another exceptional year in the international grain trade. Remarkably, the volume of grain exports from the Black Sea almost doubled, but stayed well below its 1839 peak.[45]

However, the risks involved in grain speculation were high. In part, the enormous growth of Russian grain exports via the Baltic Sea in 1847 was due to late arrivals of grain bought along the Volga during the summer of 1846. A large part of this grain was stuck *en route* between Nizhny Novgorod, Rybinsk, and St. Petersburg during the winter of 1846 and 1847. In part, this was due to the arrival of large orders issued in the fall of 1846.[46] The arrival of the large volumes that had been stored *en route* during winter provoked a significant upswing in grain exports from St. Petersburg in the spring of 1847. A few months later, in July 1847, the *hausse* in grain exports was suddenly over. As a result, the late supply of the spring of 1847 significantly exceeded foreign demand for grain. However, that was not all. Even more speculative grain transports were still on their way to St. Petersburg, but were stuck (again) in the shallow waters after Rybinsk. Merchants speculating on the continued growth of grain exports in 1847, buying the grain at high prices, now had to face extra transportation costs due to shallow water levels and loss of income due to excessive supplies and rapidly declining prices.[47] Large sums of capital invested in the grain trade literally were stuck and remained out of circulation until the Russian government took measures to secure credits in late 1847.[48] Again, Russian officials had to face the fact that the Empire was lagging behind many other nations, in its industrial as well as agricultural production, even though economic policy measures had been implemented since the 1820s, which were to improve its infrastructure and productive capacity, on the one hand, and protect the Empire's domestic industry, on the other.

The impact of Russia's self-isolation

The 1830s witnessed renewed efforts to improve the Russian Empire's transport infrastructure,[49] and increase its industrial production.[50] There were attempts to introduce flour production techniques to farmers, often referring to the example of the United States. Similarly, discussions regarding the need to improve the Empire's transport and logistics infrastructure often used the United States as example.[51] America's rapidly increasing economic power was clearly acknowledged and openly perceived as a threat:

> America, where the number of canals, railways and ships of its merchant fleet grows every year, will soon exclude us completely from the grain trade with England, if we remain in our current state.[52]

To counteract these threats, Nebolsin put up a strong argument in favour of railway construction in the Russian Empire.[53] The call for improving Russia's transport infrastructure was not new. It had been part of ongoing disputes between Russian modernists and traditionalists since the beginning of the nineteenth century,[54] and the potential benefits for the Russian Empire of canal and railway construction were obvious to external observers as well. Indeed, with some astonishment, the editor of the 1833 *Digest of all the accounts* notes that

> (…) no part of the World offers greater inducements to facilitate intercourse either by Water or Railways; the Baltic might be united with both the Black Sea, and the Caspian, at a less expence of Physical power and means than was applied to the subjugation of Poland in 1830–1831.[55]

This concise remark reveals the main deficit of the organization of the Russian state. Financial efforts were devoted to the consolidation and expansion of its military power and the oppression of any ideas threatening its autocratic rule. Modernization – in any form – was seen as a threat.[56]

During the conservative regime of Count Kankrin, who was Russian minister of finance from 1823 until 1844, there was not much room for structural innovations.[57] Kankrin, who became Russia's minister of finance one year after the introduction of a new, prohibitive customs tariff in 1822,[58] "gave his name to a set of mercantilist policies designed to strengthen the power of the state by increasing its share of the world's economic resources."[59] Kankrin's policies expressed his scepticism towards free trade and industrial development, which he considered "a grave threat to the existing social order."[60] At the same time, however, "an almighty bureaucracy"[61] hampered Kankrin's reforms. After Kankrin's retirement in 1844, the institutional underdevelopment of the Russian Empire became increasingly apparent and finally led to a deep financial crisis prior to and during the Crimean War (1853–1856). Kankrin's successors showed little interest in controlling the budget of the state: deficits and excessive spending became the order of the day and in 1844 and 1848, the Ministry of Finance recurred to signing large foreign loans to finance its expenses.[62] Through the combination of war in the Caucasus around the mid-1840s, the uprising in Cracow in 1846, and ever-growing expenses for the military, Russia's state deficits had obtained a chronical character by the early 1850s.[63] This position backfired during the Crimean War. Due to 'missing infrastructure,' Russian troops could not get to the shores of the Black Sea in time to face the joint forces of Britain, France, and Austria. The Russian defeat in the Crimean War was the defeat of a system opposed to innovation, modernization, and competition rather than a mere military defeat.

A brief interlude between 1816 and 1819 notwithstanding, the Russian Empire had returned to a protectionist economic policy in support of its domestic industries. Since the early nineteenth century, the Russian Empire intensified its efforts to substitute foreign textile imports. The Russian government developed the cotton manufacturing industry in several stages according to the different stages of cotton manufacturing – spinning, weaving, and printing. Between 1816 and 1819, only the importation of finished products was prohibited.[64] However, in 1819, the importation of all kinds of cotton textiles was allowed at relatively modest import tax rates. Russian cotton textiles production took off in 1822, when a prohibitive import tariff came into force.[65] Soon, cotton manufacturing became the Russian textile industry's main branch.[66] Even after the financial reforms of 1839–1842, the protection of the domestic cotton manufacturing industry as still in force.[67] Under these circumstances, cotton weaving could develop quickly, but the industry continued to rely partly on foreign imports of (high-quality) cotton yarn. Because of the 1822 tariff, the volume of cotton yarn imported from the United Kingdom increased from about 3,900 tonnes annually between 1822 and 1826 to almost 9,000 tonnes annually between 1842 and 1846. Afterwards, British cotton yarn imports stagnated at about 6,000 tonnes per year, as Russian cotton yarn production was now able to meet a larger share of its domestic demand.[68]

The production of cotton fabrics was concentrated in Central Russia, near Moscow and its surroundings, as well as in the towns of Shuya and Ivanovo, which contemporaries knew as "Russian Manchester,"[69] and in the provinces of Vladimir and Kostroma.[70] In many other villages, the production of simple cotton fabrics was part of the Russian peasant's annual work cycle, and a welcome occupation during the country's long winters. However, this type of organization greatly hampered the mechanization of cotton textile production; it was clear to contemporary observers like Nebolsin, that Russian cotton manufacturing was underdeveloped and backward compared to its foreign competitors.[71] This also explains why, even after 1822, cotton fabrics were still imported to Russia in large quantities. It should be noted, however, that the value of cotton fabrics imported from the United Kingdom, Prussia, and Austria declined, whereas Central Asian imports from Turkey and Persia increased.[72]

A similar reorientation occurred with metal exports from North Eurasia.[73] Among them, iron was by far the most important.[74] Traditionally, iron had been exported to Western Europe from Sweden during the seventeenth and eighteenth centuries. However, after the foundation of St. Petersburg and the development of the mining industries in the Ural Mountains and North-West Russia (Olonets),[75] Russian iron became an alternative to its Swedish counterpart.[76] Iron was one of Russia's most important export items around the mid-eighteenth century. Most of the iron was exported from St. Petersburg, a small part was exported from Arkhangelsk, and – from the late eighteenth century onwards – part of Russia's iron production was exported via the Black Sea.[77] From the mines in the Ural Mountains iron was distributed by means of the rivers Kama and Volga. Following the Volga upstream, the fair of Nizhny Novgorod and the river port of Rybinsk played a central role in the iron distribution to Central Russia and St. Petersburg. Downstream, part of the Ural iron was brought to Kazan and Samara, where it was reloaded on the land route to Orenburg and Troitsk. Iron sent in that direction was meant to be exported to Central Asia, Persia, and Transcaucasia via Astrakhan. From the Volga, iron was also sent to Rostov-on-Don in southern Russia using the overland route via Dubovka between the Volga and the Don. Finally, part of the iron mined in the Ural Mountains went up the Oka River to Tula, Moscow and the provinces of Ryazan and Tambov; part was sent along from the Oka to the Desna and further south via the Dnepr to Kyiv, Kremenchug, and Kherson. The Russo-Turkish War of 1828–1829 had a devastating effect on the latter route. Whereas they had been as high as 19,247 tonnes in 1814, only a fraction of that volume was exported from ports in the Black Sea to Turkey in 1844–1846.[78]

Russian iron exports had started to decline as early as 1800,[79] before they collapsed around 1840. The decline of North Eurasian (i.e. Russian) iron exports can be explained as the result of three changes in the production, distribution and use of iron across Europe. First, production increases in foreign countries caused a decrease in the demand for Russian iron. Second, the consumption of iron in Russia increased; the demands of the domestic iron manufacturing industry caused a decline in the excess volumes available for exportation. Third, besides Russia's old rival Sweden, the United Kingdom became the world's leading iron exporter in the first half of the nineteenth century.[80] In the early 1840s, Russian exports dwarfed compared to British and – to a lesser extent – Swedish exports. At the same time, iron exports from St. Petersburg declined strongly between the late eighteenth century and the 1840s.[81] The United Kingdom no longer needed large quantities of Russian iron and occupied potential alternative markets at the same time. As a result, only Russian iron exports via the Caspian Sea to Persia and – in particular – via the land route to Central Asia remained more or less stable throughout the first half of the nineteenth century.[82]

Sweden's progress in the iron industry was perhaps less impressive than that of the United Kingdom, but even so, the volumes exported from Sweden were five times higher than Russian exports in the early 1840s.[83] Swedish iron exports benefited from locational and price advantages, qualitative differences compared to Russian iron, and changes in the international market for iron. Sweden's iron manufactories were located closer to the sea and closer to foreign markets than Russian manufactories. According to Nebolsin, who relies on a statement published in the *Commercial Gazette* in 1849, the transportation cost of Swedish iron to the British industrial town Sheffield was 50% than that of Russian iron. This also explains why Swedish and British iron quickly took over exports to the United States in the early nineteenth century. Obviously, the duration of the trip was much longer and thus the expense much higher, when the iron had to come from the Ural Mountains first. More important, perhaps, is the fact that Swedish iron was better suited for the production of steel than Russian iron.[84] As was the case with grain and textiles, North Eurasian iron exports seem to have suffered from a combination of structural changes, among which changing consumer preferences and foreign competition stand out as key drivers for the reorientation of international commodity flows.

Last but not least, very similar observations can be made with regard to North Eurasian timber exports. Timber was one of the most significant North Eurasian export items in the eighteenth century. After 1800, the volume and structure of timber exports through the Sound experienced a number of changes. As with other commodities, a shift in the location of timber exports occurred towards the borderlands of the Baltic Sea – Scandinavia and Elbe/Oder (Prussia) – as well as to Prussian ports with direct access to North Eurasian supplies. Competition from other areas increased as well, most importantly from Norway and Sweden (outside of the Baltic), the Rhine area (via Holland), and ports on the Adriatic coast. All of these timber producing areas benefited from the fact that timber could be exported free of duty, which was not the case in the Russian Empire.[85] Competition from Scandinavia (Sweden and Norway) in the international timber trade was such, that the decline of North Eurasian timber exports to the United Kingdom, which was caused by the subsidized rise of transatlantic timber trade and the establishment of timber duties, could not be compensated with growth in other markets. Scandinavian timber occupied the markets in Denmark, France and the Mediterranean.[86]

Two major elements contribute to explaining the weak performance of timber exports from North Eurasia proper in the first half of the nineteenth century. First, the ownership structure of Russian timber hampered exports from North Eurasia proper. The state controlled the northern woods in the provinces of Olonets, Arkhangelsk, and Vologda and restricted timber exports from these areas.[87] Forests in the western provinces, however, were privately owned. Their produce was exported from Riga, the Prussian ports of Memel, Danzig, and Stettin, and – to some extent – from Russian ports on the Black Sea coast.[88] Prussia benefited in several ways from the exportation of Russian and Polish timber (and other forestry products).[89] Transportation was executed on Prussian bottoms and Prussian ports like Memel, Danzig, and Stettin gained additional income from the processing of timber prior to its exportation.[90] However, neither are the changes in the structure of North Eurasian trade limited to Russian grain exports and the breakthrough of trade via the Black Sea, or to domestic industry protection and the decline of textile imports, nor can they be reduced to the impact of protectionist tariff policies and increased domestic demand in the iron and timber trade. Based on a comparative analysis of some of the 'traditional' North Eurasian commodity flows through the Danish Sound with data compiled from British and French trade statistics, the next section reviews the reconfiguration of North Eurasian trade in the face of increasing global competition.

North Eurasian trade facing global competition

A comprehensive overview of the impact of global competition on North Eurasian trade goes well beyond the framework of this book. Nevertheless, this section attempts to show how global competition affected the supply and demand for grain, timber, hemp, flax, and linseed in different parts of Europe and across the oceans. Moreover, the increasing importance of alternative crops – such as maize and rice, as substitutes for grain; jute, as a substitute for flax; and sesame seeds, as a substitute for linseed – is briefly touched upon in this section. Perhaps these examples allow getting an idea of the kind of global competition that North Eurasian trade had to face in the first half of the nineteenth century, but the picture is by no means exhaustive, and many aspects require further research. Whereas the survey of global competition in the timber, hemp, flax, and linseed trades is succinct, it provides more detail about the challenges to the North Eurasian grain trade in the face of global competition. Special attention is paid to the impact of industrial flour-milling techniques on the structure of the international grain trade.

Hemp and flax occupy a peculiar position among the 'traditional' North Eurasian exports. Their demand rose throughout the eighteenth century,[91] and in the final decades of that century, the British government initiated several attempts to diminish its dependence on North Eurasian supplies of hemp and flax (see Chapter 5). Regardless of these efforts, however, in the 1840s, still more than 70% of all hemp and flax traded internationally originated from the Russian Empire; about 60% of all Russian hemp and flax exports went to the United Kingdom.[92] Other European production areas of considerable size were Italy and Hungary for hemp,[93] and Belgium and the Netherlands for flax.[94] The biggest advantage of Russian hemp and flax, compared to the higher quality produced in Belgium and the Netherlands, was its low price, because of which the United Kingdom contented itself with relatively rough types of hemp and flax, that needed further processing before being woven.[95] From the late 1830s, flax exports from the Russian Empire exceeded hemp exports, which had already started to decline.[96] Whereas flax exports seem to have been left untouched by changes in the structure of demand, hemp experienced competition from jute, or so-called Manila hemp, a substitute produced in Britain's overseas territories in India and on the Philippines.[97] After several decades of experimentation and testing, jute imports to the United Kingdom started to rise rapidly in the 1850s, and equalled the volume of hemp imports by the end of that decade.[98] Moreover, the demand for hemp started to decline under the impact of changes in the traditional use of hemp for shipbuilding. Cotton sails started to replace hemp-made sails and iron chains started to replace tows.[99]

Competition from Prussian ports in hemp and flax exports from North Eurasia becomes most apparent in the 1850s,[100] but compared to the rapid rise of jute imports to the United Kingdom, this was a minor change. Under the threat of global competition, the Russian government made some efforts to upgrade its hemp and flax industry by granting premiums to producers applying Flemish techniques for the production of 'first class' flax.[101]

However, the opportunities for developing additional markets for Russian hemp and flax exports turned out to be rather limited. Only France emerged as a hemp and flax importer of some significance in the 1840s. Hemp imports from Russia to France had a hard time competing with increasing production in Italy and Hungary.[102] In the 1850s, Russian hemp exports had dwindled and were replaced with Italian hemp exports, at least insofar as exports to France were concerned. Flax was imported to France from Russia and Belgium. Occasionally, Russian flax was even re-exported from the United Kingdom. Significant increases in the tonnage of exports to France notwithstanding, Russian flax exports to France grew at a lower rate than those of Belgian suppliers, and in the 1850s, more flax was imported to France from Belgium than from the Russian Empire. Flax exports through the Danish

Sound to the United Kingdom, either directly from Russian ports, or via Prussian ports, remained more or less stable in the 1840s and 1850s, and flax exports to France even continued to rise.[103] However, compared to the rapid growth of Belgian flax exports to France, on the one hand, and of jute imports from the East Indies to the United Kingdom, on the other, it becomes clear that – here as well – North Eurasian trade lost track of its global competitors.

Similar observations can be made with regard to linseed and timber exports through the Danish Sound, even though the actual patterns of global competition and their underlying causes were different from those of hemp and flax. In the case of linseed, a process of substitution with sesame seed imports from the East Indies seems to have occurred in the 1840s and 1850s.[104] In the case of timber, it can be observed that the supply of timber to the United Kingdom, which used to be a North Eurasian affair until the late eighteenth century, changed its direction after 1800. More than anything else, the British timber duties seem to have had a significant, but temporary impact on the reconfiguration of North Eurasian timber exports. This becomes obvious when the volumes exported from the British American Colonies and Europe are compared. At the same time, it becomes clear that – after the abolition of the timber duties – European timber exports from North Eurasia recovered quickly.

Insofar as grain is concerned, among the new areas of production, the United States, the British American Colonies, Egypt, and Walachia and Moldavia, the Ottoman Principalities on the Danube became the most important competitors of North Eurasia in the first half of the nineteenth century (see Table 6.3). However, whereas the Ottoman Principalities competed with Russia supplying the same product (wheat), the competition of the United States and the British American Colonies was of a different nature. Rather than wheat, it supplied wheat flour (and maize) to the United Kingdom. Wheat flour was a ready-to-use industrial product, which occupied less transport and storage space and was therefore more cost efficient than corn itself.[105] Wheat figures prominently in much of the literature on the rise of the Atlantic economy and the American "grain invasion" of Britain in the nineteenth century.[106] The latter term stems from the observation that, since the 1830s and especially after the start of the abolition of the Corn Laws in 1842, the United States massively entered the British market as a wheat supplier, whereas until then, Prussia, Russia, and "Germany" had dominated the British wheat market.[107]

Traditionally, this change is attributed to a narrowing price gap between American and British wheat, and thus of increasing market integration. More recently, strong cases have been made for the predominance of other factors, such as falling domestic transport costs and the expansion of American wheat supplies.[108] However, the predominant focus on wheat exports to Britain has compelled researchers to gather wheat and its processed, ready-to-use form 'wheat flour' together into one single category 'wheat.' Thus, significant differences in their production, value and transportation costs remain to be addressed.[109]

Table 6.3 Origin of wheat, wheat flour, other grain, and maize imported to the United Kingdom, 1840–1864

	Wheat					*Wheat flour*				
	NE	*EU*	*TUR*	*ATL*	*Other*	*NE*	*EU*	*TUR*	*ATL*	*Other*
1840–1844	255.3	228.9	7.5	15.8	23.3	0.6	4.1	0.0	48.1	1.5
1845–1849	268.0	241.9	37.5	60.4	54.4	0.7	16.3	0.1	132.9	8.1
1850–1854	416.4	303.6	178.3	115.1	40.6	0.3	73.2	0.1	137.6	4.8
1855–1859	263.5	226.6	119.3	139.1	62.5	0.7	70.8	0.1	79.7	3.5
1860–1864	514.3	164.0	128.8	613.0	43.4	1.2	89.5	0.2	188.2	7.2
	Other grain					*Maize*				
	NE	*EU*	*TUR*	*ATL*	*Other*	*NE*	*EU*	*TUR*	*ATL*	*Other*
1840–1844	96.2	151.0	16.9	8.0	18.1					
1845–1849	205.1	447.0	177.2	266.3	102.1					
1850–1854	180.9	401.2	250.2	75.8	69.6	25.5		132.4	95.7	70.9
1855–1859	124.6	196.2	24.0	0.0	86.6	40.9		96.9	108.2	67.9
1860–1864	145.9	285.5	59.3	0.0	112.6	50.4		213.5	209.1	53.6

Source: Statistical abstracts.
Note: Five-year averages, in '000 tonnes. NE = North Eurasia (=Russia – Baltic & White Sea, Russia – Black Sea, Prussia); EU = Denmark & Duchies, Sweden, Hanse Towns, Germany, Holland, France, Italian States, Spain; TUR = Walachia & Moldavia, Turkey Proper, Turkish Dominions, Egypt; ATL = British North America, United States.

Competition from the side of the Ottoman Empire took off as soon as previous restrictions for shipping on the Danube were abolished in the Anglo-Turkish commercial convention of Balta Liman (1838), which "(...) placed the whole of the Ottoman Empire on a virtually free trade status, (...)."[110] Foreign representations quickly appeared in the ports of Galaç and Braila to facilitate grain exports from the Danubian Principalities of Moldavia and Walachia. The growth of these ports entailed the decline of the neighbouring Russian ports in Bessarabia. Russia tried to hinder the Danubian Principalities' grain trade in several ways, thus contributing to its self-isolation and – eventually – to the outbreak of the Crimean War.[111] Wheat and maize exports to Constantinople were complemented with exports to *porto franco* ports in the Mediterranean, and direct exports to France and the United Kingdom. According to Nebolsin, within 10 years, the volume of wheat exports from Galaç and Braila more than doubled. Maize exports experienced a sixfold increase (see Table 6.3).[112]

The most important competitor of North Eurasian grain exports to Europe were the United States, which – in addition to wheat – exported increasing amounts of wheat flour (see Table 6.3). The breakthrough of the United States as wheat flour exporter seems to have occurred between 1835 and 1845, when some major infrastructural issues in the centre of the United States (Ohio and Mississippi) were resolved, and wheat and wheat flour exports from the American ports on the East coast became feasible.[113] Besides higher incomes from the sales of wheat flour, the main benefit of flour production lies in the reduction of transportation costs.[114] Even though wheat prices in Russia's Black Sea ports were much lower than in New York, this initial advantage melted away in the face of other costs, such as freight and insurance costs, the cost of time spent *en route*, the time needed to settle payments and the time and cost of producing flour in London.[115] Wheat's initial price advantage compared to wheat flour exported from the USA was as high as 48%. Transportation costs on the route from Odessa to London reduced this advantage to only 15%.[116] Freight and insurance rates were higher on the route from Odessa to London than from New York to the capital of the United Kingdom. Moreover, it cost twice as much time to import wheat from Odessa than from New York to London and, upon arrival in London, the remaining cost advantage of about 15% was lost in the production of wheat flour. On top of all that, the more advanced cashless payment settlement system between New York and London secured quicker payment settlements than between Odessa and London. Whereas an English merchant could easily settle his payments using bills of exchange in New York, he was forced to pay part of his sums in hard currency and part in bills of exchange on different places in Odessa. All of this, of course, added to the burden of settling the accounts,[117] and exerted a negative impact on the competitiveness of the Russian grain trade.

From one quest to another...

The first two sections of this chapter showed that the reconfiguration of North Eurasian trade in the first half of the nineteenth century had its roots in the opening of the Black Sea for international trade as well as in the increasingly adverse position of the United Kingdom towards its dependence on Russian grain and raw materials. Moreover, it paid attention to the role of 'modern' commercial infrastructure (or its absence) as a driving force for the empirically observed reconfiguration.

Long-term changes in the demand and supply of certain foodstuffs, raw materials, and manufactures affected the tonnage and geography of the distribution of these commodities in North Eurasian trade. The rise of the United Kingdom as the major importer of North Eurasian commodities provoked changes in the demand for foodstuffs, raw materials and manufactures. Rye, for example, which was grown predominantly in North-West Russia, had been a cornerstone of the Dutch commercial system and dominated trade through the Danish Sound until the mid-eighteenth century. The volume of rye exports through the Danish Sound stagnated, however, whereas that of wheat exports started to rise from the mid-eighteenth century onwards, in particular, after the emergence on the scene of Great Britain as a wheat importer from the Baltic (see Chapter 4). Alongside the usual short-term upswings and depressions in the volume of grain exports from North Eurasia, which show the impact of climatic variation on the size of grain harvests and the availability (or lack) of excess supplies for exportation, the North Eurasian grain trade in the first half of the nineteenth century was marked by the relocation of a significant part of its activities towards the coast of the Black Sea, on the one hand, and Prussian ports on the southern Baltic coast, on the other. Most importantly, this relocation affected the North Eurasian wheat trade, which had been driven by increasing British demand since the early 1780s. Russo-Prussian transit regulations supported this relocation (see Chapter 5). In the first half of the nineteenth century, North Eurasian trade had to bear with global competition in the production and supply of some of its most important commodities. The increasing global competition resulted from Britain's protracted global search for alternative supplies of naval stores, on the one hand, and the diffusion of industrial flour-milling techniques in the United States, on the other. As soon as a more or less reliable transport infrastructure from the Mid-West of the United States to its ports on the East coast was in place, grain supplies from the United States benefited from a triple advantage over most North Eurasian supplies: (1) transatlantic deliveries were faster than those from North Eurasia; (2) the transport costs for flour were lower than for grain; and (3) flour was a ready-to-use industrial product, whereas grain would still have to be processed at its final destination first.

Insofar as commercial exchange itself is concerned, first, the impact of a movement towards free trade in the United Kingdom was discussed, which eventually led to the repeal of the Navigation Laws,[118] on the one hand, and a series of reforms and later the abolition of the timber duties and the Corn Laws,[119] on the other. Second, the British search for viable alternative sources of supply for grain, naval stores and some types of textile manufactures (mostly raven duck and sailcloth), which had been imported predominantly from North Eurasia until the late 1840s was described. Third, the impact of a number of drastic changes in Russia's commercial legislation was discussed, pointing out, in particular, the role of the prohibitive system of textile imports and protectionist measures in support of Russia's domestic industries. Transport infrastructure played a double role in the reconfiguration of North Eurasian trade in the first half of the nineteenth century. On the one hand, steam shipping and railway construction started to alter the organization of international commodity distribution, leading to the rise of novel gateways for North Eurasian trade in the Southern Baltic area as well as in Western Mediterranean. On the other hand, the absence of such infrastructural developments in the Russian Empire was no less significant for the development of North Eurasian trade in the first half of the nineteenth century. The lack of transport innovations and the non-realization of a national system of commodity distribution and trade had a devastating effect on the competitiveness of the Russian Empire as a major supplier of grain and naval stores. Because of the increasing number of ports with easier access and superior port infrastructure, British commerce became less and less inclined to trade directly with the distant ports of the Russian Empire, be it

St. Petersburg in the easternmost edge of the Baltic, Arkhangelsk on the White Sea coast or Odessa on the northern shores of the Black Sea. At least partly, intermediate ports successfully challenged direct Anglo-Russian trade. These ports benefited from two advantages: they could be reached more easily with steam ships and had storage facilities that made the supply of goods more predictable and less hazardous. Last but not least, the relocation of activities towards intermediate ports in the Mediterranean and the Southern Baltic fit well into the isolation of the Russian Empire after 1839 and the establishment of an anti-Russian block in European international relations during the 1840s and 1850s.

Its increasing European isolation reinforced Russia's efforts to secure its predominant political and commercial position in the landlocked parts of Central and East Asia, most importantly in the Caucasus, along the shores of the Caspian Sea, in the territories of the former Khanates and the Amur basin. Russia's reorientation was inspired – at least in part – by the assumption that it would be able to develop markets for its products in Persia, Central Asia, and China, since they had no industry at all to compete with the Russian Empire.[120] China was an important market for Russian textiles and furs: in the first half of the 1840s, 43% of Russia's textile exports and 62% of its fur exports entered China via Kyakhta.[121] The growth of Russia's textile exports to China resulted from the substitution of the transit of Prussian woollen cloth with Polish cloth exports to China in the 1820s, and the subsequent prohibition of the latter after the Polish uprising of 1830–1831.[122] After a brief prohibition between 1816 and 1819, a tariff convention with Prussia allowed for the transit of Prussian woollen cloth to Asia.[123] Within a short period, Prussian transit started to pose a threat to Russia's infant textile industry.[124] The 1822 tariff dealt with such threats and supported the development of the domestic textile industry. After 1822, Prussian transit of woollen cloth decreased rapidly. However, it would take until 1831 before the impact of the 1822 tariff regulations on the domestic textile industry became apparent. First, because of a ten-year period of subsidized trade granted to Transcaucasia in 1821, foreign cloth could be traded freely there (at 5% import tax).[125] The November uprising (1830–1831) put an end to the transit of Polish cloth through Russia. Starting 1832, it was allowed for another three years, before being forbidden altogether.[126] The Russian textile industry could secure at least part of the Chinese market in this way, supplying China with rather rough but warm textiles made after Polish and Prussian examples. However, the quality of Russian textiles was rather low and finer types of cloth continued to be imported to Russia from other countries as well.; the transit of small quantities of 'other woollen fabrics' via Russia to China was maintained as well.[127] However, since 1846, a premium supported the exportation of cotton fabrics to Asia.[128] It had become clear that the United Kingdom and the United States threatened Russian textile supplies to Persia and China. For the time being, Russian cotton textiles continued to monopolize Central Asian markets, but the rapid development of the British textile trade with Persia via Trebizond to Tabriz since the 1830s,[129] and of British and American textiles traded via the Chinese Treaty Ports marked the final blow to the quest for North Eurasian trade.

However, Russia's reorientation towards the vast and disputed land border between North and South Eurasia again brought it in the orbit of the British Empire, which itself longed to control these areas.[130] After the Crimean War, with its devastating outcome for the Russian Empire, neither the Baltic nor the Black Sea stood in the focus of international commercial and political relations any longer. The times of diplomatic tension and (threats of) war during the late seventeenth and throughout the eighteenth century, when the Baltic and the quasi-monopolistic access it provided to much-desired supplies of naval stores and raw materials were gone. The United Kingdom looked elsewhere to secure its supply of raw materials and foodstuffs and to sell its manufactures; access to North Eurasia was no longer as high on the agenda of its international relations as it had been throughout the eighteenth century. More and more, attention shifted towards intermediate ports with good connections to North Eurasia rather than with North Eurasia proper. In the meantime, the Caucasus, Central Asia, and China gained relevance in the political and economic isolation of the Russian Empire, which was a declared policy goal of the British Empire since the late 1830s at the latest. The Russian Empire itself also shifted its attention towards the long, complex and poorly accessible land border between North and South Eurasia in an attempt to secure the less-developed Central Asian and Chinese markets for its manufactures, while attempting to strengthen its presence in the Amur basin at the same time. The United Kingdom strived for the isolation of Russia in the wake of the 1839 treaty with the Ottoman Empire, which itself became a preamble of the Crimean War. After the Opium War of 1839–1842, the Chinese Treaty Ports offered an excellent opportunity to isolate the Russian Empire further and hamper another significant branch of its international trade. Insofar as roles of the White Sea, the Baltic and the Black Sea were concerned, the quest for North Eurasian trade was over.

Notes

1 Schroeder, *The transformation of European politics*, 517–582.

2 The Treaty of Kiel had been signed by the United Kingdom, Sweden and Denmark-Norway in early 1814 and foresaw for Swedish Pomerania to be handed over to Denmark. In return, Norway would enter into a personal union with Sweden, as had been requested in 1813 by the elected heir to the Swedish throne, Jean Baptiste Bernadotte (1763–1844). Norway refused. A Norwegian constitutional movement strived for independence and even fought a brief war with Sweden in the course of 1814. The matter was settled at the Congress of Vienna, where the Prussian prime minister Karl August von Hardenberg proposed an exchange of territories, in which Swedish Pomerania was handed over to the Prussian King. On the Scandinavian Peninsula, the troubles between

Norway and Sweden were solved when the *de facto* ruler of the Kingdom of Sweden, Jean Baptiste Bernadotte, made an important concession. In return for accepting (with few changes) the Norwegian constitution, the childless King of Sweden, Charles XIII, was crowned King of Norway. Upon Charles XIII's death in 1818, the illustrious Bernadotte, who had become the elected heir (heir-presumptive) back in 1810, accepted the name Charles XIV John as King of Sweden and Charles III John as King of Norway.

3 *Tetradas* [VSWG-JDA], 1_turnover: *Estimated total turnover.*

4 *Tetradas* [VSWG-JDA], 8_CIES_Bex_FS: *Barley, Oats, Rye, Wheat.*

5 *Tetradas* [VSWG-JDA], 8_CIES_Bex_FS: *Wheat flour, Rye flour.*

6 *Tetradas* [VSWG-JDA], 8_CIES_Bex_FS: *Barley, Oats, Rye, Wheat.*

7 Perren, "Structural change," 425. However strong the growth of grain imports to the United Kingdom since the late eighteenth century may have been, it should not be overlooked that, until 1860, about 75% of all wheat available on the British domestic market was home-produced. 19% was imported as wheat and 5%–7% was imported as wheat flour. From about 1860 onwards, the volume and share of imported wheat in total available wheat started to change. By 1914, 71% was imported; its estimated volume had risen to 73.2 million cwt.

8 Barnes, *A history of the English corn laws*, 117–218; Fairlie, "The nineteenth-century corn law"; Fairlie, "The corn laws"; Williamson, "The impact of the corn laws," 124–125; Sharp, "1846 and all that."

9 Herlihy, *Russian grain*, 110–117; Nebolsin, *Statističeskoe obozrenie*, 88–91; 94–95; 120–121. In France, which usually did not need much foreign grain, a fixed tariff was in force until 1819. Between 1819 and 1832, grain imports were prohibited unless certain conditions were met. On 15 April 1832, France introduced its own Corn Laws, but the grain trade at the *porto franco* of Marseille was not affected by them.

10 Herlihy is more nuanced in her assessment of the impact of the Corn Laws:

> The grain trade under the policy of the 'sliding scale' [of 1828] (...) had a double impact: It stimulated Russian grain production undoubtedly, and attracted large investments into the ships and storage facilities needed to handle it, but it did not reward the Russian producers with the amount of profit that might have been expected from their labors.
>
> (see Herlihy, *Russian grain*, 116)

11 Nebolsin, *Statističeskoe obozrenie*, 99. Grigorij Pavlovič Nebolsin (often referred to as Nebol'sin) (1811–1896) was an economist and geographer with a long career at the service of the Department of foreign trade and ministry of finance of the Russian Empire. At the age of 18, he became the editor of the Commercial Gazette (*Ru.* Kommerčeskaja Gazeta) and held this position for 30 years (1829–1859). Most of his works rely on in-depth analyses of Russian trade statistics, and outline his ideas about the development of Russian trade and industry. Although his works are often cited, their use is mostly limited to extracting some relevant statistical information; his views on the development of Russia's foreign trade have received far less attention so far. In 1868, Nebolsin was appointed as member of the State Council of the Russian Empire (*Ru.* Gosudarstvennyj Sovet Rossijskoj Imperii). See Šilov and Kuz'min, *Členy Gosudarstvennogo soveta.*

12 Nebolsin, *Statističeskoe obozrenie*, 88–114; Zolotov, *Vnešnjaja torgovlja*, 50–56; Herlihy, *Russian grain*, 116–117.

13 Nebolsin, *Statističeskoe obozrenie*, 69–84; 91; 101; 103; 105; 118; 120.

14 Herlihy, *Russian grain*, 16–23. Herlihy developed the concept of 'deposit trade' to describe the structure of the international grain market, and analyzes the impact of the Corn Laws on the deposit trade, but she does not take into account the impact of the Navigation Laws.

15 Herlihy, *Russian grain*, 20. A similar opinion is found in: Puryear, "Odessa," 194–195.
16 Nebolsin, *Statističeskoe obozrenie*, 57; 110. In 1839–1841 the following amounts of Russian grain were brought to Prussia by river: 187,027 *četvert'* wheat, 261,643 *četvert'* rye, 21,608 *četvert'* barley and 46,098 *četvert'* oats. From the Kingdom of Poland, the following quantities were brought to Danzig via the Vistula: 1,194,578 *četvert'* wheat, 217,140 *četvert'* rye and a negligible quantity of barley.
17 Nebolsin, *Statističeskoe obozrenie*, 107–109.
18 Nebolsin, *Statističeskoe obozrenie*, 109.
19 Jones, *Bread upon the waters*.
20 Nebolsin, *Statističeskoe obozrenie*, 55–57. For a case study on the 'deposit trade' in Livorno, see Herlihy, *Russian grain*, 175–205; Herlihy, "Russian wheat."
21 Nebolsin, *Statističeskoe obozrenie*, 47–52.
22 *Tetradas* [VSWG-JDA], 7_PIES_Copenhagen: *Exports of foodstuffs*; 7_PIES_Danzig: *Exports of foodstuffs*; 7_PIES_StPetersburg: *Exports of foodstuffs*; 7_PIES_Stettin: *Exports of foodstuffs*.
23 *Tetradas* [VSWG-JDA], 8_CIES_Bex_FS: *Rye flour, Wheat flour*.
24 *Tetradas* [VSWG-JDA], 8_CIES_Bex_FS: *Barley, Oats, Rye, Wheat*.
25 *Tetradas* [VSWG-JDA], 8_CIES_Bex_FS: *Rye flour, Wheat flour*.
26 Herlihy, *Russian grain*, 86–87; Puryear, "Odessa," 196.
27 Puryear, "Odessa," 193–194; Herlihy, *Russian grain*, 97–101; Ardeleanu, "The opening and development," 30–32.
28 The early development of Odessa is strongly associated with the life and work of the first governor of New Russia, Le Duc de Richelieu. See, e.g.: Herlihy, *Odessa*, 21–48; Družinina, *Južnaja Ukraina*, 187–202; Anthoine, *Essai historique*, 50–78.
29 Polevchtchikova, "Espoirs et déceptions"; Puryear, "Odessa," 198; 200.
30 Puryear, "Odessa," 200.
31 Petmezas and Papadopoulou (eds). *Black Sea Historical Statistics*.
32 Nebolsin, *Statističeskoe obozrenie*, 12–16.
33 Nebolsin, *Statističeskoe obozrenie*, 54.
34 Nebolsin, *Statističeskoe obozrenie*, 11–21.
35 Nebolsin, *Statističeskoe obozrenie*, 47.
36 Nebolsin, *Statističeskoe obozrenie*, 46.
37 Nebolsin, *Statističeskoe obozrenie*, 49–50.
38 Nebolsin, *Statističeskoe obozrenie*, 56.
39 For some statistics on the overland connection between Volga and Don, see Stuckenberg, *Beschreibung*, 464–466.
40 See Blackwell, *The beginnings*, 264–268; Jones, "Getting the goods." Noteworthy is the extensive elder literature on the subject, as well as the recent renewed interest in the canal systems of European Russia, see Stuckenberg, *Beschreibung*, 188–191; 337–445; Širokova et al., *Tichvinskaj vodnaja sistema*; Širokova et al., *Vyšnevolockaja vodnaja sistema*; Martynov and Sazonova, "Istoričeskaja geografija."
41 Nebolsin, *Statističeskoe obozrenie*, 29–31; for a descriptive account of the journeys of iron caravans from the Ural Mountains to St. Petersburg, see Kafengauz, *Istorija*, 395–422.
42 Blackwell, *The beginnings*, 77.
43 Nebolsin, *Statističeskoe obozrenie*, 30–31.
44 Nebolsin, *Statističeskoe obozrenie*, 32.
45 *Gosudarstvennaja vnešnjaja torgovlja*.
46 Nebolsin, *Statističeskoe obozrenie*, 35–36.
47 Nebolsin, *Statističeskoe obozrenie*, 36–43; 61–62.
48 Nebolsin, *Statističeskoe obozrenie*, 43–44. Probably, these are the measures referred to in Herlihy's description of government initiatives to promote the

growth of Odessa. Based on an Italian newspaper article of 5 October 1847, Herlihy writes that

> [e]fforts were also made to make credit available in this capital-starved land. In 1847, in order to aid wheat merchants, the tsar ordered the State Bank to advance bank notes to all merchants who desired them, to the amount of one-half of the value of their stored cereals.
>
> (see Herlihy, *Russian grain*, 87)

The mechanisms of the Russian government's reaction to what appears to be a speculation bubble in the grain trade are largely unknown and represent a research desideratum.

49 Nebolsin, *Statističeskoe obozrenie*, 180–200; Rieber, "The formation of La Grande Société"; Haywood, *The beginnings*; Haywood, *Russia enters the railway age*.
50 Nebolsin, *Statističeskoe obozrenie*, 174.
51 Nebolsin, *Statističeskoe obozrenie*, 174–175; 185–191.
52 Nebolsin, *Statističeskoe obozrenie*, 189.
53 Nebolsin, *Statističeskoe obozrenie*, 189–200.
54 The theoretical background of this discussion is dealt with in: Blackwell, *The beginnings*, 123–148.
55 Marshall, *Digest of all the accounts*, 54.
56 For a different opinion, especially with regard to Nicholas I's position towards railway development, see Haywood, *The beginnings*; Haywood, *Russia enters the railway age*.
57 Kipp, "M.Kh. Reutern," 437.
58 Blioch, *Finansy Rossii*, I, 173; PSZ, XXXVIII, 28964.
59 Kipp, "M.Kh. Reutern," 437.
60 Kipp, "M.Kh. Reutern," 437.
61 Blioch, *Finansy Rossii*, I, 244.
62 Blioch, *Finansy Rossii*, I, 249–250; 257.
63 Blioch, *Finansy Rossii*, I, 281–282.
64 Nebolsin, *Statističeskoe obozrenie*, II, 355–356; Blackwell, *The beginnings*, 172.
65 Sobolev, *Tamožennaja politika*, 31; Blackwell, *The beginnings*, 173. The tariff of 1822 also "(…) closed the doors of the Ukrainian market to foreign competition for many decades, and provided a lucrative outlet for Muscovite textile manufactures." (See Blackwell, *The beginnings*, 79).
66 Nebolsin, *Statističeskoe obozrenie*, II, 355.
67 Nebolsin, *Statističeskoe obozrenie*, II, 356; Sobolev, *Tamožennaja politika*, 32–35.
68 Nebolsin, *Statističeskoe obozrenie*, II, 356–357.
69 Gestwa, "Das 'Russische Manchester'."
70 Nebolsin, *Statističeskoe obozrenie*, II, 357–360. Ivanovo was a village (selo), owned by the Sheremetyev family.
71 Nebolsin, *Statističeskoe obozrenie*, II, 359–366.
72 Nebolsin, *Statističeskoe obozrenie*, II. 367.
73 The focus of this paragraph is on metal exports only; for imports of iron and other metals to Russia, see Nebolsin, *Statističeskoe obozrenie*, II, 205–212.
74 On different types of iron produced in Russia, see Nebolsin, *Statističeskoe obozrenie*, II, 213–214.
75 In addition to the mining industries, iron manufactories emerged in Central Russia, in the provinces of Vladimir, Nizhny Novgorod, Tambov, Ryazan, Kaluga, Tula and Oryol. See Nebolsin, *Statističeskoe obozrenie*, II, 210.
76 *Tetradas* [VSWG-JDA], 8_CIES_Bex_RM: *Iron*; 8_CIES_Bex_MF: *Iron staves*.
77 Nebolsin, *Statističeskoe obozrenie*, II, 217.
78 Nebolsin, *Statističeskoe obozrenie*, II, 212–218.

79 *Tetradas* [VSWG-JDA], 8_CIES_Bex_RM: *Iron*; 8_CIES_Bex_MF: *Iron staves*.
80 Nebolsin, *Statističeskoe obozrenie*, II, 214; 218–219; 222.
81 *Tetradas* [VSWG-JDA], 8_CIES_Bex_RM: *Iron*; 8_CIES_Bex_MF: *Iron staves*; 7_PIES_StPetersburg: *Exports of raw materials*.
82 Nebolsin, *Statističeskoe obozrenie*, II, 218–219; 233.
83 Nebolsin, *Statističeskoe obozrenie*, II, 222.
84 Nebolsin, *Statističeskoe obozrenie*, II, 222–230.
85 Nebolsin, *Statističeskoe obozrenie*, II, 165–168. Special tariffs applied to Finland and the Kingdom of Poland.
86 Nebolsin, *Statističeskoe obozrenie*, II, 180–183.
87 Nebolsin *Statističeskoe obozrenie*, II, 160–165.
88 Nebolsin, *Statističeskoe obozrenie*, II, 163–164.
89 Timber was transported from the Kingdom of Poland to Danzig via the Vistula and Stettin via the Bromberg canal. See Nebolsin, *Statističeskoe obozrenie*, II, 174–175.
90 Nebolsin, *Statističeskoe obozrenie*, II, 178–179; *Tetradas* [VSWG-JDA], 7_PIES_Danzig: *Exports of raw materials*; 7_PIES_Memel: *Exports of raw materials*; 7_PIES_Stettin: *Exports of raw materials*.
91 *Tetradas* [VSWG-JDA], 8_CIES_Bex_RM: *Flax, Hemp*.
92 Nebolsin, *Statističeskoe obozrenie*, II, 2; 28.
93 Hungarian hemp was exported across the Mediterranean from Fiume. See Nebolsin *Statističeskoe obozrenie*, II, 30–31.
94 Nebolsin, *Statističeskoe obozrenie*, II, 30–34. In Spain, *esparto* was cultivated as a substitute for hemp. Large quantities of hemp and flax were produced in Prussia and the German States, but most of it was meant for the domestic industries rather than for exportation.
95 Nebolsin, *Statističeskoe obozrenie*, II, 19.
96 *Tetradas* [VSWG-JDA], 8_CIES_Bex_RM: *Flax, Hemp*.
97 Nebolsin, *Statističeskoe obozrenie*, II, 7.
98 Miskell & Whatley, "'Juteopolis' in the Making."
99 Nebolsin, *Statističeskoe obozrenie*, II, 7. Nebolsin adds that the construction of steam ships and ships with iron hulls also had a negative impact on the demand for hemp, but he does not explain why.
100 Nebolsin, *Statističeskoe obozrenie*, II, 25; *Tetradas* [VSWG-JDA], 8_CIES_Bex_RM: *Flax, Hemp*.
101 Nebolsin, *Statističeskoe obozrenie*, II, 21–26.
102 Nebolsin, *Statističeskoe obozrenie*, II, 30–34.
103 *Tetradas* [VSWG-JDA], 8_CIES_Bex_RM: *Flax, Hemp*.
104 Cf. the corresponding figures in *Tableau général*, 1829–1861.
105 In a return to an order of the House of Commons in 1852, a certain Mr Cayley gives the following proportions for conversion into equivalent quarters of grain is proposed for different types of meal and flour. Wheat flour – 392 lb, oatmeal – 176 lb, rye meal – 424 lb and other meal – 348 lb to the quarter of grain. One quarter of grain is equivalent to 112 lb. This means that it needs about 3.5 quarters of wheat to produce one quarter of wheat flour. See Cayley, *Return to an order*.
106 Sharp, "1846 and all that," 1.
107 Sharp, "1846 and all that," 3.
108 Persson, "Mind the gap!"; Sharp, "1846 and all that," 2. The traditional argument is expressed in: Harley, "Transportation"; O'Rourke and Williamson, *Globalization and history*. Sharp argues that domestic transport costs in the United States must be neglected, because the data for domestic transportation costs are not available before the 1850s (Sharp, "1846 and all that," 11). He argues that

the supply variable captures this aspect and adds that "it is not clear that the transportation improvements meant reduced costs of getting the wheat to the east coast, since it had to travel longer distances as the centre of gravity of wheat production moved westwards." (Sharp, "1846 and all that," 11).

109 E.g. Sharp, "1846 and all that," 3.

110 Puryear, "Odessa," 204–206.

111 This enduring diplomatic issue is known is historiography as the 'Sulina Channel Question.' See Ardeleanu, *International trade* for the most recent, in-depth analysis. Furthermore, see Florescu, "The Rumanian principalities," 63–67; Puryear, "Odessa," 209–211.

112 Nebolsin, *Statističeskoe obozrenie*, 150–151.

113 About the 'transportation revolution' in the United States, and its impact on the American grain trade, see Clark, *The grain trade*; Taylor, *The transportation revolution*; Taaffe et al., *Geography of transportation*, 73–108.

114 Nebolsin, *Statističeskoe obozrenie*, 161–162.

115 Nebolsin, *Statističeskoe obozrenie*, 167–168.

116 Nebolsin, *Statističeskoe obozrenie*, 166.

117 Nebolsin, *Statističeskoe obozrenie*, 167.

118 Palmer, *Politics, shipping, and the repeal.*

119 Sharp, "1846 and all that."

120 Blackwell, *The beginnings*, 172.

121 Nebolsin, *Statističeskoe obozrenie*, 338.

122 Nebolsin, *Statističeskoe obozrenie*, II, 374–376.

123 Nebolsin, *Statističeskoe obozrenie*, II, 374.

124 Nebolsin, *Statističeskoe obozrenie*, II, 374.

125 Sobolev, *Tamožennaja politika*, 31–36.

126 Nebolsin, *Statističeskoe obozrenie*, II, 376.

127 Nebolsin, *Statističeskoe obozrenie*, II, 387–391.

128 Nebolsin, *Statističeskoe obozrenie*, II, 370–371.

129 Issawi, "The Tabriz-Trabzon trade." British, French, German and Swiss cotton textiles were brought to Trebizond via Constantinople or via the Leipzig fairs.

130 In this sense, the political economy of Russia's expansion in the Caucasus, including the French and British responses as well as an analysis of the emergence of Tiflis and Trebizond as new gateways of international trade, requires further study. First insights may be obtained from the following sources: Anthoine, *Essai historique*, 304–370; LeDonne, "Geopolitics," 30–31; Van Regemorter, "Le mythe génois."

References

[Mr Cayley]. *Return to an order of the honourable the house of commons dated 16 November 1852.* London 1852.

Anthoine, M. Baron de Saint-Joseph. *Essai historique sur le commerce et la navigation de la Mer-noire, ou Voyage et entreprises pour établir des rapports commerciaux et maritimes entre les ports de la Mer-Noire et ceux de la Méditerranée. Seconde édition.* Paris 1820.

Ardeleanu, Constantin. *International trade and diplomacy at the lower Danube. The Sulina question and the economic premises of the Crimean War (1829–1853).* Brăila 2014.

Ardeleanu, Constantin. "The opening and development of the Black Sea for international trade and shipping (1774–1853)." *Euxeinos* 14 (2014): 30–52.

Barnes, Donald Grove. *A history of the English corn laws from 1660–1846.* New York 1965.

Blackwell, William L. *The beginnings of Russian industrialization, 1800–1860*. Princeton 1968.

Blioch, Ivan Stanislavovič. *Finansy Rossii XIX stoletija. Istorija – Statistika. Tom I.* Sankt-Peterburg 1882.

Clark, John G. *The grain trade in the Old Northwest*. Westport 1980 (reprint 1966).

Družinina, Elena Ioasafovna. *Južnaja Ukraina v 1800–1825 gg.* Moskva 1970.

Fairlie, Susan Elisabeth. *The Anglo-Russian grain trade 1815–1861 [Thesis submitted for the degree Doctor of Philosophy (Faculty of Arts) in the Universtiy of London]*. London 1959.

Fairlie, Susan Elisabeth. "The corn laws and British wheat production, 1829–76." *The Economic History Review* 22, 1 (1969): 88–110.

Fairlie, Susan Elisabeth. "The nineteenth-century corn law reconsidered." *The Economic History Review* 18, 3 (1965): 562–575.

Florescu, Radu R. "The Rumanian principalities and the origins of the Crimean War." *The Slavonic and East European Review* 43, 100 (1964): 46–67.

Gestwa, Klaus. "Das 'russische Manchester' und die Grafenfamilie Šeremetev. Baumwollgewerbe und Gutsherrschaft auf dem Landgut Ivanovo, 1741–1861." *Jahrbücher für Geschichte Osteuropas, Neue Folge* 47 (1999): 20–39.

Gosudarstvennaja vnešnjaja torgovlja v raznych ee vidach za … god. Sankt-Peterburg 1812–1862.

Harley, C. Knick. "Transportation, the World Wheat Trade, and the Kuznets Cycle, 1850–1913." *Explorations in Economic History* 17 (1980): 218–250.

Haywood, Richard Mowbray. *The beginnings of railway development in Russia in the reign of Nicholas I, 1835–1842*. Durham 1969.

Haywood, Richard Mowbray. *Russia enters the railway age, 1842–1855*. Boulder 1998.

Herlihy, Patricia. *Odessa. A history, 1794–1914*. Cambridge 1986.

Herlihy, Patricia. "Russian wheat and the port of Livorno, 1794–1865." *The Journal of European Economic History* 5 (1976): 45–68.

Herlihy, Patricia Anne McGahey. *Russian grain and Mediterranean markets, 1774–1861*. University of Pennsylvania Dissertation. Philadelphia 1963.

Issawi, Charles. "The Tabriz-Trabzon trade, 1830–1900. Rise and decline of a route." *International Journal of Middle East Studies* 1, 1 (1970): 18–27.

Jones, Robert E. *Bread upon the waters. The St. Petersburg grain trade and the Russian economy, 1703–1811*. Pittsburgh 2013.

Jones, Robert E. "Getting the goods to St. Petersburg: Water transport from the interior 1703–1811." *Slavic Review* 43, 3 (1984): 413–433.

Kafengauz, B.B. *Istorija chozjajstva Demidovych v XVIII–XIX vv. Opyt issledevanija po istorii ural'skoj metallurgii, Tom 1*. Moskva / Leningrad 1949.

Kipp, Jacob W. "M.Kh. Reutern on the Russian state and economy. A liberal bureaucrat during the Crimean Era, 1854–1860." *The Journal of Modern History* 47, 3 (1975): 437–459.

LeDonne, John P. "Geopolitics, logistics, and grain. Russia's ambitions in the Black Sea basin, 1737–1834." *The International History Review* 28, 1 (2006): 1–41.

Marshall, J. *A digest of all the accounts, related to the population, productions, revenues, financial operations, manufactures, shipping, colonies, commerce, &c. &c., of the United Kingdom of Great Britain and Ireland, diffused through more than 600 volumes of journals, reports, and papers, presented to parliament through the last thirty-five years, in two parts. With a separate index to each*. London 1833.

Martynov, Vasilii; Sazonova, Irina. "Istoričeskaja geografija putej soobščenija severo-zapada Rossii: 'ėpocha kanalov' (XVIII – pervaja polovina XIX vv.)." *Pskovskij regionologičeskij žurnal* 31, 1 (2017): 119–137.

Miskell, Louise; Whatley, C.A. "Juteopolis in the making. Linen and the industrial transformation of Dundee, c. 1820–1850." *Textile History* 30, 2 (1999): 176–198.

Nebolsin, Grigorij. *Statističeskoe obozrenie vnešnej torgovli Rossii.* Sankt-Peterburg 1850.

O'Rourke, K.H.; Williamson, J.G. *Globalization and history.* London 1999.

Palmer, Sarah. *Politics, shipping, and the repeal of the Navigation laws.* Manchester 1990.

Perren, Richard. "Structural change and market growth in the food industry. Flour milling in Britain, Europe, and America, 1850–1914." *The Economic History Review, New Series* 43, 3 (1990): 420–437.

Persson, Karl Gunnar. "Mind the gap! transport costs and price convergence in the Atlantic economy, 1850–1900." *European Review of Economic History* 8, 2 (2004): 125–147.

Petmezas, Socrates; Papadopoulou, Alexandra (eds). *Black Sea Historical Statistics, 1812–1914.* Published online at www.blacksea.gr.

Polevchtchikova, Elena. "Espoirs et déceptions d'Odessa dans le premier quart du XIXe siècle." *Cahiers Slaves* 14 (2016): 91–104.

PSZ: *Polnoe Sobranie Zakonov Rossijskoj Imperii, poveleniem Gosudarja Imperatora Nikolaja Pavloviča sostavlennoe.* 45 volumes. Sankt Petersburg 1830.

Puryear, Vernon J. "Odessa. Its rise and international importance, 1815–1850." *Pacific Historical Review* 3, 2 (1834): 192–215.

Rieber, Alfred J. "The formation of La Grande Société des Chemins de Fer Russes." *Jahrbücher für Geschichte Osteuropas, Neue Folge* 21, 3 (1973): 375–391.

Schroeder, Paul W. *The transformation of European politics, 1763–1848.* Oxford 2003 (reprint 1994).

Sharp, Paul R. *1846 and all that. The rise and fall of British wheat protection in the nineteenth century.* Department of Economics, University of Copenhagen Discussion Paper 06–14, 2006.

Šilov, Denis Nikolaevič, Kuz'min, Jurij Anatol'evič. *Členy Gosudarstvennogo soveta Rossijskoj Imperii, 1801–1906. Biobibliografičeskij spravočnik.* St. Petersburg 2007.

Širokova, V.A.; Snytko, V.A.; Česnov, V.M.; Frolova, N.L.; Nizovcev, V.A.; Dmitruk, N.G.; Širokov, R.S. *Vyšnevolockaja vodnaja sistema. Retrospektiva i sovremennost'. Gidrologo-ėkologičeskaja obstanovka i landšaftnye izmenenija v rajone vodnogo puti. ėkspedicionnye issledovanija: sostojanie, itogi, perspektivy. Moskva 2011.*

Širokova, V.A.; Snytko, V.A.; Nizovcev, V.A.; Frolova, N.L.; Dmitruk, N.G.; Česnov, V.M.; Ozerova, N.A.; Širokov, R.S. *Tichvinskaja vodnaja sistema. Retrospektiva i sovremennost'.Gidrologo-ėkologičeskaja obstanovka i landšaftnye izmenenija v rajone vodnogo puti.* Moskva 2013.

Sobolev, Michail Nikolaevič. *Tamožennaja politika Rossii vo vtoroj polovine XIX veka. Čast' 1.* Moskva 2012.

Statistical abstract for the United Kingdom in each year from 1840 to 1853. [s.l.] 1854.

Statistical abstract for the United Kingdom in each of the last fifteen years, from 1850 to 1864. [s.l.] 1865.

Stuckenberg, J.Ch. *Beschreibung aller, im Russischen Reiche gegrabenen oder projectirten, schiff- und flossbaren Kanaele, in historisch-statistisch-technischer Beziehung, nach den vollständigsten und zuverlässigsten Quellen verfasst, und von der Kaiserlichen*

Sankt-Petersburgischen Akademie der Wissenschaften eines Demidowschen Preises gewürdigt. Mit einer Karte. St. Petersburg 1841.

Taaffe, Edward J.; Gauthier, Howard L.; O'Kelly, Morton E. *Geography of transportation*. Second Edition. New Jersey 1996.

Tableau général du commerce de la France avec ses colonies et les puissances étrangères pendant l'année... [1829–1860]. Paris 1829–1861.

Taylor, George Rogers. *The transportation revolution, 1815–1860*. Armonk / London 1977 (reprint 1951).

Tetradas [VSWG-JDA]: *Tetradas: Tonnage estimates of trade through the Danish Sound, 1670–1856 (Replication data and selected statistics). Version: 1*. VSWG – Journal of Social and Economic History. Dataset, edited by Werner Scheltjens. https://journaldata.zbw.eu/dataset/tetradas

Van Regemorter, Jean-Louis. "Le mythe génois en Mer Noire. La France, la Russie et le commerce d'Asie par la route de Géorgie (1821–1831)." *Annales. Histoire, Sciences Sociales* 19, 3 (1964): 492–521.

Williamson, Jeffrey G. "The impact of the Corn Laws just prior to repeal." *Explorations in Economic History* 27, 2 (1990): 123–156.

Zolotov, Vladimir Aleksandrovič. *Vnešnjaja torgovlja Južnoj Rossii v pervoj polovine XIX veka*. Rostov 1963.

7 Conclusions

The previous chapters provided a long-term analysis of the impact on international trade of the protracted struggle between Britain, France, Prussia, Russia, and Sweden for economic power and political influence in the northern part of the Eurasian continent between ca. 1660 and 1860. Aware of the importance of access to resources as a means to strengthen and protect the inextricable bond between commercial and naval power, all western and northern European nations were preoccupied, more or less intensively, with the issue of North Eurasian trade. As a gateway for obtaining overland access to Asian goods, the Baltic figured prominently in European reflections about the potential economic significance of the land route through Russia to Siberia, Persia, India, and China. The preoccupation with access to North Eurasian foodstuffs and raw materials, on the one hand, and the perceived significance of the overland route to Asia, on the other, contributed to the development of a worldview, in which North Eurasia was conceptualized as the continental counterpart of the world oceans. This worldview was advocated prominently by Gottfried Wilhelm Leibniz in his writings about Muscovy and China, and had inspired Peter the Great and his successors in their political, military and commercial policies since the turn of the eighteenth century. Based on an unprecedented mass of empirical data about commodities flowing in and out of North Eurasia, and a study of primary sources and secondary literature about the commercial and diplomatic relations between the main political entities with a stake in North Eurasia's riches, this book has outlined the main stages of the international pursuit of North Eurasian trade between ca. 1660 and 1860.

The book started with an exploratory analysis of the tonnage estimates of trade through the Danish Sound (Chapter 1). The estimates revealed that, in 1670, the turnover of Baltic commercial exchange amounted to 426,978 tonnes, whereas, in 1856, it had risen to 2.8 million tonnes. During this period of almost two centuries, new commodities started to dominate imports and exports, and new centres of gravity emerged and replaced formerly dominant gateways. Between the establishment of the Sound dues in 1429 and their abolition in 1857, the Baltic had evolved from a basin of regional trade, in which members of individual cities could successfully defend their commercial interests, to an arena of world trade, where the leading powers of the time tried to secure and leverage their national interests.

Since the closing decades of the seventeenth century, the dominance of the Dutch as intermediaries of trade through the Danish Sound was threatened. Different parties – both more and less powerful – tried to benefit from the increasing Western European demand for North Eurasian grain and raw materials as well as from the perceived potential of the North Eurasian land route to Persia and China. Whereas the Baltic had been the 'backwaters' of the Dutch during most of the seventeenth century, their position was challenged in the eighteenth century, leading to a novel constellation in the first half of the nineteenth century, when – more than anything else – the Baltic had become the 'backwaters' of the British. Amsterdam lost its significance in 'Baltic trade' in the course of the eighteenth century, and only played a secondary role in international commerce after the French Wars. Contrastingly, London and a number of other English and Scottish ports, like Hull, Newcastle, Dundee, and Liverpool, rose to prominence during the eighteenth century, and strengthened their lead in the nineteenth century. Similar changes also occurred in the Baltic Sea basin itself. Alongside the ports of Danzig, Königsberg, and Riga, which had dominated Baltic trade for centuries, novel ports emerged, competed with, and eventually outstripped those traditional outlets in the course of the eighteenth century. Among these new ports, St. Petersburg, Memel, and Stettin were the most important. Significantly, in the first half of the nineteenth century, exports from Prussian ports exceeded those of their Russian counterparts, indicating an increasing concentration of commercial activity in the southern Baltic area. By the time of the abolition of the Danish Sound dues in March 1857, the centre of gravity in trade through the Sound had shifted away from the Russian ports in the eastern Baltic area (Riga, St. Petersburg) towards Prussia and – to a lesser extent – South Sweden. Russia's trade through the Danish Sound stagnated and declined after 1840.

The commodities of trade through the Danish Sound changed significantly between the latter part of the seventeenth century and the mid-nineteenth century. For a long time, grain dominated the export trade though the Danish Sound, followed by timber and iron exports. Grain exports from ports in the Baltic were matched with imports of salt, wine and overseas goods from ports on the French Atlantic and the Iberian Peninsula. Starting from the early eighteenth century, timber, hemp, flax, tar, pitch, tallow, and iron exports through the Danish Sound increased and by the mid-1720s, their estimated tonnage equalled that of grain exports. The tonnage of raw materials exports through the Sound continued to increase more or less gradually until the end of the eighteenth century, whereas short-term upswings rather than steady growth determined foodstuff exports. Only in the late 1790s, when Britain had become a net importer of North Eurasian grain, the estimated tonnages exported through the Danish Sound maintained a high level for a number of years. During the first half of the nineteenth century foodstuff exports through the Danish Sound were – again – highly unpredictable and volatile, whereas raw materials exports resumed their more regular growth pattern, after being interrupted by the Continental Blockade. After 1839, however, the volume of both grain and raw materials exports through the Danish Sound started to decline. The decline was not evenly distributed: whereas the export trade in some commodities, such as iron, stagnated and declined rapidly after 1840, the exportation of other items, such as flax, continued to grow. In the meantime, British imports of sugar, salt and especially coal caused a significant increase in the share of imports in Baltic commercial exchange.

Finally, a shift from the North Sea (Dutch Republic, later Britain) to the Baltic was observed in the domiciles of shipmasters carrying trade through the Danish Sound between 1670 and 1856. This shift became most obvious during periods of warfare in the eighteenth century, such as the Seven Years' War, the American War of Independence, the Fourth Anglo-Dutch War and the French Wars. In particular, the neutrality of Scandinavian shipmasters seems to have contributed significantly to the relocation of maritime transport services during these periods. In the first half of the nineteenth century, Prussia, Mecklenburg, and Finland (then part of the Russian Empire) joined Sweden and Denmark as the main suppliers of carrier services for Baltic trade. In the North Sea basin, only the United Kingdom remained as a significant supplier of maritime transport services for Baltic commercial exchange; the Low Countries had lost their previous significance and only played a secondary role.

The exploratory analysis served as the starting point for assessing the long-term impact on the structure of trade through the Danish Sound of territorial expansion, international politics, industrial and infrastructural development, and conflicting commercial interests. Throughout the analysis, trade through the Danish Sound served as a proxy for North Eurasian trade. The analysis identified four main stages in the international pursuit of North Eurasian trade between ca. 1660 and 1860. The first stage is that of the *emergence* of the Baltic as a privileged outlet for North Eurasian trade, and the beginnings of the quest for North Eurasian trade (1670–1721). The second stage is that of the *consolidation* of the Baltic's special role in international commercial relations with North Eurasia (1703–1766). The third stage in the quest for North Eurasian trade sees the international tension around the Baltic reaching a *peak*, before turning into a state of *disorder* (1764–1814). The fourth and final stage is that of the *reconfiguration* of North Eurasian trade in the first half of the nineteenth century. These four stages constituted the core of the book.

Chapter 3 described the *emergence* of the Baltic as a privileged outlet for North Eurasian trade, and the beginnings of the quest for North Eurasian trade. The first two sections of Chapter 3 showed that the emergence of the Baltic as an area of vested interests in European commerce was determined by a combination of factors, such as: the widely spread eagerness to break Dutch commercial predominance in the Baltic, the increasing British and

French awareness of the strategic significance of North Eurasian trade via the Baltic Sea, the roles of Sweden and Muscovy as adversaries in a long-standing struggle for North Eurasian markets, an upsurge of commercial interest in Central Asia by Europe's leading economic powers, and the acknowledgement of Muscovy's strategic role in Western Europe's trade with Central Asia, Persia and China. Although the significance attached to them greatly exceeded their (potential) monetary and economic value, the perception of 'new' commercial opportunities, 'new' trade routes and 'new' areas of trade in the increasingly competitive international environment of the late seventeenth century marked the start of a radically new phase in the political economy of 'Baltic trade.' Around 1700, the Baltic no longer served as 'backwaters' of the Dutch and their commercial system, but had become the arena of processes of state-building and power politics with a very broad scope. The Baltic no longer was a 'lake' of regional importance. The contradictions between the mercantilist systems of the Swedes and the Russians boosted the conflict potential of the Baltic as a border basin of North Eurasia, and paved the way for a long period of warfare in the Baltic between 1700 and 1721.

The third section of Chapter 3 maintained a focus on the long-term impact on the structure of trade through the Danish Sound of the Great Northern War (1700–1721). Against the background of ongoing military and diplomatic activities, a detailed analysis was provided of the growing international concern with Russia's advances along the Baltic Sea coast. Special attention was paid to the dual role of Great Britain in 'Baltic affairs' during the final phase of the Great Northern War. On the one hand, Britain was keen to establish trade relations with Russia since the foundation of St. Petersburg in 1703; on the other, it was increasingly concerned about Russia's rapid expansion in the Baltic. The third section of Chapter 3 described in detail how, alarmed by Russia's rapid westward expansion, the occupation of Mecklenburg and the far-reaching plans to establish an entrepôt fur Russian trade in Wismar in 1716, the British changed their tactics during the final phase of the Great Northern War. Well aware of its precarious dependency of raw materials from the Russian interior, Britain now sought to contain Russia's expansion in the Baltic, without giving up on her ambition to sign a commercial treaty with the Tsar. It was shown that, among other things, the British requested permission for their subjects to trade in Kazan and Astrakhan on the Volga, which indicates that British commercial interests were not limited to Russia's Baltic ports alone, but also comprised access to North Eurasia for the transit of Central Asian goods.

Chapter 4 described how infrastructural developments in North Eurasia, on the one hand, and the increasing importance of novel patterns of international trade, which complemented and started to replace the 'traditional' Dutch trade through the Danish Sound, on the other, contributed to the *consolidation* of the Baltic's special role in European international commercial relations in the first half of the eighteenth century. The first section of Chapter 4 was devoted to the establishment of St. Petersburg on the banks of the Neva, and the construction of a distribution system connecting St. Petersburg with the Volga and – thus – with the Caspian Sea, the Ural Mountains, and Siberia. The wide-ranging efforts to promote St. Petersburg were implemented at the expense of Arkhangelsk, which lost its former significance as outlet for North Eurasian commodities. Although the significance of the infrastructural developments initiated after the foundation of St. Petersburg should not be underestimated, construction works and plans to create an infrastructure of land routes, rivers and canals were developed almost exclusively with the 'two Russian capitals' (Moscow and St. Petersburg) in mind; it would be premature to speak of the development of a 'national' transport and distribution system.

Nevertheless, as was discussed in the second section of Chapter 4, the enduring pressure upon existing structures was strong enough to provoke the rise of new patterns of distribution and trade in North Eurasia, and to sustain the centrality of St. Petersburg as the main gateway of Russia's foreign trade. First of all, the shift of foreign trade from the coast of the White Sea to the Baltic forced Russian and foreign merchants alike to restructure their business. As a result, St. Petersburg could assume a leading role in Russia's foreign trade within a remarkably short period. Moreover, the rise of St. Petersburg was reinforced by the expansion of textile manufacturing near Moscow, and of the metallurgic industry in the Ural Mountains, both of which were now able to deliver their produce to St. Petersburg via a complex system of waterways and canals. Second, the former Swedish ports in the eastern Baltic area obtained different roles under Russian rule. These changes affected the structure of trade through the Danish Sound as a whole, and strengthened the complementarity of ports in the Baltic in the first half of the eighteenth century. Although some ports dealt with similar commodities, regional specialization prevailed. The latter, in turn, affected the structure of the import and export trade of the main proponents of Baltic commercial exchange: The Dutch Republic and Great Britain. Rather than being competitors, their involvement in Baltic commercial exchange had distinct characteristics, which can be explained by the clear differences in their respective structures of supply and demand. Third and finally, it was shown that the consolidation of the Russian Empire as one of the main political and economic actors in North Eurasia also had a positive impact on the transit trade with Asian goods through North Eurasia.

The third section of Chapter 4 was devoted to British advances in North Eurasian trade. It described how British commercial interests suffered from a long crisis in Anglo-Russian diplomatic relations in the 1720s, from which they recovered around 1730, and which found consolidation in the groundbreaking Anglo-Russian treaty of commerce in 1734. Chapter 4 paid particular attention to the North Eurasian elements in the Anglo-Russian commercial treaty. First, Britain's pursuit of a commercial treaty with Russia took place in the context of an ongoing battle between Britain and Prussia for lucrative military woollen cloth contracts with Russia. Second, Britain recurrently used the argument to procure naval stores from its own

American plantations rather than from Russia if the latter would not give up its Prussian cloth supplies. Third, when British merchants obtained the right to transit goods to and from Persia via Russia, like the Armenians in the seventeenth century, they also obtained several additional rights and privileges, such as the right of shipbuilding in Kazan on the Volga and a number of privileges for passage and cargo handling in St. Petersburg, Astrakhan, Saratov, and Tsaritsyn. Thanks to the commercial treaty with Russia, the British were now in a highly favourable position to take control of the overland trade with Central Asia, Persia, and China. Protests from Armenian and Russian merchants against British competition became louder and led to the prohibition of British transit trade with Persia in 1746. Although with the abrogation of that particular part of the Anglo-Russian treaty, the opportunity to take control of the overland route from Asia to Europe was lost, Britain retained significant advantages in many other aspects of North Eurasian trade.

The remainder of Chapter 4 analysed the attempts of Britain's long-term rival, France, to break Britain's increasingly strong position in Russia's foreign trade. France's attempt to reverse the existing order in North Eurasian trade was embedded in a complex international political constellation in which – besides France itself – Britain, Prussia, and Russia played leading roles. In this context, attention was drawn to the protocols of the Russian Imperial Court in 1756, which were published 1912. These protocols provide a detailed insight into the underlying goals of Russian diplomacy around the mid-1750s, and the prospects of strategic territorial gains during the war with Prussia. First, Russia wanted to break the growing power of the Prussian King. Then, Russia would negotiate an exchange of territories with Poland-Lithuania: Courland would become Russian and Poland-Lithuania would receive East Prussia in exchange. Finally, it was anticipated that Russia would gain access to the Black Sea, and would be able to incorporate Ukrainian territories into the Empire. This, in turn, would bring the Russian Empire in a good position to strengthen the anti-Turkish coalition, on the one hand, and to redirect commodity flows from the Baltic to the Black Sea, on the other. It is the latter point, in particular, in which France saw an opportunity to weaken Britain's commercial dominance in North Eurasian trade. The Russian plans themselves showed the ongoing Russian concern with the grand direction of North Eurasian commodity flows and their control. Throughout the Seven Years' War, France and Russia tried to establish trade via the Black Sea. In the meantime, since 1757, Britain and Russia had started to negotiate the renewal of their 1734 commercial treaty. The debates between both parties lasted for about ten years and bore witness of the increasing self-consciousness of the Russian Empire in matters concerning their international trade. At last, a new Anglo-Russian commercial treaty was signed in 1766, in which Britain, again, had to accept that transit rights for Asian goods did not make it into the treaty. More important, however, is the fact that, after the Seven Years' War, Prussia was in a stronger position that ever before to have an impact on the structure of trade through the Danish Sound.

Chapter 5 was devoted to the latter part of the eighteenth century, when conflicting commercial and political interests in North Eurasian trade reached a *peak*, before turning into a state of disorder during the French Wars. Against the background of groundbreaking territorial developments on the American continent and the breakthrough of British industrialization, the first section of Chapter 5 described how Anglo-Russian trade, which had been identified as a prime mover of change in the preceding chapter, developed further after the Seven Years' War and the American War of Independence. It was demonstrated how the (temporary) loss of the North American market provoked a significant increase in the exportation of naval stores (including iron) from North Eurasian ports in the Baltic (and on the White Sea coast) to Britain. At the same time, however, Britain's self-perceived dependence on Russian 'naval stores' reached new levels as their demand exploded in the wake of the American War of Independence. Furthermore, it was substantiated that Russian attempts to bypass Britain in the establishment of (direct) foreign trade relations provoked the further increase of tension between Russia and Britain, on the one hand, and the relocation of part of British Baltic trade towards Prussia, on the other. Prussia itself was guided by the ambition of increasing its share in 'Baltic trade' at the cost of Poland-Lithuania and Russia.

The second section of Chapter 5 addressed the significant territorial and regime changes that occurred in North Eurasia's border basins in the latter decades of the eighteenth century, and highlighted the Russian Empire's, Prussia's and Britain's predominant role in these territorial changes. The Russian Empire and Prussia (quite literally) expanded their economic and political influence on the European scene at the cost of Poland-Lithuania (partitions of 1772, 1793 and 1795). Moreover, Russia finally recovered access to the Black Sea after another war with the Ottoman Empire (1768–1774). The second section of Chapter 5 paid particular attention to Prussia's economic policies in the annexed territories of Poland-Lithuania, and especially to Prussia's battle against Danzig, and demonstrated how they provoked an important shift in commodity flows from the hinterland of the Baltic ports. Different connections between the Russian heartland and potential maritime outlets were sought, including Prussian ports like Memel as well as newly established ports on the coast of the Black Sea. Moreover, in the second section of Chapter 5, the British role in the Eastern Crisis (1787–1791), was highlighted. This crisis evolved around two issues: Danzig on the Baltic Sea coast, and Ochakiv on the Black Sea coast. In the Baltic, Prussia still longed for the port of Danzig and the strategically located trading city of Thorn on the Vistula, but neither Britain nor Russia and Poland were ready to grant Prussia such territorial expansion. On the southern front, access to Black Sea ports was the primary concern of the Russian Empire. The cessation of the strategic fortress of Ochakiv played an essential role in the Russian Empire's further consolidation on the Black Sea coast, but Britain was opposed to the idea. The second section of Chapter 5 described the decisive impact of Britain's pursuit of its economic interests in the Baltic and the Black Sea.

After a failed attempt to establish a free port in Danzig in 1790, Britain no longer opposed to Prussia's claims on Danzig, and accepted Russia's territorial gains on the Black Sea coast as well, arguing that this turn of events would be in their best commercial interest. These strategic decisions had far-reaching consequences, as is shown in the remainder of this section of Chapter 5. Poland-Lithuania was partitioned a second (1793) and third time (1795), and Prussia became the leading power in trade through the Danish Sound. Odessa was founded near the fortress of Ochakiv, and the rise of Russia's Black Sea trade began. In the meantime, Revolutionary France had embarked upon its policy of 'economic strangulation' that would preoccupy Europe for the next two decades.

The third section of Chapter 5 dealt with the impact of the Continental Blockade (1806–1813) and the Russo-Turkish War (1806–1812) on North Eurasian trade. It shed light on the different ways that were sought to continue trade with and on the European continent. Scattered data from Russian sources was used to show that the closure of the Danish Sound immediately led to an upswing of import and export trade via the western overland border between Austria, Prussia, and Russia, via the White Sea port of Arkhangelsk and, perhaps most significantly, via Russia's Black Sea ports. Moreover, the impact of the treaty of Tilsit and Russia's subsequent adherence to Napoleon's Continental System was illuminated based on a descriptive account of the Continental Blockade's remarkable effect on the transit trade through Russia. It was substantiated that, between 1807 and 1810, the direction of transit changed from 'Europe to Asia' to 'Asia to Europe.' Finally, the period 1810–1813 was discussed, when the breaches in the Napoleonic system became more and more numerous, and Russia eventually ended its alliance with France. During the second phase of the Continental Blockade, the 'traditional' structure of North Eurasian trade was threatened from two sides. First, the Continental Blockade had reinforced the British search for alternative supplies of raw materials, which now booked its first successes. Second, countries on the European continent had started to take protectionist measures against British commercial predominance. Thus, during the final phase of the Continental Blockade, customs tariffs and commercial policies designed to strengthen and protect (infant) domestic industries, on the one hand, and limit the importation of manufactured goods, on the other, were implemented on the European continent. The impact of these threats to the 'traditional' structure of North Eurasian trade was discussed in Chapter 6.

Chapter 6 dealt with the *reconfiguration* of North Eurasian trade in the first half of the nineteenth century. The chapter showed that this reconfiguration had its roots in the opening of the Black Sea for international trade, the onset of industrialization in (small) parts of North Eurasia, and the emergence of competing productive areas in Western Europe, the Mediterranean, the United States, and Latin America. Moreover, it paid attention to the role of 'modern' commercial infrastructure (or its absence) as a driving force for change in commodity flows through North Eurasia. The first section of Chapter 6 was devoted to the impact of the opening of the Black Sea on grain exports through the Danish Sound. Changes in the demand for different sorts of grain led to a partial relocation of North Eurasian grain exports from the Baltic to the Black Sea. The volume of rye exports through the Danish Sound stagnated, whereas that of wheat exports started to rise from the mid-eighteenth century onwards, in particular after the emergence on the scene of Britain as a wheat importer from North Eurasia. The growth of the Black Sea grain trade was placed within the broader context of international competition. It was described how, due to the increasing number of ports with easier access and superior port infrastructure, British commerce became less and less inclined to trade directly with the distant ports of the Russian Empire, be it St. Petersburg, Arkhangelsk, or Odessa. At least partly, intermediate ports successfully challenged *direct* Anglo-Russian trade. These intermediate ports benefited from two advantages: they could be reached more easily with steam ships, and had storage facilities that made the supply of goods more predictable and less hazardous. Moreover, the relocation of activities towards intermediate ports in the Mediterranean and the Southern Baltic fit well into the isolation of the Russian Empire after 1839, and the establishment of an anti-Russian block in European international relations during the 1840s and 1850s.

The second section of Chapter 6 elaborated upon the issue of global competition and its impact on North Eurasian trade. Based on a survey of selected commodity flows, it was substantiated that North Eurasia's role in the supply of foodstuffs and raw materials was already under threat at the start of the nineteenth century. Indeed, North Eurasian trade had to bear with global competition in the production and supply of some of its most important commodities, which resulted from Britain's protracted global search for alternative supplies of naval stores, on the one hand, and the diffusion of industrial production techniques in the United States, on the other. The United Kingdom looked elsewhere to secure its supply of raw materials and foodstuffs and to sell its manufactures; access to North Eurasia was no longer as high on the agenda of its international relations as it had been throughout the eighteenth century. In the wake of production increases in Ireland, Western Europe, Scandinavia, parts of the Mediterranean, and across the Atlantic, as well as the rapidly increasing importance of ready-to-use grain flour rather than grain itself, of alternative crops, such as maize and rice, and of substitutes for the traditional North Eurasian naval stores, such as Indian jute and Manila hemp, exports from North Eurasia via the Baltic or the Black Sea stagnated and declined relative to competing global areas of production. Among the latter, the United States, the British American Colonies, and the Ottoman Principalities on the Danube became the most important competitors of North Eurasia, at least insofar as grain exports to the United Kingdom are concerned. Whereas the Ottoman Principalities competed with Russia and Prussia supplying the same product (wheat), the competition of the United States and the British American Colonies was of a different nature. Rather than wheat, they supplied wheat flour (and maize) to the United Kingdom. Wheat flour was a ready-to-use industrial product, which occupied less transport and storage space and was therefore more cost efficient than corn itself. Statistical data were compiled to substantiate that, as soon as a more or less reliable transport infrastructure from the Mid-West of the USA to its ports on the East coast was in place, grain supplies from the USA benefited from a triple advantage over (most of) North Eurasian supplies: (1) transatlantic deliveries were faster than those from North Eurasia, (2) the transport costs for flour were lower than for grain, and (3) flour was a ready-to-use industrial product, whereas grain would still have to be processed at its final destination first.

The third and final section of Chapter 6 presented a brief outlook on yet another complex set of changes that unfolded in North Eurasia's western border basins (and in the Black Sea, in particular) since the early nineteenth century. It highlighted the impact of failed French efforts to revive the overland route for Asian goods through the Russian Empire via Tiflis and Odessa. Against the background of Russia's renewed efforts to secure a predominant political and commercial position in the landlocked parts of Central and East Asia, most importantly in the Caucasus, the Caspian Sea, the territories of the former Khanates, and the Amur basin, the reorientation of political and commercial interests towards the vast and disputed land border between North and South Eurasia, and the rise of diplomatic tension and commercial competition with the British Empire, which itself longed for controlling these borderlands, was briefly introduced. Finally, it was argued that, after the Crimean War, with its devastating outcome for the Russian Empire, neither the Baltic nor the Black Sea stood in the focus of international commercial and political relations any longer, for some time at least. The times of diplomatic tension and (threats of) war during the late seventeenth and throughout the eighteenth century, when the Baltic and the quasi-monopolistic access it provided to much-desired supplies of foodstuffs and raw materials were gone.

Appendix
A note on statistics

This book makes ample use of the electronic database of the Sound Toll Registers Online project (short: STRO). Without the groundbreaking digitization of the Danish Sound toll registers, a unique source for European economic history of the pre- and early industrial period, this book could not have been written. The first version of (part of) the electronic database was published in 2013, and data entry was finalized in January 2020. The first efforts to deal with the intricacies of the registers in their electronic form have made clear that the premodern nature of the data gathered in the electronic database, and most importantly the mass of non-standardized cargo registrations with their large variety of different weights and measures, poses (almost) unsurmountable problems. Therefore, most researchers have worked either with relatively small, well-defined parts of the database, or have applied more or less sophisticated methods of counting passages and cargoes, thus avoiding the issues associated with premodern weights and measures.[1] For the present study, the first attempt ever was made to convert all premodern weights and measures in STRO to metric tonnes for the period from 1670 until 1856. Knowing that weights and measures differed from product to product and from place to place, these parameters were taken into account in the conversion process. Although it is obvious that a complete and flawless conversion could not be attained, the homogenization and standardization of about four million cargo registrations, and the conversion of their related weights and measures into metric tonnage estimates, has created a range of new possibilities for analysing trade through the Danish Sound as a proxy for North Eurasian trade.

The analytical chapters of this book explore only a fraction of these new possibilities as they deal with long-term structural changes in international trade through the Danish Sound at a high level of aggregation. Most of the data used in the present study was aggregated so as to find and explore general trends rather than short-term variations. However, thanks to the bottom-up methodology that has been applied during the homogenization, standardization, and conversion of the electronic database of the Danish Sound toll registers, the results of these data manipulation processes can also be used at different levels of analysis. Moreover, the auxiliary tables containing the basic information about the process from 'raw' to converted data are available in electronic form as part of the present study. They may be used, for example, to link with the earlier part of the Danish Sound toll registers, i.e. the years prior to 1670, which have not been dealt with in this study. They could also be employed as a starting point for 'enhancing' other, more or less similar electronic databases. The data produced within the framework of this study is available to all in their entirety, including all omissions, mistakes, explanations, and references.

The bottom-up approach pursued here secures the option to return to the highest level of detail, i.e. the individual registration, at any point during the process of creating and exploring time series. It steers clear of any unwarranted quantification, making sure that relevant alphanumeric data, such as information about ports, cargoes, or shipmasters, can be retrieved at all times. The registrations of ships passing through the Danish Sound were treated as singular events. Aggregated (annual) time series based upon these events were created to examine cycles and long-term structural changes. The critical advantage of this methodology lies in the simple fact that – like in Braudel's famous conceptualization of time[2] – the level of events is not detached from that of cycles and structures. Quantifications and long-time series retain their relation with the event level. As such, they differ fundamentally from mainstream methods of quantification. It is hoped that future research will benefit from this approach, for example, in the pursuit of in-depth analyses of aspects of the general analysis attempted in this study.

Notes

1 For examples, see: Veluwenkamp and Scheltjens, *Early modern shipping and trade.*
2 Braudel, 'Histoire et Sciences Sociales,' 725–753.

References

Braudel, Fernand. "Histoire et Sciences Sociales. La longue durée." *Annales. Histoire, Sciences Sociales* 13, 4 (1958): 725–753.

Veluwenkamp, Jan Willem; Scheltjens, Werner (eds.). *Early modern shipping and trade. Novel approaches using Sound Toll Registers Online.* Leiden / Boston 2018.

Index

Note: Page numbers followed by "n" denote endnotes.

For Product Safety Concerns and Information please contact our EU
representative GPSR@taylorandfrancis.com
Taylor & Francis Verlag GmbH, Kaufingerstraße 24, 80331 München, Germany

www.ingramcontent.com/pod-product-compliance
Ingram Content Group UK Ltd.
Pitfield, Milton Keynes, MK11 3LW, UK
UKHW020009200926
475702UK00015B/2561

* 9 7 8 0 3 6 7 6 8 3 4 8 1 *